Also by Bob Woodward

Plan of Attack

Bush at War

Maestro: Greenspan's Fed and the American Boom

Shadow: Five Presidents and the Legacy of Watergate

The Choice

The Agenda: Inside the Clinton White House

The Commanders

Veil: The Secret Wars of the CIA 1981-1987

Wired: The Short Life and Fast Times of John Belushi

The Final Days (with Carl Bernstein)

All the President's Men (with Carl Bernstein)

Bob Woodward & Scott Armstrong

The

Brethren

Inside the Supreme Court

SIMON & SCHUSTER PAPERBACKS

New York   London   Toronto   Sydney

SIMON & SCHUSTER
Rockefeller Center
1230 Avenue of the Americas
New York, NY 10020

First Simon & Schuster paperback edition 2005

SIMON & SCHUSTER PAPERBACKS and colophon are registered trademarks
of Simon & Schuster, Inc.

For information about special discounts for bulk purchases,
please contact Simon & Schuster Special Sales at
1-800-456-6798 or business@simonandschuster.com

Manufactured in the United States of America

10 9 8 7 6 5 4 3 2 1

The Library of Congress has cataloged the hardcover edition as follows:
Woodward, Bob.
The Brethren.
Includes Index.
1. United States. Supreme Court. 1. Armstrong, Scott, Joint Author.   II. Title.

ISBN-13: 978-0-671-24110-0
ISBN-13: 978-0-7432-7402-9 (Pbk)

To Katharine Graham, Chairman of the Board,
The Washington Post Company,
for her unwavering commitment to an independent press
and the First Amendment.
And to our children, Tali, Thane and Tracey.

Contents

Author's Note

Two people labored as long and as hard on this book as the authors.

Al Kamen, a former reporter for the *Rocky Mountain News*, assisted us in the reporting, writing and editing of this book. He was the chief negotiator and buffer between us. His thoroughness, skepticism and sense of fairness contributed immeasurably. No person has ever offered us as much intelligence, endurance, tact, patience and friendship.

Benjamin Weiser, now a reporter for *The Washington Post*, helped in the research, writing, editing and reporting. A devoted and resourceful assistant, no one could have been more loyal and trusted.

This book is as much theirs as ours.

Acknowledgments

This book has two sponsors, Benjamin C. Bradlee, the executive editor of *The Washington Post,* and Richard Snyder, president of Simon and Schuster. Without their support and encouragement this book would have been impossible. No other newspaper editor or book publisher would have been as willing to assume the risks inherent in a detailed examination of an independent branch of government whose authority, traditions and protocols have put it beyond the reach of journalism.

At Simon and Schuster, we also owe special thanks to Sophie Sorkin, Frank Metz, Edward Schneider, Wayne Kirn, Gwen Edelman, Alberta Harbutt, Joni Evans, Harriet Ripinsky.

To Alice Mayhew, our editor, we give our respect and affection for her constant support and guidance as she nurtured this book to completion.

At *The Washington Post* we also thank Katharine Graham, Donald Graham, Howard Simons, the late Laurence Stern, Elizabeth Shelton, Julia Lee, Carol Leggett, Lucia New, Rita Buxbaum, Adam Dobrin.

A critical reading and numerous suggestions were provided by Karen De Young, Marc Lackritz, Ann Moore, Jim Moore, Bob Reich, Ronald Rotunda, Bob Wellen and Douglas Woodlock.

Tom Farber helped greatly with suggestions and writing.

Milt Benjamin, our colleague at the *Post,* devoted several months to recrafting, editing and rewriting the initial drafts. We will never be able to thank him enough.

We owe and give our greatest thanks to our sources.

Washington, D.C.
August 1979

Introduction

THE UNITED STATES SUPREME COURT, the highest court in the
land, is the final forum for appeal in the American judiciary.
The Court has interpreted the Constitution and has decided the
country's preeminent legal disputes for nearly two centuries.
Virtually every issue of significance in American society eventually
arrives at the Supreme Court. Its decisions ultimately affect the
rights and freedom of every citizen—poor, rich, blacks, Indians,
pregnant women, those accused of crime, those on death row,
newspaper publishers, pornographers, environmentalists, businessmen, baseball players, prisoners and Presidents.

For those nearly two hundred years, the Court has made its decisions in absolute secrecy, handing down its judgments in formal
written opinions. Only these opinions, final and unreviewable, are
published. No American institution has so completely controlled
the way it is viewed by the public. The Court's deliberative
process—its internal debates, the tentative positions taken by the
Justices, the preliminary votes, the various drafts of written opinions, the negotiations, confrontations and compromises—is hidden
from public view.

The Court has developed certain traditions and rules, largely unwritten, that are designed to preserve the secrecy of its deliberations. The few previous attempts to describe the Court's internal
workings—biographies of particular Justices or histories of individual cases—have been published years, often decades, after the
events, or have reflected the viewpoints of only a few Justices.

Much of recent history, notably the period that included the

Vietnam War and the multiple scandals known as Watergate, suggests that the detailed steps of decision making, the often hidden motives of the decision makers, can be as important as the eventual decisions themselves. Yet the Court, unlike the Congress and the Presidency, has by and large escaped public scrutiny. And because its members are not subject to periodic reelection, but are appointed for life, the Court is less disposed to allow its decision making to become public. Little is usually known about the Justices when they are appointed, and after taking office they limit their public exposure to the Court's published opinions and occasional, largely ceremonial, appearances.

The Brethren is an account of the inner workings of the Supreme Court from 1969 to 1976—the first seven years of Warren E. Burger's tenure as Chief Justice of the United States. To ensure that our inquiry would in no way interfere with the ongoing work of the Court, we limited our investigation to those years. We interviewed no one about any cases that reached the Court after 1976.

We chose to examine the contemporary Court in order to obtain fresh recollections, to deal with topical issues and to involve sitting Justices. This book is not intended as a comprehensive review of all the important decisions made during the period. The cases we examine generally reflect the interest, time and importance assigned to them by the Justices themselves. As a result, some cases of prominence or importance—but which provide no insight into the internal dynamics of the Court—have been dealt with only briefly or not at all. The Court conducts its business during an annual session called a *term*, which begins each October and continues until the last opinion is announced in June or early July. The Court recess runs from then until the next October.

Normally, there are seven decision-making steps in each case the Court takes.

1. The decision to take the case requires that the Court note its jurisdiction or formally *grant cert.* Under the Court's procedures, the Justices have discretion in selecting which cases they will consider. Each year, they decide to hear fewer than two hundred of the five thousand cases that are filed. At least four of the nine Justices must vote to hear a case. These votes are cast in a secret confer-

ence attended only by the Justices, and the actual vote is ordinarily not disclosed.

2. Once the Court agrees to hear a case, it is scheduled for *written and oral argument* by the lawyers for the opposing sides. The written arguments, called legal briefs, are filed with the Court and are available to the public. The oral arguments are presented to the Justices publicly in the courtroom; a half-hour is usually allotted to each side.

3. A few days after oral arguments, the Justices discuss the case at a closed meeting called the *case conference*. There is a preliminary discussion and an initial vote is taken. Like all appellate courts, the Supreme Court normally uses the facts already developed from testimony and information presented to the lower trial court. The Supreme Court can reinterpret the laws, the U.S. Constitution, and prior cases. On this basis, the decisions of lower courts are affirmed or reversed. As in the cert conference, at which Justices decide which cases to hear, only the Justices attend the case conferences. (The nine members of the Court often refer to themselves collectively as the conference.)

4. The next crucial step is the selection of one of the nine Justices to write a majority opinion. By tradition, the Chief Justice, if he is in the initial majority, can *assign* himself or another member of the majority to write the opinion. When he is not in the majority, the senior Justice in the majority makes the assignment.

5. While one Justice is writing the majority opinion, others may also be drafting a *dissent* or a separate *concurrence*. It can be months before these opinions—a majority, dissent or concurrence—are sent out or circulated to the other Justices. In some cases, the majority opinion goes through dozens of drafts, as both the opinion and the reasoning may be changed to accommodate other members of a potential majority or to win over wavering Justices. As the Justices read the drafts, they may shift their votes from one opinion to another. On some occasions, what had initially appeared to be a majority vanishes and a dissenting opinion picks up enough votes to become the tentative majority opinion of the Court.

6. In the next to last stage, the Justices *join* a majority or a dissenting opinion. Justices often view the timing, the sequence and

the explanations offered for *"joins"* as crucial to their efforts to put together and hold a majority.

7. In announcing and publishing the final *opinion*, the Justices choose how much of their reasoning to make public. Only the final versions of these opinions are available in law libraries. The published majority opinion provides the legal precedents which guide future decisions by lower courts and the Supreme Court itself.

We began this project in the summer of 1977 as two laymen lacking a comprehensive knowledge of the law. We read as many of the cases and as much of the background material about the period as time would allow. We found the work of Derrick Bell, Paul Brest, Lyle Denniston, Fred Graham, Eugene Gressman, Gerald Gunther, Richard Kluger, Nathan Lewin, Anthony Lewis, John Mac-Kenzie, Michael Meltsner, John Nowak, Ronald Rotunda, Nina Totenberg and Laurence Tribe particularly helpful. We thank them, and countless others on whose writings we have drawn.

Most of the information in this book is based on interviews with more than two hundred people, including several Justices, more than 170 former law clerks, and several dozen former employees of the Court. Chief Justice Warren E. Burger declined to assist us in any way. Virtually all the interviews were conducted "on background," meaning that the identity of the source will be kept confidential. This assurance of confidentiality to our sources was necessary to secure their cooperation.

The sources who helped us were persons of remarkable intelligence. They had unusually precise recall about the handling of cases that came before the Court, particularly the important ones. However, the core documentation for this book came from unpublished material that was made available to us by dozens of sources who had access to the documents. We obtained internal memoranda between Justices, letters, notes taken at conference, case assignment sheets, diaries, unpublished drafts of opinions and, in several instances, drafts that were never circulated even to the other Justices. By the time we had concluded our research, we had filled eight file drawers with thousands of pages of documents from the chambers of eleven of the twelve Justices who served during the period 1969 to 1976. The sole exception was the chambers of Justice John P. Stevens, who joined the Court during the last six months of the period covered in this book.

For each of the seven terms we describe, we had at least one, usually two, and often three or four reliable sources in each Justice's chamber, in no case fewer than 20 sources per term. Where documents are quoted, we have had direct access to the originals or to copies. We have attributed thoughts, feelings, conclusions, predispositions and motivations to each of the Justices. This information comes from the Justices themselves, their diaries or memoranda, their statements to clerks or colleagues, or their positions as regularly enunciated in their published Court opinions. No characterization of a Justice could be comprehensive, but we believe those that are provided help explain the decisions and actions.

New documentation about the Burger Court will likely be available in the future. It may support additional interpretations of these events and these men. The account that follows is based on the information and documentation available to us.

Bob Woodward
Scott Armstrong

"A court which is final and unreviewable needs more careful scrutiny than any other. Unreviewable power is the most likely to self-indulge itself and the least likely to engage in dispassionate self-analysis . . . In a country like ours, no public institution, or the people who operate it, can be above public debate."

WARREN E. BURGER,
Circuit Court of Appeals Judge, to
Ohio Judicial Conference on
September 4, 1968—nine months
before being named Chief Justice
of the United States

Prologue

Prologue

ARL WARREN, the Chief Justice of the United States, hailed the elevator operator as if he were campaigning, stepped in and rode to the basement of the Supreme Court Building, where the Court limousine was waiting. Warren easily guided his bulky, 6-foot-1-inch, 220-pound frame into the back seat. Though he was seventy-seven, the Chief still had great stamina and resilience.

Four young men got into the car with him that fine November Saturday in 1968. They were his clerks, recent law graduates, who for one year were his confidential assistants, ghost writers, extra sons and intimates. They knew the "Warren Era" was about to end. As Chief Justice for fifteen years, Warren had led a judicial revolution that reshaped many social and political relationships in America. The Warren Court had often plunged the country into bitter controversy as it decreed an end to publicly supported racial discrimination, banned prayer in the public schools, and extended constitutional guarantees to blacks, poor people, Communists, and those who were questioned, arrested or charged by the police. Warren's clerks revered him as a symbol, the spirit of much that had happened. The former crusading prosecutor, three-term governor of California, and Republican vice-presidential nominee had had, as Chief Justice, a greater impact on the country than most Presidents.

The clerks loved their jobs. The way things worked in the Chief's chambers gave them tremendous influence. Warren told them how he wanted the cases to come out. But the legal research and the drafting of Court opinions—even those that had made Warren and his Court famous and infamous—were their domain.

Warren was not an abstract thinker, nor was he a gifted scholar. He was more interested in the basic fairness of decisions than the legal rationales.

They headed west, downtown, turned into 16th Street and pulled into the circular driveway of the University Club, a private eating and athletic club next to the Soviet Embassy, four blocks north of the White House. The staff was expecting them. This was a Saturday ritual. Warren was comfortable here. His clerks were less so. They never asked him how he could belong to a club that had no black members.

With his clerks in tow, Warren bounded up the thick-carpeted steps to the grill. It was early for lunch, not yet noon, and the room was empty. Warren liked to start promptly so they would have time for drinks and lunch before the football game. They sat in wooden captain's chairs at a table near the television and ordered drinks. The Chief had his usual gimlet. He was pensive. They ordered another round. Warren reminisced, told political stories, chatted about sports, and then turned to the recent past, to Richard Nixon's election. The Chief thought it was a catastrophe for the country. He could find no redeeming qualities in his fellow California Republican. Nixon was weak, indirect, awkward and double-dealing, and frequently mean-spirited. Throughout the 1968 presidential campaign, Nixon had run against Warren and his Court as much as he had run against his Democratic rival, Senator Hubert Humphrey. Playing on prejudice and rage, particularly in the South, Nixon had promised that his appointees to the Supreme Court would be different.

It was unlikely that a Nixon Court would reverse all the Warren Court's decisions. Though Justices John Harlan, Potter Stewart and Byron White had dissented from some of the famous Warren decisions, each of them had strong reservations on the matter of the Court's reversing itself. They believed firmly in the doctrine of *stare decisis*—the principle that precedent governs, that the Court is a continuing body making law that does not change abruptly merely because Justices are replaced.

But as Warren and his clerks moved to lunch, the Chief expressed his frustration and his foreboding about a Nixon presidency. Earlier that year, before the election, Warren had tried to ensure a liberal successor by submitting his resignation to President Lyndon B. Johnson. The Senate had rejected Johnson's nominee, Associate Justice Abe Fortas, as a "crony" of the President. All that had been accomplished was that Nixon now had Warren's resignation on his desk, and he would name the next Chief Justice.

Warren was haunted by the prospect. Supreme Court appointments were unpredictable, of course. There was, he told his clerks, no telling what a President might do. He had never imagined that Dwight Eisenhower would pick him in 1953. Ike said he had chosen Warren for his "middle of the road philosophy." Later Eisenhower remarked that the appointment was "the biggest damned- fool mistake I ever made."* Well, Warren said, Ike was no lawyer. The clerks smiled. But Richard Nixon was, and he had campaign promises to fulfill. He must have learned from Eisenhower's experience. He would choose a man with clearly defined views, an experienced judge who had been tested publicly on the issues. The President would look for a reliable, predictable man who was committed to Nixon's own philosophy.

"Who?" asked the clerks.

"Why don't we all write down on a piece of paper who we think the nominee will be?" Warren suggested with a grin.

One clerk tore a sheet of paper into five strips and they sealed their choices in an envelope to be opened after Nixon had named his man.

Warren bent slightly over the polished wooden table to conceal the name he wrote.

Warren E. Burger.

Three months later, on the morning of February 4, 1969, Warren Burger, sixty-one, was in his spacious chambers on the fifth floor of the Court of Appeals on Pennsylvania Avenue, almost midway between the White House and the Supreme Court. President Nixon,

---

* Congressional Quarterly's *The Supreme Court: Justice and the Law,* 2nd ed., p. 163.

who had been in office only two weeks, had invited him to swear in several high-ranking government officials at the White House. When he arrived at the mansion, Burger was instantly admitted at the gate.

Nixon and Burger first met at the Republican National Convention in 1948. Nixon was a freshman Congressman and Burger was floor manager for his home-state candidate, Minnesota Governor Harold Stassen. At the next convention, four years later, Burger played an important role in Eisenhower's nomination. He was named assistant attorney general in charge of the Claims Division in the Justice Department, and in 1956 he was appointed to the United States Court of Appeals for the District of Columbia.* On that famously liberal court, Burger became the vocal dissenter whose law-and-order opinions made the headlines. He was no bleeding heart or social activist, but a professional judge, a man of solid achievement.

Now at the White House, the ceremonial swearings-in lasted only a few minutes, but afterward the President invited Burger to the Oval Office. Nixon emphasized the fact that as head of the Executive Branch he was deeply concerned about the judiciary. There was a lot to be done.

Burger could not agree more, he told the President.

Nixon told him that in one of his campaign addresses he had used two points from a speech Burger had given in 1967 at Ripon College in Wisconsin. *U.S. News & World Report* had reprinted it

---

* There are three levels of courts in the federal judiciary:
— District Courts with about 600 judges; these judges, at the first step in the federal system, hear and try cases.
— Circuit Courts of Appeal; there are eleven of these intermediate circuits numbered First (New England states) through Tenth (Western states) plus the Circuit for the District of Columbia. There are from four to fourteen appeals court judges in each circuit. These judges hear appeals from the district courts and interpret the Constitution, Supreme Court rulings and federal laws.
— The Supreme Court, with nine members, reviews decisions made by both federal courts and state courts and handles other matters, such as disputes between states.

under the title "What to Do About Crime in U.S." The men agreed that *U.S. News* was the country's best weekly news magazine, a Republican voice in an overwhelmingly liberal press. Burger had brought a copy of the article with him.

In his speech Burger had charged that criminal trials were too often long delayed and subsequently encumbered with too many appeals, retrials and other procedural protections for the accused that had been devised by the courts.

Burger had argued that five-to-ten-year delays in criminal trials undermined the public's confidence in the judicial system. Decent people felt anger, frustration and bitterness, while the criminal was encouraged to think that his free lawyer would somewhere find a technical loophole that would let him off. He had pointed to progressive countries like Holland, Denmark and Sweden, which had simpler and faster criminal justice systems. Their prisons were better and were directed more toward rehabilitation. The murder rate in Sweden was 4 percent of that in the United States. He had stressed that the United States system was presently tilted toward the criminal and needed to be corrected.

Richard Nixon was impressed. This was a voice of reason, of enlightened conservatism—firm, direct and fair. Judge Burger knew what he was talking about. The President questioned him in some detail. He found the answers solid, reflecting his own views, and supported with evidence. Burger had ideas about improving the efficiency of judges. By reducing the time wasted on routine administrative tasks and mediating minor pretrial wrangles among lawyers, a judge could focus on his real job of hearing cases. Burger also was obviously not a judge who focused only on individual cases. He was concerned about the system, the prosecutors, the accused, the victims of crime, the prisons, the effect of home, school, church and community in teaching young people discipline and respect.

The President was eager to appoint solid conservatives to federal judgeships throughout the country. As chairman of a prestigious American Bar Association committee, Burger had traveled around the country and must know many people who could qualify. The President wanted to appoint men of Burger's caliber to the federal bench, including the Supreme Court. Though the meeting was lasting longer than he had planned, the President buzzed for his White House counsel, John Ehrlichman.

Ehrlichman came down from his second-floor office in the West Wing. Nixon introduced them. "Judge Burger has brought with him an article that is excellent. Make sure that copies are circulated to others on the White House staff," Nixon said. He added that Burger had constructive, solid ideas on the judicial system as well as for their anticrime campaign. Judge Burger was a man who had done his homework. "Please make an appointment with him to talk," the President said, "and put into effect what he says." The chat had turned into a seventy-minute meeting.

Ehrlichman left, concluding that if ever a man was campaigning for elevation in the judiciary, it was Warren Burger. He was perfect, clearly politically astute, and he was pushing all the right buttons for the President. Burger and Ehrlichman never had their follow-up meeting, but from press accounts and bar association talk, Burger knew that Nixon had designated Attorney General John Mitchell, his former campaign manager and law partner, to help find him new judges, including a new Chief Justice.

Mitchell, Burger understood, was the "heavy hitter," the one closest to the President. Privately, Burger had expressed doubts to friends whether a New York bond lawyer had the experience to be the nation's top law-enforcement officer.

On February 18, Mitchell asked for Burger's help. Shortly thereafter, Burger called at his office in the Justice Department. Knowing that Burger had numerous contacts in legal and judicial circles, Mitchell sought recommendations for nominees to the federal bench. Burger offered some names, and Mitchell wrote down the suggestions. Richard Kleindienst, Mitchell's deputy, sat in on the end of the hour-long meeting. After Burger left, Mitchell remarked, "In my opinion there goes the next Chief Justice of the United States."

A month passed. On April 4, Burger wrote a letter to Mitchell on his personal stationery. "In one of our early conversations you asked me to give you my observations on District Judges and others over the country who might warrant consideration for appointment or promotion," Burger said. He offered three immediate suggestions, adding that "each of these men is especially well qualified." One of the three names he sent was a federal district judge in Florida, G. Harrold Carswell. Burger also promised to send along other recommendations "from time to time." Mitchell responded with a thank-you note the same day. Later that month, Burger received an invitation to a White House dinner that the President would give on April 23 to honor Chief Justice Warren.

Burger arrived with his wife at the White House early to have time to look over the guest list. All the important Republicans were there, including Vice President Spiro Agnew, as well as all the Associate Justices of the Supreme Court. Burger was the only lower court judge invited. "If you get a feeling they're looking us over," he told his wife, "act natural."

Supreme Court Justice John Harlan, a conservative Eisenhower appointee, greeted Burger. "I'm glad you're here," he said warmly.

The President's toast to Warren was glowing, and Warren in turn rose to praise Nixon. He was concluding his forty years of public service, he said, with "no malice in my heart."

The next day, Burger's long-time archenemy on the appeals court, liberal Chief Judge David L. Bazelon, approached him. Cordially, he pointed out that Burger was the only district or circuit judge at the dinner. "Looks like you're it," Bazelon said.

"No," Burger said, brushing off his old adversary. To Burger, the fifty-nine-year-old Bazelon was a meddler—the self-appointed protector of every racial minority, poor person and criminal defendant.

But Washington reporters had also picked up the possible significance of Burger's White House invitation and began asking him about it. Burger was humble. He neither knew nor expected anything. Asked about other candidates for Chief Justice whose names were making the rounds, such as Secretary of State William Rogers, Burger downgraded each one. "No, no," he would tell reporters confidentially, "he wouldn't be good." The media made Burger a dark-horse candidate, but there was still a frontrunner—Associate Justice Potter Stewart.

*　　*　　*

A week later, the morning of Wednesday, April 30, Stewart arrived at the Supreme Court late. He hated starting early. Stewart had impressive academic and establishment credentials. Born into a distinguished and wealthy family of Ohio Republicans, he had studied at Hotchkiss and Yale University, where he was Phi Beta Kappa and the editor of the *Yale Daily News*, before enrolling at Yale Law School, where he was a top student. At age thirty-nine he was appointed by Eisenhower to the Sixth Circuit Court of Appeals. "I can promise you he is not too old," a leading Senate supporter had said. Stewart quickly came to love the work. He remarked that it involved "all the fun of practicing law without the bother of clients." Four years later, in late 1958, Eisenhower elevated Stewart to the Supreme Court, one of the youngest Justices in history. For a decade, he had dissented from most of the major Warren Court opinions. Now, at fifty-four, he was at his prime, perhaps ready for the final step.

That morning Stewart went straight to his chambers, staring at the marble floor, by habit avoiding eye contact with those he met along the way. A shy man, Stewart was of average height and build, with thin brown hair combed straight back from a receding hairline. In the men's club atmosphere of the Court, Stewart had found a comfortable shelter. The job was nearly perfect, providing both the prominence of a high government post and intellectual satisfaction, without overexertion. Reaching his chambers, he called John Ehrlichman at the White House. Stewart said he wanted a brief appointment with the President.

Ehrlichman called back shortly. Would three o'clock be okay? He fished for a clue, saying that he had told the President only that it was some matter involving the Court. "Was that enough to tell him?"

Yes, that was enough, Stewart said. Now he was committed to meet with the President, but he still had several hours to think. Stewart knew that he had supporters from Ohio, the Middle West and in G.O.P. circles, who were urging that he be made Chief Justice. But did he really want it? Admittedly, he was ambitious, and there had been a certain natural progression to his career, always up, always the best. If he got the job, the new era would become "the Stewart Court." Technically, the Chief was only first among equals, but the post of Chief Justice had definite prestige.

On the other hand, the Chief's vote counted no more than that of any of the other eight Justices. The Chief also had the additional chores of administering the Court and managing the building. In terms of pure lawyering, it was better to be an Associate Justice. All law and no nonsense. Did he want to be involved in all the tedious little decisions? To oversee committees and groups like the Judicial Conference, which was a "board of directors" of the federal judiciary and the judges' lobby? No, he concluded, he did not want to be bothered. If he got the job of Chief, he would rarely see his family and have even less time to relax. His summers at his Bowen Brook Farm in New Hampshire would be disrupted. On a superficial level, there were big plusses. On a deeper level, there were not so many. Less law. More bureaucracy.

There were other considerations. Stewart had seen what President Johnson's feeble attempt to get his friend Abe Fortas moved from Associate to Chief had done to the Court. There had been other troubled times when Associates had been promoted. Stewart thought two of the most unharmonious times at the Court had been in 1910, when Justice Edward D. White had been made Chief, and again in 1941, when Justice Harlan Fiske Stone was elevated above his peers.

The process of getting confirmed might be both contentious and some fun, Stewart thought. A likely target for critics might be his 1964 opinion ruling that a French film, *The Lovers*, was not hardcore pornography (*Jacobellis v. Ohio*). He could not define obscenity, he had written, but "I know it when I see it." It might not be the height of legal sophistication, but the remark expressed Stewart's Middle Western pragmatism.

The biggest adjustment would be a loss of privacy. Associate Justices could live private and relatively anonymous lives. Stewart could walk about Washington unnoticed, eat lunch without interruption. There were few autograph seekers. That would change. The job of Chief was considered by some to be the most powerful position after the presidency. There would be another F.B.I. check, a Senate investigation, and hearings before the Senate Judiciary

Committee. The press would become more interested in him. He would be in the limelight. And when he got down to it, that was perhaps the biggest problem. When he had been nominated for the Court in 1958, then Deputy Attorney General William Rogers had asked Stewart if there was anything in his past that might embarrass him or the administration. Stewart had thought of some things—an editorial he had written for the *Yale Daily News* endorsing Democrat Franklin D. Roosevelt for President in 1936; or perhaps that particularly drunken evening in his sophomore year. But nothing serious. Now it was a little different. Was it fair to his family? Would he have to wonder whether his private business might appear in the newspapers, if only in a gossip column?

Stewart left his chambers in plenty of time to be at the White House before 3 P.M. His stomach knotted as he drove through the Washington traffic. He was being awfully presumptuous. The President had not offered him the job. But if he took himself out of the running, he wouldn't have to deal with temptation if it came. If the position were actually offered, it would be harder to say no. Stewart drove through the White House gates and was escorted into the Oval Office.

Nixon greeted him warmly.

Stewart said that it had been a great thing for the President to have had the dinner for Warren.

The President talked about whom he might pick as his Chief Justice. "Potter," Nixon said, "there has been an awful lot of support for you."

Stewart said he knew that there had been speculation, the inevitable lists. But he had come, he said, to tell the President that he didn't want it, that he didn't want to be considered, that he wanted to be out of the running.

"Why?" Nixon asked in surprise.

Stewart recited his speech. In his opinion there were inherent, perhaps insurmountable, problems in promoting one of the sitting Justices. Historically it had not worked. The Chief Justice had a special role to play as leader of the Court and it might disturb relationships that had been worked out over the years to appoint one of the eight Associates to be Chief. Promoting a sitting Justice would not be the best way, Stewart said.

Nixon paused. "Let me remember who is on the Court," he said. First he mentioned the hapless Fortas. Nixon looked at Stewart. Slowly he listed the others.

Fortas, Stewart thought? Was the President thinking of appointing Fortas? No, absolutely not; out of the question. But Stewart realized it was possible that Nixon was thinking of another sitting member. The only other Republican was John Harlan, but he was almost seventy and nearly blind. Perhaps Nixon was thinking of a Democrat?

Stewart mentioned that Roosevelt had elevated Harlan Stone, a Republican, to Chief Justice on the eve of World War II as a nonpartisan act of national unity. Maybe that wouldn't be a bad idea, appointing a Democrat.

Nixon went down the list of Democrats. There was William Brennan, who had been appointed by Eisenhower, and there was Byron White . . . could Nixon be thinking of White? Unlikely. White had been a Kennedy appointee, and Stewart knew what Nixon thought of the Kennedys.

Then Nixon mentioned Fortas again. Why? Stewart wondered. Why was Nixon bringing up Fortas? Did he want some reaction? Stewart had little to say about Fortas. It was obvious that it had been a mistake for Johnson to attempt the eleventh-hour elevation of his close friend and adviser. It had hurt the Court, had made for strange, uneasy relations among the members. Stewart said it would be better not to put the Court through that again, nominating someone from the ranks. But Stewart was a little uneasy. He mentioned his own position again and, in a general way, the needs and desires of his wife and children, their high regard for privacy. "It would be unfair to my family," he said.

Nixon said he understood. He asked more questions about the Court and its members. He was keenly interested, concerned about the federal courts. There was much to do, and as President he wanted to help.

Finally the two men stood and shook hands, and Stewart left. The meeting had taken longer than he had expected, but he felt a sense of relief.

As he drove back, Stewart regretted that he had given phony reasons for taking himself out, but it had been necessary to protect his family. It was odd the way the President kept bringing Fortas up. What was that about? Stewart wasn't sure he had done the right thing, but he felt better than he had felt in a long while.

Nixon was giving a good deal of thought to the Court. He wanted to make good on his campaign pledge to turn it around. Replacing Warren was not enough to break the back of the working Warren majority—which had included Warren himself; Fortas; Thurgood Marshall, the first black member of the Court, who had been appointed by Lyndon Johnson; William J. Brennan, another Eisenhower appointee who had turned out differently than Ike had expected; and William O. Douglas, seventy, a radical libertarian famous for his controversial writings and life, both on and off the bench. Nixon snickered about Douglas's fourth wife, Cathy, who was twenty-five and a law student. "Some law firm will love to get her," he told Ehrlichman.

The five-man liberal majority had support on race and civil rights issues from Byron White and Hugo Black. A new conservative Chief Justice, with Stewart and Harlan, the only Republicans on the Court besides Warren, would still give the Court only three "strict constructionists"—those who opposed a sweeping, liberal interpretation of the Constitution. White and Black might join the conservatives in certain criminal cases, but one could never be sure. The President needed at least another seat to turn things around, and Douglas seemed most vulnerable to a quiet administration investigation. On taking office, Nixon lost no time putting various federal agencies to work on it. The Internal Revenue Service began an audit of Douglas's tax returns only five days after the President's inauguration. At the same time, the F.B.I. was compiling information on Douglas's connections with Las Vegas casino owner Albert Parvin. Douglas was a director of the Albert Parvin Foundation. But the Douglas investigations were slow in bearing fruit.

Now, unexpectedly, another track opened up. John Mitchell's Justice Department was providing assistance to *Life* magazine in its attempt to establish that in 1966 Abe Fortas had accepted a

$20,000 fee from a foundation funded by millionaire industrialist Louis Wolfson.* At that time Wolfson had been under investigation by the Securities and Exchange Commission, and had apparently bragged that his friend Fortas was going to use his influence to help. Wolfson was indicted and later convicted, and Fortas secretly returned the $20,000.

When Nixon was informed of the investigation, he realized that Fortas's actions were perhaps not necessarily criminal. But there was an opportunity not only to get Fortas off the Court but to discredit his strident liberalism. The Fortas investigation became one of Mitchell's first action projects, and Nixon demanded almost minute-by-minute reports, personally calling the shots from the Oval Office.

On May 1, Mitchell received a memo from Assistant Attorney General William H. Rehnquist. If Fortas had helped Wolfson, it said, they could prosecute him. The next day, May 2, Ehrlichman received a single copy of the advance proofs of the *Life* article. Spread over six pages, it was headlined, "Fortas of the Supreme Court: A Question of Ethics." Mitchell had an aide call every major news organization in town to alert them. When the article was released on Sunday afternoon, May 4, Washington exploded. Republicans called for impeachment. Democrats and liberals were stunned.

But Nixon didn't want an impeachment. It would take too long and might in the end hurt the Court. All Nixon wanted was Fortas's seat, and he wanted it intact, not devalued. Resignation was the obvious short cut. With the departure of Fortas and Warren, Nixon

---

* In a June 2, 1969, memo to Attorney General Mitchell, F.B.I. Director J. Edgar Hoover stated that a reliable source had informed the F.B.I. that, "in connection with the investigation involving former Supreme Court Associate Justice Abe Fortas, the Department furnished considerable information to William Lambert, writer for *Life* magazine, which not only enabled Lambert to expose the Fortas tie-in with the Wolfson Foundation but additionally kept Lambert advised" regarding its own investigation into the matter. It is perhaps significant that Hoover did not name any individual, but simply "the Department of Justice." It suggests that his reliable sources indicated that the leaks were official, perhaps authorized by Mitchell.

could name two justices. That would end the control of the liberals. In his first year, he would have altered the character of the Court.

On Tuesday, May 6, Wolfson surrendered to government investigators a document that showed that the $20,000 was not a one-time payment. The Wolfson Foundation had agreed to pay Fortas $20,000 a year for the rest of his life, or to his widow for as long as she lived.

When Mitchell arrived at Dulles Airport at 1:30 A.M. after a trip to New York, his aides showed him the documents. Mitchell was incredulous. He thought they might be phony. He was assured they were not. The news was forwarded to the President. Nixon and Mitchell agreed that the Attorney General should go to Earl Warren. With the Congress and editorial writers howling for Fortas's head, pressure from inside the Court might force the issue.

Entering the Court through the basement garage, Mitchell called on Warren in his chambers at eleven-thirty Wednesday morning. The meeting was to be confidential. Laying out the documents in his possession and referring to others, Mitchell outlined the developing case against Fortas. There was not only the contract specifying the annual payment, but he was about to obtain some Wolfson-Fortas correspondence in which the S.E.C. case was discussed. In one letter Wolfson asked Fortas's help in obtaining a presidential pardon.

Warren thanked Mitchell and said that he appreciated the information. Mitchell mentioned how embarrassing this was for everyone. Approaching the subject delicately, he said that if Fortas were to resign voluntarily, the criminal investigation would "die of its own weight." An investigation would harm both Fortas and the Court more than a resignation would. Warren got the message.

From the beginning, Warren had been appalled at the disclosures about Fortas and had felt that Fortas must quit. The argument was now more compelling. After securing the support of several of the other Justices, Warren launched a week-long campaign to get Fortas to resign. Only Douglas resisted overtly. He had been Fortas's professor and mentor at Yale Law School and later in Washington. Douglas himself had discussed retiring, but, loath to give Nixon a seat to fill, he decided not to retire while the Court was still under attack.

Nonetheless Douglas was surprised by Fortas's transgression. "God, how did Abe do such a stupid thing?" Douglas asked.

In Warren's view, Fortas had two problems that had led him to such indiscretion. As a private lawyer in Washington and a known intimate of the President, Fortas had made a fortune. He had had to take almost a 90 percent cut in salary when he came to the Court, and he had not wanted to alter his life style.

Second, Warren concluded, as a bright man who had come to Washington during the New Deal, Fortas had made rules for others to follow, but had never thought they applied to him.

There were meetings and some heated sessions, and one week later, on Wednesday, May 14, Fortas sat down in his office and drafted his letter of resignation. He understood that all the evidence would be locked away. Jubilant, Nixon called Fortas to express his sympathy.

It was over for Fortas, but now two other Court liberals— Douglas and Brennan—came under attack for off-the-bench financial activities. Douglas was criticized for his $12,000-a-year directorship on the Albert Parvin Foundation. After thirty years on the Court, Douglas was accustomed to political attack. But the Fortas affair cast things in a different light. He decided to resign from the Foundation post on May 21.

Some conservatives went after the sixty-three-year-old Brennan. News stories had raised questions about a $15,000 real-estate investment he had with Fortas and some lower court judges, including Bazelon. Brennan was hurt by the criticism. He had grown up on the poor side of Newark and learned the rough-and-tumble of politics from his father, an Irish immigrant who was by turn a union leader, a Democratic politician, and a police commissioner. After a brief tenure with a private law firm, Brennan served as a state trial, and then an appellate court, judge. In 1956, Eisenhower elevated him from the New Jersey State Supreme Court to the U.S. Supreme Court. Brennan's life was a model of upward mobility through conscientious public service. He was furious at the press for implying that his review of decisions by other judges would be influenced by the fact that they shared common investments. He suspected that the attack was led by those who resented his central role in the Warren Court, his unflagging support for unions and civil rights groups, and his votes restricting the powers of police.

In May, Brennan decided to lower his profile. "Well, guys," he said, walking into his clerks' office, "I'm eliminating all this." He formally canceled all future speaking plans, gave up his interest in the real-estate venture, sold his stock, quit his part-time summer teaching post at New York University, and even resigned from a board at Harvard University. He gave up every activity except the Court, his family and the Church.

One clerk who felt Brennan was overreacting asked him jokingly: "Did you write the Pope?"

Brennan, the Court's only Catholic, was not amused.

The weekend after the Fortas resignation, Nixon was at Camp David, the presidential retreat in Maryland. With the liberals dazed by the Fortas revelations, it was time to choose his Chief Justice, perhaps the most important decision he would make as President. Mitchell had prepared a list of appeals court judges. Nixon wanted someone with judicial experience, someone whose views were fully predictable, not a crony or political friend, someone with integrity and administrative ability. Someone young enough to serve at least ten years.

Warren E. Burger.

On May 19, the President instructed Mitchell to begin the necessary F.B.I. investigation and report back at once. Burger checked out. On Wednesday, May 21, Nixon told Mitchell to offer Burger the appointment formally.

Only in Mitchell's office did Warren Burger learn that he was to be named Chief Justice of the United States. He accepted at once. A regular appointment to the Court would have been enough. Chief was incredible. Already he felt a kinship with these people, with Mitchell and Nixon. They were the men who had taken over the national government, and they had selected him over all others.

Nixon was obsessed with keeping the nomination secret until he could announce it on national television that night. Burger would be smuggled into the White House. They would stride before the cameras together. There would be no leak. The President was stage manager. He sent an aide out to bring Burger and his family in, and he organized the transportation, the timing, the sequence. Watching, Ehrlichman thought Nixon seemed as interested in the secrecy as he was in the appointment. Apparently Nixon felt that if he could make the announcement before a leak occurred, he would have outwitted the press.

Burger went home to prepare his family, making sure that everyone looked proper for the ceremony. They were picked up about 6 P.M., driven to the Treasury Department and guided down to the basement and through a long steam tunnel. They made their way to the White House and came up in an elevator at 6:57, three minutes before air time.

The President was waiting. He walked over to Burger.

"Well, will you take the job?" Nixon asked.

Burger paused. "You know, I know that question is somewhat facetious," he said. "But as I thought about it this afternoon, I had some concern." Of course he would accept, but he recognized that he was undertaking a tremendous responsibility.

As they stood chatting, Burger said: "Sometime when we have more time to talk, I want to thank you for this."

Nixon said he wanted the Burgers to come up for coffee after the ceremony to meet the Cabinet members and their wives. He added nervously, "I wanted to apologize for the fact that we couldn't have you to dinner because it would be too many."

"Don't worry about that, Mr. President," Burger said. "After what happened to me this afternoon, I am just going home to bed."

At 7 P.M. Nixon and Burger walked before the cameras. The next morning, the appointment was the lead story in every newspaper. *New York Times* columnist James Reston wrote that Burger was "experienced, industrious, middle-class, middle-aged, middle-of-the-road, Middle-Western, Presbyterian, orderly, and handsome." He took note of the liberals' and intellectuals' distress and added that "the old-boy network is grieving that the President did not elevate Associate Justice Stewart to the top job." *The New York Times* also quoted an unnamed judge who had worked with Burger on the Court of Appeals: "[Burger] is a very emotional guy, who somehow tends to make you take the opposition position on issues. To suggest that he can bring the Court together—as hopefully a Chief Justice should—is simply a dream."

Many who knew Burger's old foe, Bazelon, suspected that the comment was his. But Bazelon denied having talked to the press. "I was speechless and sick for a week," he said.

Burger stayed home to avoid the reporters who had gathered at the bottom of the driveway of his Arlington, Virginia, home. He requested that the reporters and cameramen be kept off the fifth floor at the Court of Appeals, where his office was, even though he was staying away. Later, he learned that the lobby had been filled with the press despite his request. "The only way they could have gotten in is Bazelon," Burger told his staff. "If I can prove it's true, I'll punch him in the nose."

Burger expected that his confirmation hearing before the Senate Judiciary Committee, which had to approve the nomination before it would be passed to the full Senate, might be a bloody battle. He envisioned a whole confederation of liberal interest groups planning to tear into him. "They're out to get me," he told his clerks as he brooded over the prospect. The opposition included Bazelon, the other liberals on the U.S. Court of Appeals for the District of Columbia, and some liberal Justices like Brennan. It also included the young coat carriers, who seemed to rotate from a clerkship with Bazelon to a clerkship at the Court, perhaps for Brennan, before taking a job on the Hill, where they were always whispering into the ears of liberals like Senator Edward M. Kennedy at hearings.

Burger was sure that Kennedy would lead the opposition on the Senate Judiciary Committee. As a Republican nominee before a heavily Democratic Senate, he would be hard pressed. Nixon's pronouncements about changing the Court were an open challenge to the liberals.

Burger went to discuss the confirmation process with the chairman of the committee, Senator James O. Eastland of Mississippi. The aging conservative was a sure supporter. Eastland recommended that Burger use Eastland's own personal attorney, Roger

Robb, already a close friend of Burger's, to assist him in the hearings. Burger took the advice. With Robb, he set up an office in the Watergate office complex, where they assembled records and previous opinions and tried to anticipate what curves the liberals might throw at Burger. They also gathered support from the organized bar associations, from law school deans, and from influential private attorneys.

Burger went to the Supreme Court one day and stopped by to see Brennan, the consensus builder in the Warren Court. Burger knew it was Brennan, with his instinct and passion for political maneuvering, who was the key strategist among the liberal bloc on the Warren Court. As Burger entered Brennan's chambers along the south corridor, he walked through the office used by Brennan's law clerks. There, hanging on a wall, was a grotesque rubber mask of Nixon, a souvenir of the counterinaugural demonstration that had been staged by antiwar activists and others opposed to the President. He recognized one of Brennan's clerks as a Bazelon clerk of the previous year. The clerk was scheduled to begin work for Kennedy on the Senate Judiciary Committee at the end of the term.

Learning that Brennan was not in the office, Burger turned to leave. On the inside of the door there was a Black Power poster with the clenched, raised fist. Burger sensed what he was up against. Brennan's law clerks did not share his values. They were part of a different world. Bazelon to Brennan to Kennedy.

On Tuesday, June 3, two weeks after his nomination, the Senate Judiciary Committee opened hearings. Burger was ready as the session opened at 10:35 A.M. Behind him in the audience sat six past presidents of the American Bar Association, eleven past presidents of the Federal Bar Association, and twelve past presidents of the District of Columbia Bar Association. All were prepared to speak in support of his nomination.

Burger was offered a few easy questions by Eastland and other members of the committee. Finally, from his hunched position, Eastland turned to the man Burger was certain would present him with a problem. "Senator Kennedy," Eastland mumbled.

"No questions, Mr. Chairman," Kennedy replied in his confident Boston accent.

Each Senator took his turn, and there was not a word of criticism. The members seemed almost to compete with each other to praise Burger and take shots at the Warren Court. The hearing was adjourned in less than two hours. Burger was ecstatic. The committee unanimously recommended his confirmation to the Senate. Six days later the Senate voted 74 to 3 to confirm him. The process from nomination to confirmation had taken only eighteen days.

A week later, only one week before he would be sworn in as Chief Justice, Burger was in his office at the Court of Appeals when he got some very distressing news. The Supreme Court had announced that it had overruled his Court of Appeals decision in a case involving the flamboyant New York black Congressman Adam Clayton Powell. The vote was an overwhelming 7 to 1, with Stewart the lone dissenter. Warren himself had written the majority opinion (*Powell v. McCormack*). The press would have a field day.

The House of Representatives had voted to deny Powell his seat because he had flouted a slander judgment and allegedly had misused funds. Burger's opinion, one of three separate ones, held for the House against Powell. Powell had appealed to the Supreme Court, and now Warren had declared for a heavy majority that Congress could not deny the Congressman his seat. The reversal was a typical example of the Warren Court's activism—mere meddling in Burger's view. He had already been overruled twice that year, but this was the first time since his nomination. There should have been some way for Warren to avoid a direct slap at him, perhaps with an unsigned opinion. Being reversed by the Supreme Court, however, would soon be a thing of the past. He could take comfort in that. In one more week, the Warren era would be over.

Burger vowed to himself that he would grasp the reins of power immediately. David Bazelon would be his model. For the past six years he had watched enviously as Bazelon used his position as Chief Judge to serve his own philosophy. As spokesman for the Court of Appeals, as its senior judge and chief administrator, Bazelon was able to assign extra law clerks, and control the office space, supplies and accouterments that make working conditions a pleasure or an annoyance. His influence with his colleagues, and especially the new judges, was legendary. They fell all too easily under his spell. For Burger, that too was now an old battle, a thing of the past.

Later that week, Burger left his office in the Court of Appeals and went out to Pennsylvania Avenue to meet the Solicitor General Erwin N. Griswold, the man responsible for arguing the federal government's cases before the Supreme Court. Griswold had the presidential commission, signed by the President and the Attorney General, that appointed Burger. It was to be delivered to the Court before the swearing-in.

Griswold and Burger took a cab to the Court, where Warren greeted them in his chambers. The Powell case was apparently on his mind. "I hated to decide for Powell," Warren told them.

Griswold thought Warren was going to explain the difficulty and awkwardness in overruling the next Chief Justice—perhaps apologize, saying that, of course, he had to call them as he saw them. Instead, Warren told them that he didn't like Powell and regretted having to decide in his favor. Powell was a disgrace, Warren said. But as a matter of law, it would be impossible to let Congress exclude members in such fashion. In denying Powell his seat, Congress had asserted an absolute and unreviewable right to determine who was suited to sit, contrary to what the Constitution said. "It was perfectly clear," Warren remarked. "There was no other way to decide it. Anybody could see that."

My God, Griswold thought, Warren must not realize that Burger was one of the lower court judges he had just overruled. Griswold knew Warren did not write his own opinions, but was he so out of touch? Griswold carefully avoided looking at Burger. He would have smiled, and perhaps Burger would not think it one bit funny. The meeting was soon over and as they walked out, Burger good-naturedly shrugged off Warren's comment. "He certainly didn't give me much credit for what I did in the Adam Clayton Powell case," he told Griswold.

Burger had heard that Warren delegated the writing of his opinions to his clerks. That was only one of the many practices that he was going to stop. As far as he was concerned, the Warren legend was a fabrication. He thought Warren was sloppy, politically motivated, interested more in results than in legal reasoning. He was a man playing to get himself a place in history, a man without intellectual honesty. Burger used to talk scornfully to his clerks about Warren's liberalism. It was late in coming, he said. Warren had been aligned with the right wing of the Republican party in California and was supposedly a states' rights champion. As governor he had strongly supported the internment of Japanese-Americans during World War II. As district attorney, he had authorized offshore searches of questionable legality outside the three-mile limit. Burger told his clerks that Warren was "right-wing when it paid to be right-wing, then had shifted when that became fashionable."

On June 23, Burger joined the members of the Court, the President, Attorney General Mitchell, other ranking Justice Department officials, including F.B.I. Director J. Edgar Hoover, and members of the legal and Republican law-enforcement establishment for his swearing-in at the Supreme Court.

Since it was the last day of the term, the Warren Court first handed down its three final opinions. The decisions, all involving criminal cases, effectively overruled three more conservative precedents. They were precisely the kinds of opinions that Nixon had campaigned against.

Nixon, dressed in a formal cutaway, showed no emotion. When the last opinion was read, Warren recognized the President. Nixon stepped to the podium. "There is only one ordeal which is more challenging than a presidential press conference, and that is to appear before the Supreme Court." He reviewed Warren's career and praised the Chief Justice. But, he added, "The Chief Justice has established a record here in this Court which will be characterized in many ways."

In response, Warren gave a lecture—his last words from the bench—which seemed directed at Nixon. There was acid in the oblique graciousness. His theme was continuity. "I might point out to you, and you might not have looked into the matter, that it is a continuing body . . . the Court develops the eternal principles of our Constitution in accordance with the problems of the day." It was Warren's way of saying that Richard Nixon too would pass. The Court, Warren said, serves only "the public interest," is guided solely by the Constitution and the "conscience" of the individual Justices. He was stepping down, Warren said, with a feeling of "deep friendship" for the other Justices "in spite of the fact that we have disagreed on so many things.

"So I leave in a happy vein, Mr. President, and I wish my successor all the happiness and success in his years on the Court, which I hope will be many."

1969 Term

1969 Term

B_Y JULY, Chief Justice Warren Burger was in his new offices. With three months before the start of the new term, and the other Justices spending the recess at home or on vacation, he intended to consolidate his power. First, he would assume control of the building itself. On July 19, Burger, in shirt sleeves, assembled his law clerks and the Marshal—the top administrative and business officer of the Court—for a tour of the large building.

Beginning in his own small office Burger remarked that it was smaller than his old one at the Court of Appeals. More distressing was the absence of an adjoining office that could be used as a workroom. As Chief Justice he was third in protocol as official representative of the United States government after the President and Vice-President. He would receive ambassadors and visiting dignitaries. "How can I entertain heads of state?" he asked, pointing to his relatively cramped quarters. It would never do. What would his guests think?

Passing through the secretaries' outer office, the procession stepped through to the most secret place of the Court, the conference room where the nine Justices met to vote and decide cases. Few outsiders had seen the conference room during the Warren years. No person—clerk, staff member or secretary—was in attendance when the Justices met, usually on Fridays, to discuss cases and take initial votes.

Burger surveyed this large, oak-paneled room and its rich carpet. A twelve-foot-long table covered in green felt stood in the center of the room under a splendid chandelier, and was surrounded by nine handsome high-backed green leather swivel chairs. A brass nameplate on the back of each chair identified its occupant. The Chief

Justice sat at one end of the table, the senior Associate Justice at the other. The other Associates sat three on one side, four on the other. Now this room, the Chief said, is perfect for entertaining guests. He told the group that in the original architect's plans, the room had been intended for the Chief Justice. Perhaps the conferences might be better in larger, more formal settings, the East and West conference rooms on the other side of the building. It might be more appropriate in that "neutral corner," Burger said. Then this room could become the Chief Justice's ceremonial office. He could also use it as a private dining room. Next, Burger led the group across the corridor to the courtroom proper. They entered from behind the bench, as the Justices did when they came to hear oral arguments or announce decisions. Burger stepped down to the pit in front of the mammoth bench. The large dignified room, with its dark-red curtains, had twenty-four marble columns rising forty-four feet, cathedral-like, to a sculpted marble panel.

The new Chief stepped to the podium from which the attorneys argued their cases to the nine Justices—without witnesses and without introduction of evidence.

Oral advocacy is an art, Burger remarked. He recalled that he had stood in the same spot when he was in the Justice Department, sixteen years ago, and had argued one of the most celebrated cases of the time for the United States government. The Solicitor General, Simon Sobeloff, had refused to argue a case that involved John Peters, a Yale University professor of medicine, who had been found disloyal and dismissed as a consultant to the Public Health Service (*Peters v. Hobby*). The finding of disloyalty had been based on anonymous accusations. Sobeloff should have resigned, Burger said, rather than refuse to argue his client's case, even though the client was the government. Sobeloff had become a great hero to the liberals and civil libertarians. But Burger's Justice Department bosses were pleased with his loyalty. That was probably the reason, Burger said, why he was rewarded with a seat on the Court of Appeals three years later. He didn't mention that he had lost the *Peters* case.

Lingering now, and reminiscing, the Chief told them how he got the job as head of the Claims Division in the Justice Department in the first place. While acting as Stassen's floor manager at the 1952

Republican convention, he had helped the Eisenhower forces in a crucial credentials battle.

Burger pointed to the Justices' nine high-backed black leather chairs. Each Justice chose his own, and the sizes and styles varied. Some were nearly a foot taller than others. Douglas's was tufted, the others were smooth. It looked unseemly, disorderly, Burger said. In the future only one kind of chair would be available.

Still at the podium, his eyes fixed on the bench, Burger remembered an interchange with Justice Hugo Black during the *Peters* case. He pointed to the center of the bench. A question had come from *there*, and he was answering it when suddenly another question had come from the end. With the Justices all in a straight line at a straight bench, they could not see or hear each other. That situation should be changed, he said, by curving the bench so each Justice could see his colleagues. The acoustics in the large room also were poor. That too should be corrected, he said, perhaps by installing microphones. The clerks fidgeted. Finally one of them suggested that the Associate Justices might be upset if the Chief went ahead with remodeling plans in their absence. Burger ignored him.

They walked to the outer corridor on the first floor onto which each Justice's suite of offices, known as *chambers*, faced. As they strolled along, Burger pointed out various problems—places in need of repainting, inadequate lighting; he would order a lighting study. There was poor utilization of office space; he would order a formal study of the use of space in the entire building. A few plants would bring life to the barren, gloomy halls. The telephone system was ancient, and the operators used old-fashioned plug-in switchboards. The cafeteria was old and run-down. There was no photocopying equipment, so the junior Justices got unreadably faint carbon copies. There were no electric typewriters that produced print-quality letters and memos. Outside, the landscaping was lackluster, and the guards did not have the snap and attentiveness of those at the White House.

In fact, Burger concluded, the Supreme Court Building with its fine workmanship, its columns, its brass doors and best wood was as grand as the White House, but it had not been kept up. A top-to-bottom reorganization was needed. The nineteenth-century administrative system might be charming, but it was inefficient. The tour lasted two hours.

While on the Court of Appeals, Burger had enjoyed lunching regularly with his clerks. On July 21, he took his Supreme Court clerks in his limousine to one of his favorite spots, the National Lawyers Club. The quiet atmosphere allowed him to unwind, to reflect and think ahead. That afternoon he was full of political reminiscences about Ike, Bill Rogers and Harold Stassen. He missed politics, he said. The press had been unfair to Ike, claiming he lacked intelligence, and to Stassen as well, making him a political joke because of his persistent and unsuccessful tries for the presidency. Newspapers manipulated the news to fit the editors' views. Take *The Washington Post.* For the last decade the editors had maintained a policy of keeping the names of the conservative and moderate appeals court judges out of the paper. At the same time the paper had played up the decisions of the liberals, especially Bazelon. The clerks were skeptical. The Chief insisted that a reporter recently departed from the *Post* had assured him that it was the case. *The New York Times* and the *Post* were anti-Nixon, pro-Bazelon and therefore anti-Burger. Both papers had attacked him. They were not reconciled to his appointment and would continue to snipe. The *Christian Science Monitor* had been ordered as the newspaper for his chambers.

His mood lightened, and he said he was happy with the way things were getting organized. He wanted to move his desk and other office furniture into the conference room and get settled in as quickly as possible. When the other Justices returned, they would be confronted with a *fait accompli.* Burger's clerks were astonished that he would try such a move without consulting the others. He seemed to be moving toward a needless confrontation.*

---

* Burger dropped his plan to make the conference room his ceremonial office when he learned through his clerks that the other Justices were opposed. They felt the room was their sanctorum. But in the meantime Burger had moved an antique desk into the room and placed it in a "T" with the conference table. When he learned of their opposition, Burger compromised. He removed the desk from the "T" but also moved the conference table to one side of the room and his desk to the other. The presence of the desk in "our room," as Black called it, still irritated the others. But no one confronted Burger directly. Burger's desk stayed.

Back at his office, Burger saw another opportunity to accomplish something where his predecessor had failed. Warren and his Court had alienated Congress over the years, particularly the older, powerful, conservative committee chairmen, who didn't like the Court's decisions and resented Warren's aloofness.

Burger phoned Representative John Rooney, Chairman of the House subcommittee that controlled the Court's spending. Warren had said privately that the crusty, gravel-voiced, sixty-five-year-old Rooney was "dictatorial and vengeful." Burger decided to charm him. The Court needed more law clerks. Rooney told Burger that Warren had requested nine more, one for each Justice. That was too many, Rooney said. Three might be a more reasonable request.

Three would be fine, Burger said.

Rooney said that as a special favor he would see if he could get the House to approve the three additional clerks.

Burger thanked Rooney for the effort.

Three days later, on July 14, the House approved three new clerks, and Rooney took to the floor to praise the new Chief Justice. The country, Rooney told his colleagues, "is in good hands when we are in the hands of Chief Justice Warren Burger. . . ."

At the Court, Burger told his clerks of his success. The lobbying and his willingness to compromise had paid off.

On July 29, Burger decided to make a move to put a damper on Warren's recent drive to impose a rigorous code of ethics for federal judges. Warren's original interest had gained some currency in the wake of the Fortas affair. But it was a tempest in a teapot, Burger said. He drafted a strong letter to the lower court judge who headed a committee that Warren had set up to formulate a code of ethics. Codes of ethics merely drew undue attention to minor problems, Burger wrote, and they gave the press more ammunition to depict judges as crooks.

Newspapers had published details about $6,000 in fees that Burger had received in the last three years as a trustee of the Mayo Foundation, which operated the Mayo Clinic in Rochester, Minnesota. The ethics question had been overheated both by Warren and the press, Burger felt. He was determined to cool it off.

In early August, the Chief turned his attention to selecting the three law clerks who were to be added to the Court. They were going to solve a problem—lack of staff. The Court was flooded each year with thousands of petitions from people who did not have attorneys and could not pay the $100 filing fee for review. The petitions might be jotted on notebook leaves or on scraps of paper. They were sometimes illegible and often incomprehensible.

These petitions constituted the bulk of the approximately five thousand that came to the Court each year. They were called *in forma pauperis* petitions, or "I.F.P.'s." The Court got only one copy of each, rather than the forty that were required of those able to pay. Most of the I.F.P.'s were from prisoners who alleged a violation of their constitutional rights. All the Justices agreed that only a few petitions had merit, but Burger thought that all I.F.P.'s were a waste of time. In a 1965 Court of Appeals opinion *(Williams v. U.S.)*, he had denounced the "Disneyland" contentions of those who had been found guilty and were still trying to get out of jail by raising technical objections.

The office of the Chief Justice was responsible for these I.F.P.'s. Generally, the petitions themselves did not go to each Justice. The Chief's clerks wrote one-page summaries of each, and these were circulated to the other chambers. If the clerk who handled the petition believed the claim to be particularly meritorious, the whole petition might be circulated. The preparation of the summaries was tedious work, but the Warren Court had granted hearings in a few cases. They had in some cases been simply vehicles for the Warren liberals to "discover" some new right for prisoners or criminals in Burger's view.

As he was getting the Chief's chambers organized, Burger's head law clerk reviewed a copy of a thirty-three-page set of instructions Warren had written for his law clerks that included a guide on how to prepare these I.F.P. memos. Burger's clerk edited the guide and sent it to the Chief for his okay.

Burger found no problems until he got to page 17, the section dealing with the clerks' responsibilities in preparing the summaries of the I.F.P.'s. Such summaries, the memo said, should pull together and accurately set forth the facts, issues and legal arguments that each petitioner had tried to make.

"Your secondary function," Warren's memo said, "is to present the arguments which petitioner *could* make based upon the facts of the case. That is, inasmuch as the I.F.P. petitioners generally do not have counsel, it is necessary for you to be their counsel, in a sense."

The Chief called in his head clerk. What's this? Burger demanded. This was a court, not the office of the public defender. That might be the way Warren's clerks operated, but it was not what his would do, Burger stated firmly. The Court was already overworked. It needn't look for more work. If some poor devil missed a point that might get his petition reviewed by the Court, well, that was his problem. In criminal cases, these people had already been found guilty and were looking for technicalities and loopholes to escape their just punishment. This secondary function would be *ignored*, Burger declared. Only arguments that had been identified by the petitioner would be summarized and sent to the other chambers.

Burger's clerks believed he had effectively devastated the Court's role as the last bastion of hope for these people. Without knowing any law, most petitioners had little chance of catching the Court's attention. The I.F.P.'s, however, were only one example, in Burger's view, of how law clerks had come to have too much power and influence.

He knew from his days at the Court of Appeals how clerks occasionally worked their little subterfuges. They could not be trusted to exercise proper judgment. Something had to be done about the clerk network. To combat this traditional underground inter-chamber communications system that Burger viewed as a rumor mill, he modified a memo on confidentiality from the previous term at the Court of Appeals. It was issued by his own senior clerk on August 12, only to his own law clerks.

CONFIDENTIAL
LAW CLERK MEMORANDUM—THE CONFIDENTIALITY OBLIGATION

... The confidentiality is not limited to the minimum and obvious aspect of preserving the security of all information *within* the Court. Equally important is the private nature of everything that transpires in the Chambers of the Justice, including what he says, what he thinks, whom he sees and what his thinking may be on a particular issue or case.

The memo noted that during the year, there develops "a communal professional life somewhat comparable to a large law firm." The various chambers, however, are not members of the same law firm, but rather different law offices coincidentally occupying the same building.

. . . some Clerks at times have had a tendency to develop a collective "Law Clerks'" decision to resolve cases on the merits before the Justices themselves have worked out the answers. Of special importance in this regard is the conversation which takes place in the Law Clerk Dining Room. Law Clerks generally view the lunch period as a unique opportunity to exchange insights and stories about their Justices. It has been customary for Law Clerks to discuss with one another the most intimate of matters relating to their Justices with the understanding that none of what is said shall go beyond the four walls of the Dining Room. While such conversation can be both educational and entertaining for the Law Clerks, the extent to which such information is not carried beyond the Dining Room is questionable.

Some of Burger's clerks thought the memo was reasonable so far. It continued:

Any matters of a confidential nature which tend to place the Chief Justice in an unfavorable light should not be revealed to other Law Clerks.

Despite the avowed confidentiality of the lunchroom, the possibility of unfavorable information being "leaked" to other Justices requires the Chief's Law Clerks to be reticent.

The Chief was worried not about leaks to outsiders, but about his clerks telling tales that would "leak" to his colleagues.

It is likely that information received from a Justice's own Law Clerk will both diminish his effectiveness with his colleagues and damage his public image more grievously than information received from other sources if only because it will be more highly credited.

Why would he assume that anything his clerks said would be negative? one of his clerks asked.

The Chief "does not want his views on a case—or those of his law clerk(s)—made known *outside* his Chambers until his final position is reached."

So, Burger's clerks were permitted to talk only to each other. They realized that they had just been dealt out of much of the fun and meaning of their clerkship, head-on discussions about votes and positions. They knew that traditionally clerks communicated openly and freely with their peers in order to better serve their Justice. Dissents had to be responsible to the majority opinions and vice versa. Research could be productively shared, language suggestions exchanged. These things were part of the process of improving their boss's final opinions. The next sentence took some of that away.

The Chief's clerks are not to reveal which opinions they are personally working on. . . . The Chief Justice has a strict rule that suggestions are to be accepted from other offices *only* after another Justice has first considered the matter and then communicated directly and formally to the Chief Justice.

So they couldn't negotiate with the other clerks. No one could be told anything, and no other chambers would receive advance soundings on the Chief's initial conclusions. They were to work under a bell jar, away from the flow of ideas and argument. The Chief, they concluded, had a view of the Court that implied that such interchanges corrupted rather than enlightened. Their disaffection grew. It was as if the Chief had prepackaged legal values and did not want the normal give-and-take to sway either him or his clerks. Even to Burger's clerks, the memo reflected his deep insecurity over control and a fear that somehow the clerks would try to manipulate him.

Burger had one more summer project. Earl Warren had feuded with and alienated the major organization of lawyers in the country, the American Bar Association. In 1958, the A.B.A. convention held in London included a committee report condemning the Warren Court for comforting the Communists and treading on states' rights. Warren had responded by resigning from the association, becoming one of the few prominent lawyers in the country who were not members.

Resolved to reopen the lines of communication to the organized legal establishment, Burger attended the A.B.A.'s summer convention in Dallas. It could help him, and he could help it. He agreed to give four speeches. Introducing himself as "Warren Burger," he circulated through the crowds, hand outstretched. Everyone jostled to get close. Burger, the country's number-one judge, was on the hustings. He savored the role, buttonholing, glad-handing, softening his image as the "law and order" judge. He dined privately with Mitchell and the A.B.A. president. His speeches and private talks were calculatedly moderate and drew standing ovations. There was a message. A new "partnership" had been born among lawyers, judges, and law professors, for so long considered separate components of the legal world, often with sharply differing views. The Chief promised to attend A.B.A. sessions "for the rest of my days."

After the convention, Burger flew to Los Angeles to attend a dinner that President Nixon was giving to honor the first astronauts to have walked on the moon.

On August 29, Hugo Black was resting in his landmark federal house in the Old Town section of Washington's suburb of Alexandria, Virginia. Black's chambers had just received a petition requesting that he intervene to prevent delay of racial desegregation in thirty-three Mississippi school districts (*Alexander v. Holmes County Board of Education*). He was being asked to act alone as the supervisory Justice for the Fifth Circuit Court of Appeals, which covered the Deep South. Each Supreme Court Justice was assigned to one or more of the eleven federal appeals courts, and was responsible for dealing with special and emergency petitions.

At eighty-three, Black was the Court's oldest Associate Justice and its senior member. Thirty-one annual pictures of the Justices circled the wall above the bookshelves in the second-story study of his house. Shriveled and slightly stooped, Black had for years amazed everyone with his vitality. Until the previous month, he had played several sets of tennis each day on his private court. But now he was about to begin his thirty-second term in rather poor health. He had recently suffered a stroke while playing tennis, a fact that had not become public. He had recovered quickly, but the illness had left him weaker. He also had trouble remembering things that had just happened.

Black, born in Clay County, Alabama, only twenty-one years after the end of the Civil War, was an ardent, almost militant, supporter of school desegregation. He had generally approved the efforts of the Fifth Circuit Court of Appeals over the last fifteen years to implement the Supreme Court's desegregation decisions. The day before, the Fifth Circuit Court of Appeals had abruptly reversed course.

Earlier in the summer, the appeals court had asked the U.S. Department of Health, Education and Welfare to submit desegregation plans for the thirty-three school districts so it could order them implemented at the beginning of the school year. H.E.W. was in charge of drawing up the plans as mandated under the 1964 Civil Rights Act, and had submitted them on time. At the last minute, however, both H.E.W. and the Justice Department had asked for extensions until December 1, because, they claimed, the plans had been hastily prepared and would result in "chaos, confusion, and a catastrophic educational setback." It was the first time the federal government had supported a desegregation delay in the federal courts. To Black's astonishment and dismay, the Fifth Circuit had granted the delay, deferring to H.E.W.'s technical expertise. What was more, no specific date for implementing the plans for the actual desegregation had been set. Black saw the administration's move as Nixon's payoff to the South. This was part of the so-called "Southern Strategy" that had helped Nixon win the presidential election.

In spite of the Court's historic 1954 ruling *(Brown v. Board of*

Education I) that segregated schools were unconstitutional, a great majority of schools in the Deep South had circumvented desegregation. A bitter fifteen-year battle had dragged the federal courts into disputes over the details of various desegregation plans. While the bickering continued, the schools remained segregated. There had been some progress in recent years, mostly in the border states, and largely as a result of prodding by H.E.W. and the Justice Department. A series of Supreme Court decisions during the last decade had nullified many of the evasive tactics that school boards had used to fight actual desegregation.

Black fretted over the Nixon administration's go-slow policy. Nixon's pronouncements during his campaign, as well as the winks, nods and private assurances, had fueled another drive of Southern resistance. Now the South had another excuse for delay and, it appeared, a powerful ally. So long as the government and the courts were involved in debating plans, there would be protracted litigation. The pace had already been far too slow.

Black loved the South. A staunch New Dealer and a Southern populist, he was Alabama's senior Senator in 1937, when Roosevelt chose him for the Court. As a young man Black had briefly been a member of the Ku Klux Klan, but he had been, in fact, always a progressive on race relations. He had learned much about the subtleties of this matter as a rising politician. He considered the Court's desegregation decisions as among its most important. It pained him to see the agony that Southerners, both white and black, endured as a result of the Court's rulings. And it hurt him, too, that many white Southerners thought him a traitor. Black blamed himself in part. He had given in to Justice Felix Frankfurter's demand that the phrase "all deliberate speed" be included in the Court's 1955 ruling *(Brown v. Board of Education II)* to set the rate at which school systems must desegregate. That was language for lawyers and it had been a grievous mistake. The phrase had given the South its weapon. For fifteen years lawyers had seized upon it to defy the law of the land. "I never should have let Felix get that into the opinion," Black often said to his clerks.

It had become an excuse for delay, and it had also thrust federal judges into the business of deciding which plans would work and which would not, which schedules were fast enough and which were not. Judges were running school systems and making decisions about school locations and the racial proportion of faculty members, matters in which they had no experience. Black felt that for the federal courts to assume this role was the old "tyranny of the judges." He had an abiding fear of judges exercising so much discretion, having seen them dismantle the New Deal and defend corporate power in the early 1930s.

Black had always advised both the other Justices and his own clerks to "go for the jugular," a word he pronounced in his soft Alabama accent to rhyme with bugler. He meant that cases weren't won or lost, nor was the law decided, on legal niceties. Judges might say they were, but that was never the real reason. In each case there was always a crucial issue to locate. The issue might be hard to find, Black said, but once found it must be addressed.

In this latest case (*Alexander v. Holmes County Board of Education*), it would be easy for Black to follow his own advice. The issue was that the Court's *Brown* decisions were not being obeyed, the pace of desegregation was too slow. So the question was how to prevail over an apparent loss of will by the usually firm Fifth Circuit Court of Appeals, as well as over an administration that was, at the very least, hedging.

Five days later, on September 3, Black received a memorandum from the Justice Department. Solicitor General Griswold was urging that Black permit the Mississippi delay. Griswold acknowledged that such a delay "means in most situations, another school year, and that is a tragedy and a default." But he argued that it was inevitable, because of the need to revamp student assignments and reschedule and reshuffle faculties.

Black found this request absurd. But as the single Justice acting on the request to overturn the Fifth Circuit, he felt the need to proceed cautiously. He wanted to overturn the delay and order desegregation at once. Immediately. Technically he had the authority and could do what he thought was proper. But the full Court might not accept his position. If a majority disagreed, they would doubtless vote to hear the case during the regular term, and they might reverse him. Black wanted to avoid angering his colleagues.

Douglas occasionally acted alone as Circuit Justice when there was no chance that his views would be supported by a majority. The full Court at times reversed Douglas, but the other Justices still resented Douglas's taking matters into his own hands.

There was another factor too: the new Chief Justice. Burger's record on civil rights issues seemed decent. The new Chief had sought out Black's opinion on a number of matters over the summer, and Black had found him well-meaning and congenial. Still, Burger was clearly Nixon's man.

Above all, Black wanted to avoid triggering a split in the Court. He decided not to overturn the delay but to set forth his own views as strongly as possible and thus show the way for the Court. He chose his words carefully, writing slowly with a pencil on a yellow legal pad. A clerk assisted him, but Black's memory problems slowed their effort. He frequently needed to be reminded of what the Court of Appeals had said. His clerk patiently told him. Black would jot down some thoughts and ask the same question. On some points, he needed to be reminded several times. It was a slow and painful struggle. "For a great many years," Black finally wrote, "Mississippi had had in effect what is called a dual system of public schools, one system for white students only and one system for Negro students only."

His frustration and impatience came through in sarcasm. Black recounted the history of the desegregation cases, including the ill-chosen "all deliberate speed" language of the 1955 Brown case (*Brown v. Board of Education II*). The time for "all deliberate speed," he wrote, had "run out." He acknowledged that the most recent 1968 Court desegregation decision (*Green v. County School Board of New Kent County*) could be interpreted as approving a "transition period" from a dual to a unitary system. That decision could also be read to say that the Court required only that the school systems have *plans* for desegregation now, not that there must be desegregation now. For Black, that was an incorrect interpretation. The time for delay, postponement, foot-dragging, transition was over. But, he wrote, "I recognize that, in certain respects, my views as stated above go beyond anything this Court has expressly held to date. . . . Although I feel there is a strong possibility that the full Court would agree with my views, I cannot say definitely that they would. . . ."

On September 5, Black issued a five-page opinion that left the Fifth Circuit's delay intact, "deplorable as it is to me," and invited the N.A.A.C.P. Legal Defense and Education Fund, Inc.—commonly known as the "Inc. Fund"—that was representing the blacks in Mississippi to "present the issue to the full Court at the earliest possible opportunity."

The opinion might force the Court to take the case. Since 1954, the Court had always been unanimous in school cases, its strong commands to desegregate joined by every member. For fifteen years, the Justices had agreed that it was essential to let the South know that not a single Justice believed in anything less than full desegregation. To preserve that unanimity, the Court could not let the Fifth Circuit delay remain in force. Black's opinion put him on record as favoring a reversal.

The Inc. Fund followed Black's suggestion and filed an emergency petition asking for a prompt hearing. On October 7, the Justice Department formally urged the Court to use its discretionary power not to hear the case, arguing that it would be better to wait and see what the Mississippi schools did after the plans were submitted on December 1. At conference on October 9, Black was able to muster the four votes required to grant the Inc. Fund cert petition.* The Justices agreed to put the case at the head of the docket and to hear oral arguments in two weeks, on October 23.

The press followed the case closely. Justice Department officials were saying that a Court decision in favor of the Inc. Fund, one that demanded immediate desegregation, would be tough to enforce because the Department did not have enough lawyers, and because the South might react violently. The President remarked at a press conference that those who wanted "instant integration"

---

* A cert petition is a document filed with the Court, making the arguments as to why the Justices should take a particular case for consideration. Under the Court's internal rules, four votes—one less than a majority—are required to accept a case. The term cert petition is used in this book to refer both to *petitions for certiorari* and, in the case of appeals, to *statements of jurisdiction.*

were as "extremist" as those who wanted "segregation forever."
Lower federal court judges who were on the battle lines, with hundreds of similar school cases before them, waited to see what signal, if any, might be forthcoming.

On the morning of Thursday, October 23, the courtroom was
packed. Two hours, twice the normal time, had been allotted for
oral argument. Jack Greenberg, chief lawyer for the Inc. Fund,
opened. He said there had been enough stalling and enough law-
lessness by the Southern school officials. He reminded the Court
that its decisions were not being obeyed. Even after the Court's
ruling of the year before, the federal court in southern Mississippi
had spent a year arguing whether blacks were innately inferior to
whites. Greenberg summed up the situation in Mississippi. A related suit against the school board of Jackson, Mississippi, was still
pending in the Fifth Circuit. The man who had filed that suit,
Medgar Evers, would not see how it came out; he had been
gunned down near his home in Jackson. "The sorriest part of the
story lies in the exercise of discretion by some United States
District Court judges in that state," Greenberg said. They had delayed, they had refused to proceed, and they had exploited "ambiguity—real ambiguities and fancied ambiguities—in the decisions
of this Court and the Court of Appeals."

Greenberg was going for everything in this case. He wanted the
Court to take away the South's tested and most effective tool for delay. During the lower court battles, school districts often remained
segregated until all appeals were exhausted. He proposed that the
burden of proof be shifted, and that the Court order that the original
H.E.W. plans be implemented. Desegregation should be the status
quo. Its opponents could argue all they wanted, litigate all they
wanted, but the schools would be desegregated during that process.
He had a further suggestion. The recalcitrant District Court should
be told to stay out of the case, and the higher court of appeals, the
Fifth Circuit, should oversee implementation of the plans.

Greenberg wanted a strong desegregate-at-once statement that
would have a straightforward symbolic effect. He did not want the
Court to focus on the practical problems of ordering instant desegregation.

Louis Oberdorfer, a private attorney and a former law clerk for Justice Black, argued for a group of lawyers in private practice whose names read like a Who's Who of the legal establishment. The group opposed any desegregation delay and offered, if necessary, to supply attorneys to help enforce desegregation in the South.

Black broke into Oberdorfer's argument as if he were asking his former clerk for advice. "The thing to do is to say that the dual system is over and that it is to go into effect today . . . to go at it now—do you agree?" he asked softly.

"I agree with that, Your Honor," Oberdorfer responded, "without knowing exactly what 'now' is."

"I mean when we issue an order," Black said. He paused, then added: "If we do."

The audience broke into loud laughter. Black was not hiding his position.

Mitchell had assigned the head of the Civil Rights Division of the Justice Department, Jerris Leonard, to present the government's case. Leonard had barely given an account of government's successes in achieving desegregation in the South when he was interrupted by questions, first from Douglas and then from Black. Trying to brush them off, Leonard stated that there were practical problems, that the situation was complicated.

"What's so complicated?" Black challenged testily.

Leonard backpedaled. "What I'm pleading with this Court is not to do something precipitous—"

That set Black off. "Could anything be precipitous in this field now?" He could not hide his contempt. "With all the years gone by since our order was given?"

Leonard continued, but he was interrupted repeatedly.

Burger's low baritone attempted to soothe the waters. "Just one question if I may. If there had been no appeal here . . . can you assure us that the plans would have been submitted on December 1?"

Leonard was happy with that question. Yes, he assured the Chief. If the Court did nothing, the new plans would be submitted by then.

Burger was satisfied. It was already the end of October. Whether the Court overturned or upheld the lower court order, the plans would be submitted in about five weeks. But White and Black forced Leonard to concede that even if the plans were in by then, the latest appeals court decision did not guarantee that desegregation would take place before the next school year. Leonard admitted that another year might go by without much progress.

"Too many plans and not enough action," Black said with a thin smile, and the audience once again burst into laughter.

The next day, Friday, October 24, the Justices met in conference to discuss the case. Tradition dictated that the Chief speak first, that he outline the issues and briefly state his view. Then the discussion would proceed in order of seniority, starting with Black. Theoretically, voting would then take place in the opposite order, starting with the junior Justice, Thurgood Marshall. But over a period of time, the formal vote had been dispensed with, since, in expressing his views, each Justice let it be known where he stood. If his position was firm, it amounted to a vote.

The Chief, sitting in his chair at the end of the table, turned to the Mississippi case, the first major case of the term. The crowded courtroom the day before, the intense press interest, the passion of the lawyers and the obvious concern and emotion of his colleagues, suggested this case would be a landmark, an enduring guide for future cases of the same type. It might be the most important case since the original *Brown* decision. The Warren Court had built much of its reputation on fifteen years of school desegregation cases. Now, Warren Burger, as Chief Justice, would guide the Court to its next milestone. It would be a test of his leadership. From what he had heard and seen, Burger realized that unanimity, the unwritten rule in these cases, was going to be difficult to achieve. His own position differed from Black's September 5 opinion. Burger didn't think the Justice Department was being wholly unreasonable. Clearly there were practical problems—problems H.E.W. and the appeals court understood better than the Supreme Court—and it was important that the plans be workable. If revised plans were submitted December 1, five weeks from now, it would not be a disaster for school desegregation. Yet Burger opposed delay for its own sake, and that was clearly what the district court in Mississippi favored. The Supreme Court should take a strong stand against that sort of stalling. It should issue a statement that there would be no delay and ask the appeals court to move as quickly as possible without prolonged debate. Perhaps the Justices could quickly issue a short, simple order opposing delay, and follow it with an opinion laying out their reasoning.

Black, sitting as senior Justice at the opposite end of the conference table, spoke next. Five weeks, he said, was not the issue. It was symbolic. Any willingness on the part of the Court to grant a delay, no matter how slight, would be perceived as a signal. All those district court judges with hundreds of similar cases in their courts, all those Southern politicians, and the Nixon administration itself, were waiting for the Court to show any sign of weakening in its resolve. To appear to waver, even for a second, would be a betrayal. Black attacked Nixon and his administration bitterly. They were allowing the South hope of further evasions. The Court must resolve the problem and reaffirm its commitment before Nixon took hold of the situation. What little progress there had been in the South and the Border States had really occurred after the Justice Department and H.E.W. had stepped in to sue school boards and to draw up plans. The Court could not permit them to drop out of the struggle now.

All that was needed in this case was a short, simple order, Black argued, not an opinion. There had already been too much writing. Every time an opinion came down, some lawyer found an ambiguity, filed a suit and got more time. To involve the Court in debating details or plans would be disastrous. That was exactly what the proponents of delay wanted. There must be no mention of plans in the order, or of timetables. Black wanted unanimity as much as anyone, but if the Court's order mentioned the word "plan," he would dissent. There must be nothing that school districts or the Nixon administration could grab onto for another round of quibbling.

Black also agreed with the Inc. Fund that everyone seemed to have this matter all backwards. Everyone seemed to think that the status quo was segregation, and that monumental efforts had to be launched to change the status quo. But the law was the status quo. And the law, laid down fifteen years before by this Court, called for single, unitary school systems. The order should explicitly reject "all deliberate speed" and demand desegregation immediately, today, at once, now. No more rhetoric. "If anybody writes," Black concluded, "I dissent."

There was a moment of stunned silence. A dissent by Black, a giant of the Court, an historic figure, would make it look as if the Court was in retreat. It would give new hope to the South's "never" faction. Several Justices spoke up out of turn to ask Black just how the Court could expect to enforce this order now. Black refused to discuss it. "You do what you want, and I'm going ahead," he said.

Next it was Douglas's turn to speak. Back from a summer in the Cascade Mountains of Washington State, Douglas was an imposing physical presence in the conference. White-haired, with a cowlick, a sinewy six-footer, he looked uncomfortable in his inexpensive business suit, rumpled white dress shirt and Dacron tie. Tanned and weathered, his face reflected his many off-season trips to all parts of the world. His twenty books, countless articles and speeches, and even the cowboy dime novels published under a pen name in his youth reflected his individualistic values. Douglas had built his life on adversity: poverty, polio, camping accidents. He had spent most of his years moving against the grain. He had been twice mentioned as a vice-presidential candidate, and once he had been offered the nomination, but he had decided against a politician's life. Nonetheless, he had never hesitated publicly to urge his internationalist views, even in the face of the fervent anti-communism of the 1950s.

Douglas's soft voice countered his authoritative tone. He rarely spoke at length in conference. He had decided years before that attempts to persuade were futile, or, even worse, counterproductive. His colleagues knew where he stood on most issues. He unabashedly accepted liberal dogma. He was for the individual over government, government over big business, and the environment over all else. But Douglas still insisted on laying out his exact resolution of each element of a case in his formal written opinions. If he could not persuade his colleagues, he could at least spread his ideas outside the Court.

Douglas wanted the Court to move aggressively on the race issue. In typewriter cadence, he clicked off several sentences on his general position, moved to his next point, kicking the table as he paused, jumped to another point without a connective, flapped his ear nervously while staring coldly across the table, and finally, again without warning, tied up his first and last points in terse summation.

To the others, the position was clear. Douglas would support Black.

John Harlan, quietly chain-smoking Larks, had been scrupulously attentive during Black's tirade. One hand rested near his grandfather's gold watch chain strung across the vest of his dark suit. Harlan had worn the same conservative suits, ordered by mail from London, virtually every day since he had come to the Court fourteen years before. Gaunt and ramrod-straight, he had a commanding presence. An ulcer operation had removed half his stomach, and he had no extra weight on his lean, 6-foot-1 frame. A Wall Street lawyer from a wealthy family, private schools, then Princeton and Oxford, John Harlan was the quintessential patrician, generally unflappable and unfailingly courteous.

His grandfather, named for the country's fourth Chief Justice, John Marshall, had been a Justice for thirty-four years. He had been known as the "Great Dissenter," the only Justice to dissent in the famous nineteenth-century case *Plessy v. Ferguson*, which had permitted segregated schools until it was finally overturned by the 1954 *Brown* ruling. Like his grandfather, Harlan viewed the law as almost a religious calling. Despite—and also because of—his near-blindness in the last few years, Harlan was the Court's hardest working member. He read about 150 words per minute, bent over, his eyes nearly touching the paper. Yet he was the Court's most prolific writer. No matter how insignificant the disagreement or how minor the case, Harlan felt compelled to spell out his views for the sake of intellectual honesty. He made one exception to that rule: school desegregation cases.

Harlan had been the "conservative conscience" of the Warren

Court, a frequent dissenter. He advocated restraint rather than activism. Despite his disagreements with Black, the two were as close as brothers. Harlan felt that he understood Black's concerns, particularly his guilt and anguish over "all deliberate speed." Yet he was offended by Black's speech, not because of the attack on Nixon—that was just Hugo—but because an order was no way to decide a major case. It would be preposterous for the Court just to say "Do it now," without offering any reasoning. The district and appeals courts needed guidance, and that required an opinion.

Black was being too emotional. Ever since his stroke, Black had been increasingly unpredictable, testy and belligerent, Harlan thought. "Difficult," Harlan called it. Black wanted to decide this case in a spasm of indignation. Harlan would not allow it. For years, internal disagreements had been festering among the Justices on the difficult details of desegregation. They had subordinated those disagreements to maintain their united front. Harlan felt that this might be the case where their differences might erupt into public view. In the current climate, the shattering of the Court's unanimity could set the Court and the country back several years or decades. But Black had laid down a challenge: Do it my way or I'll take those risks. Black was tinkering with the bottom line—unanimity.

Harlan said he agreed that delay should be rejected out of hand in strong language, but in a well-reasoned opinion. He would go along with much of what the Inc. Fund wanted—taking the case away from the federal district court in Mississippi and making sure there would be no long arguments over plans. But he was not going along with any notion of immediate desegregation. The Court—the Warren Court—had been criticized too often for its pie-in-the-sky views. Now the Burger Court had to show consideration for the realities. Instant desegregation was impossible.

Harlan also strongly disagreed with Black's notion that "all deliberate speed" was at the heart of the delays. Another phrase, or no phrase at all, would not have helped. The problem of achieving desegregation in the South was intractable, destined to take a long time no matter what the Court had said fifteen years before. But Nixon and his administration were also a new reality. Harlan was deeply suspicious of Nixon's motives. To affirm the Court of Appeals, as Burger seemed to favor, would send the wrong signal. Whatever the Court said, it should overturn the Court of Appeals. Harlan wanted to send a strong message to both Nixon and the South that the Court was not backing off. Then Harlan laid down his own challenge. He wanted unanimity, but if Black wrote a separate opinion, he too would write separately.

Brennan was disturbed to see the conference splintering. He agreed with much of what Black said, but one had to be practical. He wanted to stay in the middle. That had been his vantage point for years as the prime mover on the Warren Court. Physically smaller than his colleagues, Brennan was the most energetic advocate. He cajoled in conference, walked the halls constantly and worked the phones, polling and plotting strategy with his allies. He was thin and gray-haired, and his easy smile and bright blue eyes gave him a leprechaun's appearance as he sidled up and threw his arms around his colleagues. His warmth allowed Brennan alone to call the reserved Harlan "Johnny." It had been Brennan who had sat each Thursday with Warren preparing an orchestration for the Friday conference.

"Well, guys, it's all taken care of," Brennan often told his clerks after the sessions with Warren. With votes from Fortas, Marshall, and usually Douglas, Brennan rarely failed to put together a majority. He had dissented only three times the previous term, only thirty times in the last half decade. Now, with Burger replacing Warren and Black threatening to dissent, the situation looked bleak. So Brennan said little.

Potter Stewart spoke, and then Byron White. Both were upset by Black's threat, and his absolutist position. The school year had already begun. The Court had to recognize that. They both believed that the intricate processes of desegregating schools couldn't be accomplished over a weekend.

Stewart had been an appeals court judge before coming to the Court. He wanted to help the lower courts, not to confuse them. Black's "now" view might make good reading, but the trial courts needed to know what to do. If the Court said "now," the appeals and district court judges would simply ask, "What does that mean?" Worse, Stewart feared that the lower courts would lose faith in the Supreme Court if it came out with some abstract pronouncement.

There was no question where the final speaker at conference, Thurgood Marshall, stood on the question of school desegregation. Marshall had headed the Inc. Fund for twenty-two years, from its founding in 1939 until 1961, when John F. Kennedy appointed him to the Second Circuit Court of Appeals. The great-grandson of a slave, son of the steward at a fashionable all-white Chesapeake Bay yacht club, Marshall pioneered the civil rights battle against segregation in housing, public accommodations and schools. He won 29 of the 32 cases he argued before the Supreme Court for the Inc. Fund.

In 1965, Lyndon Johnson appointed Marshall Solicitor General. When Marshall hesitated, Johnson's closing argument was, "I want folks to walk down the hall at the Justice Department and look in the door and see a nigger sitting there." Two years later Johnson appointed Marshall to the Supreme Court. Marshall had not sought and had not wanted the appointment. He preferred the more active give-and-take of public-interest law. His jurisprudence was long settled; so at conference, Marshall was relaxed, almost intuitively reaching his common-sense solution. He had fit easily into the Warren liberal majority. Plain-spoken and direct, Marshall saw his job as casting his vote and urging his colleagues to do what was right. On the Court, he had little interest in perfecting the finger points of the law. He often told his clerks, only half jokingly, "I'll do whatever Bill [Brennan] does," sometimes even jotting "follow Bill" on his notes. He trusted Brennan's resolution of the detailed, technical questions of legal scholarship. The clerks had taken to calling Marshall "Mr. Justice Brennan-Marshall." Often he would follow White on antitrust cases. But on discrimination cases, Marshall followed no one.

Marshall had headed the team of lawyers who argued the original *Brown* cases. He remained unhappy with "all deliberate speed." He shifted his massive six-foot-one, two-hundred-and-fifty-pound body slightly as he closed in on his point. He agreed with Black that the phrase was ill-chosen. But the most important element in this case was unanimity for desegregation. There must be no suggestion that the Court was backtracking. He was a practical man. If necessary, he said, he was willing to go along with a delay to December 1 for submission of plans.

But that was not the major point. Marshall was concerned with bread-and-butter issues—getting black kids and white kids in the same schools. The key was a date for implementation of the plans, and the Fifth Circuit had not set one. Without a date, even the Justice Department admitted that implementation would not occur until the next school year. Surely the schools could do better than that, Marshall said. He proposed setting the implementation deadline for January, the beginning of the next semester.

As the Justices expressed their views, Burger grew increasingly worried. The new Chief had seen during his first weeks that many cases were not decided at conference. Feelings were tentative, disagreements subtle. Often, something had to be put down on paper before a consensus emerged. Burger knew the press would view this case as the first test of his leadership. None of the opinions argued so far was nearly ready to be issued. Burger didn't want to let things get any more out of control than they already were.

The Justices did have some points of agreement. First, the Supreme Court itself must not appear to be delaying. An expedited order would have to be issued soon—perhaps by the coming week. Second, the Court of Appeals should retain jurisdiction and, thus, control. The federal district court, which had allowed years of stalling, should not be involved. There even appeared to be a majority for reversing the appeals court's decision to grant a delay in the submission of plans. So that issue was settled. But beyond these points, there was a broad spectrum of opinion on what the Court should do and say. Should the Court set specific deadlines for the appeals court, or allow it some flexibility to work out the problem?

In keeping with the tradition that the Chief Justice assigns opinions if he is a member of the majority, Burger said he would try to work out language in a simple order that would encompass the concerns of all the Justices. That could be followed by a full opinion if they all agreed to it.

The way Burger analyzed the conference discussion, the main obstacle to a unanimous decision was Black. Douglas was following his lead. They were alone in insisting that the Court should order desegregation now and that no opinion should be written, points on which even Brennan and Marshall seemed open to compromise. If they could be kept from joining Black, then Black would almost certainly back down, despite his rhetoric in conference. Burger needed first to put together a consensus opinion with Stewart and White, whose views were closest to his own. From their comments about the need to be realistic, Burger felt that he could go along with anything they might decide on. Harlan was the next available vote. He might want to use stronger language, might be more inclined to fix a firm deadline for implementation. Both would be okay. Harlan might be able to draft something that would draw Brennan and Marshall over to their side.

After the conference, Burger met with Harlan and Stewart and asked for their help. They had been through this process before, working with widely disparate views, attempting to reach a common ground.

Harlan said that he resented Black's threat to break unanimity by dissenting. It amounted to "blackmail." He was perplexed by Black's unrealistic solution. The Court couldn't snap its fingers and create desegregation. He could see that Black was up to his old tricks, saying "Here is where I stand," and professing indifference to the others' views. Burger asked Harlan if he would draft a possible order for the Court to issue. He wanted Harlan's thoughts as a starting point.

Harlan went to his chambers to work. Normally, he would have a clerk prepare a first draft. This one he did himself. His grandfather's picture looked down on him from the wall opposite his desk. Harlan's face almost touched the paper as he pushed a ball-point pen across the pad. The writing was hardly legible.

"Proposed Order and Judgment," he wrote at the top.

"The question presented is one of paramount importance. . . . In view of the gravity of the issues and the exigency of prompt compliance with the Constitution, we deem it appropriate to enter the following order." He paused and added, " . . . with the opinion of the Court to follow this order." There simply had to be an opinion.

"The Court of Appeals . . . is reversed," he wrote, saying that the Court of Appeals should determine "forthwith" if the original H.E.W. plans were "adequate and reasonable interim means"— that was for realists like himself—"to achieve immediate desegregation." That last phrase was for Black.

But when should the order be implemented? The question had been left up in the air at conference. It wasn't clear that a single deadline could be set. Some school systems might be able to desegregate immediately.

"The earliest possible moment," Harlan wrote, adding, "and in no event later than _____ ___, _____." He left blanks. An outer limit probably should be set, perhaps midyear, but there had been no consensus.

The two-page order was immediately sent down to the Court's printing shop in the basement. Even the most tentative drafts were generally printed and copies distributed to the other chambers. Early printed drafts in cases were never released, only the final ones.

The next morning, Saturday, October 25, most of the Justices came to the Court. Black stayed home.

The Chief asked Harlan and White to his chambers to go over Harlan's draft. Burger and White had also drafted possible orders. With a few changes, however, Harlan's draft served as the basis for their agreement. They decided to leave the implementation date open, to be decided by the Fifth Circuit, since any date the Court set could be seen as a retreat. Burger then sent a memo to the other Justices telling them that Harlan and White and he had met and that this was their submission.

CONFIDENTIAL
MEMORANDUM TO THE CONFERENCE

Justice Harlan, Justice White and I met today and working from three rough, preliminary drafts of alternative dispositions developed the enclosed order to be followed by an opinion.

The draft reflects not necessarily our final view but a "passable" solution of the problem.

We have concluded, tentatively, to avoid fixing an "outside" date. I am partly persuaded to do this because of the risk that it could have overtones which might seem to invite dilatory tactics.

[Signed] WEB

When Brennan, Marshall and Douglas reviewed the proposed order, they agreed that it simply was not strong enough. The order would have to be improved before they could find it palatable, and certainly it was not going to be acceptable to Black. Marshall had been willing to compromise as long as there was an implementation deadline that insured desegregation by the next semester. But now he thought Black might be right. His insistence on "now" might be unreasonable, but it was quite likely the Court's best posture. It might be best to send a shock-wave message. An impractical order directing desegregation "now" might underscore the Court's seriousness. Also, Marshall reasoned, such an order would certainly mean desegregation by the next semester.

Marshall was also concerned that he not end up on the wrong side of a Black dissent. He did not want to be in a position where another member of the Court was claiming that he, of all people, was backing down. What the newspapers said the day after the Court issued its decision would be important. Marshall had to protect his position. He instructed his clerks to begin work on an opinion. At the same time, he did not want to lose touch with the others, so he sent one of his two clerks to talk with Harlan's clerks, to see if some compromise could be reached.

Meanwhile, Brennan decided that he too had to do something. Black, Douglas, Marshall and he could not let the more conservative quartet of Burger, Harlan, Stewart and White control the outcome by having the only drafts in circulation.* In phone conversations with Black, Brennan became convinced that Black was adamant. The collective liberal position would have to be largely

---

* It was still an eight-man Court since no replacement for Fortas had been confirmed by the Senate.

Black's if they were going to act as a bloc. Black's view was appealing. The Court had to be tough and dramatic, perhaps a little unreasonable, in order not to appear to be buckling.

After talking it over with Douglas and Marshall, Brennan threw himself into composing a draft order. He wrote that desegregation according to the "all deliberate speed" standard "is no longer Constitutionally permissible. The obligation of the federal courts is to achieve desegregation . . . NOW." The H.E.W. plans could be used if they achieve desegregation "immediately." Desegregation was the status quo.

In order to expedite action, Brennan wrote, the Court of Appeals "is requested so far as possible and necessary, to lay aside all other business of the court to carry out this mandate." Such a request from the Supreme Court was unusual. It would impress everyone with the urgency of the matter and the extent of the Court's commitment.

Black was home on Sunday, October 26, 1969, studying the Chief's proposed order. He thought it awful. He liked Brennan's proposal, which reflected his own arguments from conference two days earlier. Perhaps the others had not taken his threat to write a dissent seriously. Black decided that he had better make good on his word, and he began writing. Beginning with a history of the *Brown* decision, renewing his attack on "all deliberate speed," Black scrawled his message across a yellow legal pad in large crooked letters: "It is almost beyond belief that the factors mentioned by this Court in *Brown II*, to permit some slight delay in 1954, are precisely the same considerations relied upon in this case to justify yet another delay in 1969."

Criticizing the use of the word "interim" in the Chief's order, he wrote that

> any talk of interim orders necessarily implies that complete total and immediate abolition of the dual school system need not come about and the phrase "the earliest possible time" is ominously reminiscent of the phrase "as soon as practicable" used in *Brown II*.
>
> The time has passed for plans and promises to desegregate. The Court's order here, however, seems to be written on the premise that

schools can dally along with still more and more plans. The time for such delay I repeat we have already declared to be gone. . . .

I would have the Court issue the following order.

Black attached a copy of Brennan's order.

In case anyone missed the import of what he was doing, Black drafted a cover memo to the conference. He had it sent to the Court and printed, with a copy for each Justice.

The letter from the Chief Justice circulated in connection with the proposed order and judgment in this case suggests that the proposal now has the approval of three members of the Court.

It is possible that this proposal will obtain a majority and that the Court may want to issue the order on Monday. Should that be the case, I would not want to delay such action, but will dissent as I have in the opinion circulated herewith.

While a dissent at this time may seem premature, this procedure has been followed only to avoid further delay.

One more thought should be added about the Court's suggestion that a Court opinion will later follow this order. I am opposed to that. There has already been too much writing and not enough action in this field. Writing breeds more writing and more disagreements all of which inevitably delay action. The duty of this Court and of others is too simple to require perpetual litigation and deliberation, that duty is to extirpate all racial discrimination from our system of public schools NOW.

When Harlan read Black's memo late Sunday afternoon, he was deeply upset. Black wasn't circulating it to avoid delay; he was making a simple power play. Obviously they all wanted unanimity. Black was telling each of them that they were going to have to deal with him to get it.

Harlan hadn't discussed the case with Black after the conference, nor did he want to discuss it with him now. Black was dug in. Discussion would only aggravate matters. The only hope was Brennan and Marshall. Though they seemed to have joined Black, perhaps they could be peeled away. Harlan phoned Brennan.

Black was just being unreasonable, Harlan said. The differences among them were not that great. No one, including the Chief, was really trying to stall desegregation. They all agreed on the need to speed up the process; the question was simply how to be most effective. Harlan was willing to go along with something stronger, more emphatic, than the Chief's proposal. Burger's memo made it clear that the draft was not a final view.

Brennan agreed that Black was being unreasonable. But it was essential to maintain unanimity, and Black was not bluffing. He would dissent from anything less than a strong command to desegregate now.

Now Harlan foresaw an uphill struggle. He detected a tone of skepticism in Brennan's voice. That meant that Brennan and no doubt Marshall were firmly with Black and Douglas. Harlan knew that Brennan's ties to Black were strong, certainly more important than Brennan's to him. During the 1960s, Brennan had won votes from Black, Douglas and Marshall, but not many from Harlan, whom Brennan considered conservative. But Harlan was certain that he himself was as strong a supporter of desegregation as anyone else; it was simply that determination had to be tempered by an understanding of the practicalities, crucial to public acceptance of the Court's school opinions. He saw himself as an arbiter, and now he decided to make a last effort in that role.

The Chief was alarmed at Black's memo and his threatened dissent. If the Court's unanimity broke apart on a school case, particularly so early in his tenure, he would be declared an instant failure. He and the Court might never recover. The press would compare him unfavorably to Warren, who had held the Court together for fifteen years on these cases. They would say that the Court had collapsed in the first month of Burger's first term.

From his years on the Court of Appeals in Washington, Burger knew that circulating draft proposals forced the others to deal with the writer and his draft. It structured the debate on the writer's terms, allowing concessions to be made while preserving the overall thrust.

Burger didn't like Brennan's proposed order. It didn't seem responsive to his own original proposal. The differences didn't seem reconcilable. Burger knew that Harlan, Stewart and White were irritated with Black's memo and his proposed dissent. There was little that Burger could do about the order now. That was something for the others to work out. For the sake of unanimity, he would go along with anything they could all agree on. Burger turned instead to getting out his draft opinion, the more detailed explanation of the Court's reasoning. It could serve as a basis for uniting all of them. "I'm going to write an opinion that everyone will agree on or it will be a long time before there is anything in this case," the Chief told his clerks. It wasn't a threat. He was simply determined to show leadership.

The next two days, Monday and Tuesday, were a whirl of paper. Drafts and counterdrafts of proposed orders floated around. Scribbled ideas and proposed changes flew from chamber to chamber as the Justices added their thoughts. The main actors were the Chief, Stewart, Harlan, Brennan and Marshall. Black and Douglas had apparently decided on their view. White was leaving most of the work to the others. His main concern was unanimity.

The eight-man Court seemed deadlocked 4 to 4. Black, Douglas, Brennan and Marshall were on one side, agreeing on immediate desegregation and no full Court opinion. On the other side were Burger, Harlan, Stewart and White trying for something firm but less absolute, more practical, more sympathetic to the concerns of the Executive Branch.

Burger worked hard on his draft opinion. When it was typed he gave rough copies only to those who seemed to be on his side—Harlan, Stewart and White.

Stewart read it quickly. It confirmed his worst suspicions. Burger was a part of the Nixon administration. The draft opinion read like an administration press release. It was an unbelievable document, listing all the administrative difficulties involved in school desegregation, lauding H.E.W., flattering the administration for its efforts in the face of the problems. It was also a confused, rambling account, tracing the history of desegregation cases, offering all the arguments for delay and then, like an O. Henry short story, it ended with a surprise. No delays would be granted.

Stewart knew that if the opinion were issued, it would effectively make law out of the administrative difficulties encountered by the government in enforcing desegregation. It was a thoroughly disreputable effort. He told one of his clerks the opinion was too abstract and asked him to draft something that would stick to the facts in this case, make no dangerous statements, and steer between the Chief and Black.

In the meantime, Harlan was polishing off another draft order—one last effort to bring Brennan and Marshall over to his side. He decided to set two specific deadlines. First, the Court of Appeals would be instructed to decide on specific desegregation plans by November 10 and to issue an order putting those plans in effect. He would allow two months for the details to be worked out. Actual desegregation had to take place by December 31. Students would attend desegregated schools after that date. He still called this "interim relief." He was certain that once the desegregation was initiated, there would have to be some changes to accommodate unforeseen developments. This schedule would give the school board time to implement the plans, but told them in no uncertain terms that they could not wait until the coming year.

Harlan circulated his second draft order on Tuesday. Stewart's draft opinion was also ready. With the Chief's draft, the more conservative group now had three documents to go over. They caucused. Harlan indicated he had no support from Brennan and Marshall for his latest effort. But more significantly, the more conservative members could not begin to agree among themselves. For his part, White was unwilling to spend any more time on the issue. He disliked giving a disproportionate amount of his schedule to politically sensitive cases. The Court had over a hundred cases per term. White was more interested in the bottom line than in every intermediate step. One by one, they decided that they might as well give in and join Brennan. It was more important that the Court be unanimous, perhaps just as important that they act that week, to emphasize their commitment to desegregation. By the end of the day all four had approved the Brennan order with a few changes in wording. There would be no full opinion to follow. It was to be issued as a two-page *per curiam*, meaning that it was the opinion of the Court without a designated author. Though it was an opinion, it read like an order, with a short introduction and five numbered paragraphs directing the Fifth Circuit.

Black had won every major point. "All deliberate speed" was declared over, "no longer Constitutionally permissible." No delay would be permitted. In effect, the Court ruling said that the deadline had passed fifteen years ago. The final opinion stated, "The obligation of every school district is to terminate dual school systems at once and to operate now and hereafter only unitary schools." The Fifth Circuit was directed to issue its order "effective immediately." The H.E.W. plans could be used insofar as they helped achieve immediate and total desegregation.

Stewart thought the case was a demonstration of the new Chief's inability to lead them through a crisis. The Court's reputation was a result of its bold desegregation decisions, and Burger had done nothing to sustain that reputation. The Chief's job was to harmonize and synthesize. The Court had agreed on a two-page order and had issued it quickly, but the Justices had not agreed on its legal grounds or the reasoning behind it. Burger, Stewart concluded, had failed to bring about a true consensus.

Stewart felt that Earl Warren would have explained to Black that no one was going to dissent, period, and that they would all work something out. Black would never have pulled such a stunt with Warren.

Harlan withheld judgment on Burger. Given Black's obstinacy, any Chief Justice would have had difficulty with this situation, Harlan felt. But he did view the resolution as particularly lamentable. Though the Court had acted unanimously, it had handed down a meaningless and unworkable abstraction to the lower courts. What could "immediate" and "at once" and "now" mean to lower court judges faced with fact-finding and competing interests that had to be weighed?

Burger was elated that the decision was unanimous.

The next morning, Wednesday, October 29, six days after oral arguments, the decision was announced. The news stories noted that the decision was a setback for the Nixon administration—the end of dual school systems, and without further delay. Senator Strom Thurmond of South Carolina decried the decision, while praising the President. "The Nixon Administration stood with the South in this case."

The new Court under Burger, declared former Alabama Governor George Wallace, was "no better than the Warren Court"; the Justices were a bunch of "limousine hypocrites."

One of Burger's clerks congratulated him on standing up to the administration, saying this case would show the country that the Chief wasn't Nixon's puppet. Burger was flabbergasted. "Do you think people really think I'm a Nixon puppet?"

At the White House, the President and his strategists were content. Nixon had lined up his administration squarely in favor of reasonable delay. The Supreme Court had said no more delay. Elections could be won or lost on the question. White Southerners would be enraged by the decision, but it was the Court's fault, not his.

Nixon's Southern strategy suffered another defeat a few weeks later. The President had nominated conservative South Carolinian Clement F. Haynsworth, Jr., chief judge of the Fourth Circuit Court of Appeals, to fill Fortas's seat on the Supreme Court. But the liberals—by then recovered from the shock of the Fortas affair—had counterattacked.

Labor and civil rights groups opposed the confirmation, shrilly denouncing Haynsworth's opinions as consistently anti-union and against school desegregation. The liberals picked up the support of moderate Republicans when it was discovered that Haynsworth had participated in a case indirectly involving a company in which he held stock. It wasn't a major conflict of interest, according to experts who testified. But, added to the raw political opposition to Haynsworth, it was enough to tilt the votes against him. On November 21, the Senate rejected Haynsworth's nomination 55 to 45.

Burger had been looking forward to the arrival of a conservative vote that might help him shift the Court's direction. He blamed the White House for mishandling the nomination. Haynsworth was a victim of Washington's "jungle" politics, Burger told his clerks. While he himself knew how to operate in that jungle, the hapless

Haynsworth, Burger said, simply did not. He had not performed well at his hearing before the Senate Judiciary Committee. That had done him in.

Brennan, though he held out little hope that Haynsworth would share many of his views, had thought him nevertheless an acceptable candidate. Just after the nomination was announced, Brennan had sent Haynsworth a congratulatory note. Black also felt the Senate had made a serious mistake in rejecting Haynsworth. He told friends he thought Haynsworth was a "decent man" who would make a fine Justice. He was fond of him. The night the nomination was defeated, Black had him over for dinner at his house on Lee Street.

For the Court, the defeat meant more months without a ninth Justice. Numerous petitions for Supreme Court review were pending. Four votes were needed before the Court would take a case, and dozens of cases were on hold because they had only three votes. They had been put in a "hold for Haynsworth" file, to see if he would cast the fourth vote. Now the file was renamed "Hold for Justice X." The number of petitions waiting there grew each day.

Harlan had looked forward to Burger's arrival, and the first Friday conferences since he had come seemed more open. Everyone spoke more freely, more persuasively. There was not the sense, as there had been at times under Warren, that the debate was a sham. The Warren-Brennan pre-conference strategy sessions, during which the two Justices coordinated their positions, were things of the past.

Harlan thought it possible that if Burger and the new Justice were independent and open to reason, new majorities might emerge once Fortas's seat was filled. Harlan despised coalitions, revering reasoned discourse among independent Justices. But in the first months of Burger's tenure, the new Chief gave Harlan reason to pause. Harlan confided to his clerks that Burger seemed inclined to slide around issues in order to achieve certain results. He paid less attention to legal reasoning than Harlan thought necessary. He was willing to decide cases without explaining the logic or the Constitutional grounds, and without responding to each argument he had rejected.

Harlan did not believe that the Court should reach out to decide questions that were not specifically before it in a case. But at the same time, the Court had to address issues that were fairly presented. When faced with one of the numerous statutory cases, those calling upon the Court to interpret the meaning of a law or to establish the intent of the Congress that had passed it—the Court should not avoid its responsibility. In one such case (*Tooahnippah v. Hickel*), the issue was whether the Interior Department had the power to invalidate an American Indian's will leaving personal property to his niece and nothing to an illegitimate daughter. The vote was 7 to 1 to reverse the Interior Department's action, with Black the lone dissenter. Burger assigned himself to write the opinion for the majority. The case was a "peewee," Harlan's term for insignificant matters that came before the Court, but he objected to the Interior Department's high-handed paternalism.

When the Chief's first draft came around, Harlan discovered that Burger had limited himself to the question of whether the federal courts had either the jurisdiction or the power to review an order of the Secretary of the Interior disapproving an Indian will. The Chief had not decided the question of whether the Secretary of the Interior had properly exercised his power. Instead, the case was remanded—sent back—to the Court of Appeals for decision. Harlan was distressed that Burger would dispose of a case without addressing all the basic questions. The case might be a "peewee," but every case deserved as much time, effort and explanation as it took to make the issues clear.

Harlan wrote a memo to the other Justices suggesting that the Court resolve the real question and provide some guidance. In response, the Chief produced a second draft in which he added a single, final paragraph saying that the Department's decision was "arbitrary and capricious" and was therefore overturned.

To Harlan, this was not an adequate explanation. The Chief had not reviewed the applicable statutes and legislative history nor had he surveyed the prior administrative decisions of the Interior Department. Burger had reached the correct result, as far as Harlan was concerned, but there was simply no explanation for the decision in his draft. The Chief would overrule one particular decision of the Interior Department, but leave unclear the scope of the Secretary's power to disapprove wills.

After his own careful review, Harlan circulated an opinion explaining how the Secretary had exceeded his authority. Since he agreed with the Chief's result, he joined the Chief's opinion, but he added his own "concurring" comments to be published simultaneously with Burger's opinion.

The Chief did not like concurrences. He felt that they were often nitpicking, that they added little to the law, and that at times they split majorities. Separate opinions by each individual Justice giving his precise reasoning were generally an unnecessary exercise. They confused as much as they enlightened the lower court judges, Burger felt. Also, concurrences detracted from the main opinion and were, in some cases, almost an insult to the author assigned for the majority.

Burger decided in this case to borrow much of Harlan's concurrence, hoping that Harlan, seeing his reasoning adopted, would not publish. But Harlan still wasn't satisfied. Burger's next draft was much better, but not good enough for Harlan. Burger had reached the crux of the case, but in a mediocre way, by simply paraphrasing sentences from Harlan's opinion. He had not used Harlan's citations from prior Court decisions, or his review of the legislative history and prior administrative practices that was so critical in determining the intent of the Congress that had passed the law.

Harlan considered the Chief's new draft a half measure. Why not use the legal core of the opinion, or ask to borrow it verbatim? But he had a dilemma. If he didn't withdraw his concurrence, now that Burger had gone so far to accommodate him, the Chief might be offended. Harlan never wished to offend anyone unnecessarily. He mulled it over. Ultimately, as always, each Justice could publish what he wanted in terms of separate concurring or dissenting opinions. Despite the closeness of the Chief's latest draft to his concurrence, Harlan told his clerks, "We're going with it." He instructed that his concurrence be shortened slightly, printed, and published when the decision was announced. Harlan was determined to hold to his standard of meticulousness.

*　　　*　　　*

For Burger there were no more intimidating experiences than his first few encounters with Marshall in the marble corridors of the Court.

"What's shakin', Chiefy baby?" Marshall would sing out. Puzzled, Burger mumbled a greeting of his own. It did not take Burger long to realize the pleasure Marshall got from making him uncomfortable. Marshall had many similar stories of putting people on. A favorite of his involved unsuspecting tourists who mistakenly entered the Justices' private elevator. Finding a lone black man standing there, they said, "First floor please." "Yowsa, yowsa," Marshall responded as he pretended to operate the automated elevator and held the door for the tourists as they left. Marshall regularly recounted the story, noting the tourists' puzzlement and then confusion as they watched him walk off, and later realized who he was.

But Burger genuinely liked Marshall. After all, Burger had been a leader on a biracial committee in St. Paul that had tried to resolve police problems with the black community thirty years earlier—long before the issue was fashionable. He considered himself a moderate liberal, a Lincoln Republican, on race issues. And it was because of these values that his vote in a mid-November conference troubled him.

The case, *Evans v. Abney,* involved a segregated 100-acre public park in Macon, Georgia. The land had been willed to the city in 1911 by a Georgia segregationist, who had stipulated that it be kept a whites-only park. For a half-century the park was kept segregated, until in the 1966 term, the Supreme Court had ruled that the park must be integrated. The man's heirs subsequently sued to recover the land, saying that the purpose of his will had been violated. The Georgia courts agreed.

With some misgivings, Burger joined a 5-to-2 majority in conference to uphold the Georgia decision. Brennan and Douglas dissented; Marshall did not vote, since he had been involved in the case three years before as Solicitor General.

Brennan hammered away in his dissent, arguing that the closing of a public park was a discriminatory action by the state and the

Georgia court. It violated the equal protection guarantees of the Fourteenth Amendment.

Black, writing for the majority, was equally forceful. What the Georgia court had done was not discriminatory. The park was being closed for both blacks and whites alike, he asserted. It was a racially neutral act based on the state court's interpretation of its own racially neutral law on wills. The determination of wills had always been a state question, he argued. If the Court intervened, it would be carving out one more area of federal control. This was a state matter. It was also a question of a person's right to dispose of his property as he wished. Black felt strongly on that subject. He wanted no interference with his wish to have his Court papers destroyed when he died.

Burger agreed that the federal courts should not extend Fourteenth Amendment guarantees to such traditional areas of state control. But he wanted to avoid having his Court support the segregationists. As he frequently did, Burger went to Harlan for help. Harlan was an expert on federalism—the allocation of power between the state and federal governments. Harlan appreciated Burger's intention, but he said he could not find any part of the Constitution that prevented the Georgia court from directing that the land be returned to the heirs. And the federal courts had no power to order it in any case. In a literal sense, Black was right; it was not a discriminatory act.

Burger suggested that perhaps they could find a more limited ground than the Fourteenth Amendment and simply assert that the Georgia decision was "wrong" because the Georgia courts had misapplied the Georgia law. They should have ruled that the donor's basic intent had been to bequeath a park, that while he did want it segregated, he was primarily concerned that there be a park. Therefore, under Georgia law, the Georgia courts should have construed the will to leave the park *public* and, therefore, *integrated.*

Politely, Harlan asked on what grounds he based his decision. What part of the Constitution did Burger intend to cite to justify such a ruling?

Burger said he preferred to avoid specifying any grounds.

A federal court, Harlan reminded the Chief, even the Supreme Court, couldn't simply tell a state how to interpret its laws without providing a constitutional reason, whether it be equal protection or some other reason.

"We are the Supreme Court and we can do what we want," Burger replied.

Harlan tried again to point out that what the Chief was proposing amounted to a dramatic expansion of the Court's power to intervene in state matters. The Court, of course, could make statutory interpretations of federal laws passed by Congress. But, to Harlan's knowledge, the Court had never corrected a state court by asserting that its decision was "wrong" unless it conflicted with federal laws or with the Constitution.

There must be some way to decide it narrowly, Burger said.

No, Harlan responded, he could find none.

Burger left, still protesting that the Court had greater latitude to do what it wanted.

Harlan went into his law clerks' office and described the meeting. Harlan had never criticized anyone personally, but now he seemed both a bit bemused and a bit horrified. Burger had spent thirteen years on the District of Columbia Circuit, where there was little exposure to state law, since the District was a federal enclave and Congress passed the local laws. So it was probably an honest mistake. His new colleague had a lot to learn, Harlan indicated. He had hoped that Burger would be a more skillful legal technician. How could someone be a judge and not understand a concept familiar to most third-year law students? Harlan's smile flickered as he repeated Burger's assertion of federal judicial supremacy—The Court can do anything it wants. So much for the Chief's claims that he believed in judicial restraint.

Burger, for his part, was pondering what Harlan and Black had told him. He still didn't like it; the Georgia court decision was wrong. But he gave up. He wrote a memo to Black with copies for the conference.

"Dear Hugo,

"This is a difficult case with a result I do not relish, but the question is one for the states (states, unlike federal agencies and this

Court, are not infallible). Seeing it as a state question, I join your opinion."

Hugo Black had been ahead of his time for most of his life. Graduating from the University of Alabama Law School without high school diploma or college degree, he maintained a rigid reading schedule of "great books" to compensate for his lack of formal education. Elected to the Senate in 1926, Black became a powerful Roosevelt ally. A colorful showman in Senate hearing rooms, Black supported Roosevelt down the line and was a controversial and powerful politician when Roosevelt appointed him to the Court in 1937. In three decades on the Court, Black had seen his early dissents become majorities. Black had provided the basis for many of the Warren Court's landmark decisions, and some observers even argued that the "Black Court" would be a more appropriate title.

Still driven by a burning evangelical need to persuade his colleagues of his views, Black worked intensely at the job. But after thirty years on the Court, he no longer felt ahead of the times. He was troubled by the many reports of disruptions in courtrooms across the country. The judiciary—federal, state, even the local police courts like the one on which he had served in Alabama—was the real underwriter of American liberty. Black was fiercely protective of judicial independence and prestige. Yet antiwar and black activists had turned courtrooms into circuses. At the trial of the "Chicago Eight" in 1969, Judge Julius Hoffman was confronted with verbal and physical threats by defendants who had staged the antiwar protests at the 1968 Democratic National Convention. He had ordered one defendant, Black Panther leader Bobby Seale, shackled and gagged during the trial. In New York, another judge had been threatened repeatedly during pretrial hearings of thirteen Black Panthers. At one time he was forced to postpone the hearings until the defendants observed court decorum.

In the middle of the term, Black pushed to have the conference grant a hearing in a case (*Illinois v. Allen*) that dealt with the constitutional limits on judges to control unruly defendants. In the Allen case the judge had expelled the defendant from the courtroom. The case was thirteen years old, without any of the notoriety of the so-called political trials. But it provided the Court with an opportunity to tell trial judges how they could deal with disorderly courtroom behavior without violating the rights of the accused. Black thought that if the Court waited for the political cases to come up before it dealt with the issue, the waters would be muddied by such questions as the Vietnam War and police infiltration of black groups. The *Allen* case provided an opportunity to make a strong statement without any side issues.

After oral argument and conference, only Douglas had reservations about the Court reaching out to issue a list of constitutionally permissible actions that a judge might take to maintain order in the courtroom. The Chief assigned Black to write an opinion for the seven-member majority.

Black relished the opportunity. The Sixth Amendment guaranteed a defendant the right "to be confronted with the witnesses against him." But, Black wrote, the courts cannot be "bullied, insulted, and humiliated and their orderly progress thwarted and obstructed." Calling courts "palladiums of liberty" and "citadels of justice," Black said there were three things that could be done without violating the Constitution: binding and gagging the disorderly defendant; citing him for contempt; and expelling him until he promised to behave.

Harlan, a believer in decorum everywhere, was so anxious to get Black's opinion announced that he wrote a memo to complain that Douglas was taking too long in writing his separate dissent.

Douglas intended no delay. He prided himself on being the fastest writer on the Court. He often turned out an opinion the day after an assignment; his separate opinions were ready weeks, if not months, before the majority opinions. His clerks often called these "plane-trip specials," because they were written after the Friday conference on an airplane, as Douglas traveled to some speaking engagement. At times he mailed longhand drafts back to the Court, so that they could be printed and ready for revision upon his return. The other Justices all acknowledged Douglas's brilliance and incredible productivity; White called him a "paper factory." Douglas was so prolific that once when former Justice Charles E.

Whittaker was unable to draft a majority opinion, Douglas finished his dissent and then wrote Whittaker's majority for him.

But the others also had come to wonder if Douglas's opinions—often disorganized treatises on sociology rather than law—did not sometimes fall victim to his unrelenting pace and curiosity. Declaring "there will be no errors in my opinions," Douglas, just the same, refused to allow his clerks to edit them.

But in the *Allen* case, Douglas had misgivings about the majority's willingness to issue a broad-policy document that was clearly aimed beyond the case at hand. And for Harlan, who was far slower than he, to complain about delay was particularly galling. Harlan often took months, because he liked to write a *Harvard Law Review* article on each case, making his opinion gray in style, tone and result. "There is one thing you ought to know," Douglas told his only clerk, "I don't write law review articles like Harlan does."

Unwilling to sacrifice his candor in the interests of fraternity, Douglas fired back a flinty memo saying he would have his opinion ready when he was done and no sooner. He ridiculed Harlan's protest, noting that Harlan was taking months to produce an opinion in a discrimination case (*Adickes v. S. H. Kress & Co.*).

Douglas circulated his dissent soon after, expressing his irritation that the Court was, in effect, approving the broad use of harsh measures by judges to control defendants in controversial political trials.

The Court's opinion was announced five weeks after oral arguments, nearly a record for speed in such a seemingly routine case. And across the country, lower court judges could be confident that the Court would back their efforts to maintain order in their courtrooms.

It was late one Friday afternoon, and Burger was exhausted. A grueling, day-long conference had just ended. Unlike his colleagues, the Chief couldn't now go home immediately. He had to make sure that the conference actions on the approximately one hundred cert petitions that the Justices considered each week were given to the Court's administrative personnel. Burger hated this chore. It was work proper for a clerk or a secretary, not for a

Chief Justice. And it was hard to participate fully in the arguments, lead the discussions, and at the same time keep precise track of the Justices' votes and positions. Since no one other than the Justices was allowed in the conference room, he had to do it alone.

After each Friday conference, Burger would call in a law clerk, a secretary and the Clerk of the Court. Seated at his ceremonial desk in the conference room, they would go over the results. Three times early in the term, the published orders had incorrectly identified cases that had been accepted for full review. In fact, the petitions had been denied, and so public retractions had had to be made. The press had noticed the errors. The Chief's secretary and his law clerks had tried to help by preparing elaborate briefing books, so that the Chief had only to fill in the blanks with check marks. But it didn't seem to solve the problem. He was still making mistakes.

"Any dumb ass could pick it up," the Chief's secretary once remarked privately.

The Clerk of the Court couldn't understand it, either. Even Chief Justice Warren, notoriously bad at record keeping, learned to keep track of what went on at conference. Burger's chambers solved the problem whenever they were uncertain by calling Brennan's secretary to have her check Brennan's meticulous records.

After the votes had been given to the Clerk of the Court, Burger went into his working office to finish another task, one he enjoyed. The Chief spread a large sheet of plain butcher paper in front of him on the desk. Across the top were listed the names of the Justices. Down the left side were the names of the cases heard so far that term. The sheet was Burger's most powerful tool in controlling the Court. It represented the work load of each Justice. By tradition, the senior Justice in the majority at conference selected the Justice who was to write the court opinion for the majority. Since the Chief was considered senior to all the others, he made the assignments when he was in the majority. Burger was careful, in his first term, to make sure that he was in the majority most of the time—even if he had to adjust his views. Leadership in the Court could not be exercised from a minority position, he felt.

Since the Chief assigned most of the cases, he was also responsible for keeping the majority-opinion assignments as evenly divided as possible. With only about 120 cases that required full opinions, including several that were unsigned *per curiams,* the power to select the author—to choose, for example, Harlan or Stewart instead of Brennan or Marshall—was the power to determine the general direction of the opinion. Often, the reasoning was as important as the finding itself. The lower courts would draw on the opinion for guidance as they made their decisions. Burger reasoned that by assigning the cases, he—as Warren had done before him—could control the Court and influence the entire federal judiciary. The process would take years, and it would have to be done a step at a time. But each assignment that he controlled was an important step.

Burger carefully made sure that important cases in criminal law, racial discrimination and free speech were kept away from Douglas, Brennan and Marshall, his ideological "enemies," as he called them. If necessary, the Chief would switch his own vote to retain the assignment power, thus preventing them from writing ground-breaking decisions that expanded the Court's power or extended the application of liberal Warren Court decisions. Instead, he assigned them innocuous cases where their opinions couldn't have much impact.

Of those most likely to share his views, the Chief at first found Byron White the most compatible. White was also the most physically impressive. At six feet two and a trim 190 pounds, he was still like the tough University of Colorado football All-American who had become the National Football League rookie of the year in 1938. White won a Rhodes scholarship and then entered Yale Law School, where he passed up *Law Review* to earn money as the highest-paid professional football player of his day. Stewart, a classmate at law school, often saw White in the library in his steel-rimmed glasses, only to read about him in the next day's paper as the game-winning "Whizzer White." To Stewart and his classmates, White was both Clark Kent and Superman.

White clerked a year at the Court for Chief Justice Fred Vinson, and renewed his friendship with freshman Representative John Kennedy, whom he had known in England and later in the South

Pacific during World War II. White's fifteen years of law practice in Denver ended when he ran a nationwide Citizens for Kennedy committee during the 1960 presidential campaign. He was rewarded with the post of deputy attorney general as the number two man in Robert Kennedy's Justice Department. A year later, President Kennedy appointed White to the Court, saying that White "had excelled in everything he had attempted."

White was an aggressive Justice, relentlessly pressing his clerks to clarify their own, and thus his own, arguments. Never relaxed, always competitive, White loved to race his clerks to complete the first draft of an opinion, or to interrupt them for a basketball game on the Court's fourth-floor gymnasium, which the clerks called "the highest court in the land."

White's positions were clear and vehement. They seemed to his colleagues to come directly out of his practical experience in the Justice Department. He was tough on the enforcement of both civil rights and criminal justice. And it was this last hard line that delighted Burger. The press repeatedly pointed to White as a disappointment to the liberals. Poker-faced, sometimes harsh, but confident and capable in the law, White was only fifty-two and likely to be an influence on the Court for years to come. Even when they disagreed on criminal cases, Burger could count on White to write an opinion reasonably close to his own views. Burger put a check under White's name for a criminal-case assignment.

The law clerk working with Burger was puzzled. Burger was in the minority on that one, the clerk reminded him; therefore, the assignment was not his to make.

Burger checked his vote book. No he was not in the minority, he replied.

"But before going to conference you said you would not vote that way," the clerk said.

"I never said such a thing," Burger said crisply.

Moving on to another criminal case, the Chief assigned it to himself. With his vote it would be unanimous, and he wanted to assign himself as many unanimous decisions as possible. That would make it clear that he was leading the Court, and that everyone was falling into line with his opinions, that no one was dissenting or criticizing his work.

Excuse me, Chief, the clerk interrupted once again. How could he have been in the majority for a reversal of that conviction? This time the clerk was certain. The Chief had given his clerks a briefing after conference and had said he was for upholding.

"That was a tentative vote," Burger replied firmly.

At the next Thursday session, before the Friday conference, Burger and his head clerk reviewed the cases to be discussed. Burger stated that he would vote to reverse a lower court case.

After Burger left, the clerk sought out another of the Chief's clerks and explained what their boss had just said he would do. "If he comes back and denies it," the clerk said, "I want you to know that he said he would do it. And when he denies it, I want you to tell me that I'm not losing my memory." But Burger held to his initial position.

Once, the Clerk of the Court approached one of the Chief's clerks. "I've been meaning to ask you something for a week," he said. "I often find my recollection differs from the Chief's. Does yours?" Burger's law clerk said he was familiar with the problem and recalled some stories about conference votes and record keeping.

No, the Clerk of the Court said, he knew about that. But he was talking about the Chief's habit of reminiscing and placing himself at the center of events—saying things, doing things and making decisions all of which had been said, done or made by someone else.

After White, the Chief felt most ideologically compatible with Harlan, then Stewart, and in some cases Black. After so many years as a leading liberal, Black had in recent years become increasingly conservative. He was living proof that events were pushing people to the political right, the Chief felt. Liberalism was an experiment that had largely failed, and now one of the arch-liberals was moving back to common sense.

The criminal cases were going to be the guts of the battle at the Court, the Chief figured. This had been clearly spelled out by the President and emphasized by the press. The country had spoken in electing Nixon on a law-and-order platform. In the heated rhetoric of the day, Nixon had campaigned to help the "peace forces"—police and prosecutors—in their battle against the rising crime rate. He had especially criticized "coddling" of criminals by "soft" judges.

Burger's analysis was more sophisticated. He agreed that many of the changes in the criminal justice system brought about by the Warren Court, such as protecting suspects from police-coerced confessions and giving defendants legal counsel, were long overdue. An American Bar Association committee that Burger had chaired while he was an appeals court judge had gone further in its recommendations for providing lawyers for poor defendants than any decision of the Warren Court. But Burger did not think the route to reform was necessarily through Supreme Court decisions. From the outset he thought that if he was going to have an impact and make lasting contributions, perhaps be revered, he would have to help reform the criminal justice system through administrative change. Speedier trials must be provided to defendants. The state judges and the committees and commissions the Chief Justice served on or controlled had to be redirected to support reform.

Burger would then have to lend his prestige, his time and his energy to that huge administrative task. That meant giving speeches, going to conferences and making his views known to Congress. From the beginning, he realized there would be no instant shift in the Court's jurisprudence, even when Nixon appointed another conservative to fill Fortas's seat. For now, Burger would conduct a holding action, which was necessary to ensure that the Court wrote no sweeping new rules to hamper law enforcement. He would accomplish more by lobbying than by writing opinions, he felt.

Some cases now before the Burger Court had been filed in the closing days of the Warren Court. A few had apparently been singled out to refine and extend major Warren Court decisions. One case, *Bivens v. Six Unknown Named Agents*, particularly troubled Burger. Bivens was claiming that he had a right to sue and obtain money damages from federal agents who had broken into his home illegally, without a search warrant. Since they could maintain that they were acting officially, federal agents were normally immune from such suits.

Burger did not want the Court to open another whole remedy for alleged law enforcement abuses. And he was worried because there were five votes to hear the case, one more than the required four. Since the lower court had held that there was no right to sue, it was likely that the five who voted to grant cert wished to reverse the lower court. Burger felt that that would be a disaster. He was not firmly opposed to allowing such suits, but the Court should look at the entire problem of how to handle illegal police searches. The Court should take a range of cases, perhaps allowing damage suits but at the same time lifting some of the Warren Court's restrictions on police powers. Two of the five votes were those of Harlan and Stewart. Burger decided to appeal to them personally to withhold their votes.

Burger went to Stewart's adjacent chambers. He explained that he had a request to make in the case about civil money-damage suits against federal agents. A decision establishing such a right would be judicial activism at its worst and would add to the case load. Worse, it would be seen as another slap at the police, one more judicially mandated shackle on those fighting crime.

Stewart had no burning passion for the case, and he wanted to get along with the new Chief. Ten years of languishing under Earl Warren inclined him to agree. Obviously, Burger cared very much. He had come to ask a personal favor, so Stewart said yes. He would withhold his vote for the time being.

That left Harlan. Burger phoned ahead to see if Harlan had time to talk about an important matter. Harlan said, "Of course."

Harlan's office, one third of the way down the north corridor, was brightly lighted. Special high-intensity lights had been installed to aid his poor eyesight.

Burger sat down and outlined his request.

Harlan said he hadn't thought so at first, but now he thought the Court should hear the case. Innocent persons not charged with a crime should be able to sue federal agents who had violated their rights.

There was a more personal reason, Burger said, that made him believe the Court shouldn't hear the case. Apparently there was a majority for Harlan's point of view. But in his first year as Chief,

Burger said, a decision that would be viewed as another Court effort to tie the hands of the police would look awful. The press could make such a decision embarrassing both to him as Chief and to the Nixon administration.

Harlan could not believe that Burger was advancing such a blatantly political argument. Harlan himself felt that a judge should be wholly removed from politics. He never even voted in presidential elections. The Court was independent, removed from the political push and pull. The administration, the press, personal embarrassment—real or imagined—should have no effect on the Court or its deliberations. Harlan did not wish to lecture the Chief, however, so all this went unsaid. Aware that Burger obviously considered him an ally and a friend, Harlan simply told Burger that he did not think he could withdraw his vote.

Burger pressed.

Harlan found it difficult to say no to the Chief. He proposed a compromise. He would withhold his cert vote and they would hold the case over. He would then vote to grant a hearing for the next term.

Burger thanked him. That would do.

In considerable but controlled agitation, Harlan described Burger's visit to one of his clerks. There were, he said, reasons not to take the case. And he certainly didn't consider himself a judicial activist. But to worry about how it would "look" in the news media, or for the administration? Incredible, Harlan said, shaking his head in disbelief.

The clerk saw that Harlan was distraught. He urged him not to do as Burger wanted. But Harlan had promised, and the case was held for the next term. He would not refuse a personal request from the Chief Justice.

Often the Chief found that his conservative colleagues, with their concern with precedent, caused him as much difficulty as the liberals. In one part of a complicated criminal case (*Coleman v. Alabama*), the conference had voted 7 to 1 that a person charged with a crime did *not* have a right to an attorney at a routine preliminary appearance before a magistrate to determine whether there was sufficient evidence to bring the person to trial. Harlan, the lone dissenter, thought that the preliminary hearing was part of the prosecutorial process. Though he didn't like it, the logic of precedent dictated that the person who had been charged was entitled to an attorney.

Pleased to see Brennan upholding the conviction—refusing to extend the right to have an attorney—Burger assigned him the case. Brennan was relatively quick to circulate his majority opinion. It was not well received. Black announced that he had reconsidered and would join Harlan in dissent. Brennan was upset that his majority draft had apparently triggered Black's switch.

Burger sent Black a memo chiding him gently. Black, the avowed strict constructionist, always claimed that his judicial views were drawn literally from the Constitution, and from nowhere else. He carried a Government Printing Office pocket edition of the Constitution with him. "Dear Hugo," the Chief's memo said, "Please tell me what article or amendment covers this."

Black responded the next day. "Dear Chief, Amendment VI." He went on to quote from the amendment, which said that

"in all criminal prosecutions, the accused shall enjoy the right . . . to have the assistance of Counsel for his defense."

Although the Sixth Amendment doesn't go into detail on when, . . . it would disregard reality to say that a preliminary trial is not an important part of a prosecution under which a state is preparing to punish a man . . .

Where is there anything in the Constitution that says that although a man has the right at the time of prosecution, he cannot claim that help the first time he needs counsel?

Black's vote was firmly with Harlan.

That left the vote 6 to 2, with the Chief still on the winning side.

Next, Harlan circulated his dissent. Though he had dissented from most of the Warren Court decisions that extended rights to the accused, and still felt they were incorrect, Harlan now chastised the majority for its apparent willingness to disregard the logical implication of its recent decisions. In the landmark *Miranda* decision *(Miranda v. Arizona)* in 1966, with Harlan, Stewart and White dissenting, the Court had decided that an arrested individual had the right to an attorney. Whatever a person said without an attorney present could not be admitted in a trial or used against him, unless he waived his right.

The previous term, Harlan reminded them, the Court, with the same trio in dissent, said that those rules apply even when a suspect is questioned in his home. How, Harlan asked, could the Court now say that a potential defendant has the right to an attorney at a police station or in his own home, but not the first time he enters a courtroom?

Brennan was worried. Though he still had the votes, he was uncomfortable that the conservative Harlan was making the liberal argument. Also, Brennan could see the logic of the position. The votes would likely slip away from him sooner or later. Douglas and Marshall were not firm, and he himself was having second thoughts. If the others switched on that one section, Harlan would end up writing the whole opinion. Brennan did not want to lose control over the other sections of the opinion he had already drafted.

In a recent case *(Interstate Commerce Commission v. Black Ball Freight Service)*, Brennan had had a majority when the decision was assigned to him, and then lost it to Douglas, who had a different view. Brennan was not accustomed to having a majority stolen out from under him. "I'm not going to lose another one," he told a clerk, and he grimly instructed him to revise part of the opinion so that the result came out the opposite way. Douglas, Marshall and White soon joined Brennan's new opinion.

Burger, however, had no intention of changing his vote. The right to counsel at the preliminary hearings was something for legislatures to enact, not the Supreme Court. He dashed off a blistering dissent excoriating the new majority. It was an "odd business" that it took the Court "nearly two centuries to 'discover' a constitutional mandate to have counsel at a preliminary hearing."

Douglas read Burger's opinion and decided to respond with a separate opinion. He didn't know whether Burger would retract his dissent or tone it down and issue it as a concurrence. He had already done both several times that term. "I add a word as to why I think that a strict construction of the Constitution requires the result reached," Douglas wrote in a lecturing tone. "It did not take nearly 200 years of doubt to decide" the matter. "The question has never been reached prior to this case. We experience [on the Court] the case-by-case approach that is the only one available under our 'case' or 'controversy' jurisdiction under Article III of the Constitution." He was reminding the Chief that the Court could not reach out to decide issues that were not presented as live controversies.

When Burger did not withdraw his dissent, Douglas went ahead and published his rebuke.

As the author for the majority, Brennan wound up with six votes for the revised part of his opinion. Black, Marshall, Douglas and White and Brennan himself had switched to Harlan's view.

Potter Stewart's initial optimism about the new regime had also faded. One of his clerks, a committed liberal, had observed Burger in action at the District of Columbia Court of Appeals the previous year. He had sent early and repeated warnings to Stewart, characterizing Burger as petty, unpleasant and dishonest.

Stewart didn't want to jump to conclusions. He just laughed nervously as his clerks told new and old Burger tales, which always painted the Chief in the worst possible light. But as the term progressed and Stewart compared notes with the other Justices, particularly with his friend Harlan, his reservations about Burger turned to acute distress.

It occurred to Stewart that Burger was much like Earl Warren, inclined to shoot from the hip, or to view cases in purely political terms. In some respects, Burger was worse. At times the Chief changed his ground in a case three or four times. Legal arguments couldn't reach him. Often it seemed that all Burger cared about was upholding criminal convictions. He would go out of his way— bend the law, overlook earlier Court decisions—to hold a majority to keep someone in jail. But, unless the Chief could get at least one other Justice to go along with his hard-line views, he invariably moved toward the center, joining the most conservative position available. Stewart's clerks, and a number of others, worked out a theory of Burger's jurisprudence. The Chief would never be alone in dissent. "Always to the right but never alone," the slogan went.

Stewart was especially demoralized by the Chief's responses to a series of routine petitions that had come to the Court. Prisoners who made a claim in a federal district court that their rights had been violated in a state prosecution were, at times erroneously, denied hearings by the district court. Almost always, the intermediate court of appeals would order the district court to hold a hearing; then the state would petition directly to the Supreme Court for review of the appeals court's demand. The Supreme Court routinely denied such petitions because its prior decisions demanded the district court hearings. But Burger wanted to simply ignore previous Supreme Court decisions that provided for the prisoner's right to make such appeals, and reverse the intermediate courts without even holding oral argument.

Stewart considered Burger's position bizarre. With no knowledge of the facts in the cases before the Court, it was absurd to reverse the appeals courts. Though the Chief lobbied heavily on these cases during the term, he never got another Justice to go along with him.

Another criminal case considered early in the term involved a double jeopardy claim of a Missouri man, Bob Fred Ashe, who was alleged to have robbed six men at a private poker party (*Ashe v. Swenson*). Ashe was put on trial for robbing one of the six players and found not guilty. The prosecutors reworked their case, focusing on the witnesses that had been helpful to the prosecution and ignoring those whose testimony was not. Some witnesses' memories improved. The state then tried Ashe for robbing another of the players. This time he was convicted. Cert had been granted the year before to clarify a decision of the previous year (*Benton v. Maryland*) that said the states had to adhere to the Fifth Amendment's protection against double jeopardy, the doctrine that a person cannot be tried twice for the same offense.

The tentative vote in conference was 5 to 3 to free Ashe, though the majority couldn't agree on a single theory. The Chief was a dissenter. Black, as the senior Justice for the majority, assigned

Stewart to write the opinion. Gradually all the Justices but Burger agreed to join Stewart. Ashe would be freed. There were separate concurrences by Black, Harlan and Brennan. Stewart's opinion banned retrials in many circumstances. Brennan, joined by Douglas and Marshall, agreed with Stewart but wanted to go further and ban separate trials for each crime committed in a single criminal episode like the poker-game robbery.

Burger was furious. In the first place, he believed that, given the record in Ashe's two trials, the Court was going to impose a rule on the states that would free a guilty man. The Court, in Burger's view, should refrain from making more rules that limited a prosecutor's opportunities to bring criminals to justice. The robberies of the individual poker players were separate crimes; Ashe should be accountable for each. The Fifth Amendment stated that double jeopardy applied to the "same offense." Here there were six offenses. The majority's view, Burger reasoned, invited a criminal to commit multiple offenses, since there would be no accountability after the first one.

This time, Burger decided, he would dissent even if he stood alone. He would write an opinion that spelled out in his most dramatic prose the nature and meaning of the majority's position. The 1966 Chicago slaying of eight nurses by Richard Speck, one of the most notorious crimes of the decade, provided an interesting parallel. With that example, perhaps the other Justices and the public would understand the implications of providing criminals such a loophole. The Chief wrote that if the poker robbery was to be viewed hypothetically as akin to a man breaking into a woman's dormitory, as Speck had done, raping and killing eight women, the crimes beyond the first one were effectively "free." In effect, the Court would be encouraging mass murder.

Reading the Chief's draft, his law clerk assigned to the case thought it inflammatory to equate the poker-game robbery with the Speck murders. The draft would reflect poorly on the Chief and the Court; he removed the comparison. When Burger received the redraft, he severely reprimanded his clerk and reinserted the Speck comparison. The clerk tried once more, again without success. The dissent was then circulated.

White was amused by the Chief's choice of metaphors. If other members of the Court wanted to be inelegant, White was perfectly willing to let them. He cared only about the case's effect on precedent and about his own opinion. In the margin of his copy of Burger's draft, next to the reference to the man who had raped eight women, White wrote, "Some man!"

The dissent led Stewart to conclude that the Chief was the Douglas of the right. He was capable of circulating preposterously wild opinions in order to get press attention. Stewart was fearful that if the Chief's dissent was published, the press would indeed pick up on the notion that the new Chief Justice had accused the Court of encouraging mass murder. Stewart felt that it would be hard for a news reporter to explain that the Court was doing nothing of the kind. A complicated explanation might be cut by editors looking for sensational headlines. The Chief would look silly; the Court would seem bitterly divided.

Further, as the Chief presumably knew, Stewart's majority opinion simply cut back on prosecutors' opportunities to initiate retrials. It didn't ban them completely. Even Brennan's one-trial theory would permit multiple charges for multiple crimes, requiring only that they be presented at one trial. Multiple crimes would hardly be "free," but would make the defendant subject to a much stiffer jail sentence. Prosecutors regularly charged people with multiple counts, one for each alleged crime. That was the deterrent. The Chief was just flat wrong.

The Chief finally dropped the direct reference to the Speck murders and changed that portion of his dissent to refer to four men breaking into a college dormitory and assaulting six girls. Arguing that the "dignity of the human personality and individuality" called for retribution for each crime, he added: "No court that elevates the individual rights and human dignity of the accused to a high place—as we should do—ought to be so casual as to treat the victims as a single homogenized lump of human clay." He kept in the notion that the accompanying crimes were in effect "free."

The decision was announced April 6, 1970. For the first time, Burger was alone in dissent.

*   *   *

Two days later, Stewart returned from lunch shortly after 1 P.M. About ten people, including Thurgood Marshall and one of Burger's secretaries, were clustered about a small black-and-white portable television in his secretary's office. They were watching reports of the Senate vote on Nixon's second attempt to fill the Fortas seat. The nominee was Judge G. Harrold Carswell, now a member of the Fifth Circuit Court of Appeals.

Stewart was not aware that Burger, before his own nomination to be Chief Justice, had suggested to Mitchell that Carswell be promoted from a district to an appeals court judge. Carswell's nomination, like Haynsworth's, had run into difficulties. It had been disclosed that Carswell had said in a 1948 speech that, "Segregation of the races is proper and the only practical and correct way of life in our states. I have always so believed and I shall always so act." He had renounced the speech, but it had triggered a search into his past. The search revealed that Carswell had been involved in a plan to use a federally financed public golf course in Florida as a private segregated club.

His judicial and civil rights record also came under attack. Some legal scholars also stated that he was not fit to sit on the Supreme Court. The Dean of the Yale Law School said that Carswell "presents the most slender credentials [for the Court] of any man put forward in this century." Senator Roman Hruska, a conservative Republican from Nebraska, had inadvertently made the most damaging criticism. "There are a lot of mediocre judges and people and lawyers," he said, "and they are entitled to a little representation, aren't they?"

The group in Stewart's chambers watched a reporter repeat messages relayed from inside the Senate chamber, where no cameras were allowed. Clearly the vote was going to be very close. Spiro Agnew was standing by; as Vice-President and presiding officer of the Senate, he would vote to break a tie.

The group chatted excitedly as the voting began. It had been nearly a year since Fortas had resigned. The Court had been waiting for its next member, anxious to see whom Nixon and the Senate would finally send them.

A key Republican voted against the confirmation. Some of those watching in Stewart's office cheered. Stewart said that he didn't want any outbursts.

The vote continued. Another key Republican voted against confirmation. That was it. The final tally was 51 to 45. The group erupted in exaggerated sighs of relief, hoots and applause.

Stewart, red with fury, shouted at them to quiet down. But he went into his office elated by the vote. Carswell would have been awful for the Court. Nevertheless, Stewart was upset about the racket. It would not be good to have Burger or the press hear that there had been a celebration in Stewart's chambers.

The next day, Nixon asserted angrily: "I will not nominate another Southerner and let him be subjected to the kind of malicious character assassination accorded both Judges Haynsworth and Carswell." The speculation among the Justices and the clerks turned to what Nixon would do now. Who would be his non-Southerner?

Five days after Carswell's defeat, Republican House Minority Leader Gerald R. Ford told a press conference that he would urge that Douglas be impeached. Two days later, he delivered a long, scathing attack on Douglas from the floor of the House. Accusing Douglas of being out of touch with conventional political thought and behavior, Ford claimed that Douglas, in his recent book, *Points of Rebellion*, had endorsed riot and revolution against the "establishment." His voice ringing with moral indignation, Ford thumbed through the latest edition of *Evergreen Review*, a magazine combining social commentary, poetry, fiction and the arts. Douglas had permitted an excerpt from his book to appear in that magazine right next to pictures "perhaps more shocking than the post cards that used to be sold only in the back alleys of Paris and Panama City, Panama."

Ford turned to more serious allegations, using unconfirmed material from F.B.I. and C.I.A. files that had been provided him secretly with the approval of Attorney General Mitchell. Ford raised the specter of Fortas, another corrupt Justice. Ford charged that Douglas, because he served on the Parvin Foundation, was a "well-paid moonlighter for an organization whose ties to the international gambling fraternity have never been sufficiently explored." Ford linked Albert Parvin and his foundation, and by implication Douglas, to "known gambling figures and Mafia types." He also accused Douglas of offering legal advice to the foundation, that is, practicing law while on the federal bench, a possible ground for impeachment.

More than one hundred conservative Congressmen from both parties sponsored a resolution to set up a special bipartisan committee to investigate Douglas. The House Judiciary Committee was assigned to look into the allegations.

With Democrats in control of Congress, Douglas was relatively safe, but he considered the attack an effort to reduce the effectiveness of his "side" of the Court. Intensely political, Douglas had come to Washington in 1936 from teaching at Yale Law School to join and later head the newly created Securities and Exchange Commission. Determined to smash predatory industrial monopolies, Douglas became a member of Roosevelt's inner circle of New Deal activists. In 1939, at the age of forty, he was appointed to succeed Louis Brandeis on the Supreme Court.

Fearless to a fault, Douglas loved political controversy, taking on "the other side"—big business, environmental polluters, censors, any vested interest—and excoriating them as "powerful, crafty and ruthless." In turn, Douglas had come to expect political counterattacks. In 1953 he survived an impeachment drive launched after he voted to stay the executions of Ethel and Julius Rosenberg (despite his earlier secret votes to deny them a hearing). In 1965, Douglas's fourth marriage, this time to a twenty-three-year-old, resulted in another impeachment attempt. This time, with Fortas's blood not yet dry, the effort had to be taken seriously.

Douglas needed help, but was unaccustomed to asking for it. He normally remained aloof even from his closest colleagues, and he bothered to charm only the most casual of his acquaintances. With friends he was often cold, impatient and gruff. He was a loner, unwilling to lobby or influence his colleagues. But he needed help, and his relationship with Black had cooled as Douglas had run through his string of wives. So he turned instead to the best legal defense he could find to fight the impeachment and to organize the documentation for a rebuttal. Douglas called his close friend, Clark Clifford, a former Secretary of Defense under President Johnson. "Nixon has sicked his gorillas on me," he told him. It was the work of Nixon and Mitchell, and Ford was the front man. Douglas knew the administration was willing to play politics with the Court and that it had used "friendly persuasion" to get Fortas off the bench. He asked Clifford to lead the defense. Clifford declined. He reasoned that he was too closely identified with the Democratic Party; the whole thing would look too much like a political brawl. Douglas finally engaged Simon Rifkind, a onetime classmate at Columbia Law School. Rifkind was also a Democrat, but had served as a federal judge for years.

The attacks and investigations preoccupied Douglas. He was now determined to outlast the Nixon presidency. But since there was no forum for him as a Supreme Court Justice to defend himself, he declined public comment. He turned inward and brooded, calling friends late at night. If they succeeded in impeaching and convicting him, what would be left of all the values and freedoms he had fought for all his life? How could the Court remain independent? His "side," already damaged by the departure of Warren and Fortas, would be irreparably weakened. The liberals were in trouble. Black, old and slowing up, had good and bad days. His memory problems cropped up at unpredictable times. Even worse, as Black aged he was becoming more conservative. He was no longer a certain liberal vote.

Marshall was weak—a correct vote, a follower, but no leader, no fighter. He was not one to speak up articulately or forcefully. That left Brennan. "Bill's not a troublemaker," Douglas told an associate. Brennan was indeed a true friend, another correct vote, but really a man of the center, an organizer for the moderate-liberal position. Brennan was too willing to compromise. When things got tough, Douglas felt, Brennan did not stand up for his principles. In 1966, Brennan hired a University of California at Berkeley law graduate, Michael Tigar, as a clerk. Tigar had been a leading radical activist. When conservative columnists attacked Brennan, it became a political issue. Brennan fired Tigar the week he arrived to start work. As Douglas saw it, Brennan sacrificed the clerk to protect his personal position and his relationships with the moderate and conservative Justices. Douglas called it "scandalous," a "shocking cave-in."

During the impeachment investigation, friends and advisers from the old days would come to have lunch with Douglas, to help develop strategy and to offer suggestions. Douglas was often near tears of outrage. He felt powerless. Always suspicious, he was sure that the investigators would resort to any tactic, no matter how low or even illegal. He was more than ever convinced that his phone was tapped, that his office and perhaps even the conference room were bugged. (Even before Nixon's arrival, he had persuaded Earl Warren to have the conference room checked for listening devices. None was found.)

"Let's take a walk in the hall," Douglas told a friend who had come to discuss strategy. Many times during that year, Douglas came to Brennan's chambers and asked him to walk in the halls to discuss something privately. "I've got to go meet Bill out in the hall," Brennan would say to his clerks, his eyes twinkling. None of the other Justices seemed to take the investigation seriously enough, Douglas thought. Everyone seemed unconcerned.

Nixon wasn't sure that impeachment of Douglas was a very good idea. The evidence was thin, and Burger had signaled him that the attack was not good for the Court. Also, the President was more concerned with foreign affairs, particularly with the military escalation in Southeast Asia.

Later, when Nixon called Mitchell and said Ford should be told to "turn it off," Mitchell indicated that it would be difficult, since he himself had supplied Ford with some ammunition.* But he could put some distance between the administration and the impeachment move in a speech he was about to give to the Bar Association of the District of Columbia.

Mitchell's draft, condemning "irresponsible and malicious" criticism of the Court, was sent to Nixon, who forwarded it to Burger. Burger found it perfectly appropriate. When Burger tried to call

* See William Safire: *Before the Fall: An Inside View of the Pre-Watergate White House.*

the President, who had just given a speech on national television announcing a U.S. military incursion into Cambodia, he couldn't get through, and he decided to drop off the draft with his comments at the White House. Informed that the Chief was at the gate, Nixon invited him to come up.

"I didn't want to disturb you, Mr. President," Burger said, "but I wanted you to know that I think your speech tonight had a sense of history and destiny about it."

Nixon complained that he was already being denounced by his critics.

Burger was reassuring. He told Nixon he was sure both the speech and invasion of Cambodia would be supported by the people. "I think anyone who really listened to what you said will appreciate the guts it took to make the decision," he said. Anyone who thought about it would realize that a shrewd politician like Nixon wouldn't have done something that might damage Republican chances in the upcoming November congressional elections unless it was absolutely essential for national security.

"Speaking in the greatest confidence, Mr. Chief Justice," Nixon replied, "I am realistic enough to know that if this operation doesn't succeed—or if anything else happens that forces my public support below a point where I feel I can't be reelected—I would like you to be ready to be in the running for the nomination in 1972."*

In response to press inquiries, the White House issued a statement the next day saying that Chief Justice Burger had come to congratulate the President on his Cambodian action. Burger had the Supreme Court press officer issue a statement saying he had called at the White House on "judicial business."

Black was huddled comfortably over his law books one day in the late fall when an old friend came through his doorway. "Tommy," Black called out, greeting Thomas G. "Tommy the Cork" Corcoran, a Roosevelt brain-truster from the old days, now a lawyer in private practice in Washington. Corcoran and Black had been friends

* See *RN: The Memoirs of Richard Nixon*, p. 452.

since the 1930s, when both were zealous advocates of the New Deal. Black had introduced much of Corcoran's trust-busting legislation in the Senate and guided it through.

Now sixty-nine, Corcoran had gone over to the other side as far as Black was concerned. The charming Irish salesmanship had been fine when Corcoran was fighting the special interests. Now he represented them. His law practice was known for influence work, lobbying and backstairs deals.

Corcoran sat down in Black's office. Black had no idea why he was there. But they shared a family interest in Corcoran's twenty-eight-year-old daughter, Margaret. A Radcliffe College and Harvard Law School graduate, Margaret Corcoran had clerked for Black three years before, and was a member of Black's "family" of former law clerks. Recently she had been suffering from a series of personal problems, which Black presumed had occasioned Corcoran's visit.

The Court had done a great injustice, Corcoran told Black. Its ruling the previous term in an antitrust case against El Paso Natural Gas Company, the world's largest gas pipeline company, threatened the survival of the corporation (*Utah Public Service Commission v. El Paso Natural Gas Co.*).

Black was shocked. No one came to the Supreme Court to lobby, even to "put in a good word" for a petitioner. The mere mention of a pending case at a cocktail party was forbidden. Out-of-court contacts with Justices about cases were unethical. There was currently before the Court a petition requesting a rehearing of the El Paso case, and Corcoran had come to lobby for the company. Black cut his old friend off quickly. *No.* He shooed Corcoran out of his office.

The El Paso case had been in the federal courts for the past twelve years. It was the most celebrated and the most litigated antitrust case of the decade. It had been to the Supreme Court three times until finally, in the previous term, the company was ordered to divest itself of monopolistic holdings in the West.

The rehearing petition that was pending before the Court was a common, last-ditch, usually futile, effort of the losing side, asking the Court to reconsider what it had just done. Black thought it unlikely that El Paso would win review. The Court, which had just decided it the term before, was not going to reverse itself unless dramatically different circumstances presented themselves. As far as Black knew, there were none.

The previous term's opinion had been a 4-to-2 vote, with three Justices not participating. White and Marshall were out because they had been involved in the case while at the Justice Department; and Fortas had resigned before the decision. Black, Douglas, Brennan and Warren had formed the majority. Harlan and Stewart had dissented.*

The Court's rules provided strict guidance on rehearing petitions. Rule 58 said that the conference could not consider a petition unless it was brought up by one of the Justices from the previous majority. Those who had dissented could not propose a rehearing. The rule was logical, since, ordinarily, there was no reason to reconsider a case unless someone in the original majority had changed his mind, or had found a reason to hear the case again. Otherwise litigation would never end.

Since Warren was gone, the only remaining members of the old four-man majority were Brennan, Black and Douglas. Unless one of them took the initiative and brought up the petition at conference, it would die.

Under a long-standing tradition of the Court, new Justices—in this case the Chief and the eventual replacement for Fortas—would not even vote on rehearing petitions. That could mean that a previous decision would be left standing, even if a clear majority of dissenters and new Justices thought it was wrong. This was essential if the Court was to maintain credibility as its membership changed. The Court must be perceived as a continuing body, whose opinions do not change merely because new Justices join it.

Black could almost forgive Corcoran for his carelessness. Corcoran had been an advocate all his life; he was unable to stop pressing for his clients' interests. But in his thirty-two years on the Court, Black had never had the arm put on him in such an overt

---

* "Those Republicans will ruin us all," Black once told a clerk. "John Harlan is one of the smartest, nicest guys who ever lived; I love him. But you know, he's a Republican. You know, that's Potter's problem too," Black said.

way in his own chambers by a lawyer for a private party involved in a dispute before the Court.

Corcoran, however, was not about to give up. His lobbying efforts had been disregarded before in Washington. He was used to taking his knocks. He made an appointment with Brennan.

Brennan had no idea why Corcoran, whom he did not know well, had requested an appointment. He greeted Corcoran warmly. The two Irishmen sat and exchanged a few pleasantries. Corcoran quickly got to the point. Why was the Court determined to ruin El Paso?

Brennan was surprised.

Corcoran said that the deathbed statement of one of the gas pipeline lawyers in the case, John Sonnett, had prompted his visit. Sonnett had said that a grave injustice had been committed by the Court in its sweeping, dictatorial divestiture order against El Paso.

Brennan stood. He said that he, of course, could not and would not ever discuss a pending case, and showed Corcoran to the door. He immediately went to tell his clerks. Something awful just happened, he said. His shock was evident on his face as he described Corcoran's visit. Brennan said he had had no way of knowing beforehand what Corcoran wanted. Corcoran's name had not been on the petition for rehearing or on other briefs and papers. It was outrageous, a lawyer coming to lobby a Justice. The question was what to do now? He probably would have to disqualify himself from participating in the consideration of the rehearing petition. Disqualification is voluntary, a decision left to each individual Justice in situations where his neutrality could be questioned. Even though Corcoran had been unsuccessful and had not influenced him, Brennan suggested that the appearance of the situation might call his impartiality into question.

But, Brennan felt, the Court might have been wrong in the El Paso decision. After all, the states in the West supported El Paso because they were bothered less by monopolies than by the threat of a shortage of natural gas. Perhaps zealous trust busting was not feasible here.

*　　　　*　　　　*

The Chief believed that the 4-to-2 El Paso decision of the previous term was one of the classic excesses of the Warren Court. He wanted to grant a rehearing and a reversal. Though tradition seemed to suggest that he not participate, and though Rule 58 might keep the conference from even considering the case, Burger was looking for a way around these obstacles. The El Paso decision involved a procedural twist that, in his view, dramatized the willingness of the Warren Court to bend the rules to meet its goals.

The Chief thought it fantastic and unprecedented that all those involved in the dispute—the El Paso Company, the individual states, and the Justice Department which enforced the antitrust laws—had finally agreed to a compromise, something less than the total divestiture ordered earlier by the Court. All parties involved the term before had asked that the case be dismissed. Rule 60 of the Court said such a request for dismissal by all parties should be granted automatically.

As the Chief saw it, that should have ended the case. It was simple. How could the Court make a ruling when there was no controversy, no complaint, no dispute? But the Warren Court had refused to let the parties dismiss the case.

Incredible as it seemed, the Court had allowed a former California public-utility official to argue as a "consumer spokesman." Traditionally, an individual had no legal standing to intervene in a government antitrust suit. By law the Justice Department had the job of enforcing the antitrust statutes, and it had decided to let the twelve-year controversy die. That should have been it for the Court. But the Court had set itself up as a sort of review board, saying there had been a dispute, and the Court wanted to resolve it anyway. This was not mere judicial activism, but judicial interventionism—an arbitrary exercise by the Court of its power to do justice when no one had requested it.

The Chief felt Warren had bent the rules in this case. If the rehearing petition was granted and the preceding term's decision was eventually reversed, it would be a body blow to Warren Court activism. It would signal that the Burger Court was going to play by the rules. Overturning the decision would not be merely overruling one case with another (something that happened on the average of once a term); it would be taking the very case itself and saying that the previous Court had been wrong.

The Chief thought the obstacle of Rule 58 could be cleared. The majority of the current members of the Court should prevail, and any Justice should be able to bring up a rehearing petition. The tradition that prevented new Justices from voting made little sense. Burger planned to cast his vote despite the tradition. He thought the votes were there for a 4-to-3 victory. Harlan and Stewart, who had been vigorous dissenters in the previous term's decision, would no doubt join the Chief and the Fortas replacement, giving them four votes to defeat Brennan, Black and Douglas.

But Douglas had a strong interest in seeing that no rehearing was granted. For him, the issue was also simple, and also of fundamental importance. The Supreme Court was having some trouble getting the lower courts, as well as the Justice Department and big-business interests like El Paso, to obey its rulings. Just as segregationists in the South had in effect ignored the Court's school rulings with tricks and delays, now corporations and utilities were dodging unfavorable rulings with their high-paid country-club lawyers and delaying tactics.

In Douglas's opinion, the Court had to show its willingness to ensure that its decrees were obeyed, and divestiture of El Paso meant just that. The corporate interests were thwarting the Court; the Justices had to stand fast. There was a coalition of energy, environmental and consumer interests involved in this case. According to one press account, El Paso was making one million dollars a day by retaining its monopoly. According to another, it was spending millions lobbying Congress for legislation to guarantee that it could keep its holdings.

The Court's decision in the preceding term was necessary. Douglas was suspicious about the Justice Department's withdrawal from the case. Nixon and Mitchell had been partners in a New York law firm that had done some legal work for El Paso. Legal fees of $771,000 had been paid to the Mudge, Rose, Guthrie & Alexander firm during the 1960s.

Soon after the Corcoran visits, the conference took up the El

Paso petition. Brennan recounted to the full conference the details of Corcoran's visit, his plea, and his account of the purported deathbed statement of one of the lawyers. The lobbying effort was improper, Brennan said. Nonetheless, he felt that perhaps El Paso did have an argument, that possibly a rehearing should be granted.

Douglas interrupted sharply. That was no deathbed confession, merely a lawyer's distress at having lost a case. How could Brennan even consider it? In the first place, Brennan was wrong in suggesting that El Paso had a legitimate claim. But more important now, Douglas said, it was Corcoran's lobbying that was the issue. If the Court granted a rehearing, Tommy Corcoran would be all over town bragging about how he had stopped by Bill Brennan's office and had twisted his arm—and, in turn, how Bill Brennan had bamboozled the rest of the Court. Did they want their halls filled with influence peddlers?

"If that's the way you're going to look at it, I'll remove myself," Brennan responded.

The matter was left dangling until the next conference, but Brennan was concerned. After Fortas and Haynsworth, the Court could not afford another black eye.

Brennan went to see Harlan, a man of strict propriety. Harlan was both offended by and amused at Corcoran. The lawyer-lobbyist, he observed, just couldn't make a distinction between Congress, where he always lobbied, and the Court. Since the Supreme Court Building was geographically on "the Hill," Corcoran probably just stumbled across First Street after an attempted seduction of some Senator. The important thing was that Corcoran had not been allowed to make his arguments and had been thrown out. Harlan would have recused—disqualified—himself if Corcoran had come to him, but each Justice must decide for himself. Privately, Harlan thought Brennan should not even have expressed his tentative desire to rehear the case.

Brennan, still concerned, went to Black.

Black had not told the conference that Corcoran had also visited him. He had not wanted to hurt his old New Deal friend. But he had been quietly telling individual Justices about the episode. Now he told Brennan.

That made it even worse, Brennan felt.

They agreed on a course of action. Only Brennan, who was more upset about the appearance of the visit and was also tentatively in favor of helping El Paso, would formally remove himself from the case. With Brennan out, that left Black and Douglas from the old majority, and neither wanted the case reconsidered. Thus, no member of the old majority would propose the discussion, and the rehearing petition would be denied. Brennan soon formally notified the conference that he would not participate. He considered the matter settled.

Burger, however, wasn't happy. Corcoran's visits were stupid, but trivial. That should not interfere with the Court. Clearly the votes were there to grant a rehearing, and probably reverse the decision. Brennan's recusal had tipped the balance to 3 to 2 in Burger's favor—himself, Harlan and Stewart versus Black and Douglas. The Chief needed the vote of the Fortas replacement to win now, for without it, he lacked a quorum. For the Court to conduct any business, six members must participate.

But the others were holding him to the Rule 58 technicality that permitted consideration of the rehearing petition only on the motion of a member of the old majority, of which only Black and Douglas remained. Since they were opposed, the case could not even be discussed. The minority would have its way over the majority. As the Chief was fond of saying, that made no sense. And if it didn't make good sense, how could it make good law?

The year before, Earl Warren had pulled out all stops to get his way. Douglas had done everything to push toward a divestiture order. And now Brennan was dropping out, thus preventing the Court from readdressing the issue.

The Chief had been working on a revision of the Court's rules. He decided that Rule 58 on rehearings was too restrictive, and he wrote out a change. Instead of requiring that a Justice from the old majority propose any reconsideration of a decision, the Chief wanted the rule to read that any Justice could do so.

Burger's suggestions for revision of the rules were sent around to all the chambers. If the changes were adopted, the El Paso rehearing petition could be considered. He was confident that he had the votes.

Reading the Chief's suggested changes, Douglas immediately noticed Burger's proposal concerning Rule 58. Douglas had watched the new Chief for months. His anxiety had mounted. Now he had caught Burger red-handed, trying to change the rules to fit one case. It was crooked. Burger's lack of intellect, Douglas felt, was necessarily forgivable. This was not.

Douglas was determined to get in an early shot. He sat down at his desk to draft a dissent for publication. It was written as if the rehearing had been voted and the change of Rule 58 had been approved. He laid out the long history of the case—the Court's struggle to enforce its ruling, the petition for rehearing, Corcoran's ridiculous lobbying efforts, the Chief's proposal to change Rule 58, and the break with the traditional prohibition that new Justices not vote on rehearing petitions. Douglas tried to push the Nixon-Burger rhetoric about judicial restraint and strict constructionism down Burger's throat. He charged that the Court and its rules were being manipulated to overturn a one-year-old precedent. He portrayed the new Chief as a radical interventionist—a Justice who was sticking a knife in the heart of *stare decisis*.

If the conference consented to the rule change and granted the rehearing, Douglas would publish his ten-page memo as a dissent to the official announcement of the Court's decision to rehear the case. Douglas sent his memo to the printer and had it circulated. It went off like a bomb in the other chambers.

To those clerks who had not been informed about the Chief's proposed changes, it was an eye-opener. Clearly, the Chief and Douglas, two of the most stubborn men on the Court, were on a collision course.

Stewart and Black were worried. The Court did not normally air its disputes publicly—nor, for that matter, publish the improprieties of a member of its own bar, like the lobbyist Corcoran.

Stewart went to Douglas, who assured him that he was firm about publishing his dissent. Douglas was sure this was how to blow the whistle.

Stewart and Black spoke with the Chief. Douglas will go ahead, they warned him. Burger had to withdraw his proposed change to Rule 58. There was no choice. The Chief agreed.

On June 29, 1970, the Court announced that the El Paso rehearing was denied.

Douglas was pleased. The incident suggested that Burger would go far to win, but that when he was threatened with being put in an unfavorable light, he would back down.

Harry A. Blackmun, a veteran of eleven years' service on the Eighth Circuit Court of Appeals, was at work in his office in Rochester, Minnesota, the morning after Carswell's defeat in the Senate. At 11:05 A.M., the phone rang. It was Attorney General John Mitchell. "Can you get to D.C. and meet me at 9 A.M. tomorrow?" Mitchell asked.

"Do you know how far it is out to D.C. from here?" Blackmun replied respectfully. Rochester was a remote outpost, and there were no direct flights. "What's on your mind?" Blackmun asked.

In fact, Blackmun strongly suspected that the Nixon administration had finally found its non-Southerner to fill the Fortas seat. The sixty-one-year-old Blackmun knew that he had been on earlier lists and that the F.B.I. had conducted a routine background check on him.

Mitchell was evasive.

"Do I have to prepare anything to bring with me?"

"No, just come."

The next day at 11:15 A.M., Blackmun arrived at Mitchell's office at the Justice Department. The grilling began. Mitchell was determined to learn everything about his latest nominee. There would be no more surprises. He wanted to know if there were skeletons. He quizzed Blackmun about his finances, his social activities, his writings, and his appeals court decisions.

Assistant Attorney General Rehnquist, head of Mitchell's personal legal staff at the Justice Department—the office of Legal Counsel—joined them. He was followed two hours later by Johnnie M. Walters, the head of the Department's tax division. There would be no mistakes this time. Any area of possible trouble had to be identified.

There were some minor difficulties. Blackmun held $2,500 and $1,350 of stock in two companies, and he had ruled on cases indirectly involving them. Insubstantial as Blackmun's holdings were, Haynsworth had been hurt by disclosure of such alleged conflicts. It was decided that Walters would accompany Blackmun to Minnesota to gather the records. Everything had to be made public before or right after the announcement of the nomination.

That afternoon Mitchell and Blackmun went to see the President at the White House. Nixon had not met with Haynsworth or Carswell before their nominations, but he wanted to see Blackmun. Nixon found Blackmun's moderate conservatism perfect. A short, modest, soft-spoken man, Blackmun had been Phi Beta Kappa at Harvard, had gone on to Harvard Law School, a clerkship at the Eighth Circuit, sixteen years of private practice and about ten years as general counsel to the famous Mayo Clinic. After that he had been appointed to the Eighth Circuit by Eisenhower. He had academic credentials, practical legal experience in the Middle West, and a predictable, solid body of opinions that demonstrated a levelheaded strict-constructionist philosophy. And Burger thought highly of Blackmun. Blackmun was a decent man, consistent, wedded to routine, unlikely to venture far.

Neither Nixon nor Mitchell asked Blackmun about his judicial philosophy. The judge had three daughters in their twenties. Nixon asked if any were "hippie types." Blackmun assured him that none was.

He saw his lifelong friendship with Burger as his greatest potential problem. They had gone to grade school together, and Blackmun was best man at Burger's wedding in 1933. After Burger came to Washington in 1953, they corresponded, and they saw each other when Burger came to Minnesota to visit his family.

"Look," Nixon said, "you two grew up together. Your paths separated when you went to different high schools. But you have remained good friends. I don't see anything wrong with that." He wanted to go ahead. The administration was ready for an offensive. A detailed financial report on Blackmun was released to the Senate Judiciary Committee.

Nina Totenberg, who covered the Supreme Court for the weekly newspaper the *National Observer*, was one of Washington's most aggressive reporters, unwilling to settle for the usually placid

Court coverage. A specialist in digging out behind-the-scenes detail, Totenberg flew to Minneapolis to interview Blackmun's eighty-five-year-old mother. Mrs. Blackmun told Totenberg that the Chief Justice and her son talked to each other on the telephone almost once a week. They talked about all sorts of things, legal, political.

In an article Totenberg wrote that Mrs. Blackmun had recounted how once, the previous year, the Chief Justice had issued an open invitation to her son, "telling him that any time he needed assistance in sorting out recent Supreme Court decisions, he, the Chief Justice, would be glad to help. But Judge Blackmun, says Mrs. Blackmun, quickly declined the invitation, making it clear to the Chief Justice that he did not think receiving such assistance would be proper."

Blackmun was enraged at Totenberg. His relationship with Burger was the thing he was most sensitive about. For a moment, he considered withdrawing from the nomination. But Blackmun was ready when he faced Eastland's Senate Committee on April 29. He was tense, but determined to be candid. He knew the key was to show no arrogance, to be self-effacing. It came naturally to him.

Some of Haynsworth's opponents were chagrined at the fact that they were now supporting Blackmun. Haynsworth's alleged conflicts of interest, in retrospect, had not really amounted to more than the minor technical conflicts of interest involving Blackmun, a point Southern Senators could not resist making.

Blackmun was in Minnesota on the day of the final vote. He was trying to finish his appeals court work when two large canvas bags of cert petitions arrived from Washington. Burger soon called. "Did you get your mail?" he asked.

"Yes," Blackmun said jovially. "What's the idea?"

"You've got to go to work."

"I've got plenty of work out here," Blackmun said jokingly. "You're not my boss yet."

Burger wanted him in Washington before the term ended the next month. After a full year with only eight justices, nearly two hundred petitions for review had been held for "Justice X." In many of these cases, there were three votes to grant a hearing and Blackmun could supply the fourth. On cases that questioned the constitutionality of the death penalty, the feeling had been that the Court should not even grant a hearing until it was certain there would be nine members to review the cases.

Blackmun was overwhelmed at the prospect of making so many important decisions. When he was working on the appeals court, there was always another review authority, the Supreme Court, to correct any mistake he might make. Now, on these two hundred cases, it would be solely up to him. Blackmun was very cautious in dealing with the pending cert petitions. Burger did not want to take many of the cases. Blackmun finally voted to grant hearings in only three or four. Brennan was disappointed and concluded Burger had another vote.

The Chief was in a good mood. His first term was about to end, and there had been no major blowup. He himself couldn't have picked a better person to fill Fortas's seat.

Burger had paid attention to his administrative and housekeeping chores. He had tried to add life and warmth to the building and to his relations with the other Justices whenever possible. He had brought geraniums from his home to be planted in the courtyards. He made a personal gift of silver goblets to his fellow Justices to be used on the bench instead of the ordinary drinking glasses. The lunch hour had been extended from thirty minutes to an hour so the Justices would have more time to converse in their private dining room. (Douglas usually ate alone in his chambers and found the extended lunch period ludicrous. Black thought the additional half hour wasteful; he told Burger they might all begin to overeat.)

The Chief tried to remember each Justice's birthday or anniversary of service on the Court. On May 19, he sent out a memo:

Dear Brethren:
   Tomorrow, Wednesday, is John Harlan's birthday. If there are a sufficient number at luncheon we will break out a bottle of chilled German grape juice to take note of the occasion. Please let us know if you will be available. Would 12:30 be convenient for all?

Brennan, fiercely optimistic, had initially adopted a softer line on the new Chief than Douglas had. For years, at their regular weekly lunch, Bazelon had told Brennan tales of Burger's churlishness, but Brennan preferred to accept any plausible explanation for the Chief's actions. On substantive matters, Brennan characterized Burger as "ideologically reactionary but not evil." But his disappointment with the new Chief's style in running conferences had begun to increase. The fun and fascination Brennan had felt as the playmaker on the Warren Court was gone now. He was growing skeptical of the new Chief and about his own future role on the Court. By the end of the term, he was talking openly of resigning.

The other Justices also began to resent Burger's style.

In preparation for Blackmun's swearing-in ceremony on June 9, the Chief sent a memo saying that Blackmun would be "traveling light" and would wear only a dark business suit. Burger said he himself would "go a bit more formal but without 'cutaway.' Members are free, of course, to follow any course they desire."

Black was irritated about having someone even remind him that he could wear what clothes he wanted. Burger was much too concerned with appearances. He scrawled a note, "I shall go to the Court dressed as usual."

At the swearing-in ceremony, Blackmun took his place at the far-left side of the bench, the seat reserved for the junior member. The seat had, in the past, been occupied by Oliver Wendell Holmes, Benjamin N. Cardozo and Felix Frankfurter. Blackmun pulled out the drawer in the bench by his seat and started examining the contents. He found a copy of the Constitution stamped "O.W. Holmes," and apparently signed by Frankfurter. Suddenly White's loud whisper came from his right. "Harry! Harry, where's your spittoon?" Blackmun looked around as White snapped his fingers to one of the two pages that sat behind the bench to run errands for the Justices. "Get the Justice his spittoon," he ordered. The traditional spittoon, used as a wastebasket, appeared. Blackmun glanced down the bench. Without looking up from his papers, Douglas flipped an empty cough-drop box behind him. It had barely hit the floor before a page picked it up. Moments later, the page handed Douglas a fresh box.*

Blackmun had arrived at the busiest time of the year, the "June crunch," when the undecided votes in dozens of cases were finally cast and the results announced. These cases were often the most important and difficult to decide, the Justices having wrangled over them much of the term. By tradition and informal agreement, the Court tried to take final action on each of the argued cases before the end of the term. A decision might be issued. A case might be *dismissed as improvidently granted*—meaning that a majority had decided, at times even after oral argument, and often for technical reasons, not to decide the case. Or a case might be put over for reargument the next term. This year there were sixteen cases put over for reargument, an unusually high number.

Blackmun sat quietly at the last conferences. He had not participated in the hearings, so he could not vote. No one said anything about it to him directly, but he soon realized that they were putting over most of the cases because the vote was deadlocked 4 to 4. His vote would decide most of them.

At a special conference on Thursday, June 25, Blackmun watched as Black and Harlan squared off on two cases. The cases (*Sanks v. Georgia* and *Boddie v. Connecticut*) involved the constitutionality of state laws requiring that everyone, including the poor, pay a small court fee to fight a housing-eviction notice or to obtain a divorce. Harlan thought the fees, small as they were, violated the guarantee of due process, a guarantee that amounted to the right to have a fair hearing. The fees made it virtually impossible for the poor to get their day in court. Harlan had been assigned the cases, and he had the formal votes for his opinions. He wanted the cases to come down on Monday.

Black said he wanted more time. He had circulated his dissent in draft form only that morning. The cases were an outrage, he indicated. The Court had no license to make such a broad application of due-process guarantees. Nothing in the Constitution granted

---

* See National Geographic Society, *Equal Justice Under the Law: The Supreme Court in American Life,* rev. ed., p. 127.

equal access to the courts in civil cases, such as divorce or eviction hearings. The Constitution granted that access only in criminal cases. The Court's intent to hand down the decisions would be a revival of the notion of "substantive due process"—a generalized notion of fairness as defined by the Justices. This doctrine had been used, much to Black's dismay, to protect corporations from government regulations. "The Court doesn't enjoy a roving jurisdiction to do good," Black often told his clerks. It was not a matter of whether a law was unfair or fair, as long as it applied to everyone equally. As long as everyone had to live with it, the legislature that made the law would have to be accountable, not the Court.

Harlan was adamant. He would respond to Black by revising two footnotes. He would not rewrite the whole thing, nor would he agree to put the cases over. The Court had already put over a large number of cases and there was no reason to add this one to the list. He wanted his opinions to come down.

Black played his last chip. By tradition, a single Justice, even a dissenter, could insist that an opinion not come down until he had finished his own opinion. This was the conference's equivalent of senatorial courtesy. Black said he needed more time for his dissent in the eviction case. He really wanted the time to lobby some of the other Justices.

Harlan knew what Black was up to. He had seen this many times before.

Blackmun sat wide-eyed as the two went back and forth. Harlan seemed truly irked. If the eviction case were held over, then, Harlan pointed out, they might as well also put over the divorce-case opinion, since it relied heavily on the reasoning used in the eviction case.

A majority also wanted the opinions to come down. They urged Harlan to see if he could make the revisions by the next day's special conference. Harlan grudgingly consented. In spite of the sometimes heated argument, Harlan and Black walked out arm and arm, gently arguing as they headed down the hall to their chambers.

Harlan called in his clerks and told them what they were going to do: they would take the legal reasoning used in the eviction case and put it into the divorce case. They worked nearly all night cutting and pasting, and at conference the next day, Harlan presented his revisions.

Black wasn't satisfied with Harlan's massive effort of the previous night. "I don't want them to come down," Black said. Such a major opinion would have implications for many other cases.

Burger stepped in. He, too, wouldn't mind a little more time to go over both cases.

That did it.

Harlan was furious; Black had won again. He was still put out after conference as he prepared to go to dinner at Black's house. But by evening, all was forgiven.

Blackmun was dumbfounded. All over the country there were people who couldn't get into court on civil cases because they couldn't pay the fees. A majority of the Supreme Court had resolved the problem. But a single Justice had the power to force them all to wait. And now he was a Justice and had that same power.

1970 Term

As his second term approached, Burger worried increasingly about how his tenure would measure up against Earl Warren's. In Warren's first term, the Court had handed down the *Brown* school desegregation ruling. Over the next sixteen years, his monumental reputation for leadership and integrity had rested in large part on the continuing chain of school desegregation cases.

Burger's first term had not provided any such opportunity, but now Burger saw a wave of cases rising through the lower courts that presented the potential for a landmark decision. The Court's *per curiam* decision the term before in the Mississippi desegregation case (*Alexander v. Holmes County*) had made it clear the Court meant that desegregation was to occur now. The new cases raised the question of how it was to be achieved.

All that summer, the Supreme Court had been under fire over what seemed to be rapidly becoming the country's most volatile domestic political issue—busing. The furor had been growing since the spring of 1970, when U.S. District Court Judge James B. McMillan ordered each of the public schools of Charlotte, North Carolina, and surrounding Mecklenburg County to desegregate, not piecemeal, but totally. Like many federal judges, McMillan felt that desegregation no longer meant simply putting a single black student, a James Meredith, into an otherwise all-white school, like the University of Mississippi.

Since roughly 71 percent of the school population of the Charlotte area was white and 29 percent black, McMillan felt that a 71–29 white-black pupil ratio for *each* school should be the goal. While conceding that "variations from the norm may be unavoidable," he had radically altered school attendance zones and ordered busing for 13,000 additional students to achieve "racial balance," as it was called, in each school.

Burger felt that what McMillan had ordered amounted to forced racial mixing, an attempt to remedy residential segregation. This went far beyond the intent of the *Brown* cases, which ordered *desegregation*—the end of separate schools for blacks and whites. That was a proper task for the Court, Burger thought, and he supported it. But this was an order for *integration*.

"Desegregation" and "integration" are often used interchangeably, but they are very different matters, Burger told his clerks. "Integration" implied more—racial mixing, strict racial balance. Desirable as this might be in a perfect society, it had no legal foundation as an appropriate ruling by the Court.

Five weeks after the McMillan order, Burger published a concurrence to an opinion in another desegregation case (*Northcross v. Memphis Board of Education*). Though he did not mention McMillan's Charlotte opinion, Burger suggested that it was now time for the Court to determine how far lower court judges could go in ordering desegregation in general and busing in particular. He posed several key questions.*

Two weeks later, the President issued an extraordinary eight-thousand-word policy statement on desegregation. Though he did not address the Charlotte situation specifically, the President told how he himself would answer Burger's questions. Although he had supported the Warren Court's *Brown* decisions, Nixon found the situation far different now. The reason some black children were still going to all-black schools, he said, was that they lived in all-black neighborhoods. Children should attend their neighborhood schools, the President argued. These lower court decisions, ordering busing to equalize racial proportions in each school, went far beyond what the *Brown* decisions required. "Unless affirmed by the Supreme Court, I will not consider them as precedents to

---

* It was an area the Chief indicated he would like settled as soon as the Court was at full strength. The Fortas seat had not yet been filled at the time, and Marshall was hospitalized.

guide administration policy elsewhere," Nixon declared. He was shifting the onus of public hostility from his administration to the federal court system. A challenge had been issued.

Shortly after Nixon's statement, the Fourth Circuit Court of Appeals cut back substantially on the McMillan order, ruling out McMillan's extensive busing of elementary-school children. Calling for "reasonableness," without defining it, the majority opinion said that all-black schools need not be totally eliminated if there was "an intractable remnant of segregation" in a large black neighborhood. McMillan's extensive busing had created too great a burden on the community. He had tried too hard to reach his goal of a nearly perfect racial balance in each school, the court implied. It remanded—sent back—the case to him for further hearings.

Before McMillan had an opportunity to hold his new hearings, some black parents appealed the case to the Supreme Court (*Swann v. Charlotte-Mecklenburg Board of Education*). They wanted a quick ruling to the effect that every school must be de-segregated. Only Black, Douglas and Marshall had been prepared to postpone the end of the previous term in order to hear the case. The others agreed to hear it in October 1970. And the Court rein-stated McMillan's busing of elementary-school children until it would have a chance to rule. Therefore, McMillan's massive bus-ing plan would go into effect when the schools opened in September.

In the meantime, McMillan, encouraged both by the Fourth Circuit's ratification of some of his basic approach and by the Supreme Court's willingness to hear the case, went ahead and held his further hearings. And, once more, he ordered extensive busing of elementary-school children.

Southern politicians stumped the South chastising the Court for taking off the summer without deciding this crucial case before the school term began. Some of them suggested that the Justices were not earning their $60,000-a-year salaries.

On Monday, August 31, Burger took the unusual step of sum-moning the AP and UPI reporters who covered the Court to his chambers. The Supreme Court, he told them in a forty-five-minute background briefing, had decided not to have a summer session, because it wanted to hear several busing cases and consider the full range of issues. But, Burger said, he had placed the Charlotte case and two other pending appeals (*Davis v. Board of School Commissioners of Mobile County* and *McDaniel v. Barresi, Clarke County, Georgia*) at the head of the docket to be argued first in the new term. Burger also suggested to the reporters that the cases under review would likely produce a landmark decision. These cases, it now appeared, would be the most significant since the *Brown* decision. While all the cases involved Southern school districts, the Supreme Court's decision would likely affect every major school district in the country, North as well as South, Burger said.

The Chief knew that his ability to hold the Court together on the sensitive busing issues would be a crucial test of his leadership. Unanimity in key school desegregation cases was a tradition. But Burger had trouble seeing how unanimity could be achieved. As the term began, however, Burger found that he had an unexpected ally—Hugo Black, the previous term's militant proponent of desegregation "now." Black accepted busing in rural areas; most children were bused all their lives to one school or another. But, for all his hatred of segregation, Black viewed the urban neighborhood school as a foundation of community life. He was opposed to massive busing to achieve racial balance and wanted limits placed on the power of federal judges to order it.

"Where does the word *busing* appear in the Constitution?" Black asked his clerks. His approach struck them as almost a parody of his legendary literal-mindedness.

Desegregation, Black argued, meant children should go to the nearest available school. It did not require that they be bused beyond a neighborhood school, in order to meet some precise racial-balance formula. Massive urban busing was an attempt to "rearrange the whole country," he said. He was also sure that black parents, like white parents, did not want their children to spend unnecessary hours on a bus. He asked his messenger, Spencer Campbell, a black man who had been with him for over thirty years, what he thought of busing.

Spencer said he agreed with the Justice.

Black related the results of his private poll to his clerks. "Spencer doesn't like busing," he told them. End of discussion.

Black's clerks were convinced their boss was being unrealistic. The Court could not order immediate desegregation without adopting substantial busing, they argued. But as soon as they thought they had made some headway, Black had yet another counterargument. The power to tax was reserved for Congress. Therefore the Court could not require school districts to buy additional buses.

His clerks argued that many of the Court's decisions, including several written by Black himself, had required local governments to spend money.

Black's rebuttal was straightforward. He would allow limited busing to desegregate most schools, but he felt busing for racial balance was unnecessary.

Burger would stop by Black's chambers planning to lobby Black on the busing cases. But, for all of Black's famous "liberal" leanings, Burger found that Black had deep-seated conservative instincts. Each time, it was Black who ended up lobbying Burger.

It was clear that Burger could count on Black's vote. Burger was also confident of the position of his newest ally, Blackmun. The remainder of the Court, however, was another matter. At the opposite pole was Douglas.

For Douglas, the essence of the *Brown* cases was not that they ended segregation. He viewed the Warren Court rulings as an attack on the *stigma*—the stamp of inferiority—that segregated schools left on minorities. The only way to end that stigma, in Douglas's view, was through "integration." This was not likely to be achieved, however, with neighborhood schools. All-black neighborhoods would have all-black schools. And neighborhoods were not all-black because of random, natural development, Douglas felt. Some kind of discriminatory government action was behind most racial segregation, including that of neighborhoods. Douglas liked the sweeping way in which McMillan had gotten to the heart of the problem in his *Charlotte* decision.

McMillan had said that racial restrictions in deeds of land and actions by local and state agencies, such as zoning boards, urban-renewal agencies, public-housing authorities, and school boards had all contributed heavily to residential segregation. "There is so much state action embedded in and shaping these events that the resulting segregation is not innocent," he wrote.

Douglas subscribed to McMillan's basic premise that any school which could be labeled as predominately "white" or "black" must be integrated. More than anything else, he wanted to endorse this approach by McMillan. It was a reasonable effort to correct a clear constitutional violation.*

The other Justices were on a spectrum between Black and Douglas. Marshall would probably stand with Douglas if he felt that they could get a majority. Brennan was slightly less aggressive, convinced they could never get all Douglas wanted.

It was a question of what White, Stewart and Harlan would do.

At oral argument in the Charlotte case on October 12 and 13, Solicitor General Griswold argued for minimal busing, no quotas in individual schools, maximum use of neighborhood schools, and retention of some one-race schools. He strongly opposed strict racial balancing or any efforts by federal courts to correct for residential segregation. Judge McMillan had gone too far, he said. The Constitution did not require such extensive steps. School segregation should end, but children should be allowed to go to the school in their neighborhood—whether it was black, white, or perfectly integrated.

James M. Nabrit III, the Inc. Fund attorney representing the black parents and their children, knew he had to convince the Court that busing students to achieve full desegregation was feasible, not some crazy radical idea. Busing was already a part of most school systems, including Charlotte's. The new busing, an increase of less than 50 percent, was neither expensive nor disruptive.

The second *Brown* decision, Nabrit argued, specifically en-

---

* Douglas knew the McMillan opinion would put a nearly impossible burden on the school boards. They would have to prove that they were not responsible for the existing segregation. And unless the school board proved that, federal judges had unrestrained freedom to choose a broad remedy.

trusted the lower courts with designing appropriate desegregation remedies to meet different situations. McMillan could be affirmed, Nabrit said, "on the ground that he did not abuse his discretion in ordering a plan which remedied the wrong he found."

At the Friday conference Burger anticipated that there would be substantial disagreement among the Justices, so he suggested some preliminary ground rules. To encourage candor on such a sensitive subject, he proposed that the Justices adopt an extra measure of confidentiality, and not brief their clerks on the conference discussion. The Chief said that they should circulate only a single typewritten copy of drafts, instead of providing each Justice with the usual printed copies. This would be quicker and more secure. Burger then proposed that the Justices follow precedent set by Warren during the *Brown* cases, and put off taking even a preliminary vote for the time being. The Chief was anxious to keep the positions of the Justices fluid to avoid having Douglas and Black harden in their views. No matter what the Court finally decided on these cases, Burger wanted, above all, a unanimous opinion.

After each Justice had been given a chance to present his analysis of the cases, Burger quickly seized the initiative. It was obvious, he said, that there was no five-Justice majority for any one approach. Therefore, he would try to draft an opinion reconciling the different views.

Douglas was more than a little put out by the Chief's move. He had marked his own vote book based on each Justice's remarks. There seemed to be a 5-to-4 majority generally favoring McMillan's order. An even larger 7-to-2 majority endorsed the broad remedial powers of federal judges. The five solid votes were Douglas, Brennan, Marshall, Harlan and White.

In Douglas's view, Burger was in a minority of two with Black. As the senior Justice in the true majority, Douglas felt entitled to assign the opinion. Because of the confused conference discussion, however, he would just have to wait and see what the Chief wrote.

As he walked back to his chambers, Burger knew exactly what he wanted. If the opinion was to be unanimous, the important thing would be the wording. It would have to be a reasonable decision, with a little something for everyone—for the school boards, for the

Nixon administration, for the Inc. Fund, for the Fourth Circuit, even for Judge McMillan.

Burger quickly briefed his head clerk and set him to work on the draft. The Chief did not have sufficient time to write it himself, but he would stay more closely in touch than usual.

Stewart, meanwhile, once again read the series of opinions that Judge McMillan had written. He was becoming fascinated by this lower court judge. McMillan's final opinion, written in August, after the case had been remanded to him for additional hearings, struck Stewart as among the boldest and best lower court decisions he had ever read.

Over the summer, McMillan had conducted eight days of fact finding. Even in the face of the Fourth Circuit's criticism, he rather daringly had reinstated his original order, demonstrating its reasonableness:

- A third of the children in Charlotte were already being bused to public school;
- Few additional buses had to be purchased;
- The average bus route would be shorter;
- His order had been issued only after the school board refused three times to submit a desegregation plan;
- The school board had vastly exaggerated the number and expense of buses required to implement the plan, exaggerations that, as McMillan put it (with a footnote credit to Lewis Carroll's *Alice in Wonderland*), "border on fantasy";
- Racial balance in each school was not something he had strictly required; it was a model by which to measure successful desegregation.

In reinstating his original order, McMillan had criticized the Fourth Circuit's vague directive that he be more "reasonable." He was reinstating the order because "it does the complete job." Stewart admired McMillan's candor and the clever manner in which he had tied the order back to the facts. Since appellate courts were usually supposed to rule only on law and not on facts, except where the factual assessment was clearly erroneous, McMillan's opinion would be hard to reverse.

Looking McMillan up in *Who's Who,* Stewart found that he and McMillan were almost the same age. McMillan had gone to Harvard Law School, while Stewart attended Yale, and both had served in the Navy during World War II. McMillan was a member of the United World Federalists, a group of idealists working for world government. It seemed to Stewart that McMillan represented a courageous strain of Southern liberalism. McMillan reportedly had received death threats because of his decision, and he had been placed under police protection. But he seemed willing to have crosses burned on his lawn.

"The issue is one of Constitutional law, not politics," he had said. "A judge would ordinarily like to decide cases to suit his neighbors . . . To yield to public clamor, however, is to corrupt the judicial process."

"I've got to admire his courage," Stewart told his clerks. "Some people do cause a lot of trouble. It would be nice if it hadn't happened."

From Stewart's point of view, McMillan had put the Court on the spot. Two decades before, it would have been easier for the Court to back McMillan up. Then, Northern Democrats and Northern Republicans had given bipartisan support to the Court's desegregation orders. Although President Eisenhower had never enforced the orders with any enthusiasm, at least he had not campaigned against them as Nixon had done.

To Stewart, the evaporation of bipartisan support suggested that more than the usual amount of restraint and caution was needed. And above all, the Court's tradition of unanimity in these cases had to be maintained. That was clearly not going to be easy. McMillan's courage created a difficult impasse for the Court. The conference had only reconfirmed the enormous gulf between the extremes. The Chief seemed closely aligned with Black's antibusing stance. Stewart felt that it was highly unlikely that Burger could write an opinion that would shelter everyone under one umbrella.

Stewart saw himself in the center. And it was the center of the Court that would have to prevent the collapse of unanimity. "I don't know what the Chief is doing about this case," Stewart told one of his clerks. "Maybe we ought to have something ready." Stewart told the clerk to research the subject and pull together a memorandum drafted as an opinion. He added some directives: McMillan was about right on the justification for racial balance; racial balance was a goal against which progress in desegregation could be measured; busing and redrawing school-attendance zones were remedies within the powers of the federal courts to order; they should be catalogued and approved, though no one remedy should be glorified.

Yet, McMillan had gone too far on one matter. Stewart could support busing for junior and senior high schools; but when it came to busing elementary-school pupils, he felt that McMillan had gone too far. "They're busing babies, mere babies, mere four-year-olds," Stewart said. "I would not want a four-year-old of mine to go off on a bus for forty-five minutes."

Stewart thought the Fourth Circuit was right on this point. It had agreed with McMillan on the busing of older students, but not the younger ones. The clerk was to prepare a draft memorandum that, on this point, would reverse McMillan and uphold the Fourth Circuit.

There were other tightropes to walk in preparing the draft. Stewart felt that there should be strong language in the opinion welcoming aggressive, innovative approaches to school desegregation. The tone should be positive, to encourage the few lower court judges willing to take this kind of initiative.

But, Stewart cautioned, the sense of the conference was certainly not to go so far as to require the elimination of all one-race schools—something McMillan's opinions had implied was necessary. There were situations in which one-race schools would have to be allowed.

Overall, the draft memorandum should be written as both a legal and a political document. The media would interpret it on a superficial level. Who had won and who had lost? Had the Court reaffirmed its commitment to desegregation? Had the Nixon administration forced the Court to back down? The language had to be chosen carefully. But the tone had to be supportive of

McMillan's innovative approach. The federal district and appeals court judges were the real audience.

Stewart's clerk began his research.

On December 8, 1970, Burger's double-spaced typewritten draft was hand-delivered to each chamber. Stewart read it carefully. It was an appalling effort. The tone was entirely negative, criticizing McMillan, and not approving even the part of his order dealing with the junior and senior high-school students.

After recounting the *Brown* decisions and noting the difficulty in implementing the desegregation of Southern schools, Part III of the Chief's draft said, " . . . some of the problems we now face [may] arise from viewing *Brown I* as imposing a requirement for racial balance, *i.e.*, integration, rather than a prohibition against segregation."

Stewart saw this as potentially disastrous—certain to draw the wrath of Douglas, Brennan and Marshall.

"The ultimate remedy commanded by [the desegregation cases from 1955 to 1969] was to discontinue the dual system," the draft continued. The Chief was saying that federal judges could only restore the situation to what it would have been had there never been separate school systems for whites and blacks. This, Stewart knew, would provoke at least half of his colleagues, who wanted the decision to also correct for residential segregation.

Stewart was puzzled. Traditionally, the courts had power to correct violations of constitutional rights. Judges could do whatever was necessary to correct the situation once a violation was proved. Burger wanted to limit judges to the minimum necessary to correct a violation, whereas the consensus of the conference was to have judges do anything that was effective in correcting a violation. Effectiveness should be the measure of a remedy, Stewart felt. Lower court judges should not be second-guessed unless they grossly abused their discretion.

Burger's draft then turned to the four main issues presented in the case—racial balancing; elimination of one-race schools; altering school-attendance zones; and busing. These sections were written with one purpose, Stewart concluded. Burger wanted to

show that federal court desegregation remedies could not take residential segregation into account. The objective "does not and cannot embrace" the residential segregation, Burger had written. For
Burger, all the rest followed. Thus, trying to achieve "racial balance" in each school was not necessary, because imbalance often
resulted from residential segregation beyond the courts' power to
correct. The conference had been closely divided on this question
already. Stewart agreed with the Chief, although he found the draft
overstated and severe. Stewart would much prefer to duck this issue for the time being.

Turning to Burger's section on whether the courts could redraw
school-attendance zones, Stewart found an incredible phrase
dropped in the middle: "Absent a history of a dual school system,"
the courts could do nothing, the Chief said. That statement would
have little effect in the South, where dual systems had existed in
most locations, but it would drastically limit Northern desegregation orders.

The remainder of the draft seemed more reasonable to Stewart.
It said that busing and alteration of school zones were certainly
proper in some instances, but the age of children could be taken
into consideration. The Fourth Circuit had properly brought
McMillan to task for not considering the age of the elementary-
school children. The liberals would not like that, but Stewart
would support it.

Burger's draft neither reversed nor affirmed McMillan, but simply sent the case back to him for "reconsideration" in accordance
with the opinion. What bothered Stewart was the tone of even
those sections that endorsed McMillan. Burger said McMillan's
technique was "not an impermissible tool." The double negative
was a needless jab. The Chief also praised the "valiant efforts" of
the school boards, a seeming endorsement of their obstruction.

Stewart concluded that Burger had given a begrudging yes to
very limited busing, but that he had undercut the thrust of the
McMillan order. If published, the opinion would almost certainly
encourage segregationists to use the federal courts to try to cut
back on desegregation orders already in effect in the South. It
would also preclude efforts to use the federal courts to desegregate

Northern schools. "This will represent a complete retreat," he told his clerk. "It's disorganized and stupid."

Stewart asked his clerk to finish his research memo as quickly as possible. "I want a lot of emphasis on the remedial power of the trial court," Stewart said.

Within a week, Stewart had edited and partly restructured his clerk's memo. He sent it to the printer with the simple heading "Mr. Justice Stewart." He did not want it to be anything more than a memo. Anything suggesting that it was a separate opinion, an alternative draft, or even a dissent, would be threatening to the Chief. "I don't know whether we should circulate this now," Stewart told his clerk after the draft came back from the printer. But a few days later, Stewart told his clerk to take copies to the five other Justices who he hoped would be sympathetic—Douglas, Brennan, White, Harlan and Marshall.

Brennan did not like the Burger draft. The Chief had insulted the intelligence of the conference, Brennan felt. He was trying to frustrate the will of the majority. Brennan was not entirely pleased with Stewart's memo, but he much preferred it as a basis for discussion. He encouraged Stewart to circulate it to the full Court. That way, the Chief would at least have the benefit of seeing it.

Stewart was reluctant, however, to confront Burger with what would obviously be perceived as an alternative draft. "I got shitty opinion assignments from Earl Warren for ten years, and I'll be damned if I want to get them from Warren Burger for the next fifteen years," Stewart declared.

Brennan again urged Stewart to circulate his effort. Privately he considered Stewart far too timid, almost cowardly, for his reluctance to stand up to the Chief.

Douglas, Marshall and White also urged Stewart to circulate. Each had objections, but each felt that, as a basis for negotiation, Stewart's draft was certainly more palatable than Burger's.

Stewart realized that with the votes of the four Justices who were urging him to circulate, he had the makings of a majority. He decided to send the memo to the others, and he prepared a carefully worded cover letter indicating that the circulation was just a research memo, really nothing more than some thoughts and background prepared by his law clerk.

"They think your draft is good," Stewart told his clerk. "But don't get your hopes up."

Burger's reaction to Stewart's memo and cover letter seemed positive. The chief told Stewart that he would use the memo as the basis for yet another draft, and he quickly set his senior and most trusted law clerk back to work.

The Chief finally circulated his second draft. It was, on the whole, a major disappointment to Stewart. Despite Burger's assurances, he had incorporated little of the material in Stewart's memo. The draft was still overwhelmingly negative in tone. "We may have to dissent," Stewart told his clerk. "Your thing may be published yet."

Harlan watched the maneuvering on the cases from a dignified distance. He had assigned a law clerk to prepare a detailed research memorandum on the pertinent law, and he felt that the issue came down to whether federal judges enjoyed a sufficiently broad power to order such remedies as busing for constitutional violations. His research indicated that they had the power to set forth any remedy they deemed necessary.

Harlan had his clerk's massive research memorandum printed and presented it as a set of suggestions for revisions to Burger's draft opinion. His cover memo, restrained in tone, said the Chief's draft would be acceptable, provided that Burger made a few changes. The changes, however, amounted to deleting almost all of the Chief's draft and substituting the far longer Harlan memorandum.

Blackmun had also maintained a deliberately low profile. These were the first cases argued since his arrival on the Court. Blackmun took great pride in his progressive views on racial matters. He had, after all, authored some of the opinions of the Eighth Circuit Court of Appeals in the Little Rock desegregation cases. But he worried that McMillan's order would destroy the role played by neighborhood schools in formulating community values.

Still, Blackmun thought that the basic question was the power of judges in the lower federal courts to deal with these situations. Harlan's research had settled this, as far as Blackmun was concerned. Blackmun preferred Stewart's draft, but he was not about to disagree openly with the Chief. If only Burger would alter his own draft to remove any ambiguity about the power of lower federal courts to order busing.

Burger, however, wouldn't move. Black was not willing to budge on his opposition to busing, Burger insisted. The others would have to compromise in order to reach some consensus.

At this point, Douglas, Brennan, Marshall and White took stock. They could not live with the Chief's draft. They preferred, in varying degrees, different solutions. The Stewart draft also fell short of their aspirations, but provided them with some leverage on Burger.

Douglas, Brennan and Marshall went to Stewart's chambers. Stewart was nervous about the implications of a meeting of five Justices—a potential majority, the very sort of rump caucus Warren used to hold—so White had not been invited. Stewart emphasized that he was unwilling to take the opinion away from the Chief. His goal, he said, was to pull the conference together, not to divide it. He did not want to be a leader, or even a member, of any faction.

The other three Justices tried to reassure Stewart. He alone was in a position to rally their votes and those of White, Harlan and Blackmun. If he was unwilling to make his draft a counter opinion, he must at least take the responsibility of negotiating with the Chief.

Stewart felt pressured. But at the same time, he rationalized that he was pulling the liberal wing along into a more moderate posture, one more likely to result in a true consensus. It was clear to Stewart's clerks that he liked the idea of being the principal negotiator with the Chief.

Back in his chambers, Douglas was worried. Desegregation sentiment in the country had peaked. This time, there was a very real threat of a backlash. The antibusing sentiments salted throughout Burger's draft would appeal not just to segregationists in the South, but to a substantial blue-collar constituency in the urban

North. If Burger's opinion surfaced in its present form, it would appear to legitimize Nixon's antibusing, anti-desegregation policies. The Court would look like an instrument of Nixon's will.

For Douglas, the Court's credibility, its prestige and its independence were at stake. Normally he preferred to publish his views in a separate opinion rather than compromise with his colleagues. But this was too important. Black's desertion, his apparent support for the entire Burger effort, left Douglas unsure where the final Burger draft would come out. The key to any meaningful alternative was clearly Stewart. Stewart's memo was not that bad, as far as Douglas was concerned. His approach and his tone swept in the proper direction. But there was one major problem.

Douglas made a decision. He walked over to Stewart's chambers, and knocked on the door that led directly from the hall into Stewart's own office. Stewart was surprised to see him. "I like your memo," Douglas said, "except for one thing—the result."

In Douglas's view, the question of whether elementary-school children should be bused in Charlotte was of far less significance than the symbolism of how the Supreme Court treated Judge McMillan. It was important to endorse McMillan's logic. If it were affirmed, every district court judge would have to go to the McMillan opinion for guidance, instead of merely reading the Supreme Court's opinion. That was what Douglas wanted.

Was it absolutely necessary, Douglas asked Stewart, to reverse McMillan because he had ordered the busing of elementary-school children? Douglas had an alternative. Suppose the order affirmed McMillan—thus upholding the use of racial balance as a criterion for designing a desegregation plan—but went on to point out, in the text of the opinion, the difficulties and considerations in busing young children?

Okay, Stewart said.

Douglas left and Stewart ordered his draft changed—from reverse to affirm.

Marshall was happy to see that Stewart was willing to affirm McMillan. That was vital. But in general, Marshall had some strong reservations about Stewart's version. First of all, it was nearly as conservative as the Chief's. Worse, it was too specific. Too lawyerlike. Too well written. Stewart's draft, Marshall feared, would make all too clear the extent to which the Court was not fully backing up McMillan. Marshall felt that the goal of protecting the extensive desegregation efforts already underway in the South would best be served if the Court affirmed McMillan and accompanied the order with something like the hodgepodge prepared by Burger. Lower court judges would not be able to understand a mushy opinion like that. They would be forced to read McMillan's opinion for guidance to see what it was that the Court was affirming.

As Burger's senior clerk labored in his second-floor office, he began receiving frequent visits from a clerk who worked for Marshall. Marshall had a number of problems with Burger's first version.

Ideally, Marshall would have liked to go as far as possible in this case to maximize desegregation. But he was practical enough to recognize that sweeping changes were not about to be realized in this case. He focused, therefore, on more limited goals.

One problem with Burger's draft was the way it held that a judge should not attempt to correct for residential segregation patterns in designing school desegregation plans. That was precisely the question that judges had to weigh, Marshall felt, if there was to be any meaningful desegregation of big-city school systems, particularly in the North.

So Marshall's clerk began lobbying through Burger's clerk, trying to persuade him to move a discussion of residential segregation that had been buried in Footnote II up to the main body of the next draft. Burger at last gave in, though he refused to go along with most of the other changes sought by Marshall.

Stewart continued his negotiation with the Chief. He knew now that his alternative draft implicitly commanded the votes of at least five justices and, with Harlan, six. But the process of trying to bring Burger around was painfully slow. Stewart finally came to the conclusion that the Chief's principal commitment was to his own language. He seemed flexible on where his language and phrases appeared, as long as they were somewhere in the opinion.

So, to diminish the overall negative tone, Stewart began dispersing the Chief's most damaging sentences throughout his draft. A string of sentences in the middle of Burger's original draft, suggesting sympathy with desegregation delays, was softened by the elimination of one sentence, additions from Stewart's draft, and the relocation of some of Burger's other material. Nearly every paragraph required a drawn-out negotiation. As Stewart pushed to insert as much of his draft as possible to dilute the Burger rhetoric, the length of the opinion almost doubled.

Black remained a major obstacle. Spurning the negotiating process, Black insisted that he would not join any opinion that mentioned or approved of busing to achieve racial balance. And Burger used Black's intransigence as a lever in his negotiation with Stewart. It had been difficult to coax Black along, Burger explained. Hugo had already compromised a great deal. The others would also have to compromise.

Stewart could hardly contain his frustration in his face-to-face meetings with the Chief. Privately he knew that what the Chief painted as an 8-to-1 split was really a 7-to-2 split. As one of the two members of the minority, the Chief was doing his best to control the opinion. "If Black did not exist, Burger would have to create him," one clerk complained.

Stewart's frustration had reached its limit. He still hoped for a unanimous court. But if Black insisted on holding out, an 8-to-1 opinion would be close enough. Black would be dealt with later, once the other eight agreed. It was time to call the Chief's bluff. He let the Chief know he wanted his changes made.

Brennan, too, felt frustrated. By not writing himself, by letting Stewart—who was really in the middle—negotiate for the liberals, it was going to be difficult to get an acceptable opinion. Stewart's final draft, even with modifications, would have been barely sufficient. Now, he was making compromises with Burger that Brennan found increasingly unsatisfactory.

It was clear that the Chief had moved from his true position in order to accommodate the majority. He wanted to be the author. What had started out as an antibusing opinion was taking shape as at least a moderate endorsement of busing and McMillan. The negative tone, if it was not yet positive, was at least becoming neutral. But the Chief had not come far enough, and now he seemed to be digging in. It was time to act.

Brennan had all three of his law clerks draft a detailed memo listing his objections to the latest Burger draft. "This is my shot," Brennan told his clerks, "and I want to draw the line." Because the Chief wanted unanimity, Brennan felt there was no reason not to threaten to be as immovable as Black.

Brennan's memo made four basic points:

1. Racial balance had to be clearly endorsed as a permissible guideline against which to measure the extent of the segregation problem and the effectiveness of the desegregation solution.
2. The acceptability and appropriateness of busing needed to be clearly emphasized to the lower courts.
3. A stronger position had to be taken on eliminating one-race schools.
4. Annual readjustment of the racial composition of the schools should be made to keep them from becoming all-white or all-black again.

Brennan sent his memo to the Chief and the other Justices. Faced on all sides with insurrection, the Chief circulated still another draft. The tone, and much of the substance, was a far cry from his first draft four months earlier.

Where Burger's first draft had declared that past delays by Southern school boards in dealing with desegregation were "not now relevant," the new draft said that "the failure of local authorities to meet their constitutional responsibility aggravated" problems in desegregation.

The Chief had also declared in his first version that judges had less power in school desegregation cases than in other types of cases involving constitutional violations. Now, in a victory for Stewart, the latest draft declared them identical. Burger's section prohibiting federal judges from taking into account residential segregation had also been removed. On the other hand, Douglas's suggestion that judges be *required* to consider residential segregation had not been adopted either. Marshall's language had been adopted, specifying that courts should give "great weight" to residential segregation in designing desegregation orders if the residential segregation was at least caused in part by school board decisions—such as decisions to close or open schools in certain neighborhoods.

The racial-balance question was split down the middle, but basically it affirmed McMillan. The draft still said that the Constitution did not require it. But, on the other hand, it stated that "the very limited use made of mathematical ratios was within the . . . discretion of the District Court." In case the message was missed, the final draft praised McMillan's "patient efforts."

Not all the battles, however, had been won by the liberals. A "small number of one-race" schools was not necessarily a mark of an illegally segregated system, the draft said. But there was a "presumption" against them, and the goal should be their elimination.

Burger and Stewart had agreed on two other sections that gave the liberals some problems. The age of students, the draft said, should be taken into account in busing orders. A section tacked onto the end also made it clear that it was unnecessary to readjust the racial composition of schools each year—a defeat for Brennan.

But the bottom line—the answer to the question of how much desegregation was adequate—was a clear victory for the liberal wing of the Court. "The district judge or school authorities should make every effort to achieve the greatest possible degree of actual desegregation," the new draft said.

The Chief had abandoned his earlier language about "limitations" on busing. The new version approved McMillan's plan as "reasonable, feasible and workable." Burger had also worked out a tricky compromise that was meant to avoid offending either McMillan or the Fourth Circuit Court of Appeals headed by Judge Haynsworth. The order said that the Fourth Circuit was affirmed to the extent that it affirmed McMillan. And, it said, the remainder of McMillan's order was also affirmed. Thus, without saying so, the Court actually reversed that portion of the Fourth Circuit opinion which had not upheld McMillan.

The order was a jumble of compromises, but the new draft had one thing going for it: it had the backing of eight Justices.

Black remained unhappy. The time had come, he decided, to make his stand. He had heard all his clerks' arguments that desegregation *now*, which he had demanded the previous year, could not be accomplished without busing. He was not willing to accept that logic. They were two entirely different issues.

Black was convinced that massive forced busing would trigger a wave of militant, perhaps violent, resistance in the South. For two decades, he had believed that white parents would never desert the public schools. Now he was convinced they would take their children to private and parochial schools.

Black sent a memo to his colleagues. He would not go along with any opinions that explicitly approved compulsory busing. Unless the others acquiesced, removing the endorsement of McMillan's busing order, Black was going to dissent.

Harlan was peeved. It had been bad enough the year before, when Black had threatened to dissent in the Mississippi desegregation case unless he got his way. Now he was doing it again. These continuing blackmail attempts were outrageous. Faced with recalcitrant school boards willing to seize any difference, unanimity in school cases was an important tradition. To hold it hostage, Harlan felt, demeaned both Black and the Court.

Brennan was convinced that Black had lost touch with reality. Black wanted desegregation, but, as the Court's only Southerner, he found it hard to face the discomfort and dislocation it inevitably brought. The others decided that the only course was to accept the prospect of a Black dissent. Perhaps an 8-to-1 decision would not be that bad.

Faced with this defeat, Black began to reconsider his position. A separate dissent, he feared, might provide an encouraging signal to the remaining segregationists. He and the Chief had, after all, succeeded in preventing a flat-out endorsement of strict racial balancing, the elimination of every one-race school, and unlimited busing. Practically speaking, the final draft would cause most lower court judges to think twice before ordering massive compulsory busing of elementary-school children.

A few days later, Black sent a memo to the Chief. "Maybe it is safe to join now," Black said.

The tradition of unanimity appeared to have been saved. At the last minute, however, a final obstacle threatened to undo the months of compromise. Douglas circulated a draft dissent in another busing case (*Keyes v. School District No. 1, Denver, Colorado*) that went far beyond the carefully worded opinion in the Charlotte case. The other Justices quickly prevailed on Douglas to withdraw the draft before it provoked a response from Black or Burger.

On April 20, 1971, the Chief announced from the bench his unanimous opinions in the Charlotte and companion cases. Newspapers from coast to coast carried banner headlines declaring that the Court had backed busing. *The New York Times* featured Judge McMillan as the "Man in the News." Burger couldn't understand it. He told friends that he considered his opinion "antibusing."

It also did not take Court observers long to recognize the internal inconsistencies in the opinion. "There is a lot of conflicting language here," a judge of the Fifth Circuit Court of Appeals, where most desegregation cases had arisen, told *Newsweek* magazine. "It's almost as if there were two sets of views, laid side by side."

Stewart could see the judge's point, but he felt that the thrust of the decision could not be missed. It was rare for the Court to pat a lower court judge on the head, and to specifically approve his actions without saying that they were constitutionally required.

Another news article, citing inside sources as saying that the opinion had been pieced together by other Justices, sent Burger into a rage.

Black took the Chief aside and told him to ignore the press.

Later, when Burger gave a tea for the law clerks from all chambers, one of them asked him about the evolution of the Charlotte opinion from his first draft. "There wasn't much difference," Burger replied. "It didn't change much."

With Blackmun's addition to the Court, Burger hoped to trim back some of the Warren Court's decisions on criminal law during the 1970 term. In one case *(Relford v. Commandant)*, the Court was being asked to make a 1969 Warren Court decision *(O'Callahan v. Parker)* retroactive. The ruling required civilian, rather than military, trials for servicemen accused of non-service-related crimes.

At conference on the Friday before Christmas, Burger and Blackmun joined the dissenters in the 1969 case—Harlan, Stewart and White—to create a new majority that both opposed making the earlier decision retroactive and favored cutting back on the precedent itself.

Harlan suggested they go even further and actually overrule the 1969 case. The others in the majority were inclined to agree. As the Justices moved to other cases, however, Harlan had second thoughts. It would be precipitous, he said, to overrule the precedent. He suggested a less drastic alternative, distinguishing between the two cases in order to leave the earlier one intact. The others in the majority were satisfied.

Another case considered in December *(Harris v. New York)* challenged the scope of the Warren Court's famous *Miranda* ruling. Under *Miranda*, police were required to inform a person who had been arrested of his right to remain silent and be provided a lawyer. If the police failed to give that warning, whatever a suspect told them could not be used in a trial.

In the pending case, a lower court had made an exception to the strict commands of *Miranda* when the defendant, in testifying at his trial, had contradicted what he had first told police. The prosecutor claimed that the earlier statements had to be admitted in court in order to challenge the defendant's new testimony.

At conference, Black, Douglas, Brennan and Marshall wanted to hold the line with the *Miranda* decision. Allowing the statements to be used for any reason would undercut *Miranda*. Burger and Blackmun again joined the three *Miranda* dissenters to allow the statements to be used in the trial. And the new majority, it seemed to Burger, might be willing to go further and gut much of *Miranda*.

Harlan, however, repeated his concern that they were moving too quickly. He wanted to overrule *Miranda*, and a number of other Warren Court decisions. But to sweep away years of precedent because the membership of the Court had changed would be a serious mistake. For fourteen years, Harlan had urged *stare decisis* in his dissents from the Warren Court rulings. He would not abandon that doctrine. Harlan, the fifth vote, suggested that they stick to the narrower exception to the *Miranda* ruling presented by this one case. The others went along.

Harlan was delighted when his friend Black leaned over to him one day during oral argument and whispered some good news. Black said he was rethinking his position on one of the most controversial areas of criminal law—the so-called "exclusionary rule." Under this doctrine, the Court had held more than once that evidence obtained in an "unreasonable search" could not be used to convict the person searched even if, as a result, obviously guilty criminals went free. These decisions, beginning in 1914 with *Weeks v. U.S.*, had come to be called the "exclusionary rule," because evidence obtained in an illegal search—a weapon, a document or a piece of stolen property—had to be excluded from a criminal trial.

The rule had grown out of two theories: first, that the only way to deter police from violating the Fourth Amendment's protection against "unreasonable searches" was to prohibit the use in prosecutions of whatever they had illegally obtained; second, that evidence obtained illegally would taint a trial and make the courts partners in lawless police conduct.

Harlan was glad to hear that Black was reconsidering. Since Harlan, White, Burger and Blackmun were all, each for different reasons and to a different degree, willing to change the exclusionary rule, Black could be the needed fifth vote. Harlan also felt that since Black was a member of the original majority, there would be less of a problem in overruling the precedent.

There were before the Court several cases that dealt with various aspects of the rule. They could provide Black with a number of opportunities to revise his thinking.

The Justices who wished to modify the rule thought it had developed into a series of complicated and confusing requirements that puzzled the police more than it restrained them. The Fourth

Amendment prohibited "unreasonable" searches, but "unreasonable" had never been fully defined. It was a term Black had trouble interpreting literally. It was necessarily rooted in each Justice's subjective judgment.

The Fourth Amendment also required that police obtain a warrant, and that it be issued only when "probable cause" was shown that a search would yield specific items. Yet the Court, over the years, had allowed numerous exceptions to the warrant requirement. The exceptions allowed police to conduct warrantless searches during a lawful arrest, to seize items in "plain view," to search a person if he consented, and to search automobiles since someone could move a car before the police could get a warrant.

Since his days on the Court of Appeals, Burger had been an articulate advocate of a change in the exclusionary rule. He argued, both on and off the bench, that society had paid a monstrous price for the rule. Guilty criminals were being set free because key evidence could not be introduced at trial. Often, the police were well-meaning, but had made a technical error in securing a warrant or in documenting probable cause.

Burger agreed that evidence should be suppressed where there was genuine police misconduct, such as breaking and entering or coercion. But he was sympathetic to the cop on the beat who honestly concluded that a person had been casing a store for a burglary. That was the kind of routine and proper law enforcement that prevented crime. Yet the evidence obtained as a result of stopping and searching in such instances was often excluded for lack of "probable cause."

Burger had presented his views in a 1964 lecture at American University. "We can ponder whether any community is entitled to call itself an 'organized society' if it can find no way to solve this problem except by suppression of truth in search for truth." The argument had a strong common-sense appeal. Why should a trial designed to determine what actually happened exclude the very evidence that would best establish just that?

Burger felt that there should be a remedy such as disciplinary action against police officers who abused constitutional rights. But he also believed that the exclusionary rule had little deterrent effect on future police misconduct. Police were often unable to follow their own cases through the years of appeals where Fourth Amendment questions were eventually decided. If a conviction was overturned because of police error, the police would probably never know why.

Quoting former Justice Benjamin N. Cardozo, Burger declared that it was irrational that a "criminal go free because the constable erred." It was absurd to free a murderer because a policeman, for example, had made a minor error on an application for a search warrant.

Although Brennan was one of the strongest supporters of the exclusionary rule, he also had developed serious doubts about its effectiveness in deterring police abuses. But he could think of no practical alternative. When Harlan told him that Black was rethinking his position, Brennan was worried.

Black had never been a strong supporter of the rule, but his vote was the essential fifth. Without it, there was a chance now that the original 1914 *Weeks* case, requiring federal courts to exclude illegally obtained evidence, could be overruled. Nearly as drastic would be a decision overruling the 1961 *Mapp* case (*Mapp v. Ohio*), in which the Warren Court had decreed that the federal exclusionary rule would have to be adhered to by state as well as federal courts.

Brennan instructed his clerks not to recommend that he vote to grant cert in Fourth Amendment cases unless there had been a flagrant police violation. Since a majority of five could overrule any case they wanted, the risk was great. One case with the wrong set of facts might send Black over to the other side, wiping away major protections it had taken years to develop. Brennan told his clerks that they could not afford to take cases to "right little wrongs." Better to play it safe until it was clear what Black was going to do.

Marshall gave his clerks the same message: no free shots at the Fourth Amendment should be given. Even in cases where Marshall was convinced that police had violated the Fourth Amendment, he would not take the risk of granting cert.

Even Harlan, unsure where the cases would come out, had been reluctant to grant cert.

Word of Black's reassessment spread quickly through the clerk network. Burger's past rhetoric fueled rumors in the clerks' dining room. *"Mapp* is dead," one clerk concluded sadly. The question seemed only whether the basic federal rule, the *Weeks* case, would weather Black's reexamination.

Burger lobbied Black privately, encouraging him to provide the fifth vote to cut back. But even though Black didn't like *Mapp,* he didn't want to overrule it. He had provided the key fifth vote in the 1961 decision, joining it reluctantly, because of his belief that the same constitutional rights that applied in federal court trials ought to be equally binding on the states: whatever exclusionary rule existed for the federal government existed also for the states. The problem was that Black had never been sure what exclusionary rule should exist for the federal government.

Black's reconsideration stemmed partly from his experiences as a prosecutor and as a crusading Senate investigator. Over the years, the police had become the underdogs. The rights of the accused had been extended too far. The Court had to take into account the growing crime problem, to reappraise the balance between the needs of society for safety and the rights of the defendant.

Black was not opposed to readjusting the law. Under Warren, the Court simply had gone too far. As crime soared, the Court had brought the country's wrath upon itself. News reports of heinous and violent crime frightened Black. The nation's fear of crime had enabled Nixon, who had exploited that fear, to be elected President. The Court had to put on the brakes.

Rather than overrule *Mapp,* Black preferred to create a clear check list of what was and what was not a reasonable search; when evidence could, and when it could not be excluded. A complicated murder case *(Coolidge v. New Hampshire),* posing several major Fourth Amendment questions, offered that chance.

Edward Coolidge had been convicted of murdering a fourteen-year-old girl in 1964, after luring her from her home during a heavy snowstorm with an offer of a babysitting job. The facts were gruesome. The girl's body had been found along a highway eight days later when the snow melted. Her throat had been slashed and she had been shot in the head.

The police, without a warrant, had gone to Coolidge's home, where his wife gave them a gun that turned out to be the murder weapon, and some clothes that Coolidge had worn the night of the murder. Shortly after arresting Coolidge, the police, again without a valid warrant, searched and vacuumed Coolidge's car and found dirt and other fine particles that matched those on the murdered girl. Coolidge's lawyers argued that all the evidence should have been excluded from the trial.

At conference, Black indicated that he thought none of it should be excluded. The evidence found with the wife's consent was properly obtained. He also felt that it had been proper to search the car.

Harlan was personally inclined to agree with Black. But the *Mapp* case bound them, since *Coolidge* was a state case, so he announced that he would not join Burger, Black, White and Blackmun unless they were willing to overrule *Mapp*, freeing the states from the exclusionary rule. That was the only logical way.

Black refused. He simply wasn't willing to overrule *Mapp*.

Harlan therefore tentatively voted with Douglas, Brennan, Stewart and Marshall to exclude the evidence. Thus, even though there were five members who thought the evidence against him should be admitted, Coolidge would get a new trial and another chance to be acquitted.

Black was exasperated at Harlan's refusal to simply bend the exclusionary rule without overruling *Mapp*. He accused him of allowing the Court to turn professional criminals loose to prey upon society with impunity.*

Black's vehemence hurt Harlan's feelings. He considered airing his own frustrations in an opinion but decided against it. Harlan said that his vote would remain tentative, however, until he saw a draft opinion.

It was obvious to the others that if and when Black and Harlan found common ground—whether to just overrule *Mapp* or to modify the entire exclusionary rule—they would form a new majority

---

* Black later published these views in the case *Whitely v. Warden.* Harlan drafted but did not publish a rebuttal, because he didn't want to attack Black publicly.

with Burger, White and Blackmun. In an effort to keep that from happening in this case, Douglas, the senior Justice in the majority, assigned the opinion to Stewart, whose views were closest to Harlan's.

Stewart, however, was unsure of his own position on the car search. He asked his clerk to research the matter, and the clerk developed a car-search theory. In situations where police stumbled on a car inadvertently or made an on-the-spot arrest, a warrant might not be necessary. But where they expected to find the car when they made the arrest, they should be forced to take the time to get a valid warrant.

White found this doctrine absurd, and he wrote a lengthy dissent. Why should evidence be excluded, he asked, solely because police expected to find it? Besides, in this case there was no indication that the police had expected to find the car there. Even more distressing to White was Stewart's apparent willingness, without explicitly saying so, to undermine a case White had written during the previous term (*Chambers v. Maroney*), which had held that police should be allowed to seize whatever they found in plain view when making an arrest. The car was surely in plain view.

Harlan sent Stewart a memo. He found the White dissent persuasive. He did not believe he could join that section of Stewart's opinion. Then he called Stewart. Perhaps it was time for the Court to reconsider the entire exclusionary rule and all the Fourth Amendment ramifications. Maybe this was the case in which to do it.

Stewart could see his majority slipping away. He encouraged his clerk to write a strong critique of White's view. This began a war of footnotes between the two chambers for Harlan's vote. The number of footnotes in Stewart's draft doubled to forty.

Stewart's clerk also tailored a section specifically designed to win Harlan back. He built on Harlan's concern that the Court had to be careful not to grant too many exceptions to the Fourth Amendment's warrant requirement. If good motives and probable cause were the sole criteria for a valid search, as White was suggesting, search warrants would not be necessary. The Fourth Amendment clause that required specific warrants would be void.

When Stewart's new draft arrived in Harlan's chambers, he took it home to read. The next morning Harlan entered his chambers, as usual, through his clerks' office. "Good morning, chaps," he said brightly. "I read Stewart's draft last evening. It is not a bad opinion." That was that. Harlan was willing to join that key part of the opinion.

Then, suddenly, trouble developed for Stewart from the liberal wing. Brennan had written a dissent from the part of Stewart's opinion that upheld the house search based on the wife's consent. The question of whether someone other than the suspect could grant consent to a police search had never been fully settled by the Court. Stewart wanted to allow the evidence provided by Coolidge's wife to be used in any new trial. Since that included the murder weapon, Coolidge's new trial would likely result in another conviction.

Studying the record, Stewart's clerk found indications that the police had intimidated and coerced Coolidge's wife into cooperating. Police, prosecutors and judges could therefore conceivably read the opinion and conclude that intimidation of nonsuspects, to secure their consent to searches, was acceptable.

The solution, the clerk decided, was to distort the facts in the draft. "There is not the slightest implication of an attempt on [the police officers'] part to coerce or dominate her, or, for that matter, to direct her actions by the more subtle techniques of suggestion that are available to officials in circumstances like these," his draft stated.

Stewart bought this approach. This way, police and prosecutors would see they could conduct such searches only with voluntary cooperation.

But the intimidation and coercion of Coolidge's wife had also been noticed by one of Brennan's clerks. He had prepared a dissent pointing out the severe distortion in the Stewart draft. When Stewart's clerk learned of it, he realized that if the Brennan dissent circulated, it might well pick up Douglas and Marshall's votes and leave Stewart with no majority on that portion of the opinion. Stewart's clerk appealed to Brennan's clerk to urge Brennan not to flag the problem.

Brennan agreed. Kicking up a fuss with a sharp finger-pointing dissent could lead to a worse resolution.

*   *   *

White replied to the conference in a memo. He was unhappy with the outcome of both *Coolidge* and another exclusionary rule case. Stewart's opinion resolved nothing. He wanted the issue put over for argument in other cases the next year.

Burger replied to White's memo the same day. He agreed with many of White's observations. He wanted these cases reargued. "I have this suggestion however: that to accommodate varying views we pose the reargument questions along the following lines: (1)— Should *Mapp v. Ohio* be overruled? (2)—If *Mapp v. Ohio* is not overruled, should the scope of the Exclusionary Rule be narrowed so as to relate its application to the nature of the violation? I am not in any sense 'wedded' to this formulation of the question."

At the next conference, Harlan, the key vote, said that *Coolidge* was not the case on which to modify the rule. The facts were hopelessly convoluted. They should get rid of the Coolidge case and find a better test. He was sticking with Stewart on this one. Stewart's majority decision was announced June 21.

As the term closed, the exclusionary rule and the Fourth Amendment law stood largely where they had been when the term opened.

Blackmun wasn't having an easy time adjusting to the demands of the Court. At the Eighth Circuit Court of Appeals, he had used his clerks solely for mundane legal research. Blackmun had started to use his clerks the same way on the Supreme Court, but soon expanded their role slightly. On one occasion, he asked a clerk to research a question on jurisdiction and, as was customary, then circulated the resulting memo in his own name. It had barely left Blackmun's hands when a blistering response came in from Douglas, picking the legal research apart for overlooking obvious points. Douglas's memo was almost sadistic.

Blackmun was mortified. He realized that Douglas was right. He vowed to never again let his clerks be in a position to embarrass him in front of his colleagues. His clerks once more received very routine assignments, and Blackmun checked their work carefully.

After the first few weeks of oral argument, Burger sent Hugo

Black a note saying that he had heard that by tradition a new Justice got to pick his "maiden" majority opinion. Black explained that the courtesy was often extended to a new Justice to steer him away from controversial opinions and make sure that he got a simple, unanimous opinion as his first task. The Chief said he would defer completing the assignment sheet until he could talk with Blackmun.

With unanimity the criterion, Burger and Blackmun didn't have a wide range of choices. Most of the cases argued the first few weeks had been hotly contested. So Blackmun finally decided to take one such case *(Wyman v. James)* that raised the question of whether welfare officials needed a search warrant to inspect a welfare recipient's home. He did the research himself, meticulously inspecting the trial record. He concluded that welfare officials could cut off benefits to persons who refused to allow inspectors into their homes. Likening welfare payments to private charity, Blackmun wrote that the public "rightly expects" some assurance that its funds are being spent in the proper manner. Blackmun saw in the record some evidence that the welfare mother's two-year-old child was being abused. He wrote in a footnote: "There are indications that all was not always well with the infant Maurice (skull fracture, a dent in the hand, a possible rat bite). The picture is a sad and unhappy one." Certainly the search was justified.

Blackmun concluded that if proper notice of a caseworker's visit was given, there was no need for a search warrant. If the recipients wouldn't allow the searches, they could forgo the welfare benefits. Caseworkers weren't police. They entered people's homes to assist, not to investigate.

The dissents, first by Douglas, then by Marshall joined by Brennan, were shrill. Douglas thought Blackmun's opinion outrageous. Marshall pointed out that previous Court rulings held that fire or housing inspectors could not demand the right to search businesses without a warrant. He charged that the majority was setting one standard of protection against searches for the upper and middle classes, and another, lesser standard for the "lowly poor."

The dissenters, however, couldn't pry enough votes away from

Blackmun to deny him a majority. Stewart was unhappy, but it was Blackmun's first opinion and he wanted to join. Black couldn't understand the opinion, but he too went along. Blackmun "will learn," he told his clerks.

Traditionally the two dozen-plus Supreme Court law clerks tried to have a group lunch during the term with each Justice. Blackmun's clerks were apprehensive when he accepted the invitation. Each of Blackmun's clerks had received his own share of abuse about the welfare opinion, and they knew their fellow clerks planned to ask their boss about it at the lunch.

One of Brennan's clerks started by mentioning a law school professor who planned to use Blackmun's opinion in a course entitled: "Has the Supreme Court Lost Touch with Reality?" How could Blackmun justify his opinion? the clerk asked.

Blackmun explained that the woman wasn't eligible for welfare anyway. He cited a footnote where he had written that the record in this case showed that the woman failed to satisfy the requirements for eligibility, had a bad attitude toward the caseworkers, was reluctant to cooperate, evasive and belligerent.

The room erupted. Many of the clerks were incredulous. Blackmun seemed to think he was still on a lower court, deciding a single case. Didn't he realize that he was creating the law of the land, setting precedent? Blackmun's clerks were embarrassed. Clearly if the recipient wasn't eligible for welfare, no precedent-setting decision should have been written. It was elementary.

More than anything, however, Blackmun often seemed paralyzed by indecision. The problem was greatest on cases where his was the swing vote.

As he left the bench one day early in the term, Harlan overheard Brennan discussing a crucial case (*Younger v. Harris et al.*) with Blackmun. It had been held over for three straight years because the conference was deadlocked on the question of the power of federal courts to intervene in state court proceedings. Harlan, uncomfortable with lobbying, jokingly suggested to Brennan, "Why don't we let Harry confer by himself on these and we'll go back and get some work done."

Black also was concerned about Blackmun. "If he doesn't learn to make up his mind, he's going to jump off a bridge some day," Black remarked to his clerks. Black tried to help, and he would occasionally wander down the hall to Blackmun's chambers to provide encouragement. "Now Harry," Black once said, "you just can't agonize over it. You have just got to vote."

But Blackmun plodded along, working day and night, trying to master the record in each case, and read all previous Court decisions in every given area. Blackmun not only couldn't see the forest but was overwhelmed by each tree, Black figured. On one case in which he had voted to join Blackmun's dissent, Black walked down to see how Blackmun was doing. He found his colleague working away as usual, with piles of law books spread all over. Black looked over the work. "That's the way to it, Harry," he said. "Strike for the jugular, strike for the jugular."

The long delays were strategically bad for Blackmun. As he struggled to get out his views, other justices filed theirs and moved on to new cases. His influence was slight. When he first arrived, Blackmun warned Burger that they would be tagged the "Minnesota Twins" after the baseball team for their home towns— the Twin Cities of St. Paul and Minneapolis. It took only half a year of voting together before Blackmun's prophecy came true. He was only surprised it had taken so long.

Still, it particularly offended him, because it was clear that the Chief was the dominant twin. The notion implied that Blackmun had no judicial mind of his own. But the fact remained that he and Burger had found themselves on opposing sides only twice in the first fifty cases decided by the Court. He never seemed to disagree with the Chief when it really counted. The clerk network had another name for Blackmun: "Hip pocket Harry." Burger, they felt, controlled not only his own vote but Blackmun's as well.

Burger brooded about his public image as a "conservative." The press liked to label Justices as conservatives, liberals or moderates. That was understandable, Burger felt. Most people needed the shorthand, because they didn't read opinions or study the Court. But the labels were misleading and unfair. He didn't think of himself as a conservative. The press had cast him in that role, comparing him unfavorably with their hero Earl Warren. Burger thought of himself as moderate. Warren had been an "activist." Burger was determined to correct his image, to vote with the liberal wing, to write some "liberal" opinions. That, he confided to his clerks, would confuse his liberal detractors in the press.

In one case (*Griggs v. Duke Power Co.*), a group of black laborers at the Duke Power Company in North Carolina had protested the company's requirement that they have high-school diplomas and pass intelligence tests in order to be promoted from laborer to the higher-paying job of coal miner. The laborers charged that the tests were simply a way of discriminating against blacks. They had lost in the lower courts and had petitioned for Supreme Court review. Burger had put their cert petition on the "dead list," a list of petitions that he felt did not even need to be considered at conference. Any single Justice could remove a case from the dead list for conference discussion, but those that remained on the dead list for a conference were automatically denied.

Although Brennan was supposed to be out of the case because he had once represented the company, he got Stewart to take it off the dead list. Brennan hoped the decision would go against his former client. The case was discussed, cert granted, and oral argument heard. The black laborers won.

The Chief assigned the opinion to himself. One of his clerks did virtually all of the research and drafting. Stewart was surprised by Burger's draft. It was well-written with first-rate reasoning. He was staggered, however, by the sweeping language of the opinion. "If an employment practice which operates to exclude Negroes cannot be shown to be related to job performance, the practice is prohibited," Burger wrote.

Although the lower court had found that the company didn't intend to use the test to discriminate against blacks, Burger said that intentions were irrelevant—"Good intent or absence of discriminatory intent does not redeem employment procedures or testing mechanisms that operate as 'built-in headwinds' for minority groups." N.A.A.C.P. lawyers and the liberal press praised the unanimous decision. Burger was proud of it.

Later that term, in a sex discrimination case (*Phillips v. Martin*

Marietta), Burger wanted to rule in favor of a company that refused to hire women with preschool-age children. He strongly supported the company's policy. "I will never hire a woman clerk," Burger told his clerks. A woman would have to leave work at 6 P.M. to go home and cook dinner for her husband. His first clerk back in 1956 at the Court of Appeals had been a woman, he told them. It had not worked out well at all. As far as he was concerned, an employer could fire whomever he wanted and for whatever reason. That was the boss's prerogative.

When it was suggested that his position amounted to a declaration that part of the Civil Rights Act was unconstitutional, Burger angrily shut off the discussion. He didn't want to argue legal niceties. His experience showed him that women with young children just didn't work out as well as men in the same jobs. The employer was within his rights.

At conference, however, the majority voted the other way. Burger returned to his chambers and announced that he wanted a *per curiam* (unsigned opinion) drafted, ruling that unless the company could show that conflicting family obligations were somehow more relevant to job performance for women than for men, the company would have to lose. "It was the best I could do," Burger told his amazed clerks. The decision became another liberal opinion for the Burger Court.

A month later, Burger told his clerks that he intended to vote to uphold a state court decision ordering a community group to stop picketing near a real estate broker's home *(Organization for a Better Austin v. Keefe)*. The organization had distributed literature in the broker's neighborhood accusing him of "blockbusting" in their neighborhood some miles away. A man's home was his castle, Burger told his clerks. The broker's home shouldn't be picketed. But after conference Burger told his clerks that he was writing an opinion to overturn the state court order and allow the group to continue picketing. The order halting it, he now said, interfered with the group's First Amendment rights of free speech and peaceable assembly.

Burger would often write short dissents or concurrences to opinions scheduled to come down the following week. These short opinions were his gut reactions, often angry in tone. They expressed his notion of right and wrong, of common sense—his real political philosophy. He called them "little snappers."

His clerks usually asked to edit them. Blatant political and moral assertions could be rewritten in legal language or couched in terms of "judicial restraint," "strict constructionism," or "states' rights."

A few days later, in a calmer mood, Burger would frequently have second thoughts about these opinions. "Oh, I wasn't really serious about that," he would say briskly. "You didn't send it to the printer did you?"

"I have no plans to retire or not to retire," Hugo Black told reporters at a press conference two days before his eighty-fifth birthday in February 1971. Such questions were becoming more frequent. He was serving his thirty-third year on the Court. Only four Justices had served longer.

Privately, Black had been giving the notions of retirement and death considerable thought. The previous term, when he was hiring new clerks, he told one applicant: "You must realize that I may die. And I may retire. If you want the job with those risks, it is yours."

As the term moved into the spring, Black's health deteriorated. He was suffering from frequent painful headaches. He took aspirin and painkillers, but the medication made him sleepy and he napped more frequently. It was difficult to discuss things with him. He could latch onto some past event and begin to reminisce. It frequently was impossible for his clerks to steer the conversation to the immediate issue. Black began to stumble badly in conference. He would become tired and confused, unable to remember which case they were on. He bitterly rejected Burger's suggestion, however, that the conferences end a bit earlier to accommodate him.

Black occasionally became shrill in dissents from the bench. When Harlan's majority opinion came down in a Connecticut divorce case that had been held over from the previous term (*Boddie v. Connecticut*), Black found himself alone in dissent. "Is this strict construction?" he demanded from the bench as Burger and Blackmun, Nixon's strict constructionists, stared stonily ahead. "If ever there has been a looser construction of the Constitution in this Court's history, I fail to think what it is."

Once, Black read a dissent from the bench in a search-warrant case *(Whitely v. Warden)* in which Harlan had written that the warrant had to be based on probable cause, not simply on what one sheriff had told another. For several minutes, Black railed on, accusing Harlan and the majority of writing a decision "calculated to make many good people believe our Court actually enjoys frustrating justice by unnecessarily turning professional criminals loose to prey upon society . . ."

Harlan sadly told his clerks afterward that he wished "Black hadn't done that."

Despite his ailments, however, Black still had the energy to turn the Court his way. In one case *(United Transportation Union v. State Bar of Michigan)* Harlan circulated an apparent majority opinion, upholding some restrictions on unions that offered legal services to their members. Black wrote a stinging dissent, arguing that any restriction on the union was unconstitutional under the First Amendment.

After dropping it off at the printers, Black took off for lunch with one of his clerks. As they walked down the hall, they passed Harlan. "John," he said, "I have a little love note coming over to you this afternoon." Eventually, Black won a majority for his view.

Since 1966, Douglas had been urging the Court to take up the Vietnam War *(Mitchell v. U.S.)*. He felt strongly that Vietnam was different from other American wars; it was a war of aggression. The Court, however, had shown little stomach for the issue.

In 1967, Douglas picked up a second vote, Stewart's, to hear a case concerning whether the 1964 Gulf of Tonkin resolution amounted to a congressional authorization of the war *(Mora v. McNamara)*. But at no time had there been four votes to grant cert and bring a Vietnam War case before the Court.

Now, in 1970, Douglas saw a new opportunity *(Massachusetts v. Laird)*. The Commonwealth of Massachusetts, a hotbed of vocal war opposition, had passed a law stating that no citizen could be

required to serve in combat abroad unless the hostilities were constitutional, either under the President's powers or by explicit declaration of war by Congress. Because the state had brought the
case against the United States government, it could come directly
to the Court. It was up to the Court to decide whether to allow the
state to file it.

Douglas wrote a memo conceding that the Court could not, and
should not, address the question of whether the country should
"fight a war in Indochina," but it should address the question
"whether the Executive can authorize [such a war] without
Congressional authorization." Stewart quickly indicated his willingness to vote to hear the case. They needed two more votes.

On the surface, Hugo Black seemed like a natural ally. A pacifist
at heart, Black had been against World War II until Pearl Harbor,
against the Korean War throughout its duration, and against the
Vietnam War from the start. He felt that the Court did not handle
war issues very well. In World War II, the Justices had pretended
that eight United States residents of German heritage had no constitutional guarantees when they were found guilty of attempted
sabotage: six were executed while the Court looked the other way.
The Court had ceded to the President and the military virtual au-
tonomy in war-related matters. "You can't fight a war with the
Courts in control," Black had said. He still defended his own 1944
opinion upholding the forced relocation of Japanese-Americans on
the West Coast, but as the years passed, he did so with noticeably
less enthusiasm.

Each night as he watched the news of the Vietnam War on television, his bitterness over the senseless slaughter grew. "A waste, a
mistake," Black lamented. "We're going to pay a high price for that.
Big heroics today; wait until the death lists come in."

But Black wanted no part of the Massachusetts case. Whether
one believed that Congress had meant to authorize the Vietnam
War, or whether the President was conducting it on his own authority—either way in Black's view, the decision was a "political
decision," to be made by another co-equal branch of government.
Traditionally, the Court did not meddle in matters of foreign policy,
war powers, and national security. The Constitution had given the

Congress the power to declare war and the President the power to conduct it. It gave the Court no role in that area.

If the war were to be attacked, Black said, it should be by Congress, not by the Court. And if he were still in the Senate, he would lead the charge. But he knew that even if the Court were to take up the war, at best only Douglas, Brennan, himself and perhaps Stewart would vote against it. Most assuredly, Burger, Harlan and Blackmun would support the Nixon administration. White, a Kennedy protégé, and Marshall, a Johnson protégé, had both, in Black's view, supported their former bosses' respective war policies with the rest of the hawks.

While Douglas did not agree with Black's logic for not wanting to hear the Massachusetts case, he understood it. Douglas was far more aggrieved, however, over Brennan's position. Brennan felt that the Court could take up a "political question" like the war only if Congress explicitly opposed the war and the President continued to conduct it. As long as Congress failed to act, Brennan said, there was nothing the Court could do. Otherwise, the Court would end up dealing with moral rather than legal questions. Its credibility would be lost. This infuriated Douglas.

Seven years before, Douglas recalled, when Earl Warren had been on hand to give Brennan guidance and confidence, Brennan had been willing to bend the doctrine on political questions. Brennan had authored the first "one man, one vote" legislative reapportionment case (Baker v. Carr), when the Court addressed the question of who elects members of Congress and state legislatures—an issue previously thought to be "political." It irked Douglas that Brennan would not vote his conscience on the war now.

But while brooding over Brennan's stand, Douglas remained determined that the Court should take up the Massachusetts case. To his surprise, he picked up a third vote on the case from John Harlan.

Harlan was certainly no pacifist. He had fond memories of a camaraderie he had found while directing the Eighth Army strategic bombing group during World War II. But he thought this war was different. Something was seriously wrong, and it was wrong at the top. "What we need is some moral leadership from the White House," he observed, "and that won't come now."*

But beyond that, Harlan felt that the Court should at least hear arguments on whether it could decide such questions as the Massachusetts case posed. Douglas's point was that by not ruling on the constitutionality of the war, the Court, in effect, was sanctioning a new constitutional formulation: the President could make undeclared war as long as Congress gave him the funds. Harlan was unsure as to how he would vote on the ultimate question. But so far the Court had taken the position that individual taxpayers, draftees and soldiers had no standing from which to challenge the executive in a court case regarding the war. If a state did not have standing, Harlan mused, then who did? He voted to take the case.

Douglas's effort to bring the war before the Court stalled there. For a month, he put the case over from conference to conference. Finally conceding that the fourth vote was not coming, Douglas gave up. In November, he published a memo dissenting from the denial of cert.

Harlan's vote to hear the Massachusetts case was not a vote on the constitutionality of the war. He tended to give the benefit of the doubt to the men who, he presumed, still ran the national-security establishment. Many of the antiwar protest cases that filtered up to the Court involved civil disobedience. Like Black, Harlan had little sympathy for disruptive tactics.

One case (*Radich v. New York*), however, did bother Harlan. The

---

* Always concerned that the slightest gesture or contact with the executive might be thought to imply endorsement, Harlan declined to vote in Presidential elections (or any others) and never applauded at the President's State of the Union address. In 1967, Harlan refused to continue a tradition in which the Justices in top hats and tails annually paid their respects to the President at the White House at the opening of the Court's term. Johnson had continued to use then Justice Fortas as a principal adviser, calling him often on the red "hot line" in his office for help on the war. Fortas had even missed conference to attend White House meetings. Harlan persuaded the others to abandon the practice of calling on the President, lest Johnson try to use them to legitimize his war effort as well.

proprietor of a midtown-Manhattan art gallery had been convicted of displaying American flags in a "lewd, vulgar and disrespectful way." The flags were thirteen impressionistic sculptures, each portraying the American flag as a penis. For Harlan, the sculpture was clearly protected by the First Amendment's guarantee of free speech. It was, he presumed, a protest against the war. Harlan suggested they take the case and overturn the conviction. To his surprise, no other Justice was interested in hearing it. Douglas had recused himself from the case, since the law firm that had defended him against impeachment was representing the art gallery's manager.

Harlan asked that the decision be put over a week so he could circulate a memorandum. He was not used to writing dissents from the denial of cert. It was not his style to air the Court's disagreements in public. But this was an exceptional case. He had a clerk prepare a stern memo pointing out that it was "self evident" that the case was substantial. The ploy worked. Brennan, Stewart and Marshall joined him in granting cert.

But Harlan could see that it was a loser. There was no fifth vote. After oral argument, the vote was 4 to 4. According to tradition in tie votes, the conviction would be affirmed without an opinion.

Harlan's view of the First Amendment was not always so expansive. Paul Cohen, a young antiwar protester, had been sentenced to thirty days in jail for disturbing the peace by wearing a jacket with the words "Fuck the Draft" inscribed on the back. Harlan termed this case (Cohen v. California) a "peewee."

When they had first granted cert on the case, Black had vehemently disagreed with Harlan. His interpretation of the First Amendment was literal: "Congress shall make no law . . . abridging the freedom of speech."

"I read 'no law . . . abridging' to mean no law abridging," he had stated emphatically in a 1959 opinion (Smith v. California).

Black found the conviction of Cohen so outrageous that he insisted that the Court summarily reverse the conviction without even holding oral argument. Harlan's strong opposition prevented the summary reversal, and only reluctantly did he agree to have it argued.

Many clerks, however, saw the case as symbolically important. Sentiment against the Vietnam War was at its height. Many of the clerks opposed the war, and felt a little guilty that they had signed up for a year with an establishment institution like the Supreme Court. Most agreed with the sentiments on Cohen's jacket, and one way or another many had themselves avoided military service. In a vote on whom to invite to a question-and-answer lunch, one of their top choices had been the outspoken antiwar activist and actress Jane Fonda.

The antiwar movement was part of the clerks' culture, and its slogans part of their politics. The obscenities used to denounce Vietnam and the draft were important political expressions. Clearly, if the First Amendment protected speech of any kind, it protected political speech. Abrasive, outrageous expressions were sometimes called for. "Fuck the Draft" was hardly the most extreme. A decision against Cohen, in essence banning "Fuck the Draft" from the jackets and posters of the antiwar movement, could have deeper ramifications, some clerks believed. Police throughout the country were looking for grounds on which to curtail the activism unleashed by the war.

In Stewart's chamber, it looked to the clerks as if the Court was about to say that vulgar antiwar protests were not protected speech. Both flag sculptures and jacket slogans would be banned. The Court was desperately out of touch with the times. And, perhaps, with the Constitution. One of the clerks fashioned a makeshift patch combining the themes and put it on the back of his suit coat. "Fuck the Flag," it said. He wore it for several hours around the chambers before deciding that he did not want to test the Court's tolerance for political speech in its own building.

At oral argument on February 22, the Chief attempted to signal Cohen's attorney to not use the vile slogan in the courtroom. " . . . You may proceed whenever you are ready," Burger said. " . . . the Court is thoroughly familiar with the factual setting of this case and it will not be necessary for you . . . to dwell on the facts."

But Cohen's lawyer, Melville B. Nimmer, acting on behalf of the A.C.L.U., thought that the case would be lost if he didn't say the word at least once. To not utter it would be conceding that the word was or should be unspeakable.

"At Mr. Chief Justice's suggestion," the lawyer responded, "I certainly will keep very brief the statement of facts . . . What this young man did was to walk through a courthouse corridor . . . wearing a jacket on which were inscribed the words 'Fuck the Draft.'"

The Chief's irritation was evident in his tone for the rest of oral argument. The Justices avoided using the word *fuck* in their questioning of the lawyers, referring instead to "that word."

The ritual that Harlan enjoyed most was sitting with his clerks on Thursday afternoons, reviewing the cases argued that week in preparation for the Friday conference. The afternoon of February 25, the clerk he had assigned to the Fuck-the-Draft case reviewed the details at length, pointing out that according to Harlan's prior opinions, the slogan was clearly protected by the First Amendment. Cohen's conviction was for the content of the message on his jacket, for his opposition to the war, and not for some disruptive conduct.

For Harlan, and for all of his colleagues except Douglas and Black, there were exceptions to what was protected speech under the First Amendment. The clerk went down the list to assure Harlan that none was involved.

Did the words advocate an insurrectionary act—the overthrow of the government or interference with the draft? No, they merely conveyed Cohen's view of the war and of the draft.

Did the words immediately endanger observers—like shouting "Fire!" in a crowded theater? No, of course not.

Did the words incite a noisy disruption? No, the only one in the courthouse apparently bothered by them was the arresting officer.

Did the words provoke a violent reaction from observers, so-called "fighting words"? No, again only the arresting officer seemed concerned. He had tried and failed to get the judge to hold Cohen in contempt.

Were the words "offensive" to unconsenting viewers? This was the most difficult problem for Harlan. Some passersby in the corridor might have been offended. But they could have limited their exposure by moving away, the clerk argued. The only captive audience would have been the one in the courtroom where Cohen appeared, but there he folded his coat over his arm, so that the spectators were not exposed. Moreover, the clerk reasoned, a certain amount of "offensive" exposure had to be expected in public.

Were the words themselves "obscene"? Certainly the use Cohen had made of the word *fuck* was not meant to be erotic, or to appeal to "prurient" interests. It did not depict explicit sexual activity. Surely, the state of California could not purge the word from public discourse.

Harlan was still not sure how he would vote the next day, but he admitted that he now saw the case in a different light. The war was a continuing subject of protest. That protest was an exercise of free speech. And the various levels of government—federal, state and local—were doing their best to curtail that protest. Why should a jacket be different from a flag sculpture? Perhaps he was being inconsistent.

At conference the next afternoon, the Chief referred to the case as the "screw the draft" case. He voted to uphold the conviction. To everyone's surprise, Black's position had changed drastically. He did not offer his absolutist position. Instead, he agreed with the Chief: this was a question not of political speech but rather of the pernicious use of a vile word. Cohen's jacket slogan was not protected "speech," but unprotected "conduct," he said. Cohen could be prosecuted.

With his most boisterous drawl, Black claimed that he was not deviating from his absolutism. Conduct was different from speech. His favorite example was picketing a courthouse. It was unacceptable *conduct*, not speech. People could not "tramp up and down the streets by the thousands" and threaten others, for example.

Douglas and the other First Amendment liberals—Brennan, Stewart and Marshall, who grumbled that it wasn't a case worth "giving blood on"—all lined up in favor of reversing the conviction. White and Blackmun sided with the Chief and Black.

Harlan provided the day's second surprise. He had thought it over, and he was now leaning toward overturning the conviction. But he was still not sure. He wanted the case put over for a week. He needed more time to consider it.

The others agreed.

Douglas's clerk joked about how the "magic word" set off such severe reactions in the "Bad B's," as he referred to Black, Burger and Blackmun. Douglas was disappointed that Black had deserted his long-standing First Amendment position. Perhaps Black was simply too old to understand these issues any more, to pursue the reasoning necessary to draw consistent parallels. But Harlan's hesitation offered little encouragement. He would likely end up voting to uphold the conviction. He too was out of touch with the country. The key would be Black, Douglas figured.

Black's clerks kept a constant pressure on their boss to revise his stance, but the word *fuck* offended Black's moral sensibilities. For all the freedoms he espoused, Black was priggish, especially about vulgar language. Never had his son heard him utter an obscene word. "Crook" was his strongest expletive. "What if Elizabeth [his wife] were in that corridor," he asked. "Why should she have to see that word?" Wearing the offensive jacket was conduct, not speech. The clerks could not move him.

The day before the next conference, Harlan's clerk mentioned the Cohen case. "We don't have to spend time on that," Harlan said. "I've made up my mind." He was now firm to reverse Cohen's conviction. He was determined to be consistent; the slogan was no less speech than the flag sculptures were. He could not understand Black's sensitivity to the word. "I wouldn't mind telling my wife, or your wife, or anyone's wife, about the slogan," Harlan told his clerks.

At the Friday conference, the voting went quickly, since everyone had had a week to consider. Harlan indicated that he had switched his position and would vote to reverse. Douglas, the senior member of the new 5-to-4 majority, realized that Harlan was the shakiest vote. Over the course of thirty-two years on the Court, he had learned that the best way to hold a swing vote was to assign that Justice to write the decision. "John, I'm assigning the opinion to you," Douglas said.

Harlan then said that he would prefer a narrow ruling, not one broadly declaring the use of these particular words to be protected speech.

"That's not enough for me, John," Stewart said. Like Douglas he wanted the slogan declared to be speech that was protected by the First Amendment.

Harlan assented quickly. If he wrote the decision on narrower grounds, Stewart and Douglas would concur separately and Brennan and Marshall might well join one of them. Harlan's majority would soon become a concurrence to someone else's majority.

Harlan and his clerk were pleased to have the opinion. They turned immediately to the drafting. Traditionally the Court had held that expletives like *fuck* were devoid of any social value. Suddenly to say that the word had value would certainly go beyond Harlan's previously expressed views and those of the other members. But if the slogan itself were protected, there must be some basis for protecting the words individually. The person expressing his political views ought to be able to choose from his own lexicon of expression. "One man's vulgarity is another's lyric," the clerk wrote.

When he had completed the draft, the clerk read it to Harlan and they discussed each section as they went. Harlan was generally pleased, though slow to warm to the protection afforded the word itself. He did not want to move recklessly in such a delicate field. He said that he would take the draft home overnight and reread it in his study. The next morning, Harlan announced that the draft was fine as it was. He was taking a major step, but he was behind it wholeheartedly.

The draft circulated shortly thereafter. The Chief was less than pleased when he read it in late May. He never expected to see Harlan glorifying such filth. Cohen should be spanked, and here Harlan was congratulating him.

"This case may seem at first blush too inconsequential to find its way into our books, but the issue it presents is of no small constitutional significance," Harlan's draft began.

Worse still, Harlan repeated the facts in detail, including the offending phrase, by quoting the lower court opinion. Raising such a word to a level of protected speech was more than the Chief could stomach. He sat down and scrawled out a short dissent. It helped blow off steam, but it also let his colleagues know about his strong feelings. On May 25, he sent his dissent to the conference. "I will probably add the following, which is the most restrained utterance I can manage," the Chief's memo began. His dissent was typed on the bottom half of the page. "I, too, join in a word of protest that this Court's limited resources of time should be devoted to such a case as this. It is a measure of a lack of a sense of priorities and with all deference, I submit that Mr. Justice Harlan's 'first blush' was the correct reaction. It is nothing short of absurd nonsense that juvenile delinquents and their emotionally unstable outbursts should command the attention of this Court."

Blackmun too was deeply offended by Cohen. "Cohen's absurd and immature antic, in my view, was mainly conduct and little speech," he wrote.

Sensing the exaggerated tone of reactions, Black decided not to write an opinion; Burger dropped his own opinion and joined Blackmun's instead; White found even Blackmun's opinion too severe and joined only part of it.

Burger was still angry on June 7 when the case was set for announcement. In the light-oak-paneled robing room, a messenger—selected for the task because he was taller than any of the Justices—was helping Harlan into his robe.

"John, you're not going to use 'that word' in delivering the opinion, are you?" Burger asked.

Harlan had been deeply amused at Burger's concern. He had no intention of uttering the word aloud in open court, but he sidestepped the question. He enjoyed "twitting" the Chief, as he called it.

"It would be the end of the Court if you use it, John," the Chief asserted.

Harlan chuckled. It was time for Court. They paraded out the door after the Chief in order of seniority—Black, Douglas and then Harlan—along a red carpet placed in the hall between the robing room and the courtroom. As the case was announced, Harlan bent over in his chair to review his notes, his forehead almost touching the bench as his eyes strained to read. He straightened up and repeated most of it from memory. His occasional sideways glances to see if the Chief was still paying attention were almost imperceptible. The Chief sat in rigid and pained stoicism, waiting for the offending word. Harlan paused, glanced again at the Chief, and proceeded, still without uttering the word. Finally, he finished without ever using it.

Tuesday, April 20, was a long day for the Chief. It was 6 P.M. when he finally got around to hearing an emergency petition from the Justice Department seeking reinstatement of a lower court order to evict more than a thousand Vietnam Veterans Against the War who were camping on the Mall in Washington.

Solicitor General Griswold argued that the veterans posed a real danger to security because antiwar protesters had advertised plans to shut down the city. Former Attorney General Ramsey Clark, the son of retired Supreme Court Justice Tom Clark, appeared for the veterans. He argued that the government had no business anticipating unlawful conduct.

Burger reinstated the order to evict the veterans, but given the late hour, he said, the order would not be effective until the next day. Justice Department lawyers, convinced that Burger's order would be appealed the next day to the full Court, were reluctant to evict the veterans, who had been peaceful so far.

Just before noon the following day, a dozen veterans delivered a letter to Burger's chambers decrying his decision. Protests at the Court were a new phenomenon, but the Chief's response to the delegation milling around the large entrance hall awaiting his reaction was quick and to the point. The Court police gave the demonstrators one minute to leave the building and then arrested them.

Inside, the Court was hearing oral argument on its last regularly scheduled case of the day. Next, they would hear the appeal of the Chief's decision the day before. Suddenly, a uniformed veteran stood silently, his right fist clenched in the air. A marshal scurried down the aisle and directed him to sit down. The veteran refused. A scuffle ensued.

The lawyer arguing the case did his best to hold the attention of the nine wide-eyed Justices watching over his shoulder the marshals forcibly ejecting the veteran from the audience. On the way out, the man shouted: "Remember the Vets!"

As the veterans' injunction case was called, Douglas rose and left the courtroom. He had to recuse himself from this case. Ramsey Clark's law firm had represented him during the impeachment hearings.

At the conference following the argument, Stewart and Marshall made it clear that they were irritated. Since the ban was not to take effect until later, there had been no reason for the Chief to have acted alone the day before. The full Court could have been convened. Now, if the majority disagreed, they would have to overrule the Chief, embarrassing both him and the Court. The Court had overridden only one such decision in the past twenty years.

Stewart and Marshall were concerned that the Justices were being asked to do the dirty work of the Executive Branch. The Court could become a tool for the Nixon administration's suppression of war opposition. And the case was precisely the sort that Stewart feared. Normally, the Justices had the luxury of time. They watched an issue mature as it made its way up to them, and by the time it arrived, the lawyers had sifted the issues. In this instance the Court's action would be part of a still unfolding drama.

Marshall urged that they reject the Justice Department's plea, because it was based on the presumption that the veterans were going to break the law. The Nixon administration was seeking to govern with Court injunctions.

The others—Black, Harlan, Brennan, White and Blackmun— were unhappy. If the government was correct, the antiwar protesters were going to close Washington. If the government was wrong, the Justices would be evicting a peaceful group before their protest was over. But to overrule him would be a personal affront to the Chief. And they were willing to stand with him. Stewart and Marshall decided not to publish their disagreement. A unanimous order reaffirming Burger's initial order was signed and distributed by 5 P.M.

The veterans voted 480 to 400 to stay on the Mall. They would not be forced out. Though armed with the Supreme Court order it had so desperately sought, the administration decided not to evict them. Harlan was struck by Nixon's willingness to force an issue and then, after he had gotten grudging approval, to back down. These were self-inflicted wounds, Harlan said.

Shortly before nine o'clock the next morning, several hundred veterans appeared at the Court to demand that it rule on the constitutionality of the war. About 150 of them stood on the Court's steps, leaving a fifteen-foot corridor in the center leading to the two huge sliding bronze doors. They clasped their arms around one another and, shoulder to shoulder, swayed side-to-side singing "God Bless America" and reciting the Pledge of Allegiance. "All we are saying is rule on the war now!" they chanted, brandishing toy M-16 rifles and waving American flags.

Inside, Burger was informed of the demonstration. He ordered Perry Lippett, Marshal of the Court, to have the steps cleared. So, for the first time on a day when the Court was open, Lippett ordered the massive bronze doors closed. The doors, each with four panels tracing the evolution of the law from ancient Greece and Rome to early America, made an imposing crash as the thirteen tons of bronze slid shut.

Lippett passed on the Chief's instructions to the police of the Supreme Court and of the District of Columbia. As the D.C. riot police moved in to arrest the protesters, the veterans turned and waved to former Chief Justice Earl Warren, who was watching, ghostlike, from his office window overlooking the front steps.

Marshall had seen enough of the effects of Burger's paranoia. He was apparently listening to scare stories from the Court police that demonstrators posed a real threat to the Court's security.

Burger already had a gun-carrying chauffeur and guards that followed him wherever he went, even inside the Court building. He wore dark glasses and a hat in public to avoid being recognized as he prowled Georgetown antique shops. He at times used a false name when he traveled. He had brought in the kind of metal detectors used at airports to screen spectators entering the courtroom. But this time, he had gone too far.

Marshall dictated a one-and-a-half-page, single-spaced memo to the conference. It was not combative in tone, but there was no question to whom it was addressed. The Court had overreacted when the government came to them claiming that the veterans were a menace to the safety of Washington, Marshall said. The Chief, and then the full Court, had agreed to prohibit the veterans from sleeping on the Mall because the government claimed pre-emptive action was necessary to protect the Congress, the White House, even the Court. Now, the Marshal of the Court had overre-acted. The arrest of the veterans on the steps was unnecessary, he said. The Court was in no position to anticipate what visitors or demonstrators *might* do.

Naturally, no member of the Court would ever condone such clearly unconstitutional police tactics, Marshall said. But just the same, the arrests discredited the entire institution. Similar arrests in other situations would no doubt result in litigation. Who would finally rule on those cases, Marshall wondered, if the Supreme Court itself had permitted such clearly unconstitutional arrests?

Marshall was not sure that the Chief understood. But the local U.S. District Court made the issue crystal clear, as it dismissed all charges after finding that there was no evidence of any violence in the demonstration. "Inconvenience alone," a lower court judge held, "doesn't warrant a criminal prosecution."*

Brennan was the only Justice who really wanted to hear the Cassius Clay case (*Clay v. U.S.*).

Clay, who had changed his name to Muhammad Ali in 1964, had been sentenced to prison for five years for refusing in 1966 to take the traditional step forward and be inducted into the Army. The former world heavyweight-boxing champion based his refusal on religious grounds, claiming that, as a Black Muslim, he was a con-scientious objector and thus entitled to exemption from military service.

Apart from the complicated war and draft issues, there were racial overtones to the case. Ali was one of America's best-known and most popular black athletes. His appeals had taken six years and, stripped of his title by the World Boxing Association, the fighter had been banned from boxing for nearly four years at a loss

---

* The next week, over ten thousand antiwar demonstrators were summarily ar-rested under what then Assistant Attorney General William H. Rehnquist called "qualified" martial law. Federal officials cited the arrests at the Court as prece-dent. These arrests were subsequently declared illegal by a federal court.

to him of millions of dollars in purses. Public sympathy was growing for Ali, but at the same time the Black Muslim faith had been portrayed as separatist, antiwhite and bizarre.

The case had already come up to the Court two terms before, and the conference had voted not to hear it, thus letting Ali's conviction stand. A last-minute revelation by the government that Ali had been overheard on a national-security wiretap had prevented the decision from being announced. The technicality had allowed the Court to send the case back to the lower court for further hearings.

The Justices had hoped it would not come up the ladder again, but when it did, Brennan finally persuaded his colleagues to grant cert.

Given Ali's prominence, the Justices would allow him the satisfaction of having his case reviewed by the highest court in the land, a satisfaction given to few defendants. None of the Justices believed Ali had a chance of winning.

At oral argument, Solicitor General Griswold pointed out that Ali had left little doubt that "if the Vietcong were attacking his people, the Muslims would become involved in that war." Moreover, Ali had been quoted in the press as saying, "I am a member of the Muslims and we don't go to war unless they are declared by Allah himself. I don't have no personal quarrel with those Vietcongs." Since Ali would participate in a holy war, he was not really a conscientious objector, Griswold said.

On Friday, April 23, with Marshall recused because he had been Solicitor General when the case began, the conference decided, 5 to 3, that it agreed with Griswold. Ali was not really a conscientious objector and should go to jail.

The Chief immediately assigned Harlan to write the majority view. But as Harlan's clerk began preparing a draft opinion, he was persuaded by another clerk who had read Alex Haley's *Autobiography of Malcolm X* to reconsider the question of Ali's opposition to war. Reading the *Message to the Black Man,* one of the most trusted texts of the Black Muslims, the clerk became convinced that Ali's willingness to fight in a holy war was irrelevant. For all practical purposes, Ali was opposed to all wars.

Harlan was not inclined to buy any of this. But he agreed to take home his clerk's background materials and study them in the specially illuminated library of his Georgetown townhouse. The next morning, he had a surprise for his clerks. He had read the materials and he agreed wholeheartedly, wanting them incorporated, as written, into his draft. Harlan was persuaded that the government had mistakenly painted Ali as a racist, misinterpreting the doctrine of the Black Muslims despite the Justice Department's own hearing examiner's finding that Ali was sincerely opposed to all wars.

Harlan wanted to confront the Justice Department's misrepresentation and state explicitly that there had been "no basis in fact" all along for them to say that Ali was not really opposed to all shooting wars. Because there had been no indication outside Harlan's chambers that his view had changed, when his memo suggesting reversal of the conviction was circulated, it exploded in the Court. Burger was beside himself. How could Harlan shift sides without notifying him? He was even more irritated by the incorporation of Black Muslim doctrine in the opinion. The draft said that Black Muslim doctrine teaches "that Islam is the religion of peace . . . and that war-making is the habit of the race of devils [whites] . . . [and that Islam] forbids its members to carry arms or weapons of any kind." Harlan had become an apologist for the Black Muslims, Burger told a clerk. Moreover, his switch tied the vote, 4 to 4. That would, however, still mean that Ali would go to jail.

The Chief was not about to shift his own vote. Nor were Black, White or Blackmun, the other members of the original majority. They were particularly disturbed that Harlan wanted to stress the government's twisting of the facts. Harlan's view could mean that all Black Muslims would be eligible for the conscientious objector status.

The Court year was coming to a close. If the Court remained deadlocked, Ali would finally go to jail for draft evasion. Since decisions in which the Justices were equally divided were not accompanied by opinions, Ali would never know why he had lost. It would be as if the Court had never taken the case.

Stewart was particularly upset by this prospect. He proposed an alternative: the Court could simply set Ali free, citing a technical error by the Justice Department. The proposal had several advantages. For one, the ruling in this case would not become a precedent. It also would not broaden the categories under which others might claim to be conscientious objectors.

Gradually, all but the Chief agreed to go along with Stewart's plan, giving Ali seven votes.* That left Burger with a problem. If he dissented, it might be interpreted as a racist vote. He decided to join the others. An 8-to-0 decision would be a good lift for black people, he concluded.

Stewart drafted the final unanimous *per curiam*. Ali's victory was announced on June 28. He heard the news in Chicago. "I thank Allah," Ali said, "and I thank the Supreme Court for recognizing the sincerity of the religious teachings that I've accepted." He did not know how close he had come to going to jail.

As the end of the term approached, Black's health continued to deteriorate. One day during the last week in May, he was returning to his chambers following conference when his knees buckled. By the time his clerks reached him and carried him into his office, he was shivering with a high fever. "They are after all my old majorities," he babbled as his clerks wrapped him in a blanket.

Black recovered from the fever, but his strength was seriously depleted. Disabling headaches plagued him, and his cheerful whistle as he strolled through the marble halls was suddenly missing.

For Black, who advocated positive thinking as the cure for every malady, the idea that he was no longer in full control of his own destiny was torture. For years, he had talked of how Holmes, Brandeis and Cardozo had lingered on at the Court, unable to perform their work competently. But Black was determined to remain. He had resisted Warren's and then Douglas's hints that he resign, and he had done his best to ignore Harlan's remarks that perhaps

---

* Douglas's concurrence retained language making it obvious that it was originally a dissent. His clerk, who normally would have corrected it, refused to work further on the opinion after Douglas insisted on retaining an incorrect statement of the Black Muslim position on holy wars.

they both had stayed on too long. Now, in his thirty-fourth term, he had kept on his desk a small card bearing the exact lengths of service of John Marshall and Stephen J. Field. Both had served thirty-four terms and he would surpass both in a few months. But, finally, he was no longer sure that he could hold out.

On June 13, however, Black read a lengthy article in that Sunday's *New York Times* with unusual interest. It was the first installment of a top-secret government history of United States involvement in Vietnam. The *Times* cited numerous documents showing that government officials had lied to the American people about the war for three decades. The articles were based on a massive study, commissioned by former Secretary of Defense Robert S. McNamara, covering the period 1945–1967. The entire forty-seven-volume set, called *The Pentagon Papers*, was considered extremely sensitive. Black was pleased to see the press expose what he regarded as a long, sordid story.

The series continued the next day. But on Tuesday, June 15, Attorney General John Mitchell, arguing that the articles endangered the national security, obtained an order in federal District Court in New York enjoining further publication.

Black was stunned. "They're actually stopping it," he said to his clerks. In his view, that was an obvious violation of the First Amendment. The press was free; it could not be stopped from publishing material the government thought damaging to the national security. That was prior restraint; it was an absurd notion.

On Friday, June 18, publication of *The Pentagon Papers* began in *The Washington Post*, which had also obtained portions of the secret war study. The government lost twice in federal courts, before securing a temporary restraining order against the *Post*. By the following Thursday, June 24, both cases were before the Supreme Court (*New York Times v. U.S.* and *U.S. v. The Washington Post*). For Black, the developments were like a shot of adrenaline.

Both papers had been stopped from publishing the war series for almost a week. Each day's delay, in Black's view, was a defeat for the press and for the First Amendment. The authors of the First Amendment had anticipated that the press's ongoing critique of the government would involve great risk.

Black geared up for what was clearly going to be a historic test, and this case was not going to be easy. Black felt that Brennan and Marshall, as well as Douglas, would probably join him in favor of the newspapers' right to publish. The Chief, Harlan and Blackmun would likely be on the other side. That left Stewart and White for the fifth vote that Black needed. White was never a great supporter of First Amendment freedoms. He might sympathize with the Justice Department in this case, or he might fear what the papers would say about John Kennedy's role in the war. No one really knew what the *Times* or *Post* had.

Stewart was the key. As an establishment Republican, Stewart might back the administration's position, but he had good First Amendment credentials. At times, Black thought he had the votes to win; at other times, he was not so sure. One thing was certain: his headaches were less severe.

Harlan was exceedingly upset with the haphazard way in which the Pentagon Papers case had arrived at the Court. The Justices were considering a case less than twenty-four hours after the appeals. To make matters worse, they were going to decide immediately both on cert and on whether to continue the injunction. The case had come to them so quickly that it was impossible to calculate what consequences might result from an erroneous decision.

In 1931, in *Near v. Minnesota*, the Court had suggested that the government probably could prevent someone from publishing "the sailing dates of transports or the number and location of troops." Harlan read that to mean that when the national security was endangered, it had to be balanced against First Amendment freedoms. Harlan wanted to send the Pentagon Papers case back to the lower courts. He wanted a stronger foundation on which to base a decision. Why should the Court be required to make an instantaneous decision on an issue of such apparent magnitude? The injunctions should be continued until the Court could make some responsible determination. Harlan resolved not to be pushed into a hasty decision.

The last thing Stewart wanted was a delay. The temporary injunctions had been in force too long already. He would not accept any drawn-out decision making while the newspapers were kept from publishing. It wasn't really the great battle of the First Amendment and national security that it appeared on the surface. The issue was basic and factual. Were there in the documents matters that, if published, could truly threaten the national security?

Stewart would not accept the government's claim of national security on its face. The government had lied too much about the war already. At the same time, Stewart wanted to make sure that nothing in the papers was so sensitive that disclosure might result in deaths. It was difficult. A lot rested on the Court's decision, and he was possibly the swing vote. Contrary to his normal practice, he sought little advice from his clerks. "You're only the clerks," he said gently, "and I will have to decide for myself."

With the term substantially over, Stewart knew that normal procedures would have to be expedited if the Justices took the case. They would need a special session, maybe that weekend, to hear oral arguments, and they would have to render a decision almost at once. The prior-restraint issue virtually required that they act immediately. To delay would be to decide the case in favor of the government.

On Friday, June 25, eight Justices convened for the last regularly scheduled conference of the term; Douglas was already in Goose Prairie, Washington, where he had a cabin. The Justices quickly took up the question of whether the *Times* case should be granted cert.

Black took an absolute First Amendment stand. The *Times* and *Post* should be free to publish what they want. The Court should not even hear the case, and it should lift the injunctions immediately.

Douglas had phoned in his position. He agreed with Black. Brennan and Marshall, for different reasons, took this position too. To accept the cases and proceed in a normal manner would set a precedent for stopping the presses while courts tried to ascertain how much damage the articles might cause. These four Justices were ready to grant cert immediately and let publication resume at once. Normally only four votes were necessary to grant cert. But the two cases were being brought as emergency appeals and, under the Court's internal rules, that required a fifth vote.

Burger, Harlan, White and Blackmun all wanted to hear argument in October and continue the injunction until then. So Stewart held the crucial vote. He was unwilling to prevent publication until the fall. He was ready to grant cert now.

Harlan was annoyed by the haste with which the cases had been propelled through the lower courts. The Court's most shameful and wrenching episodes had come from acting hastily. He preferred to let the *New York Times* case return for an additional hearing in the lower federal court. Then, if an appeal was still sought, it could be considered with the *Post* case at some later date, next fall. He was willing that the temporary injunction against publication continue for weeks or months. But Stewart said that if that happened, he would join the four votes for a summary decision in favor of the newspapers and would lift the injunction against them. Without an injunction, the case would be moot, purely academic and publication would continue. Reluctantly Harlan joined the others in voting to grant cert. The expedited oral argument was immediately scheduled for the next day.

Griswold realized that he had some fast work to do. He calculated that it would take ten weeks to read the entire forty-seven-volume history—which was obviously impractical—so he called in three top national-security officials to help sift out the most important "Top Secret" documents. They suggested that forty-one items—some entire volumes—be listed.

Griswold was amazed. To try to exclude so much of the material would hurt their case. He had already warned Attorney General Mitchell that the case should never have been started, that the government could never win. Any "dirt" in the papers was "all on Johnson and not you," Griswold had told him. Mitchell had replied that if Griswold didn't press ahead, the administration would find someone else to argue the case.

Griswold filed the long list with the Court by 5 P.M. But he knew that to make the national-security claim credible, he must create a shorter, more persuasive list. By the next morning, he had managed to pare down the number of alleged national-security items to eleven, although one item comprised four volumes that detailed diplomatic efforts to end the war and secure the return of American prisoners of war.

By mid-morning Saturday, a long line of people had formed out-side the Court. Many had been waiting hours in hope of attending the oral argument.

That morning, when Griswold filed the shorter list as part of a se-cret brief, he also requested that the oral argument be held in se-cret, without press or public present. This was the procedure the lower courts had followed for at least part of the argument. It would allow him to discuss "top secret" and even more highly clas-sified items.

The sealed record had been placed in the conference room, with security guards stationed at the doors. A memo over Burger's name had been posted there—" . . . the Conference Room is, 'off limits' due to material placed there for the Justices."

The Chief was taking the national-security aspects of the case at face value. He expressed his fear that some antiwar clerk might gain access and leak the papers.

Black joked with his clerks that he would not look at the sealed record anyway. To do so was inconsistent with his First Amend-ment views. After all, he regularly passed up the opportunity to view the pornographic movies that came into the Court. Individual judgments were unnecessary. Every book, every newspaper arti-cle, every movie was protected. But he knew that the clerks were concerned that he might see this as he had seen the *Cohen* Fuck-the-Draft case, as something other than free speech, and vote the wrong way. "Somehow I'll find a way to call this conduct rather than speech," he quipped.

The Justices arrived and met briefly to discuss Griswold's re-quest for a closed hearing. The request itself had been secret; the lawyers for the two newspapers had not been told. Black, Douglas, Brennan and Marshall wanted the arguments to be open. Burger, Harlan and Blackmun were willing to close them. Stewart and White wanted some better indication of what extraordinary cir-cumstances justified secret proceedings. The record from the lower courts revealed that little of the matters that had been dis-cussed was of sufficient sensitivity to warrant excluding the public. Stewart said that secret proceedings would hurt the Court's repu-tation.

In addition, Griswold's credibility with the Justices had not been helped by his forecast of two months before that there would be mass insurrection if the veterans were allowed to camp on the Mall. He had embroiled the Court in a needless controversy. Stewart and White were not about to be taken in again. They voted with the four others to deny the motion.

At 11 A.M., the Chief opened the session before a packed courtroom. Douglas had flown back from Goose Prairie.

Griswold sat at the government counsel's table across from the lawyers for the two newspapers. Beneath the table were three boxes containing the forty-seven volumes of the Pentagon Papers. "The heart of our case," Griswold said, "is that the publication of the materials specified in my closed brief will . . . materially affect the security of the United States . . . [and] the process of the termination of the war . . . [and] of recovering prisoners."

Griswold presumed that he had no hope of winning Black, Douglas, Brennan or Marshall. He focused his appeal on the other five. A more general, less restricted concept of national security was required, Griswold argued, than was mentioned in the 1931 decision suggesting a ban on publication of "sailing dates" and "location of troops."

Stewart and White pressed Griswold. The potential harm must be *immediate* to justify prior restraint?

No, Griswold argued, it would be too narrow a standard to require that publication result in "a war tomorrow morning, when there's a war now going on." National security had to include peace overtures, for instance, and ongoing negotiation for the release of prisoners of war, and even more remote negotiations such as the Strategic Arms Limitation Talks (SALT) or Middle East peace plans. These were processes, chains of events, that could be "irreparably" harmed by publication of certain details. This would surely harm "national security" in a way that would justify prior restraint.

Yale Law Professor Alexander Bickel, a renowned constitutional scholar, argued next for the *Times*. He pointed out carefully that the *New York Times*'s position was not absolute. There might be cases when national security considerations would justify prior restraint. This, however, was not such a case, he said.

Eleven days had already passed since the original disclosures, and no catastrophes had occurred. Government concerns about potential national-security crises were nothing but speculation and surmise. The link between publication and consequences, Bickel argued, must be "direct and immediate and visible."

"Let us assume," Stewart said, "that when the members of the Court go back and open up this sealed record we find something there that absolutely convinces us that its disclosure would result in the sentencing to death of a hundred young men whose only offense had been that they were nineteen years old and had low draft numbers. What should we do?"

Bickel assured him that nothing of the kind would be found. "I am as confident as I can be of anything that Your Honor will not find that when you get back to your chambers," Bickel said.

If such evidence did appear, Stewart pressed, "you would say the Constitution requires that it be published, and that these men die, is that it?"

"No," Bickel responded, "I am afraid that my inclinations to humanity overcome the somewhat more abstract devotion to the First Amendment in a case of that sort."

Unable to restrain himself any longer, Douglas broke into Bickel's argument. "Do you read [the First Amendment] to mean that Congress may make some laws abridging freedom of the press?"

"No, sir," Bickel answered. "Only in that I have conceded, for purpose of this argument, that some limitations, some impairment of the absoluteness of that prohibition is possible—"

"That is a very strange argument for the *Times* to be making," Douglas snapped.

Argument ended at noon. As the Justices returned to the robing room, Stewart insisted that instead of proceeding to lunch they should each immediately read the record. They should waste no time in voting. The prior-restraint issue called for an immediate decision.

Harlan disagreed. First, the case had been allowed to sail through the lower courts with insufficient time to render a considered judgment. Now Stewart was recommending that they rush even faster. But the others agreed with Stewart. They would read the record and reconvene that afternoon.

As the Justices returned to their chambers, Black echoed Douglas's amazement over the unexpected stand taken by Bickel. "Too bad the *New York Times* couldn't find someone who believes in the First Amendment," he said.

But beneath the surface, Black was deeply worried. As he saw it, only Brennan would stand with Douglas and him on the ground that the First Amendment prohibited the stopping of publication. Marshall and White were not prepared to say newspapers had an absolute right to publish. They thought the government should prosecute the newspapers afterward, rather than stop publication before the fact. Stewart wanted to find a factual basis on which to decide the case. If the sealed record demonstrated the clear and direct causal link to a danger to the national security, his vote was probably lost. Burger, Harlan and Blackmun seemed determined to send the case back to the lower courts for further hearings. Whichever side got two of the three undecided votes—Stewart, White and Marshall—would have the decision.

Black was particularly concerned about Stewart. "I just don't know about Potter," he said. "I just don't know how he'll come out."

It was clear from the start, when Stewart and White had voted to grant cert, that neither would take an absolutist First Amendment position. For both, it would come down to the sealed record. Had the government proved that the material was truly dangerous? "We're all in real trouble," Black told his clerks.

The papers that Griswold had filed with the Court remained under guard in the conference room.

Douglas had none of Black's reluctance about reading the sealed record. Unwilling to abide by the Chief's restrictions that all the material be kept in the conference room, protected by Pentagon security guards stationed outside, Douglas took the materials to his chamber and raised no objection when his clerks read the exhibits.

Douglas was totally unimpressed with what he found. His many trips to Vietnam, his own writing on the area (*North from Malaya*), and his close friendships with Vietnamese officials (including the late Ngo Dinh Diem, with whom he stayed on his visits) had made him intimately familiar with Southeast Asia. With characteristic vanity, he told his colleagues that there was nothing in the materials he had not known or assumed.

Harlan, unable with his poor eyesight to read the documents, also picked up a set of the papers in the conference room, stuffed them into a manila envelope, and headed back to his chambers. Entering as usual through his clerks' office, he handed one clerk the materials and told him he wanted him to begin reading the papers aloud to him in his office in a few minutes.

Harlan was barely out of the room when Blackmun burst through the door. He apologized profusely. He had been trying to catch Harlan, he told the clerk. Obviously embarrassed, Blackmun explained that the Chief had sent him to retrieve Harlan's copy of the record. No one was to remove the papers from the conference room, he explained. Taking the exhibits from the clerk, Blackmun left.

When he heard what had happened, Harlan was upset. But reluctant to criticize his colleagues before his clerks, he returned to the conference room, where Blackmun read the material to him.

Stewart looked through the sealed exhibits in the conference room with an almost boyish curiosity about the secrets contained in the documents. Both the enormous publicity and the complicated legal question made this the best case to come along in years. It was the kind of issue that Stewart thought central to the Court's role. It would be hard to decide. "I've seen things that shake me," Stewart told his clerks later, pacing excitedly about his chambers. It wasn't "frivolous." "There is no question that there is some stuff in there that could get people killed, and I hope it never gets out." But he remained unsure whether its publication would immediately and gravely affect national security.

There was an air of uncertainty late that afternoon, as the nine Justices convened in the conference room.

The Chief was determined to send the case back for additional hearings; the government should have another chance to prove the national security was in jeopardy. Black and Douglas said the newspapers should be permitted to publish immediately. Harlan again argued that the Court had moved too precipitously, but if he were forced to reach a decision on the merits of the case now, he would vote for the government. Brennan's disgust with the war and the government had come to a head; he voted for the newspapers. Publication could be enjoined only in one circumstance—that the nation be in a declared war.

The crux of the issue, as Stewart saw it, was a matter of facts. The lawyers for the newspapers had acknowledged that they were not arguing against prior restraint in all cases. The question was whether, in this case, today, the government had proved its point. Would some grave, irreparable harm come to the country if the newspapers continued publishing the papers? He agreed that publication was probably not in the national interest, but would it cause immediate and irreparable harm? Stewart was not sure. The burden of proof was clearly with the government. It was close, but the government had not met the burden, Stewart concluded. He would vote to let the newspapers publish. That gave Black his fifth vote.

White and Marshall took nearly identical views: the government had taken the wrong course in seeking injunctions against the newspapers. It could prosecute them after publication if it could prove that they had violated laws against disclosing classified secrets. Both Justices would vote to lift the injunctions. Though they could imagine situations in which prior restraint was permissible, it was not called for here.

Blackmun joined the Chief and Harlan. That made it 6 to 3.

The logic now demanded that the decision be released as soon as possible. No one would be assigned to write for the majority. The Justices would issue a brief *per curiam* with the result, and each man would write his separate opinion. There was really no time for anything else.

Douglas, as usual, was first off the mark. By the end of Saturday, he had finished a draft. By Sunday, he had polished it. On Monday, he was back in Goose Prairie.

Brennan was also anxious to get away. The ferry tickets to his annual summer vacation spot, the island of Nantucket off the Massachusetts coast, had been purchased weeks in advance. He had planned to leave on Monday.

For Black, this decision represented the most important First Amendment opinion of his career—a final accomplishment in his efforts to gain acceptance for First Amendment values. First among the priorities of a free press was exposing the secrets of government, especially those calculated to fool a nation into shipping its sons off to be "murdered" on foreign shores, he stated. Even as he wrote, he realized how deeply and seriously the government had misled its people about the war. "They've deceived us all this time," he said to one of his clerks. He felt personally betrayed. He had known how foolish this war had been, but now he regretted that the Court had not taken some stand earlier to protect the public from the deceptions. He resolved to incorporate into his opinion a stronger condemnation of the war itself. He cast about for the precise language he wanted. The words just would not come.

But after sleeping on it, Black arrived in chambers and summoned his clerks. He had found the words in an old Southern drinking song, "I'm a Good Old Rebel." Enthusiastically he sang it for them.

I'm a good old rebel,
Now that's just what I am,
For this "Fair Land of Freedom"
I do not care a damn;
I hates the Yankee nation
And everything they do,
I hates the Declaration
of Independence, too.

Three hundred thousand Yankees
Is stiff in Southern dust;
We got three hundred thousand,
Before they conquered us;
They died of Southern fever,
And Southern steel and shot,
I wish they was three million,
Instead of what we got.

He rewrote his draft:

> ... paramount among the responsibilities of a free press is the duty to
> prevent any part of the government from deceiving the people and
> sending them off to distant lands to die of foreign fevers and foreign
> shot and shell. In my view, far from deserving condemnation for their
> courageous reporting, the *New York Times*, the *Washington Post*, and
> other newspapers should be commended for serving the purpose that
> the Founding Fathers saw so clearly. In revealing the workings of
> government that led to the Vietnam War, the newspapers nobly did
> precisely that which the Founders hoped and trusted they would do.

Black spent nearly every minute of his time polishing his lesson
on the history and meaning of the First Amendment. He was oblivious to the other chambers. He wanted his opinion to be perfect.

There was little for Harlan to do other than outline his reasoning
why the Court's action was "almost irresponsibly feverish." He was
still upset with Stewart for rushing them. Although he voted with
the government, he would, in future cases, require that each national-security claim be made personally by a cabinet secretary.

As the Justices worked on their opinions, Harlan was flabbergasted to learn that the Chief had received a telephone call from
James "Scotty" Reston, a vice-president and senior columnist for
The New York Times. Burger told Harlan that Reston had asked for
a meeting.

"About what?" Burger had asked.

"The Pentagon Papers case," Reston had told him.

Shocked at the impropriety of Reston's overture, Burger had terminated the conversation.

Harlan was not sure that the Chief was construing Reston's call
fairly. The Chief presented the incident as if Reston were clearly
trying to influence the outcome of the case. Given the Chief's
overreaction, Harlan thought Reston was lucky not to have been
held in contempt. And he was hardly surprised at the apparent display of arrogance.

Harlan recalled when he had first been introduced to Reston at a
cocktail party in Connecticut. When he had been told that Harlan

never voted in elections, lest it give him a partisan interest in issues that came before the Court, Reston appeared visibly shocked. "He doesn't vote?" Reston had asked Harlan's wife. "That's strange. All of us at *The New York Times* vote."*

Harlan still marveled at the pomposity of a man who could confuse the role of a newspaper with the role of the Court.

The Chief agreed with Harlan that the cases had been considered too quickly. Maybe it was easy for Douglas and Black. They didn't need briefs or orals, and they didn't care what was in the sealed brief. But for him, it was not such a simple matter. "We do not know the facts . . ." he wrote in dissent. "No District Judge knew all the facts. No Court of Appeals Judge knew all the facts. No member of this Court knows all the facts."

Burger was also bothered by the newspapers' willingness to receive stolen property.

> It is hardly believable that a newspaper long regarded as a great institution in American life would fail to perform one of the basic and simple duties of every citizen with respect to the discovery or possession of stolen property or secret government documents. This duty was to report [to] responsible public officers. This duty rests on taxi drivers, Justices, and the *New York Times*.

Struck by the similarity between the administration's appeal for the Court to protect the nation's secrets and the Court's own need for secrecy, Burger added a last-minute footnote:

> There may be an analogy with respect to this Court. No statute gives this Court express power to establish and enforce the utmost security measures for the secrecy of our deliberations and records. Yet I have little doubt as to the inherent power of the Court to protect the confidentiality of its internal operations by whatever judicial measures may be required.

---

* Reston said in an interview that he recalls neither the call to Burger nor the discussion with Mrs. Harlan.

At 2:30 P.M., Wednesday, June 30, four days after the argument and conference, Burger announced the 6-to-3 decision in favor of the newspapers. He chose to read the short *per curiam* himself, despite the fact that he was among the three dissenters.

The other chambers were deeply unhappy with the Chief's usurpation of the majority's right to present its own opinion. Black, not Burger, should be announcing the decision. But the tone of the opinion gave the impression of unanimity among the Court, despite the split. And it expressed a strong presumption against prior restraint, which the government carried the burden of justifying. The district courts had said the government had not met that burden in this case. Concluded Burger: "We agree."

In conversations with reporters later, and in a speech to the American Bar Association the next week, the Chief referred to the Pentagon Papers case as "actually unanimous."

Shortly after the *Pentagon Papers* decision was announced, Griswold asked to see the Chief. He informed Burger that he had been privy to some extremely reliable leaks on voting patterns within the Court, including the temporary deadlock in the Ali case, and that he regularly learned which cases would come down each Monday. He had known precisely when the Pentagon Papers case would be announced, Griswold said. He had wanted to tell the Chief earlier, but had decided to wait until the term's work was complete. Griswold expressed concern about the confidentiality of the conference. He did not elaborate, but he remarked simply that some members of his staff knew some clerks at the Court. The Chief thanked him.

It was clear when he brought the issue up at conference that Burger was upset. The F.B.I., he said, should interview each clerk, and conduct lie-detector tests. Personally, Burger said, he avoided the possibility of leaks by not telling his own clerks about votes or discussion at conference.

"You can tell he doesn't talk to his clerks by reading his opinions," Brennan later remarked.

When the other Justices objected to the lie-detector tests, the Chief backed down and appointed a committee on security to be chaired by Stewart and to consider the matter further.

The Chief took one other step as well. In the future, the law clerks would no longer schedule basketball games against teams from the Solicitor General's office.

Douglas was especially pleased with the outcome of the Pentagon Papers case. He was now confident that he could gather the votes to grant cert on the constitutionality of the war if the right case were to come along. Brennan and Black were now ready to consider it. With Stewart and Harlan, he would have a comfortable margin of at least five to grant cert.

1971 Term

1971 Term

IN LATE AUGUST 1971, the Chief invited his new clerks to join him for lunch. It was a last-minute invitation. Several arrived at the ground-floor Ladies Dining Room carrying their cafeteria lunches on trays. Since they had come to the Court at various times over the summer, Burger's clerks had had only fleeting contact with their boss.

Alvin Wright, the Chief's messenger and valet, stood in the doorway wearing a white waiter's jacket. The sight of the familiar messenger dressed as a waiter was startling enough, but suddenly Wright pivoted and snapped to attention. "The Chief Justice of the United States of America," he called out.

By reflex, the clerks rose.

"You've got to be shitting me," one mumbled in the face of a hostile stare from Burger's senior clerk.

Burger strolled into the room, greeted each clerk graciously, and took his place at the head of the table. The antique table was covered with a linen cloth and set with the Court Historical Society's china and silver. Here in this dining room with pale-yellow walls covered with portraits of the wives of the former Chief Justices, Burger felt comfortable. He had taken a great interest in the proper refurbishing of this room. Newly acquired antiques, financed through the Society with donations from prominent Washingtonians and members of the bar, were selected by the Chief with great care. The room itself was a vestige of an age when the Court's oral arguments were among Washington's premier social events attended by the Justices' wives and their guests.

Burger enjoyed entertaining in the midst of this elegant collection of period pieces. The guests that he invited to dinners here were as carefully selected as the décor, drawn for the most part from admirers he encountered as he moved through social Washington. But the esteem of outsiders was not enough. Burger genuinely sought understanding and respect from the young men who came each year to work as his clerks. He missed the relaxed days of the Court of Appeals, when he often took his clerks to his house in Arlington and cooked them a gourmet meal. Now, with the press of Court and administrative duties, he was lucky to manage lunch with his clerks once a month.

Burger began this gathering with an introduction to the approaching term. Lamenting the fact that both John Harlan and Hugo Black had recently been hospitalized, he told some anecdotes about the warm affection that existed between these ideological opponents. He emphasized his respect and admiration for the two legal giants.

The Chief also expressed concern about Marshall's recent emergency appendectomy. Marshall had not allowed the news media to know about complications that had arisen from a stomach ulcer. And though Douglas was healthy, he had had his heart "pacemaker" batteries replaced three months before.

The message was clear. Reluctantly but inevitably, the Chief was having to assume additional burdens of leadership. One of the most pressing problems of the approaching term was the evident confusion of the lower federal courts in the wake of the Charlotte desegregation and busing decision. Many district judges had ordered massive busing in an apparent attempt to achieve racial balance in each school, the Chief explained. This had provoked a massive public outcry. It was all unnecessary, the Chief said. The Charlotte decision did not require racial balance. He told the clerks how he had struggled to overcome Black's adamant opposition to any busing. Only his personal effort had allowed the Court to come down with a unanimous decision.

One of the clerks, familiar with the case from a year's clerking at the Fourth Circuit Court of Appeals, politely challenged Burger. In the Charlotte case, the Supreme Court had approved Judge McMillan's order and McMillan had used racial balance in devising the busing remedy.

No, the Chief explained patiently, as the author of the opinion he knew what the Court was trying to achieve. Since the original school desegregation decisions in 1954 and 1955, the lower courts had been confused about whether the Supreme Court was calling for desegregation or for integration. Clearly, the Court was calling only for desegregation. Forced racial mixing, racial balance, or total integration had not been demanded.

Federal district judges in about twenty desegregation cases in large Southern metropolitan regions had misread the Charlotte opinion, Burger told them, and the result had been orders for massive busing. As it happened, he had an emergency request on his desk from the Winston-Salem, North Carolina, school district to stay a busing plan ordered by a district court judge. The judge had mistakenly ordered busing to achieve racial balance. Burger said he would end the unnecessary confusion over busing by writing a single-justice opinion to accompany his order. This would be no *"post hoc"* repair job, Burger said, but simply a clarification.

The clerks had heard the rumors of the rancorous debates over the Charlotte case. Varying scenarios placed Stewart, Brennan, Harlan, Douglas and even Marshall in key roles resolving a conflict brought to a head by the obstinacy of both Black and the Chief. Now, they were bewildered to find that Burger expected them to believe that he had been the single author of the final opinion. Several wondered whether the Chief even understood what he had "authored" in the Charlotte case. He was espousing the position he had been forced to surrender last term.

Burger turned to other matters, pausing briefly here and there before spinning off in new directions. Several clerks glanced at their watches. They had hundreds of cert petitions and scores of memos to complete. The Chief's head clerk noticed that the nodding of one of the new clerks was becoming more and more pronounced. He seemed to be asleep. A nudge was passed along the perimeter of the table.

It was nearly three o'clock when Burger got up and returned to his office to deal with the Winston-Salem case. He telephoned several of the other Justices, some of whom were not yet back in Washington.

Brennan was adamantly opposed to a stay. The lower court had acted properly, he declared. Several of the Justices also expressed their opposition. On the other hand, the week before, Black had issued a stay order in a similar busing case (Corpus Christi), saying that the situation was too confused to be considered on the spur of the moment. Burger did not want to grant the stay on his own; his intention could too easily be misunderstood. He did, however, want to make the point that integration and strict racial balance were not required. He finally thought that he knew how to achieve both objectives. He wrote that an inadequate record and the fact that only one week remained before the schools were scheduled to open made it impossible to grant a stay in the Winston-Salem case. But any interpretation that the Charlotte opinion required racial balance was "disturbing," and might involve "misreadings." He believed the district and appeals court judges in Winston-Salem had read the Charlotte opinion to mean that racial balance was required. The Chief wanted to send a message to those judges and all other lower court judges.

In the Charlotte opinion, the others had insisted on saying that racial balance was not simply a means to assess whether there was a violation of the law, but that it was "a useful starting point *in shaping a remedy* to correct past Constitutional violations." Some selective editing was needed, Burger concluded.

He wrote that racial balance was "an obvious and necessary starting point to decide whether in fact any violation existed," and he stopped there, leaving out any reference to its use in shaping a remedy. Then he carefully chose from the Charlotte opinion the language that he felt was important. "If we were to read the holding of the District Court to require, as a matter of substantive constitutional right, any particular degree of racial balance or mixing, *that approach would then be disapproved and we would be obliged to reverse.* The constitutional command to desegregate schools does not mean that every school in every community must always reflect the racial composition of the school system as a whole." To be sure that no one missed the point, the Chief added the emphasis. He released his ten-page opinion on August 31, the day after the schools opened in Winston-Salem.

Brennan was especially unhappy with the tone. The order had been written as if it were meant to be construed as a majority opinion, as if the Chief were speaking for the Court. Burger had mischaracterized the case, Brennan told his clerks. The Court had settled all this last year.

There were, Brennan was well aware, vague, even contradictory notions in the Charlotte opinion. That had been inevitable, given the demand for unanimity. But the lower court judges had interpreted it correctly, as Brennan had hoped they would. Now, in order to put the brakes on the lower courts, Burger was trying to confuse the situation all over again. Brennan was offended that the Chief in his opinion would go so far as to offer his view that three hours average daily busing was excessive. Brennan agreed, in fact, with this view, but it was inappropriate for the Chief to offer his personal standard.

Burger had also suggested that if the busing was too extensive, students should be allowed to transfer to schools nearer their homes. This was an invitation to school districts to subvert desegregation orders, Brennan thought. One of Brennan's clerks joked that Nixon—who the month before had ordered the Department of Health, Education and Welfare to hold busing to "the minimum required by law"—had given Burger his marching orders.

No, Brennan responded, Warren Burger did not need Richard Nixon on this issue.

Tension over Burger's unilateral redefinition of the Charlotte case was eclipsed by the rapid physical deterioration of Black and Harlan.

The Pentagon Papers case turned out to be only a temporary reprieve for Black. His headaches had resumed with greater frequency and intensity. Douglas counseled Black to resign. But Black would not accept the advice.

He had checked into the Bethesda Naval Medical Center for four days in mid-July and returned for two more days of tests later in the month. Despite his doctor's conclusions to the contrary, Black was certain that he had cancer. He had lost his appetite and weighed barely 115 pounds when his doctors asked his family to bring him back to the hospital in mid-August. Two days before he entered, he asked a former clerk, Lou Oberdorfer, a prominent Washington attorney, to draft a letter of resignation. Oberdorfer brought a copy to Black the next night. Black left the date open, but he signed it. "This," he said, "will protect the Court."

Black entered the hospital the next morning, August 27. Harlan, undergoing diagnostic testing for recurring back pains, was in the next room.

In contrast to Black, Harlan continued to run his chambers from his hospital bed. Nearly blind, he could not even see the ash from his own cigarette, but he doggedly prepared for the coming term. One day a clerk brought in an emergency petition. Harlan remained in bed as he discussed the case with the clerk. They agreed that the petition should be denied. Harlan bent down, his eyes virtually to the paper, wrote his name, and handed the paper to his clerk. The clerk saw no signature. He looked over at Harlan.

"Justice Harlan, you just denied your sheet," the clerk said gently, pointing to the scrawl on the linen. Harlan smiled and tried again, signing the paper this time.

Black didn't want to see any visitors. He was convinced that he was going to die. Nixon sent a letter saying he wanted to pay him a visit. Black declined. Burger came by to chat but Black didn't respond. Harlan tried repeatedly to cheer Black, and he failed.

"I can't see," Black told one of his sons. "I've got to quit. . . . And I'll tell you something else, John Harlan can't see a thing. He ought to get off the Court, too."*

Black's major concern, from the moment he entered the hospital, was to make sure that his most private papers, memos and conference notes were burned. Publication would inhibit the free exchange of ideas in the future. He felt that he had been treated unfairly in the late Justice Harold H. Burton's diary, in which Burton had written that Black at first resisted desegregation. Black had also been shattered by the biography of former Justice Harlan Fiske Stone, written by Alpheus Thomas Mason. Black had told

---

* See Hugo Black, Jr., *My Father: A Remembrance*, p. 249.

Burger that when he read Stone's biography, he had discovered for the first time that Stone couldn't stand him.

Black didn't want that kind of use made of his private papers. He ordered his son, Hugo, Jr., to burn them. His son stalled for a time, hoping that his father's condition would improve, but Black's health continued to deteriorate. His papers were finally retrieved and burned. On September 17, Black's messenger delivered his letter of resignation to Nixon. He was eighty-five. He had served thirty-four terms.

At about the same time, Harlan received the news he had feared. The tests showed that he had cancer. Harlan decided to resign, but he delayed his announcement to avoid detracting from the attention and the adulation he knew Black would receive. On September 23, Harlan submitted his letter of resignation. He was seventy-one and had served sixteen terms.

Two days later, Black died.*

With the Court down to seven Justices, the conference met quickly to revise its schedule. The Justices realized the Court might be shorthanded for some time if there were protracted confirmation battles.

A number of capital punishment cases, scheduled for argument the first day of the term only two weeks away, were the first to be postponed. Such cases would require a full nine-man court. In any case, Burger was interested in deferring as many cases as possible. With Harlan and Black gone, Douglas's anticipated votes to grant cert in the war cases were gone. Burger was certain that Nixon's new appointees would be natural allies.

But when the administration made its move, it seemed to Burger

* The minister selected to deliver the eulogy went to Black's library and found various books that Black had underlined, including *The Greening of America,* by Charles Reich, one of his former clerks. The minister selected some of the underlined portions to read at the funeral. During the eulogy, Brennan gently nudged Stewart. "Hugo would turn over in his grave if he heard that," Brennan said. Only Black's intimates knew that Black thought Reich's book absurd, and that Black underlined the sections he *disliked.*

that Nixon had learned nothing from the Haynsworth-Carswell disasters. The first name that was sent to the American Bar Association screening committee was conservative Republican Congressman Richard Poff of Virginia. The prospect was greeted unenthusiastically in legal circles. It seemed unlikely that the A.B.A. committee would give Poff anything approaching a strong endorsement. Poff quickly withdrew his name.

Other possibilities were leaked. One that caused an uproar in the press and legal establishment was Democratic Senator Robert Byrd of West Virginia. Nixon wanted Byrd's name sent to the screening committee, even though Byrd, a law school graduate, had never been admitted to the bar and had never practiced law.

From the hospital, Harlan expressed his concern to Stewart about the men being mentioned as possible successors. They were both puzzled by Nixon's seeming willingness to denigrate the Court by once more nominating lackluster, even obviously unacceptable, candidates. The rest of the Court shared Harlan's worry.

Nixon had two criteria. He was still looking for a Southerner, and he wanted another "first" for his administration. He wanted to appoint the first woman to the Court.

Mitchell quickly came up with a male candidate from Arkansas, a local municipal bond lawyer, Herschel Friday. On Thursday afternoon, October 7, Mitchell and Rehnquist interviewed him. The following morning, they interviewed their top woman candidate, Mildred Lillie, a California Court of Appeals judge.

The White House counsel, John Dean, was sent to interview the candidates. Mitchell had lost some credibility with the President in the wake of the Haynsworth and Carswell failures. Friday was a good lawyer, Dean reported, but he would make Carswell look good as a Senate witness. He knew very little constitutional law and would have trouble being confirmed. Lillie had similar problems, Dean said. The A.B.A. committee probably wouldn't approve her, since she lacked sufficient judicial experience.*

Rehnquist was also unimpressed. "Christ, we've got to be able to

---

* See John Dean, *Blind Ambition*, p. 50.

do better than this," he told Kleindienst. He preferred New York Court of Appeals Judge Charles D. Breitel, a brilliant conservative jurist.

But Mitchell was satisfied. On Tuesday, October 12, he sent the names of Friday and Lillie to the A.B.A. committee.

Burger was increasingly worried. Another Nixon attempt to appoint someone without qualifications, leading to another drawn-out battle with the Senate, would severely damage the Court's prestige. The possibility that the Court might have to limp along for an entire term with seven justices, because of White House bungling, was intolerable. The Chief had discussed the need for prompt and careful selection of candidates with Mitchell on several occasions since Black's and Harlan's resignations. The message didn't seem to be getting through.

On October 13, Burger once more tried to get the point across in a "personal and confidential" letter to Mitchell. Burger asked Mitchell and his "client" (Nixon) to keep the Court's needs in mind. "It is beyond dispute, I think, that the Court as an institution has been sorely damaged in this last decade."

Reminding him of the embarrassment caused by L.B.J.'s effort to replace Chief Justice Warren with Fortas, and the subsequent scandal over Fortas's finances, Burger noted that the "completely unwarranted rejection of Judge Haynsworth and the subsequent rejection of Judge Carswell were also bruising episodes.

"The loss in September of two strong and able Justices—one of whom had become virtually a legend—is a blow of a different character but, nevertheless, a new injury to the institution," Burger said. The Chief said that he understood Nixon's desire to appoint a woman to the Court, but argued against a "woman appointed simply because she is a woman."

Burger also expressed sympathy for Nixon's wish to appoint a Southerner. "As I indicated to you in our conversation some weeks ago and again more recently, I recognize that geographical factors cannot be ignored by the President."

The Chief proposed that the President consider two candidates from the South in addition to Herschel Friday, whom he described as an attorney of "very superior professional qualifications." One was Lewis Powell, sixty-four, a private attorney in Richmond and a former president of the A.B.A. The other was Federal District Judge Frank Johnson of Alabama, a liberal with a strong civil rights record. Burger also put forward the names of seven other judges from the Northeast as possibilities.

The following afternoon, Mitchell and Burger met in the Attorney General's office. Two hours later, Mitchell told reporters that the administration was considering nine candidates besides Friday and Lillie.

By Monday, October 18, the head of the screening committee reported that the main candidates, Lillie and Friday, would have serious trouble getting A.B.A. approval. The formal vote would be on Wednesday. Nixon and Mitchell didn't wait. At 8:20 A.M. Tuesday, Mitchell phoned Lewis Powell at the Waldorf-Astoria Hotel in New York. "I am authorized by the President to offer you an appointment to the Supreme Court," Mitchell said.

Powell declined. He reminded Mitchell of a letter he had written shortly after the Carswell defeat. At the time he had heard that he was on a small list of those under consideration, and he had written Mitchell to say that he didn't want the job, that at sixty-two he was too old to begin a new career. Now, Powell reminded Mitchell, he was two years older.

Mitchell was aware of the age problem. The President had agreed when Powell's name came up two years earlier that he was too old. He wouldn't have enough time on the Court to really influence it. But now the situation was more urgent. Powell could get confirmed.

Mitchell asked Powell if he would remain by the phone and promised that he would call him back at 10:30 A.M. Powell waited. It was almost 11:15 A.M. when Mitchell called to ask Powell to reconsider. Powell declined again.

Solicitor General Griswold suggested to Mitchell that Powell might react differently to a direct appeal from the President. Powell had barely arrived home in Richmond that night when the phone rang. It was the White House. President Nixon pushed hard. Powell had a "duty" to accept—a duty to the South, to the law, the Court, the President, the country, Nixon said.

Powell told him that he would consider it, but even as he said it, he realized that he couldn't turn down the President.

Powell had been offered Hugo Black's seat. A candidate was still needed for Harlan's. Kleindienst got ready to review the likeliest nominees with Mitchell. Rehnquist, who had participated in most of the meetings, was also preparing for the meeting when Kleindienst told him to forget it. "We're going to be talking about you," Kleindienst said.

Nixon had certain concerns about nominating Rehnquist. It would look like an "in-house" appointment, and Rehnquist was relatively unknown in establishment legal circles. A former clerk to Justice Robert Jackson in 1952, Rehnquist had practiced law for sixteen years in Phoenix where he was part of the Goldwater wing of the Republican party. He had joined the Justice Department to head the Office of Legal Counsel as an assistant attorney general in 1969. He had been, in effect, Attorney General Mitchell's lawyer.

Nixon had some trouble remembering Rehnquist's name; he once called him "Renchburg." He was also somewhat taken aback by the easygoing lawyer's appearance, once referring to him as "that clown" because of his long sideburns and pink shirts. But Rehnquist was very bright and extremely conservative. And at forty-seven, he could be expected to serve many years.

On Thursday night, October 21, in a televised address, Nixon announced the nominations of Powell and Rehnquist.

Nixon thought Powell would be confirmed easily. He was a native Virginian and he had impressive credentials: Phi Beta Kappa from Washington and Lee College in 1929; first in his class at Washington and Lee Law School after completing the three-year course in only two years; a year of graduate work at Harvard Law School; private practice with a prestigious law firm; directorships in eleven major corporations; President of the A.B.A. in 1964–65; President of the American College of Trial Lawyers, 1968–1970; and member of Lyndon Johnson's National Crime Commission.

Powell was a political moderate. As Vice-President of the National Legal Aid and Defender Association, he had played an important role in securing organized bar support for legal services for the poor. As Chairman of the Richmond School Board from

1952 to 1961, he kept the Richmond schools open in spite of segregationist pressure to close them in the wake of the *Brown* decisions.

Rehnquist too had excellent credentials: an undergraduate and master's degree from Stanford; a master's in history from Harvard; and Editor of the *Law Review* at Stanford Law School.

But Rehnquist might have more trouble than Powell in getting through the Senate. Richard Kleindienst, the Deputy Attorney General, had brought him to Washington in 1968 to serve as Assistant Attorney General to advise the department on legal strategy. He had performed brilliantly for the administration—justifying its anticrime measures, its wiretapping of domestic radicals, and the mass arrests during the previous spring's demonstrations. Rehnquist might have done his job too well. He might run into fire from congressional liberals. Blacks also seemed certain to oppose his nomination. Rehnquist had testified against a Phoenix civil rights act as recently as 1964, and in favor of limited school desegregation in 1967.

But Nixon had a plan: the two nominations would be sent to the Senate as a package. Powell's supporters worked hard to untie the knot, to try to see that Powell and Rehnquist were not even so much as photographed together in visits to Capitol Hill. Shortly after his nomination, Powell and a group of supporters called on the Senate Judiciary Committee chairman, the conservative James Eastland.

Eastland sat behind his desk, silently puffing his cigar. "You're going to be confirmed," he told Powell.

Powell thanked him.

"Do you know why you're going to be confirmed?" Eastland asked.

No, he replied.

"Because," Eastland drawled, "they think you're going to die."

Eastland was offended by the efforts of Powell's friends to separate his nomination from Rehnquist's. Rehnquist had captured Eastland's affections during his appearances on the Hill. The Senator had heard enough from Powell's supporters about how Rehnquist was a lowbrow, not up to the standards of the Supreme

Court. To Eastland, that just meant that Rehnquist represented ordinary folk, Middle America. The confirmations, he declared, would be "double or nothing."

Eastland got word that the A.B.A. screening committee was not going to give Rehnquist a favorable recommendation. The committee's authority was only advisory, but an adverse vote might damage Rehnquist's chances by making him seem unqualified. Eastland found that prospect incredible. Rehnquist was no dullard. He had been first in his class at Stanford Law School. There had to be a raw political motive behind this, and Eastland decided to expose it. The Chairman passed the word to the A.B.A. committee that if it didn't approve Rehnquist, he would subpoena each of the twelve members to testify about their reasons under oath. Subpoenas were typed; travel plans prepared. Staff members were ready to fan out around the country.

The A.B.A. panel voted on November 2. Powell was unanimously given the highest possible rating. The committee, apparently buckling to Eastland's threat, then voted 9 to 3 to give Rehnquist the highest rating, and even the minority stated that it was "not opposed" to his nomination.

The Senate Committee's questioning of Powell in early November was perfunctory. A brief controversy arose over an article that Powell had written for the local Richmond paper four months earlier. The article had attacked the "radical left" and linked it to "foreign Communist enemies." Wiretapping of domestic radicals without obtaining warrants was reasonable and necessary, Powell had written; there was no real distinction between "external and internal threats" to the national security. But the flap over the article was minimal. Powell was confirmed by the Senate on December 6 by a vote of 89 to 1.

Rehnquist received a rougher grilling. His most serious problem arose when a memo surfaced that he had written in the Brown case, when he was clerking for Justice Jackson nineteen years earlier. The memo recommended that the Court not order school desegregation. "Separate but equal" facilities were all that was constitutionally required, Rehnquist had stated.

Rehnquist testified that he had written the memorandum, but he denied that it had reflected his views. He was merely summarizing Jackson's views for the conference.

Rehnquist's account was disputed by a lawyer who had clerked with him on the Court, and by Jackson's secretary. Press reports played up the discrepancies in testimony.* But the Committee dropped the matter. In two full days of hearings, the liberals could do no more than establish that Rehnquist was every bit as conservative as he appeared to be when defending administration policies. On December 10, the Senate voted to confirm him 68 to 26.

The new Justices were to be sworn in after the holidays.

In spite of their philosophical differences, Blackmun admired Douglas for the passion in his opinions. He was particularly moved by the poetic force of a Douglas dissent in an environmental case *(Sierra Club v. Morton)* that was argued in November.

Because the Sierra Club could not prove that any of its members would be individually affected, the Court had thrown out the conservation group's suit to block the conversion of eighty acres of wilderness into a Walt Disney recreation complex and ski resort.**

> Those who hike it, fish it, hunt it, camp in it, frequent it, or visit it merely to sit in solitude and wonderment are legitimate spokesmen for it, whether they may be few or many. . . .
>
> The voice of the inanimate object . . . should not be stilled . . . before these priceless bits of Americana . . . are forever lost or are so transformed as to be reduced to the eventual rubble of our urban environment; the voice of the existing beneficiaries of these environmental wonders should be heard.

---

* Douglas, the only remaining member of the Court that had decided the Brown cases, examined a copy of Rehnquist's testimony. Rehnquist was correct, he told clerks. The views were, in fact, Jackson's. But see also Richard Kluger, *Simple Justice*, pp. 605–610.

** In order to have standing to bring a case, anyone bringing suit must have been directly affected by the action under question. "Why didn't the Sierra Club have one goddamn member walk through the park and then there would have been standing to sue," White remarked, before joining the four-member majority.

Blackmun did not feel that he could join Douglas's dissent. It was too personal. But he would vote with him, and he would provide the mathematical equivalent of Douglas's imagery. He made some calculations. The expected daily influx of tourists—14,000—would arrive over a new 29.2-mile, two-lane highway through Sequoia National Park. Assuming they came in the fewest possible number of vehicles, with four passengers apiece, that would mean 3,500 vehicles per day. Just one round trip per car would mean 300 each hour in each direction. A vehicle would pass every six seconds. "Is this the way we perpetuate the wilderness and its beauty, solitude, and quiet?" Blackmun asked.

He suggested that the Sierra Club refile, with individual members as parties to the suit, thus giving them the "standing" that the Court had ruled the Club as a whole lacked. Alternatively, he proposed that the Court might broaden its traditional definition of standing to allow suits like this.

Douglas was delighted by Blackmun's support and by his somewhat radical approach to broaden standing. He sought him out. "You like the out of doors, don't you, Harry?" Douglas said, patting Blackmun on the back. He did not need to say more.

After months of struggling with the knowledge that Douglas held him in professional contempt, Blackmun felt they were suddenly bonded, two naturalists among despoilers of the environment. He felt closer to Douglas.

Early in the morning of April 19, Blackmun dispatched a law clerk to Douglas's chamber, with a memo—" . . . Mr. Justice Blackmun desires to deliver his dissent orally from the bench but . . . will not do so unless you also deliver your dissent orally. He therefore requests that you dissent orally today."

Douglas read his dissent aloud.

Douglas had long wanted the Court to face the abortion issue head on. The laws in effect in most states, prohibiting or severely restricting the availability of abortions, were infringements of a woman's personal liberty. The broad constitutional guarantee of "liberty," he felt, included the right of a woman to control her body.

Douglas realized, however, that a majority of his colleagues were not likely to give such a sweeping reading to the Constitution on this increasingly volatile issue. He knew also that the two cases now before the Court—challenging restrictive abortion laws in Georgia and Texas *(Doe v. Bolton* and *Roe v. Wade)*—did not signal any sudden willingness on the part of the Court to grapple with the broad question of abortions. They had been taken only to determine whether to expand a series of recent rulings limiting the intervention of federal courts in state court proceedings. Could women and doctors who felt that state prosecutions for abortions violated their constitutional rights, go into federal courts to stop the state? And could they go directly into federal courts even before going through all possible appeals in the state court system? Douglas knew the Chief wanted to say no to both these jurisdiction questions. He knew the Chief hoped to use these two cases to reduce the number of federal court cases brought by activist attorneys. The two abortion cases were not to be argued primarily about abortion rights, but about jurisdiction. Douglas was doubly discouraged, believing that his side was also going to lose on the jurisdiction issue.

Since Powell and Rehnquist still had not been sworn in, the cases were going to be decided by a seven-man Court. The Chief, Stewart, White and Blackmun seemed firmly opposed to taking an expansive view of the range of civil rights cases that could be brought to federal court. So, jurisdiction or abortion, either way it looked like at least a 4-to-3 defeat.

In one case, Sarah Weddington, a poised but inexperienced advocate before the Court, argued on behalf of the women hoping to overturn an 1856 Texas law restricting abortions. Unaware the Court was focusing on jurisdiction questions, she immediately began discussing the woman's constitutional right to an abortion.

Stewart pointed out that there were several threshold questions to be dealt with first, including the jurisdiction issue.

Stewart's questions drew Douglas's attention. As always during oral argument, he was a flurry of activity. Douglas listened with one ear, wrote, listened a moment, requested a book from the library, listened again, asked an occasional question, signed his correspondence for the day, listened again, made sarcastic comments to the Chief on his left or Stewart on his right. Now, for a change,

Douglas stopped dead. He jotted a quick note to his clerks. "I need considerable research" on the jurisdiction question, he wrote. "Would one of you take it on?"

Weddington replied to Stewart that she saw no jurisdiction problem. Under earlier Court decisions, federal courts could intervene in state courts when constitutional issues had been raised. The Court had a number of bases for striking down Texas's abortion law. "We had originally brought the suit alleging both the due process clause, equal protection clause, the Ninth Amendment, and a variety of others," Weddington began. "Since—"

"And anything else that might have been appropriate?" White interjected sarcastically.

"Yes, yeah," Weddington said, dissolving into laughter for a moment.

But White had pinned Weddington where he wanted her. She had made a broad constitutional claim, the kind a majority of the Court normally opposed.

"Well, do you or don't you say that the constitutional right you insist on reaches up until the time of birth, or what?" White asked.

" . . . The Constitution, as I see it, gives protection to people after birth," she offered.

Douglas then turned the questioning back to the issue they were supposed to be considering, the federal jurisdiction question, and Weddington's time soon lapsed.

When Assistant Attorney General of Texas, Jay Floyd, began presenting the state's case, Marshall returned to the issue of abortion. When, he inquired, does an unborn fetus come to have full constitutional rights?

"At any time, Mr. Justice; we make no distinction . . ." Floyd replied. "There is life from the moment of impregnation."

"And do you have any scientific data to support that?" Marshall asked.

"Well, we begin, Mr. Justice, in our brief, with the development of the human embryo, carrying it through to the development of the fetus, from about seven to nine days after conception," Floyd answered.

"Well, what about six days?" Marshall asked, eliciting a mild chuckle from the audience.

"We don't know," Floyd acknowledged.

"But this statute goes all the way back to one hour," Marshall said, clearly enjoying himself.

"I don't—Mr. Justice, it—there are unanswerable questions in this field, I—" Floyd, flustered, was interrupted by laughter around him.

"I appreciate it, I appreciate it," Marshall chanted, leaning back in exaggerated satisfaction with Floyd's befuddlement.

"This is an artless statement on our part," Floyd offered.

"I withdraw the question," Marshall said, trailing off.

Laughter nearly drowned out Floyd as he continued.

The Court turned to the Georgia case. Margie Pitts Hames summarized her client's case against a Georgia law that required abortions to be approved by two doctors and a hospital committee. This case was different from the Texas case, she insisted. There was no question of jurisdiction here, she argued.

Blackmun, energized for the first time that morning, asked questions about why the women who were suing had not sued the hospital as well as the state of Georgia. He also questioned Hames closely on the widespread practice of requiring that medical panels—not simply one doctor—approve certain types of abortion, thus making them difficult to obtain.

Blackmun's tone was hostile throughout. Overall, he had found the quality of oral argument in these cases poor. The abortion issue deserved a better presentation.

The rule of thumb at the Court was that oral arguments rarely win a case, but occasionally lose one. The Texas Attorney General would certainly have hurt his case had it not been for the fact that the case would be decided on the question of jurisdiction.

As the father of three outspoken women and the husband of another, Blackmun was sensitive to the abortion issue. Even more, as a former counsel to the Mayo Clinic, he sympathized with the doctor who was interrupted in his medical practice by the state, and told how he could or could not treat his patients. On the other hand, Blackmun generally felt the states should have the right to enforce their legislative will.

*   *   *

Stewart thought that abortion was one of those emotional issues that the Court rarely handled well. Yet it was becoming too important to ignore. Abortion was a political issue. Women were coming into their own, as Stewart learned from his daughter Harriet, a strong, independent woman.

As Stewart saw it, abortion was becoming one reasonable solution to population control. Poor people, in particular, were consistently victims of archaic and artificially complicated laws. The public was ready for abortion reform.

Still, these were issues of the very sort that made Stewart uncomfortable. Precisely because of their political nature, the Court should avoid them. But the state legislatures were always so far behind. Few seemed likely to amend their abortion laws. Much as Stewart disliked the Court's being involved in this kind of controversy, this was perhaps an instance where it had to be involved.

Stewart had no intention, however, of declaring himself the Court's leading activist. The abortion advocates argued that the Court should extend its 1965 decision in a Connecticut birth-control case, *Griswold v. Connecticut*. A majority of the Justices had held in that case that, although no right to privacy was explicitly stated in the Constitution, it was implied from a number of the Amendments. They had ruled that Connecticut could not prohibit married couples from using birth-control devices. Abortion advocates wanted that constitutional right to privacy extended to abortion.

Stewart thought that the abortion advocates' argument was too drastic. He had dissented from the 1965 decision, and he was reluctant to renounce his position. It was simply unnecessary for the Court to create another new constitutionally based right.

In a case the previous year (*U.S. v. Vuitch*), when the Court had upheld restrictions on abortion in the District of Columbia, Douglas had argued in dissent that a physician's judgment on abortion was a professional judgment that should not be second-guessed. Maybe this was the approach.

Stewart thought he could expand Douglas's argument to show that some anti-abortion statutes inhibited a doctor's ability to exercise his best judgment. Since a state-licensed doctor was a professional, the laws should not interfere with his judgment on behalf of his patient. On that theory, Stewart could vote to knock out the Georgia law—which required that abortions be approved by two doctors and a hospital committee—without creating an explicit constitutional right to abortion. But he did not want to be the one to raise this issue in conference.

Douglas had presented this rationale the year before. Since he was the Justice most likely to point out any inconsistency by Stewart with his past positions, one of Stewart's clerks went to Douglas's chambers. Stewart was considering voting against the Georgia abortion law, he told one of Douglas's clerks. If Douglas were to resurrect his reasoning, it might help.

The clerks compared notes. It seemed that Blackmun had also asked his clerks to research the same point. Blackmun's high regard for doctors might make him susceptible to this argument. The message from Stewart's clerk was relayed to Douglas.

Douglas was not impressed. Stewart was a patrician, a Rockefeller Republican; his constituencies were not the poor or women. He was "off in a cloud," hobbled by the *noblesse oblige* of America's upper class. Stewart was more concerned with the appearance of his jurisprudence than with its substance. Douglas was convinced that Stewart was out of touch with three quarters of American society. He used to make fun of Stewart's elitist Yale background. No, Douglas decided, there would be no special assistance for Stewart. As always, Douglas would present his own thoughts and let the others fend for themselves.

The buzzer summoned the seven Justices to conference that Thursday. Douglas's travel plans had caused it to be scheduled a day early.

Before dealing with the abortion cases, the conference took up *Mitchum v. Foster,* a case which involved a Florida "adult" bookstore that had been shut down by a state judge for peddling obscene materials. *Mitchum* posed a similar question of jurisdiction that was presented in the abortion cases. Could the bookstore owner go into federal court before the state courts had finished with the case?

Stewart concluded that, despite restrictions the Court had previously placed on federal-court intervention, the doctrine of nonintervention had its limits. The federal courts must be allowed to intervene wherever a glaring constitutional violation was taking place. Contrary to Douglas's expectation, Stewart joined Douglas, Brennan and Marshall to make it 4 to 3 for asserting federal jurisdiction.

Since the jurisdiction question here was the same as in the abortion cases, the Court had effectively decided the abortion jurisdiction issue as well. The Court *did* have jurisdiction. Suddenly, unexpectedly, the Court found itself faced with the underlying constitutional issue in the abortion cases. Did women have a right to obtain abortions?

The Chief had some difficulty in summarizing the cases. The Georgia law, requiring approval by two other doctors and then a hospital committee, put unusual restrictions on a physician who wanted to perform an abortion.

As Stewart had hoped, the discussion focused on the professional rights of a doctor seeking to perform an abortion, rather than on the rights of a woman trying to obtain one. Both Stewart and Blackmun were sympathetic to the arguments for lifting some restrictions on physicians. Each Justice focused on a different aspect of the case. As discussion continued, their positions emerged:

The Chief strongly in favor of upholding the state abortion laws, but not casting a clear vote;

White also for upholding;

Douglas, Brennan and Marshall strongly in favor of striking down the abortion laws on broad grounds of women's constitutional rights;

Stewart and Blackmun in favor of striking down at least portions of some of the laws, if only on narrower grounds of professional discretion.

These are difficult cases, the Chief said. No one could really tell how they would come out until the final drafting was done. The cases might even be candidates for reargument after the two new Justices were sworn in.

Brennan and Marshall counted the vote 5 to 2—Douglas, Brennan, Marshall, Stewart and Blackmun for striking the laws; the Chief and White dissenting.

Douglas, however, thought there were only four votes to strike the laws. Blackmun's vote was far from certain. He could not be counted on to split with the Chief on such an important issue.

For his part, Blackmun was for some kind of limited ruling against portions of the law, but he had not decided what to do.

White believed the vote was three for striking—Douglas, Brennan and Marshall; three for upholding—White, Stewart and Blackmun; and the Chief, who had passed, but clearly had strong feelings for upholding.

Stewart told his clerks, "We're going to face the abortion issue squarely," and there seemed to him to be a majority to strike the laws. The puzzle was Blackmun.

The Chief's assignment sheet circulated the following afternoon. Each case was listed on the left side in order of the oral argument, the name of the Justice assigned to write each decision on the right.

It took Douglas several moments to grasp the pattern of the assignments, and then he was flabbergasted. The Chief had assigned four cases in which Douglas was sure the Chief was not a member of the majority. These included the two abortion cases, which the Chief had assigned to Blackmun. He could barely control his rage as he ran down the list. Was there some mistake? He asked a clerk to check his notes from the conference. Douglas kept a docket book in which he recorded his tabulation of the votes. It was as he suspected.

In the Florida bookstore case, which raised a similar jurisdictional question as the abortion cases, and in which the Chief was a member of the minority, Burger had not only assigned the case but assigned it to another member of the minority. Douglas was all the more incredulous, since this case provided the basis for jurisdiction in the two abortion cases.

In another case (*Gooding v. Wilson*), the Chief had assigned a case in which he and Blackmun were a two-vote minority. Douglas, as the senior justice in the majority, had already assigned this case at conference to Brennan.

In a fifth case (*Alexander v. Louisiana*), the Chief had been in the majority but had assigned Stewart, a member of the minority, to write. Stewart sent the Chief a memo declining for that reason.

Never, in Douglas's thirty-three years on the court, had any Chief Justice tried to assign from the minority in such fashion. For two terms now there had been incidents when the Chief had pleaded ignorance, had claimed he hadn't voted, had changed his vote. Until now they had been isolated instances.

At the first conference of the term, in a prison case *(Younger v. Gilmore)*, the Chief had taken a position against the other six and, to Douglas's astonishment, attempted to assign the decision to himself.

Douglas had always been deferential to the Chief. As much as he despised Burger, he knew the Chief Justice's prestige determined the Court's: to an extent, its reputation could not be greater than his. Douglas might have differed with other Chief Justices, but he always respected their office. Occasionally, as in Warren's case, the Chief provided brilliant leadership. Douglas was not one to block a Chief's prerogatives; normally, he tended to his own business.

But the prison case had been too much. Douglas had simply gone ahead and assigned Marshall to write a majority *per curiam.* He had then informed Burger that he had made the assignment because the Chief had not been in the majority. The incident had hurt Burger's feelings. He had not voted at conference, he explained in a memo. He had merely given his preliminary view. By the time of the assignment, he had become a member of the majority. He would have drafted a fitting majority opinion. But that time, the Chief had backed down.

Since then, Douglas had let other misassignments slip by. "God, I miss Hugo," Douglas lamented to friends whenever Burger manipulated assignments. "Burger would never have dared pull that if Hugo were around." As senior Associate Justice, Black had helped keep the Chief within bounds. To Douglas's dismay, that role now fell almost exclusively to him.

Four misassignments at one time, however, was simply too much to let pass. Douglas was convinced that as the senior member of the majority, he should have assigned all four of the cases. What particularly bothered him was that the Chief had given the abortion cases to Blackmun, his personal ally. Blackmun had voted with the Chief nearly every time the previous term. The Chief might as well have assigned the abortion cases to himself.

On Saturday, December 18, Douglas drafted a scathing memo to Burger, with copies to the other Justices. He, not the Chief, should have assigned the opinions in four of the cases. And, Douglas added, he would assign the opinions as he saw fit.

The Chief's response was back in a day. He conceded error in two of the cases, but insisted that the voting in the two abortion cases was too complicated. "There were . . . literally not enough columns to mark up an accurate reflection of the voting," Burger wrote. "I therefore marked down no votes and said this was a case that would have to stand or fall on the writing, when it was done.

"That is still my view of how to handle these two sensitive cases, which, I might add, are quite probable candidates for reargument."

Douglas ascribed to Burger the most blatant political motives. Nixon favored restrictive abortion laws. Faced with the possibility that the Court might strike abortion laws down in a presidential-election year, the Chief wanted to stall the opinion, Douglas concluded.

Blackmun was by far the slowest writer on the Court. The year was nearly half over and he had yet to produce a first circulation in a simple business case that had been argued the first week (*Port of Portland v. U.S.*). It was the kind of case in which Douglas produced drafts within one week of conference. But in the abortion cases, Douglas had a deeper worry. The Chief was trying to manipulate the outcome.

Blackmun might circulate a draft striking portions of the restrictive abortion laws. But as a judicial craftsman, his work was crude. A poor draft would be likely to scare off Stewart, who was already queasy, and leave only four votes. Or if Blackmun himself were to desert the position—a distinct possibility—precious time would be lost. Either defection would leave only a four-man majority. It would be difficult to argue that such a major decision should be handed down on a 4-to-3 vote. There would be increasing pressure to put the cases over for rehearing with the two new Nixon Justices. This was no doubt exactly the sort of case that Nixon had in mind when he chose Powell and Rehnquist.

Blackmun was both pleased and frightened by the assignment. It was a no-win proposition. No matter what he wrote, the opinion would be controversial. Abortion was too emotional, the split in society too great. Either way, he would be hated and vilified.

But from Blackmun's point of view, the Chief had had little choice but to select him. Burger could not afford to take on such a controversial case himself, particularly from the minority. Douglas was the Court's mischievous liberal, the rebel, and couldn't be the author. Any abortion opinion Douglas wrote would be widely questioned outside the Court, and his extreme views might split rather than unify the existing majority. Lastly, Blackmun had noticed a deterioration in the quality of Douglas's opinions; they had become increasingly superficial.

Brennan was certainly as firm a vote for striking down the state abortion laws as there was on the Court. But Brennan was the Court's only Catholic. As such, Blackmun reasoned, he could not be expected to be willing to take the heat from Catholic anti-abortion groups. Marshall could not be the author for similar reasons: an opinion by the Court's only black could be unfairly perceived as specifically designed for blacks. That left only Stewart. Blackmun believed that Stewart would certainly relish the assignment, but he clearly had trouble going very far.

Blackmun was convinced that he alone had the medical background and sufficient patience to sift through the voluminous record for the scientific data on which to base a decision. He was deeply disturbed by Douglas's assumption that the Chief had some malicious intent in assigning the abortion cases to him. He was *not* a Minnesota Twin.

True, Blackmun had known the Chief since they were small children and had gone to Sunday school together. They had lived four or five blocks apart in the blue-collar Daytons Bluff section of St. Paul. Neither family had much money during the Depression. The two boys had kept in touch until Blackmun went to a technical high school.

Blackmun's seven years at Harvard, however, put the two men worlds apart. Burger had finished local college and night law school in six years and was already practicing law when Blackmun came back to clerk for a judge on the Court of Appeals. Blackmun was best man at Burger's wedding, but the two drifted apart again as they established very different law practices.

Blackmun tried to tell his story every chance he got. His hands in his pockets, jingling change uncomfortably, he would explain how he had practiced in Minneapolis, where large law firms concentrated on serving major American corporations. Burger had practiced in St. Paul, across the river, in the political, wheeler-dealer atmosphere of a state capital.

"A Minneapolis firm," Blackmun would say, "will never practice in St. Paul or vice versa." Left unsaid was the disdain so obvious in the Minneapolis legal community for St. Paul lawyers.

But Blackmun was a hesitant and reserved storyteller, and he was never sure that the others got the message. Douglas, however, should have realized by now that Harry Blackmun was no Warren Burger twin.

Blackmun had long thought Burger an uncontrollable, blustery braggart. Now, once again in close contact with him, he was at once put off and amused by the Chief's exaggerated pomposity, his callous disregard for the feelings of his colleagues, his self-aggrandizing style. "He's been doing that since he was four," he once told Stewart.

Blackmun was just as aware as Douglas was of the Chief's attempts to use his position to manipulate the Court. Douglas was correct to despise that sort of thing. But this time, Blackmun felt, Douglas was wrong. When he arrived at the Court, Blackmun had assumed the Chief's job as scrivener for the conference. Burger had finally given up trying to keep track of all the votes and positions taken in conference, and had asked Blackmun to keep notes and stay behind to brief the Clerk of the Court. Even then the Chief sometimes misstated the results. Blackmun would deftly field the Chief's hesitations, filling in when he faltered. When Burger misinformed the Clerk of the Court, Blackmun's cough would cue him.

"Do you recall what happened there, Harry?" the Chief would then say. "My notes seem to be a bit sporadic."

Blackmun would fill in the correct information as if Burger had initiated the request.

Part of the problem was that the Chief spread himself too thin. He accepted too many social, speaking and ceremonial engagements, and exhibited too little affection for the monastic, scholarly side of the Court's life. As a result, Burger was often unprepared for orals or conference. Too often, he had to wait and listen in order to figure out which issues were crucial to the outcome. His grasp of the cases came from the summaries, usually a page or less, of the cert memos his clerks prepared. The Chief rarely read the briefs or the record before oral argument.

The problem was compounded by Burger's willingness to change his position in conference, or his unwillingness to commit himself before he had figured out which side had a majority. Then, joining the majority, he could control the assignment. Burger had strained his relationship with everyone at the table to the breaking point. It was as offensive to Blackmun as it was to the others. But one had to understand the Chief. For all his faults, here was a self-made man who had come up the ladder rung by rung. Blackmun did not begrudge him his attempts at leadership.

The abortion assignment really amounted to nothing more than a request that Blackmun take first crack at organizing the issues. It was one of those times when the conference had floundered, when the briefs and oral arguments had been inadequate, when the seemingly decisive issue in the case, jurisdiction, had evaporated. The Court had been left holding the bull by the tail.

Blackmun was not so naïve as to think that the Chief had given him the abortion cases with the intention of having him find a broad constitutional right to abortion. But he was distressed by Douglas's implicit suggestion that he was unfit for the assignment or was somehow involved in a deception.

Blackmun also knew that he, after all, had a unique appreciation of the problems and strengths of the medical profession. At Mayo, he had watched as Doctors Edward C. Kendall and Philip S. Hench won the Nobel Prize for research in arthritis. He rejoiced with other doctors after their first successful heart-bypass operation, then suffered with them after they lost their next four patients. He sat up late nights with the surgical staff to review hospital deaths in biweekly meetings, and recalled them in detail. He grew to respect what dedicated physicians could accomplish. These had been terribly exciting years for Blackmun. He called them the best ten years of his life.

If a state licensed a physician to practice medicine, it was entrusting him with the right to make medical decisions. State laws restricting abortions interfered with those medical judgments. Physicians were always somewhat unsure about the possible legal ramifications of their judgments. To completely restrict an operation like abortion, normally no more dangerous than minor surgery, or to permit it only with the approval of a hospital committee or the concurrence of other doctors, was a needless infringement of the discretion of the medical profession.

Blackmun would do anything he could to reduce the anxiety of his colleagues except to spurn the assignment. The case was not so much a legal task as an opportunity for the Court to ratify the best possible medical opinion. He would take the first crack at the abortion case. At the least, he could prepare a memo to clarify the issues.

As was his custom, Douglas rushed through a first draft on the cases five days after conference. He decided not to circulate it, but to sit back and wait for Blackmun. He was still bitter toward Burger, whom he had taken to calling "this Chief," reserving "The Chief" as an accolade fitting only for retired Chief Justice Earl Warren. But Douglas broke his usual rule against lobbying and paid a visit to Blackmun. Though he would have much preferred that Brennan write the draft, he told Blackmun, "Harry, I would have assigned the opinion to you anyway."

Reassured, Blackmun withdrew to his regular hideaway, the Justices' second-floor library, where he worked through the winter and spring, initially without even a law clerk to help with research.

Brennan too had little choice but to wait for Blackmun's draft. But in the interval, he spotted a case that he felt might help Blackmun develop a constitutional grounding for a right to abortion. Brennan was writing a majority opinion overturning birth-control activist Bill Baird's conviction for distributing birth-control devices without a license (*Eisenstadt v. Baird*). He wanted to use the case to extend to individuals the right to privacy that was given to married couples by the 1965 Connecticut birth-control case.

Brennan was aware that he was unlikely to get agreement on

such a sweeping extension. He circulated his opinion with a carefully worded paragraph at the end. "If the right to privacy means anything, it is the right of the individual, married or single, to be free from unwarranted government intrusion into matters so fundamentally affecting a person as the decision whether to bear or beget a child."

That case dealt only with contraception—the decision to "beget" a child. He included the reference to the decision to "bear" a child with the abortion case in mind. Brennan hoped the language would help establish a constitutional basis, under the right to privacy, for a woman's right to abortion.

Since the last paragraph was not the basis for the decision, Stewart could join it without renouncing his dissent in the 1965 case. Brennan got Stewart's vote.

But Blackmun was holding back. The Chief was lobbying Blackmun not to join Brennan's draft. Brennan's clerks urged their boss to lobby Blackmun.

Brennan refused. Blackmun reminded him, he said, of former Justice Charles E. Whittaker, who had been paralyzed by indecisiveness. Whittaker's indecision had ended in a nervous breakdown and his resignation. Former Justice Felix Frankfurter had misunderstood Whittaker's indecision and had spent hours lobbying him. Instead of influencing him, Frankfurter had drawn Whittaker's resentment. No, Brennan said, he would not lobby Blackmun.

Blackmun finally decided not to join Brennan's opinion, but simply to concur in the result. That worried Brennan. Without adopting some logic similar to that provided in the contraception case, Blackmun would have difficulty establishing a right to abortion on grounds of privacy.

With the official arrival of Powell and Rehnquist, the Chief scheduled a January conference to discuss which cases should be put over for reargument before the new nine-man Court. Burger suggested that cases with a 4-to-3 vote should be reargued. His list included the abortion cases, as well as the Florida adult-bookstore case that had settled the question of federal jurisdiction.

Douglas, Brennan, Marshall and Stewart objected vigorously.

The Court had an obligation to dispose of every case it could, Douglas argued, leaving the second half of the term free for important cases they had still to deal with, including the death penalty.

The Chief was equally determined. The 4-to-3 cases, particularly those in which two new conservative members might likely change the outcome, should be put over. As always, the majority would determine what cases to put over, but Burger argued that the new Justices should be allowed to vote on whether these cases should be reargued.

That was impossible, Douglas insisted. The new Justices could not vote. Their votes could determine the outcome of the very cases being debated. The internal operating rules, though they were unwritten, must be inviolable.

White said it was important that the Court not discredit itself by deciding cases one way and then shifting and deciding them the other way. Two votes added to the minority side of a 4-to-3 would become a new 5-to-4 majority. The others stirred uncomfortably in their seats. They were unsure of their ground and no one wanted to force the issue.

Powell and Rehnquist said they would prefer not to participate in any vote on whether to hold the cases over for reargument. It was up to the other seven. Powell added that he wasn't sure how he would come out on the cases, particularly the abortion cases. They should not be reargued for him.

One 4-to-3 case involved an antiwar demonstrator who had cursed at a policeman (*Gooding v. Wilson*). The Chief said it should be reargued.

Douglas was sure the vote had been 5 to 2. "Who was the third vote to reverse?" he asked.

"White," the Chief replied.

His jaw jutting out, White stared at the Chief. No, he was with the majority, he stated. The issue of reargument was finally dropped.

Brennan was relieved. In fact, they didn't even have a draft in the abortion case. Maybe they were getting ahead of themselves. If Blackmun and Stewart shifted positions, then he, Douglas and

Marshall might be on the short end of a 4-to-3, themselves demanding that the abortion cases be put over.

Blackmun spent his time—apart from oral argument, conferences and a bare minimum of office routine—in the Justices' library. Awesome quantities of medical, as well as legal, books were regularly carried in. But all indications pointed toward no circulation of a first draft until much later in the spring.

Burger had not yet given up on the federal jurisdiction issue. If he could derail the opinion on this important subject, the abortion issue would not have to be decided. On January 25, 1972, the Chief circulated a memo and a historical analysis raising three problems with the federal jurisdiction issue settled in the Florida bookstore case that Douglas had assigned to Stewart.

Stewart was not yet prepared to respond. Instead of circulating his opinion, he circulated a memo that Harlan had prepared over the summer on the history of the issue.

Douglas then had one of his clerks get out an elaborate memo on the issue. Unusually detailed and well documented, it responded to each of the questions the Chief had raised. The four-member majority on jurisdiction held firm.

In early April, since several significant opinions remained to be settled, the Chief called for a special conference to deal with the crush of argued and reargued cases. It had to be worked in around the Chief's extensive ceremonial calendar, Douglas's speaking engagements, and long-standing commitments of the other Justices. Burger's secretary called each chamber, double- and triple-checked, and a time was finally set for early in the week.

Shortly before the conference, Marshall asked for a postponement in order to attend a family funeral. A new date, Wednesday, April 12, was set and confirmed. But when Marshall returned from the funeral, he was startled to learn that the conference had taken place at the original time without him. He called the Chief's office. Had not the conference been rescheduled for April 12?

Yes, Burger's secretary explained. But in the interim, the Chief had learned that former Justice James F. Byrnes's funeral had been scheduled for April 12. So the Chief had decided to hold the conference according to the original schedule.*

Marshall was weary of the Chief's unilateral decision making for the conference. He dictated a short memo. No conference had ever been held before, under any Chief Justice, without informing all members of the Court. Now, under Warren Burger, the Court had taken to holding conferences without one of its members.

The Chief's racial priorities were clear, Marshall sniped privately. A chance to appear in public with the President, who had also attended the Byrnes funeral, was obviously more important to Burger than Marshall's attendance at conference.

The other Justices were mortified. They had not objected on Marshall's behalf. The conference was repeated, every vote retaken. No decision came out differently.

While Blackmun continued to labor on the abortion decision, the Court, now at full strength, took up a case involving antiwar demonstrators who had distributed literature at a shopping center in Portland, Oregon (Lloyd v. Tanner). The protesters had been ejected by shopping center guards.

The Chief was unsure of his position. Technically, a shopping center was private property. But the demonstrators were exercising free speech in what was, in effect, a public place, with numerous stores and thousands of people coming and going all day. Was the demonstrators' action protected by the First Amendment?

Marshall argued that the case was "on all fours" (identical) with his opinion in 1968 (Almalgamated Food Employees Union v. Logan Valley Plaza), in which he had written that union pickets could not be stopped from picketing a grocery store in a private shopping center. Marshall was proud of that decision. Now, he spoke firmly and knowledgeably about the case before the Court. The outcome should be obvious.

---

* After retiring from the Court, Byrnes had become governor of South Carolina. In the famous Brown school cases he had personally hired John W. Davis, the preeminent Supreme Court advocate of his time, to argue the segregationist position against Marshall, who represented the Inc. Fund.

Douglas, Brennan and Stewart agreed. White had some reservations. There was a limit to free speech on private property.
Blackmun, Powell and Rehnquist, each with a slightly different
view, sided with White.

With the Chief still undecided, the vote seemed to be tied 4 to 4,
and Marshall had little doubt as to where Burger would finally
come out. He returned to his chambers that day a beaten man. For
the first time, his clerks saw him truly depressed about the future
of the Court. Powell and Rehnquist were going to make a big difference. It was not just a close vote in one case. It was the first
wave of full-scale revisionism. The work of the Warren Court
would be destroyed.

Douglas returned to his chambers, however, with a different
view of the tie. Since the Chief was apparently undecided, Douglas was the senior Justice with a position in the case. He would assign. Because of Marshall's expertise and interest in the area,
Douglas selected him to write the *Lloyd* opinion.

But on April 24, with Douglas out of town, a memo from the
Chief came around assigning Powell to write the Lloyd case. When
Douglas returned, he was incensed. He prepared a new memo.
His careless and crimped scrawl was ordinarily legible only to the
trained eye. Now he hacked paragraphs on his legal pad so quickly
that the words flowed together.

"Dear Chief Justice:" he wrote instead of the usual "Dear Chief."

> You apparently misunderstand. *Lloyd* is already assigned to
> Thurgood and he's at work on an opinion. Whether he will command
> a majority, no one knows.
>
> Under the Constitution and Acts of Congress, there are no provi-
> sions for assignment of opinions. Historically, the Chief Justice has
> made the assignment if he is in the majority. Historically, the senior
> in the majority assigns the opinion if the Chief Justice is in the mi-
> nority.
>
> You led the Conference battle against affirmance and that is your
> privilege. But it is also the privilege of the majority, absent the Chief
> Justice, to make the assignment. Hence, [the *Lloyd* case] was as-
> signed and is assigned.

The tragedy of compromising on this simple procedure is illustrated by last Term's *Swann* [The Charlotte busing case]. You who
were a minority of two kept the opinion for yourself and faithfully
wrote the minority position which the majority could not accept.
Potter wrote the majority view and a majority agreed to it. It was not
circulated because we thought you should see it. After much effort
your minority opinion was transformed, the majority view prevailed,
and the result was unanimous.

But *Swann* illustrated the wasted time and effort and the frayed relations which result when the traditional assignment procedure is not
followed.

If the Conference wants to authorize you to assign all opinions,
that will be a new procedure. Though opposed to it, I will acquiesce.
But unless we make a frank reversal in our policy, any group in the
majority should and must make the assignment.

This is a two-edge sword. Byron (fifth in seniority) might well head
up five members of the Court, you, Bill Brennan, Potter Stewart and
I being the minority; and we might feel very strongly about it. But in
that event it is for Byron to make the assignment. It is not for us in
the minority to try to outwit Byron by saying "I reserve my vote" and
then recast it to control the assignment. That only leads to a frayed
and bitter Court full of needless strains and quarrels.

[The *Lloyd* case] stays assigned to Thurgood.

Douglas omitted the ordinary closing salutation and directed
that copies of the memo, with its mocking, patronizing tone, should
go to all the Justices.

There were no more cases to be argued. Douglas had pitched his
battle on the last assignment of the year. Never a man to procrasti-
nate before wreaking havoc, he sent the memo out on Monday,
May 1.

Brennan and Marshall were worried. In principle, Douglas was
right. They too doubted the Chief's sincerity in reserving his vote.
As usual, he was maneuvering to make sure he could assign the
case regardless of how the vote went. But if the vote was 4 to 4 with
the Chief reserved, then the Court would go whichever way the
Chief voted. If Burger assigned Powell, Powell might as well write

it. Marshall could write all he wanted, he would never command a majority.

Marshall realized that he was writing his opinion as a dissent. There was always a chance that he might win White's vote, but he was very pessimistic about it since he had been shooting for White's vote all year without much success. All through the term, one of White's clerks had tried to convince Marshall's clerks that he could deliver White's vote on a certain case if Marshall would change a particular sentence. Bullshit, Marshall said. All of them—Marshall, his clerk and White's clerk—knew that Byron White listened to Byron White and to no one else. Marshall was bitterly resigned that he was on the losing side in the *Lloyd* case. And Douglas was not helping with this frontal attack on the Chief.

The Chief was surprised by Douglas's memo. It had never occurred to him that he might be wrong on this assignment. He wrote a note explaining patiently that the case, as he saw it, was 5 to 4 with himself the senior in the majority. Powell would write. Anyone else could also write. They would see who got five votes.

Behind Douglas's back, Burger was less diplomatic. Any unnamed person who thought he was assigning cases improperly was "stupid" or "lying," he told other Justices and friends—at best, simply wrong.

Powell's opinion declared that private property rights were precisely that, private. In the balance, they must prevail over the First Amendment rights of protesters. It won the expected five votes. Powell had carefully sidestepped overruling Marshall's 1968 opinion directly. But he infuriated Marshall by using language from the dissenting opinions in the earlier case. How could Powell claim he was not overruling when he had taken the dissenting position almost exactly, Marshall wondered.

Marshall had his clerk rework his dissent, adding uncharacteristically harsh words. "I am aware that the composition of this Court has radically changed in four years. The fact remains that [the earlier case, *Logan Valley*] is binding unless and until it is overruled."

Marshall was so irritated that he switched his vote from a Powell opinion in the case *(Kleindienst v. Mandel)* of a Belgian Communist barred from receiving a visa to speak in the United States.

Marshall was now sure that the First Amendment was threatened by the Nixon Court. The only choice was to stand firmly with Douglas and Brennan.

Blackmun began each day by breakfasting with his clerks in the Court's public cafeteria, and clerks from the other chambers had a standing invitation to join them. Blackmun would often spot a clerk from another chamber eating alone and invite him over. He seemed, at first, the most open, unassuming and gracious of the Justices.

Breakfast-table conversation generally began with sports, usually baseball, and then moved on to the morning's headlines. There was an unspoken rule that any discussion of cases was off limits. Where other Justices might openly debate cases with the clerks, Blackmun awkwardly sidestepped each attempt. The law in general was similarly out of bounds. Blackmun turned the most philosophical of discussions about law around to his own experience, or to the clerk's family, or the performance of a younger sibling in school.

The clerks in his own chambers saw a different side of Blackmun which betrayed more of the pressure that he felt. The stories were petty. An office window left open all night might set him off on a tirade. It was not the security that worried Blackmun, but the broken social contract—all clerks were supposed to close all windows each night. Number-two pencils, needle-sharp, neatly displayed in the pencil holder, need include only one number three or a cracked point to elicit a harsh word. If Blackmun wanted a document photocopied, and somehow the wrong one came back, he might simply fling it aside. An interruption, even for some important question, might be repulsed testily.

The mystery of the Blackmun personality deepened. His outbursts varied in intensity and usually passed quickly. "Impatient moods," his secretary called them. But they made life more difficult; they added an extra tension.

Yet none of his Court family—clerks, secretaries or his messenger—judged Blackmun harshly. They all knew well enough the extraordinary pressures, real and imagined, that he worked under.

From his first day at the Court, Blackmun had felt unworthy, unqualified, unable to perform up to standard. He felt he could equal the Chief and Marshall, but not the others. He became increasingly withdrawn and professorial. He did not enjoy charting new paths for the law. He was still learning. The issues were too grave, the information too sparse. Each new question was barely answered, even tentatively, when two more questions appeared on the horizon. Blackmun knew that his colleagues were concerned about what they perceived as his indecisiveness. But what others saw as an inability to make decisions, he felt to be a deliberate withholding of final judgment until all the facts were in, all the arguments marshaled, analyzed, documented.

It was a horribly lonely task. Blackmun worked by himself, beginning with a long memo from one of his clerks, reading each of the major briefs, carefully digesting each of the major opinions that circulated, laboriously drafting his own opinions, checking each citation himself, refining his work through a dozen drafts to take into account each Justice's observations. He was unwilling, moreover, to debate the basic issues in a case, even in chambers with his own clerks. He preferred that they write him memos.

Wearing a gray or blue cardigan sweater, Blackmun hid away in the recesses of the Justices' library, and his office had instructions not to disturb him there. The phone did not ring there, and not even the Chief violated his solitude. Working at a long mahogany table lined on the opposite edge with a double row of books, Blackmun took meticulous notes. He spent most of his time sorting facts and fitting them to the law in a desperate attempt to discover inevitable conclusions. He tried to reduce his risks by mastering every detail, as if the case were some huge math problem. Blackmun felt that if all the steps were taken, there could be only one answer.

These abortion cases were his greatest challenge since he came to the Court. Beyond the normal desire to produce an opinion that would win the respect of his peers in the legal community, Blackmun also wanted an opinion that the medical community would accept, one that would free physicians to exercise their professional judgment.

As general counsel at the Mayo Clinic, Blackmun had advised the staff on the legality of abortions the hospital had performed. Many of them would not have qualified under the Texas and Georgia laws now in question.

Blackmun plowed through both common law and the history of English and American law on the subject. He was surprised to find that abortion had been commonly accepted for thousands of years, and that only in the nineteenth century had it become a crime in the United States. At that time, abortion had been a very risky operation, often fatal. The criminal laws had been enacted largely to protect pregnant women.

The use of antiseptics and the availability of antibiotics now made abortion relatively safe, particularly in the first few months of pregnancy. The mortality rates for women undergoing early abortions were presently lower than the mortality rates for women with normal childbirths. That medical reality was central for Blackmun. It was itself a strong medical justification for permitting early abortions.

A decision to abort was one that Blackmun hoped he would never face in his own family. He presumed that his three daughters felt that early abortions should be allowed. He claimed to be unsure of his wife Dottie's position. But she told one of his clerks, who favored lifting the restrictions, that she was doing everything she could to encourage her husband in that direction. "You and I are working on the same thing," she said. "Me at home and you at work."

By mid-May, after five months of work, Blackmun was still laboring over his memorandum. Finally, he let one of his clerks look over a draft. As usual, he made it clear that he did not want any editing. The clerk was astonished. It was crudely written and poorly organized. It did not settle on any analytical framework, nor did it explain on what basis Blackmun had arrived at the apparent conclusion that women had a right to privacy, and thus a right to abortion. Blackmun had avoided extending the right of privacy, or stating that the right to abortion stemmed from that right. He seemed to be saying that a woman could get an abortion in the early period of pregnancy. The reason, however, was lost in a convoluted discussion of the "viability of the fetus," the point at which the fetus could live outside the womb. Blackmun had added the general notion that as the length of the pregnancy increased, the states' interest in regulating or prohibiting abortions also increased. But there was no real guidance from which conclusions could be drawn. Blackmun had simply asserted that the Texas law was vague and thus unconstitutional.

The clerk realized that the opinion could not settle any constitutional question. It did not assert, or even imply, that abortion restrictions in the early months of pregnancy were unconstitutional. The result of this opinion would be that restrictive laws, if properly defined by the states, could be constitutional.

The draft seemed to fly in the face of Blackmun's statements to his clerks. "We want to definitely solve this," he had told them. But he seemed to be avoiding a solution.

In the Georgia case, he had found that the law infringed on a doctor's professional judgment, his right to give advice to his patients. Blackmun proceeded from the doctor's point of view; a woman's right to seek and receive medical advice did not seem an issue.

Blackmun's clerk, who favored an opinion that would establish a woman's constitutional right to abortion, began the laborious task of trying to rehabilitate the draft. But Blackmun resisted any modification of his basic reasoning or his conclusions. He circulated the memo to all chambers with few changes.

Stewart was disturbed by the draft. Aside from its inelegant construction and language, it seemed to create a *new* affirmative constitutional right to abortion that was not rooted in any part of the Constitution. Stewart had been expecting a majority opinion. Blackmun's memo did not even have the tone of an opinion, merely of a tentative discussion.

Stewart decided to write his own concurrence, specifying that family-planning decisions, including early abortions, were among the rights encompassed by the Ninth Amendment, which says that the people retain other, unspecified rights beyond those enumerated in the Constitution. Rather than identify the rights that women or doctors have, Stewart preferred to say that states could not properly interfere in individuals' decisions to have early abortions. He circulated his memo two weeks after Blackmun's but immediately joined Blackmun's original.

Douglas saw no shortage of problems with the Blackmun draft, but Blackmun had come a long way. At least it was a step in the right direction. Though Douglas was still holding on to his concurrence, he did not circulate it. Instead, he joined Blackmun.

At the time, the Court was considering an antitrust case against a utility company, the Otter Tail Power Company, which operated in Minnesota. Douglas saw an opportunity to flatter Blackmun. "Harry, you're not a Minnesota Twin with the Chief," he told him. "I am the real Minnesota Twin. . . . We were both born in Minnesota and you were not" (*Otter Tail Power Co. v. U.S.*).

Blackmun appreciated the point.

"Furthermore, Harry, I belong to the Otter Tail County regulars. You can't belong, because you weren't born there."

Douglas regaled Blackmun with stories of his father's life as an itinerant preacher in Otter Tail County, and he praised Blackmun's abortion draft. It was one of the finest presentations of an issue he had ever seen, he said.

Blackmun was ecstatic. Douglas, the greatest living jurist, had freed him of the stigma of being Burger's double. Soon, Blackmun had five votes—his own and those of Douglas, Brennan, Marshall and Stewart. It was one more than he needed; it would have been a majority even if Powell and Rehnquist had participated.

For White the term had its ups and downs like any other year at the Court. He had been a fierce competitor all his life. He loved to take control of a case, pick out the weaknesses in the other Justices' positions, and then watch them react to his own twists and turns as he pushed his own point of view. When he could not, which was often, he took his frustrations to the third-floor gym to play in the clerks' regular full-court basketball game.

Muscling out men thirty years his junior under the boards, White delighted in playing a more competitive game than they did. He dominated the games by alternating savage and effective drives to the basket with accurate two-hand push shots from twenty feet.

White consistently pushed off the clerk trying to cover him, calling every conceivable foul against the hapless clerk, while bitching about every foul called against himself. He regularly took the impermissible third step before shooting. The game was serious business for White. Each man was on his own. Teamwork was valuable in order to win, not for its own sake.

One Friday afternoon White was out of position for a rebound, but he went up throwing a hip. A clerk pulled in the ball and White came crashing down off balance and injured his ankle.

The Justice came to the office on crutches the next Monday: he would be off the basketball court for the rest of the season. He asked the clerks to keep the reason for his injury secret. The clerks bought him a Fussball game, a modern version of the ancient game of skittles. It was competition, so White enjoyed it, but it lacked for him the thrill of a contact sport like basketball—or law.

On Friday, May 26, Byron White read a draft dissent to Blackmun's abortion decision that one of his clerks had prepared. He then remolded it to his liking. The structure of Blackmun's opinion was juvenile; striking the Texas law for vagueness was simply stupid. The law might have several defects, but vagueness was not among them. The law could not be more specific in delineating the circumstance when abortion was available—it was only to protect the life of the mother.

Blackmun was disturbed by White's attack, but whether it made sense or not, it showed him that he had more work to do. The more he studied and agonized over his own memo, the less pleased he was. He needed more information, more facts, more insight. What was the history of the proscription in the Hippocratic oath which forbade doctors from performing abortions? What was the medical state of the art of sustaining a fetus outside the womb? When did life really begin? When was a fetus fully viable? What were the positions of the American Medical Association, the American Psychiatric Association, the American Public Health Association?

These and dozens of other questions plagued Blackmun. His opinion needed to be stronger. It needed more votes, which could mean wider public acceptance. A nine-man court was essential to bring down such a controversial opinion. "I think we can get Powell," he told his clerks.

One Saturday toward the end of May, the Chief paid Blackmun a visit, leaving his armed chauffeur-bodyguard in the outer office. Blackmun's clerks waited anxiously for hours to find out what case the Chief was lobbying. The Chief finally left, but Blackmun also departed without a word to his clerks. The next week, the Chief shifted sides to provide the crucial fifth vote for Blackmun's majority in an antitrust case against professional baseball (*Flood v. Kuhn*).

The following Saturday, June 3, Blackmun drafted a memorandum withdrawing his abortion opinion. It was already late in the term, he wrote. Such a sensitive case required more research, more consideration. It would take him some time both to accommodate the suggestions of those in the majority, and to respond to the dissenters. Perhaps it would be best if the cases were reargued in the fall. He asked that all copies of his draft memo be returned.

Douglas was once again enraged. The end of the year always involved a crunch. Of course, there was tremendous pressure to put out major opinions without the time to fully refine them. That was the nature of their work. The pressure affected them all. It was typical that Blackmun could not make up his mind and let his opinion go. Douglas had heard that the Chief had been lobbying Blackmun. This time, Burger had gone too far. The opinion had five firm votes. It ought to come down. It was not like cases with only four votes that might change when Powell's and Rehnquist's votes were added. Douglas also did not want to give the Chief the summer to sway Blackmun.

Burger was taking the position that there were now five votes to put the case over to the next term—Blackmun, White, Powell, Rehnquist and himself. Douglas couldn't believe it. Burger and White were in the minority; they should have no say in what the majority did. And Powell and Rehnquist had not taken part; obviously they could not vote on whether the case should be put over.

The looming confrontation worried Blackmun. There were no written rules on such questions, and Douglas's apparent willingness to push to a showdown would further inflame the issue.

Finally, Blackmun turned to Brennan, who was sympathetic. Obviously the opinion could not come down if its author did not want it to come down. But Brennan also wanted it out as soon as possible.

Blackmun said he understood that Douglas did not trust him, but insisted that he was firm for striking down the abortion law. The vote would go the same way the next year. They might even pick up Powell. That would make the result more acceptable to the public. He would be able to draft a better opinion over the summer.

Brennan was not so certain of Blackmun's firmness. At the same time, he did not want to alienate him. He agreed to tell Douglas that he too was going to vote to put the case over for reargument. He was fairly certain Marshall and Stewart would join. That would leave Douglas protesting alone.

Douglas was not pleased by the news of Brennan's defection. But the battle was not yet over. He dashed off a memo, rushed it to the secretaries for typing and to the printers for a first draft. This time, Douglas threatened to play his ace. If the conference insisted on putting the cases over for reargument, he would dissent from such an order, and he would publish the full text of his dissent. Douglas reiterated the protest he had made in December about the Chief's assigning the case to Blackmun, Burger's response and his subsequent intransigence. The senior member of the majority should have assigned the case, Douglas said, and continued:

> When, however, the minority seeks to control the assignment, there is a destructive force at work in the Court. When a Chief Justice tries to bend the Court to his will by manipulating assignments, the integrity of the institution is imperilled.
>
> Historically, this institution has been composed of fiercely independent men with fiercely opposed views. There have been—and will always be—clashes of views. But up to now the Conference, though deeply disagreeing on legal and constitutional issues, has been a group marked by good-will. Up until now a majority view, no matter how unacceptable to the minority, has been honored as such. And up until now the incumbents have honored and revered the institution more than their own view of the public good.

Perhaps the purpose of THE CHIEF JUSTICE, a member of the minority in the *Abortion Cases*, in assigning the opinions was to try to keep control of the merits. If that was the aim, he was unsuccessful. Opinions in these two cases have been circulated and each commands the votes of five members of the Court. Those votes are firm, the Justices having spent many, many hours since last October mulling over every detail of the cases. The cases should therefore be announced.

The plea that the cases be reargued is merely strategy by a minority somehow to suppress the majority view with the hope that exigencies of time will change the result. That might be achieved of course by death or conceivably retirement.

Douglas knew a fifth Nixon appointment was a real possibility on a Court with a seventy-four-year-old man with a pacemaker; with Marshall, who was chronically ill; and with Brennan, who occasionally threatened to quit.

But that kind of strategy dilutes the integrity of the Court and makes the decisions here depend on the manipulative skills of a Chief Justice. The *Abortion Cases* are symptomatic. This is an election year. Both political parties have made abortion an issue. What the parties say or do is none of our business. We sit here not to make the path of any candidate easier or more difficult. We decide questions only on their constitutional merits. To prolong these *Abortion Cases* into the next election would in the eyes of many be a political gesture unworthy of the Court.

Each of us is sovereign in his own right. Each arrived on his own. Each is beholden to no one.

Borrowing a line from a speech he had given in September in Portland, Douglas then made it clear that, despite what he had said earlier, he did in fact view the Chief and Blackmun as Nixon's Minnesota Twins. "Russia once gave its Chief Justice two votes; but that was too strong even for the Russians. . . .

"I dissent with the deepest regret that we are allowing the consensus of the Court to be frustrated."

Douglas refined his draft three times, circulated it, and left for Goose Prairie.

The Court erupted in debate over whether Douglas was bluffing or was really willing to publish the document. Though sympathetic to his views, Brennan, Marshall and Stewart could not believe that Douglas would go through with it. No one in the history of the Court had published such a dissent. The Chief might be a scoundrel, but making public the Court's inner machinations was a form of treason. And the reference to the Russian Chief Justice with two votes was particularly rough. They pleaded with Douglas to reconsider. His dissent would undermine the Court's credibility, the principal source of its power. Its strength derived from the public belief that the Court was trustworthy, a nonpolitical deliberative body. Did he intend to undermine all that?

Douglas insisted. He would publish what he felt like publishing. And he would publish this if the request to put over the abortion decision was not withdrawn.

But, the others argued, what good would it do to drag their internal problems into public view?

It would have a sobering influence on Blackmun, Douglas retorted. It would make it harder for him to change his mind over the summer.

Brennan's impatience with Douglas turned to anger. Douglas had become an intellectually lazy, petulant, prodigal child. He was not providing leadership. Douglas was never around when he was needed. His departure for Goose Prairie was typical. He was not even, for that matter, pulling his share of the load, though he certainly contributed more than his share to the tension. The ultimate source of conflict was the Chief. But Douglas too was at fault.

Finally, Brennan gave up arguing.

Blackmun then took it up, pleading with Douglas to reconsider. He insisted that he was committed to his opinion. He would bring it down the same way the next term; more research would perhaps pick up another vote.

Douglas was unconvinced. He needed time to think it over. His clerks would remain instructed to publish the opinion if the cases were put over for reargument.

But Blackmun had made his point. Douglas finally decided that he couldn't publish. It would endanger next term's vote on the abortion cases.

No longer speaking to his own clerks, whom he blamed for slow mail delivery to Goose Prairie, Douglas called Brennan and told him to have his dissent held. A memo came around to the Justices from Douglas's chamber asking for all the copies back.

The conference agreed to put over the abortion cases, but they would not announce their decision until the final day of the term.

Earlier at the March 24 conference, Stewart had found himself the senior member of a majority for the first time in his career. The case (*Flood v. Kuhn*) concerned Curt Flood, a former star outfielder for the St. Louis Cardinals, who had refused to be traded to the Philadelphia Phillies. He had filed an antitrust suit against professional baseball. Flood wanted to break the reserve clause that allowed teams to trade baseball players without their consent.

Oral argument had failed to clarify the issues. Former Justice Arthur Goldberg, in his first appearance before the Court since resigning in 1965 to become Ambassador to the United Nations, had offered such a poor presentation of Flood's case that his former colleagues were embarrassed.

Powell withdrew from the case, because he held stock in Anheuser-Busch, Inc., whose principal owner, August Busch, Jr., also owned the St. Louis Cardinals. The Chief, Douglas and Brennan voted for Flood, leaving Stewart to assign the opinion for a five-member majority.

Stewart thought that the opinion would be easy to write. The Court had twice before decided that baseball was exempt from the antitrust laws. It was, Stewart said, "a case of '*stare decisis*' double dipped." There seemed little chance of losing the majority as long as the two earlier precedents were followed. He assigned the opinion to Blackmun.

Blackmun was delighted. Apart from the abortion assignment, he felt that he had suffered under the Chief, receiving poor opinions to write, including more than his share of tax and Indian cases. He thought that if the antitrust laws were applied to baseball, its unique position as the national pastime would be undermined. A devoted fan first of the Chicago Cubs and later the Minnesota Twins, he welcomed this chance to be one of the boys.

With his usual devotion to detail, Blackmun turned to the *Baseball Encyclopedia,* which he kept on the shelf behind his desk. He set down minimum lifetime performance standards—numbers of games played, lifetime batting averages or earned-run averages. He picked out representative stars from each of the teams, positions, and decades of organized baseball. Then, closeted away in the Justices' library, Blackmun wrote an opening section that was an ode to baseball. In three extended paragraphs, he traced the history of professional baseball. He continued with a list of "the many names, celebrated for one reason or another, that have sparked the diamond and its environs and that have provided timber for recaptured thrills, for reminiscence and comparisons, and for conversation and anticipation in season and off season: Ty Cobb, Babe Ruth . . ." There were more than seventy names. "The list seems endless," Blackmun wrote. He paid homage to the verse "Casey at the Bat," and other baseball literature. When he had finished, Blackmun circulated his draft.

Brennan was surprised. He thought Blackmun had been in the library researching the abortion cases, not playing with baseball cards.

One of Rehnquist's clerks called Blackmun's chambers and joked that Camilo Pascual, a former Washington Senators pitcher, should have been included in the list of greats.

Blackmun's clerk phoned back the next day. "The Justice recalls seeing Pascual pitch and remembers his fantastic curve ball. But he pulled out his Encyclopedia and looked up his record. He decided Pascual's 174 wins were not enough. It is difficult to make these judgments of who to include but Justice Blackmun felt that Pascual is just not in the same category with Christy Matthewson's 373 wins. I hope you will understand."

Calling Blackmun's chambers to request that some favorite player be included became a new game for the clerks.

Stewart was embarrassed that he had assigned the opinion to Blackmun. He tried to nudge him into recognizing the inappropriateness of the opening section, jokingly telling him that he would go along with the opinion if Blackmun would add a member of Stewart's home-town team, the Cincinnati Reds.

Blackmun added a Red.

Marshall registered his protest. The list included no black baseball players. Blackmun explained that most of the players on his list antedated World War II. Blacks had been excluded from the major leagues until 1947.

That was the point exactly, Marshall replied.

Three black players were added—Jackie Robinson, Roy Campanella and Satchel Paige.

Marshall decided to switch anyhow and write his own opinion in Flood's favor. The Court was now split 4 to 4, and word circulated that White was considering following Marshall. That would give him a majority.

White owed a great deal to professional sports. His career in football had paid for a first-rate law school education. He remembered the years he had spent touring the country playing football. In those days, teams were real teams, brotherhoods of young men. It was different now. There were too many prima donnas, concerned only with their own statistics. White had difficulty feeling sorry for Curt Flood, who had turned down a $100,000 annual salary.

The antitrust issues were not easy in the case. White thought that if the federal laws did not apply, state antitrust laws might. His clerks used his hesitation to negotiate small changes in the Marshall opinion. White would probably join if the changes were made, one clerk offered.

When Marshall balked at a change that seemed trivial, his clerk protested that it was necessary to get White's vote.

"Says who?" Marshall asked.

A White clerk, he was told.

"He'll never join," Marshall responded.

Finally, White indicated he would stay with Blackmun's opinion against Flood. But he flatly refused to join the section listing the baseball greats.

Blackmun ignored the insult. He still had only four votes. If the tie stood, no opinion would be published.

At the end of May, Powell's clerks made a last-ditch effort to get him back in the case. They knew that he favored Flood's position. Since he would be voting against the major leagues, he could not be accused of a conflict of interest, his clerks argued. He would only be hurting his own interests. It was in fact possible that he could be accused of conflict if he did not vote.

No, Powell told them. He was out and he would stay out.

The Court was still deadlocked in the last half of May. After all his work, it seemed that Blackmun was to be deprived of his opinion. The Chief's Saturday visit to Blackmun, and Blackmun's subsequent withdrawal of the abortion opinion, had spawned vicious rumors among the clerks of vote trading. Then, as the term drew to a close, Burger announced that he would switch to the Blackmun opinion in the Flood case, giving him the fifth vote. He too, however, initially declined to join the first section.

After the opinion had come down, a clerk asked Blackmun why he hadn't included Mel Ott, the famous New York Giants right fielder on his list of baseball greats.

Blackmun insisted that he had included Ott.

The clerk said that the name was not in the printed opinion.

Blackmun said he would never forgive himself.

Earlier in the term, White's clerks had quickly fallen into the routine of Court life. Metal library carts full of cert petitions rolled into the chambers each week, and, as the term progressed, the time needed for processing each petition dropped from hours to minutes. But the improved pace did little to reduce the boredom of sifting through endless formalized pleas. Only the obscenity cases provided a break in the monotony. Many of these petitions were accompanied by the exhibits from the original trials—full-length motion pictures, tiny reels of peep-show film, boxes of magazines, books, an occasional set of glossy photos or playing cards. The exhibits circulated among the chambers for perusal by clerks and Justices.

As one of White's clerks went through the exhibits in two cases (*Hartstein v. Missouri* and *Wiener v. California*), his interest went beyond mere titillation.

In 1967, the Court had given up a decade-long effort to define obscenity, and acknowledged the subjectivity of the task. It had declared *(Redrup v. New York)* that any material held not to be obscene by a majority of the Justices, regardless of their personal definitions of obscenity, was protected by the First Amendment. The Court had since reversed more than two dozen obscenity convictions under the *Redrup* decision.

In the pending cases, White's clerk checked to see whether the material violated his boss's personal definition of hard-core pornography. It was a definition that White had never written into an opinion—no erect penises, no intercourse, no oral or anal sodomy. For White, no erections and no insertions equaled no obscenity. His clerk noted also that there was no evidence that the materials had been shown to minors or adults who had not willingly sought out the material. So he typed out his recommendation: "Reverse on Redrup." The lower court decision holding the materials obscene would be reversed without an opinion or oral argument. The Court would not further confuse the lower courts by expressing the Justices' lack of agreement. The clerk noted that White need not view the exhibits. They were clearly not obscene.

White sat at his oversized, glass-topped partners' desk reviewing his clerk's recommendations. When he came to the obscenity cases—and the recommendation that he skip viewing the exhibits—White bellowed, "Are you kidding?" He got up and went into the clerk's office, standing next to the chair reserved for him there, his feet apart as if he were ready for a physical challenge. Above the chair there were two Daumier prints of a famous Paris obscenity trial; White had bought them in Europe. One portrayed a woman flashing her breasts at a panel of judges, who reeled back in horror. White had given a third print to Brennan, who had put it in a closet.

White's clerks often urged him to adopt the absolutist First Amendment position of Black and Douglas. They would hold that any exceptions to the First Amendment put the Court on a "slippery slope," where one exception justified another, and then another, until there would be little, if anything, left of the First Amendment.

As often as they brought it up, White insisted he would have none of it. "Don't give me that 'slippery slope' argument again," he would say. One step did not necessarily lead to another, reasonable lines could be drawn. "The important thing is to know when and how to stop the real censorship of ideas."

"Send in the exhibits," White now commanded the clerk. He felt obliged to view them before voting to reverse the lower courts.

The exhibits were no worse than the usual collection of pornography that found its way to the Court week after week. White flipped through the material. He quickly saw enough. White did not loathe pornography, as Blackmun and Burger did. It was simply that these were things for his son's eyes, perhaps, but never for his wife's or daughter's. He was bothered less by the material than by its ready availability in every major city across the country.

White also wanted an end to the waste of time spent in reviewing and "Redrupping" individual cases. He decided for the first time not to give Brennan, Stewart, Marshall and Douglas a fifth vote for reversing the obscenity convictions in these two pending cases. He was going to join the Chief and Blackmun in a dissent. He wanted to handle the obscenity cases differently, though he wasn't sure how.

White's move irked Brennan. Of course White was exasperated by the endless obscenity cases. So were all the Justices. "I'm sick and tired of seeing this goddamn shit," Brennan complained. But what choice did they have?

Brennan realized that the *Redrup* approach forced the lower courts to go back each time to the original exhibits to try to deduce what the Court had most recently ruled. Most of them had gotten the point. The Court was not inclined to allow the lower courts to deem obscene anything but the most explicit hard-core pornography.

Brennan was not ready to buy Douglas's absolutist position that nothing could be banned. But neither did he feel that the Court could sit back and let local bluenoses censor whatever they thought would stain the soul. The *Redrup* procedure was better than nothing—as long as he had the votes.

Brennan, like White, had his own private definition of obscenity: no erections. He was willing to accept penetration as long as the pictures passed what his clerks referred to as the "limp dick" standard. Oral sex was tolerable if there was no erection. In these two cases, the material passed Brennan's test.

Stewart was another vote to *Redrup*. Years before *(Jacobellis v. Ohio, 1964)*, Stewart had written that only "hard-core" pornography could be banned, but conceded the subjective nature of any definition: "I shall not today attempt to further define the kind of materials I understand to be embraced within that shorthand definition; and perhaps I could never succeed in doing so," Stewart had said. "But I know it when I see it."

He had seen it during World War II, when he served as a Navy lieutenant. In Casablanca, as watch officer for his ship, he had seen his men bring back locally produced pornography. He knew the difference between that hardest of hard-core and much of what came to the Court. He called it his "Casablanca Test."

Marshall, as usual more amused than shocked by the exhibits in the pending obscenity cases, was also a vote to *Redrup*. And Douglas, of course, was a fourth vote.

Since Black's departure, Douglas was the only First Amendment absolutist on the Court. He and Black had been certain that it was impossible to define obscenity. Any laws banning it, therefore, were doomed to be vague and unconstitutional. There could never be an obscenity law clear enough to meet the constitutional requirement that a person must know beforehand whether he is acting illegally.

The Court's sin, Douglas felt, had been to make obscenity an exception to the First Amendment in the first place. And the original sinner, the father of obscenity law, the author of the first Court opinion that had attempted a definition, was Bill Brennan. In a 1957 case *(Roth v. United States)*, Brennan had written an opinion holding that there was one category of expression, obscenity, that was not speech, and thus was not protected by the First Amendment and could properly be banned.

Douglas knew that Brennan had developed his definitions to

protect serious literary works—James Joyce's *Ulysses*, William Faulkner's *Sanctuary*, Erskine Caldwell's *God's Little Acre*—from overzealous prosecutors and judges. Under Brennan's definition, material was obscene if, to "the average person, applying contemporary community standards, the dominant theme of the material taken as a whole appeals to the prurient interest." But lower courts continued to ban material Brennan thought was obviously not obscene. For a plurality, in a 1966 opinion *(Memoirs of a Woman of Pleasure [Fanny Hill] v. Massachusetts)*, Brennan had next tried a formulation holding that material had to be "utterly without redeeming social value" before it could be banned. This placed the burden on prosecutors to prove that nothing in a work redeemed it. Pornographers then took to citing medical reports or throwing in lines from Shakespeare to protect the product.

In Douglas's view, these efforts by the Court to define obscenity were absurd. The only remotely rational development, he felt, had occurred in a 1969 case *(Stanley v. Georgia)* when Marshall had said obscenity was largely a personal privacy question. He had written, "If the First Amendment means anything, it means that a state has no business telling a man, sitting alone in his own house, what books he may read or what films he must watch."

As defense lawyers attempted to expand the logic of *Stanley*, hundreds of cases began working their way up to the Court. If there was a constitutional right to possess obscene material in one's home, then there was a right to buy it. If there was a right to buy it, there was a right to sell it. If there was a right to sell it, there was a right to distribute it. If there was a right to distribute it, then there must be a constitutional right to write, photograph or film it. Or so their logic went.

If the privacy logic could be extended all the way, the lawyers argued, the distinction between obscene and not obscene would become largely irrelevant. There would be no need to define obscenity as long as people had the right to see and read what they wished. But Brennan had hesitated over *Stanley*, and during the previous two terms had refused to provide the liberals a crucial fifth vote to extend the logic. Now, with White shifting and two new Nixon Justices taking their seats, Douglas feared that a majority might modify Brennan's old definitions and declare a war on pornography—and soon on free speech.

The Chief could hardly wait for three obscenity cases that were to be among the first argued to the full nine-man Court. He considered it fortunate that the Warren Court liberals had never gotten five votes to agree on a definition; that would have settled the law. Their lack of agreement gave him an opportunity to leave his mark in an area of the law on which the Court had been stumbling for fourteen years. There had to be a way to suppress pornography and still protect free speech, he felt.

The January 21 conference, with Powell and Rehnquist now in attendance, was a test of endurance. By the time the Justices got to the three obscenity cases, their energies had measurably faded. The first case *(Miller v. California)* was the most difficult, in that it raised questions about the definition of obscenity. The conference put it aside and turned to two cases that involved extending the *Stanley* privacy decision.*

The discussion was complex, the positions difficult to follow, but Douglas counted votes quickly. Stewart and Marshall were ready to vote with him to extend the *Stanley* decision to cover both cases. To Douglas's surprise, Powell also joined them. In an effort to bring himself up to par on constitutional law before he arrived at the Court, Powell had asked associates at his old law firm to prepare memoranda on major areas. One of their recommendations had been to extend the *Stanley* privacy doctrine. Powell was willing to follow the advice, at least tentatively. Brennan and Blackmun seemed ready to go along with the four in one case, but not the other.

The Chief waited and spoke last. He was willing to go along in one case, perhaps both. "I'll try my hand at the opinions," he said.

There was nothing fashionable about the boisterous older black man at the corner table of Washington's Trader Vic's restaurant. Amid a Polynesian décor of palm leaves and bamboo, and in the

---

* *U.S. v. Orito* and *U.S. v. Twelve 200-Foot Reels of Super 8 mm. Film.*

din of the luncheon crowd on April 27, two younger men atten-
tively listened to him.

The older man's heavy dark-brown horn-rimmed glasses seemed
several sizes too small, pinching his massive head. His loud high-
pitched "Hee, hee, hee" lasted fully ten seconds as he wheezed at
his own jokes.

Marshall was lunching with two of White's clerks. He had turned
to his favorite pastime of reminiscing as a respite from the pressures of the Court. An accomplished raconteur, he needed little encouragement to get him started. He would tell stories of Baltimore
ghetto life in a resilient family; night riders chasing him along
country back roads in the South; courtroom encounters with bigots
and buffoons; the little boy in Mississippi who asked him "What's
that?" as Marshall ate an orange outside a courthouse; General
Douglas MacArthur and the Army's racism.

Often Marshall would corner one of his clerks after lunch and
spend hours in the special chair they reserved for him in their office. By the time he had worn out his own clerks' patience, clerks
from other chambers might have wandered in for a new round of
the endless storytelling. But they could always leave. His own
clerks had nowhere to go.

At one point, his clerks tried piling books on Marshall's chair to
discourage him from settling in for the afternoon. They underesti-
mated their boss's stamina. Marshall had spent years standing in
courtrooms, corridors and schoolhouses. Finally, the clerks took to
hiding in his second-floor office.

The first two years of Burger's reign had had their difficult moments for Marshall. He had always seen Burger as an inappropriate caretaker of a seat that had belonged to a man of the stature of
Earl Warren. But his annoyance with the new Chief's style never
eroded his respect for the office of Chief Justice.

Now, however, as the four Nixon appointees increasingly joined
White and occasionally Stewart to chip away at Warren Court
precedents, Marshall felt the outlook was grim. He seemed to grow
weary, more discouraged. "I'm going fishing, you kids can fight the
battles," he would tell his clerks. "What difference does it make?
Why fight when you can just dissent?"

Some clerks in other chambers came to the conclusion that Marshall was unfit to sit on the Court. He was not willing to do his homework, not willing to prepare for his cases, not of the intellectual caliber of Douglas, White, Stewart or Brennan, not combative enough to take on the others in conference.

Marshall's own clerks felt that he knew where he stood on every issue of importance to him. He might not prepare extensively for either oral argument or conference, but his ability to think on his feet—a talent developed during years on the road for the Inc. Fund—made him an incisive questioner at oral argument. And, when he chose to speak, he was a skilled debater at conference.

One of the issues that Marshall enjoyed arguing with his clerks was the question of what was obscene. He loved to take conservative positions with them, maintaining that anything hard-core could be and should be totally banned. What was so important about it? First Amendment principles are not at stake in this case, he would bellow. Dirty pictures are.

What about his liberal opinion for the Court in *Stanley?* his clerks would ask.

He had meant only to protect people's privacy in their own homes, he would claim with a grin. Publishers, distributors, sellers could be stopped.

But, a clerk once pointed out, "You said that the right to privacy must go further than the home."

"No," Marshall retorted. He had never said that.

Yes, the clerk insisted.

No, never, Marshall was sure. "Show me."

The clerk brought the bound opinions.

Marshall read the relevant section.

"That's not my opinion, that's the opinion of [a clerk from the prior term]," he declared. Opening the volume flat, he tore the page out. "There. It's not there now, is it?"

At Trader Vic's, Marshall had just launched into another story when he suddenly stopped. He stared at his watch a moment. It was about 1:50.

"My God, I almost forgot," he said in a stricken tone. "It's movie day, we have to get back."

Movie day was the humorous highpoint of most terms. Year after year, several of the Justices and most of the clerks went either into a basement storeroom or to one of the larger conference rooms to watch feature films that were exhibits in obscenity cases that had been appealed to the Court.

Douglas, and Black during his years on the Court, never went. In their view, nothing could be banned. "If I want to go see that film, I should pay my money," Black once said, and he wondered aloud why nine men, many in their seventies, should make judgments about sexuality. The Court was acting as a "Supreme Board of Censors," he said.

Burger too preferred not to go.

But the others sat on folding chairs with their clerks, watching such films as *I Am Curious (Yellow)* projected onto a white wall. During his later years, Harlan watched the films from the first row, a few feet from the screen, able only to make out the general outlines. His clerk or another Justice would describe the action. "By Jove," Harlan would exclaim. "Extraordinary."

Clerks frequently mocked Stewart's approach to obscenity, calling out in the darkened room: "That's it, that's it, I know it when I see it."

Marshall's quips were the best. The previous term, a pornographic movie had used the familiar ruse of posing as an educational film. The actor playing a psychologist had concluded by stating, "And so our nymphomaniac subject was never cured." Marshall retorted, "Yeah, but I am."

Now the lights were about to go off as Marshall and White's clerks plunged through the door to see *Vixen*, a "soft-core" feature with nudity but no explicit intercourse.

The last thirteen minutes consisted of an attempted hijacking of the plane carrying the female protagonist by an Irish Communist bound for Cuba. He gave a talk on the comparative merits of Communist and Western societies. "Ah, the redeeming social value," Marshall said.

The clerks were disappointed that the movie was such soft-core.

Powell left after the first film.

The second movie was *Sexual Freedom in Denmark*, a feature

documentary that had been released two years before. A very serious commentator explained the harmful effects of liberal Danish sexual attitudes, and showed a photograph of a penis in the last stages of syphilis. The dull narrative was punctuated by drawings of sexual and reproductive functions in color.

Blackmun sat stone-faced, ignoring the banter from Marshall and the clerks. Marshall turned to him when the lights came on as the projectionist changed reels. "Well, Harry, I didn't learn anything, how about you?"

Blushing, Blackmun joined the rest of the room in a hearty laugh.

The second reel had the first hard-breathing segment as two women made love. Then the film returned to its clinical, documentary style. Blackmun found it distasteful. The film's tone, if not its content, degraded women. That alone was enough to predispose him against all pornography.

Back in chambers, Powell's clerks remarked to him that *Vixen* had been disappointing. Two clerks confessed that they had seen all the movies of the director Russ Meyer—the master of sex-exploitation films. Yale Law School had even presented a Russ Meyer festival.

Powell's gaunt face was expressionless. He had never before seen such a film, he explained slowly. He had had no idea such movies were even made. He was shocked and disgusted. He did not wish to discuss it further.

Powell's clerks were amazed. There could not have been a milder movie for him to have seen. There had been nothing more than nudity, and facial and bodily expressions that suggested orgasm. How would he have reacted to the hard-core peep-show reels with nothing but explicit sex from beginning to end?

His clerks decided not to let any other clerks know of Powell's reactions. His vote would be crucial. He was a reasonable man. Perhaps when the shock had faded a bit, his initial distaste could be overcome.

As the spring wore on and the conference waited for the Chief's circulation, the liberals were encouraged by two cases.

Douglas found a case that pointed up the danger of obscenity laws. A radical underground paper in Madison, Wisconsin, had been run out of business, and its publisher had been harassed with a two-year prison sentence and a $2,000 fine for publishing "obscene" pictures and poems. The obscenity laws had been only a means for suppression of unpopular papers, Douglas contended. He was pleased when all the others agreed. They seemed a hair's breadth from at least establishing that printed material without illustrations could never be obscene *(Kois v. Wisconsin)*.

The Chief assigned a *per curiam* opinion to Rehnquist. Though striking down the conviction, Rehnquist stopped short of where the others were willing to go. He did not write that purely textual material could never be obscene.

Douglas's second victory of the spring came in a case in which the movie *Carmen Baby,* a loose contemporary adaptation of Bizet's opera, had been declared obscene. The female lead's body had been displayed on an outdoor movie screen in Richland, Washington, and had been visible to neighborhood children *(Rabe v. Washington)*.

Douglas argued that the movie would not be obscene if shown indoors, and since the statute said nothing about location, it was too vague a factor to have forewarned the theater manager. Pleased that all his colleagues except Rehnquist and the Chief agreed, Douglas assigned himself the opinion. He had never authored an opinion that accepted a definition of obscenity, however, and chose to write this one as a *per curiam,* so that it would be anonymous.

Douglas was a bit surprised when the Chief filed a two-paragraph concurrence, "a little snapper." If the law in question had explicitly required that certain movies not be exhibited to unwilling viewers and children, it would have been constitutional, the Chief wrote. Douglas took some consolation that at least Burger was thinking about the distinction between public and private exhibition. Certainly that would be a factor in any extension of the *Stanley* privacy doctrine.

The two cases also encouraged Brennan. The conference seemed to be creeping toward a consensus. Even Douglas and Rehnquist, polar opposites, were moving toward the center.

On Friday, May 19, Burger finally circulated his first memo on the obscenity cases argued in January. To the astonishment of most of the justices, the twenty-one-page opinion set out once more to redefine obscenity, rather than extend the *Stanley* privacy doctrine.

First, Burger encouraged the lower courts to be more flexible, to apply local, not national, standards, in defining what was obscene. He quoted an Earl Warren opinion (*Jacobellis v. Ohio*) opposing national standards. He would accept Warren's analysis: "In a society that prides itself—and properly so—in supporting pluralism and diversity there is no sound reason for the law to say that what is found tolerable in the portrayal of sexual activities in Los Angeles or Las Vegas must be accepted in Maine and Vermont."

Local juries representing the "conscience of the community," Burger wrote, could determine what was acceptable for their communities. Anyone who did not agree with him, Burger said, did not believe in the American jury system. The Court's general definition of obscenity should be loosened to allow more prosecutions to succeed, he said. "The statement that material should be 'utterly' without redeeming social value is clearly too sweeping . . . Courts have seen patently spurious inserts to season filth with a dash of the race problem, foreign policy, or the evils of 'war profiteering.'"

"Utterly without redeeming social value" was a problem, the Chief said, because he had "never been sure just what this phrase means, but neither—very likely—are most lay jurors so that we could disregard it without great risk."

Instead, Burger wrote, works henceforth should have "literary, artistic, political, or social value" to avoid being declared obscene. Publishers would have to show that they met this standard. Prosecutors would not have to show that they didn't. That would shift the burden of proof, and make prosecutions easier.

To deal with the most "egregious abuse" of obscenity laws by local prosecutors and judges, the Chief proposed that the Court continue to review them individually and *Redrup* them.

"In the long run this Court cannot act as an efficient Super Censor, and the sooner we leave the problem to the states the better off we and the public will be."

Brennan carefully searched Burger's draft for a sign that he was still open to the *Stanley* privacy approach. The Chief had put emphasis on "public activities with respect to obscene materials," had described pornography as an "intolerable nuisance . . . to a community," and had cited the *Stanley* case. If taken literally, Burger seemed to distinguish between "public" and "private" displays of obscenity, and to view the problem as merely controlling dissemination. That fit Brennan's own view. "Boys, do you think the Chief really means this?" he asked his clerks.

The clerks were skeptical of the Chief's motives and logic. He was watering down Brennan's definition of obscenity to allow easier prosecution of pornographers. But Brennan felt that if the Chief were willing to extend the *Stanley* privacy logic, it really didn't matter if he wanted to rewrite the definition. Consenting adults would still be allowed to see and read what they wanted, regardless of whether it was obscene.

Brennan thought he might push the Chief a bit further. He had already had his clerks prepare a draft opinion that partly renounced his old approach and, instead, extended the Stanley logic. But to send the draft around just now might be too provocative; clearly, it had been prepared beforehand. Worse, the Chief would see it as a blatant attempt to steal the majority opinion from him. So Brennan decided to alter his draft and try to persuade Burger that it was close enough to his own view to be incorporated into his opinion. The Chief's work was a rough draft, almost conversational in tone. Certainly he would not object to a few suggestions.

However, the timing was important. There were six weeks before the term was to end. If something could be circulated in the second week of June, there would be no time for the Chief to rewrite his own opinion in response. Unless he adopted much of Brennan's memo as his own, he would take the chance that Brennan would get a majority.

In three weeks Brennan was ready with his memo. It began informally, but the thirty-seven-page document was structured as a majority opinion. Brennan admitted that he had been wrong in 1957, wrong in later attempts to define obscenity, wrong not to vote for *Stanley,* and wrong not to extend it.

Brennan was willing, however, to retain a definition of obscenity for public places in order to protect children and unwilling viewers. State laws could prohibit any unsolicited example of pornography, or require that it be kept out of sight or in an area prominently labeled "adult materials." Flashy, explicit signs would have to come down. Still shots of sexual conduct from obscene movies would have to be taken off theater displays. Live sex shows in public could be banned.

Brennan had tailored his draft to capture at least the ground the Chief seemed willing to give. Books without pictures, and mere nudity, could not be banned.

Douglas was pleased to see Brennan's confession, but it was too little too late. He continued to hammer at him to go all the way: nothing could be banned. If Brennan retained a definition of obscenity—even to protect children and unwilling adults—the courts could some day use it to censor materials for consenting adults, Douglas argued.

Brennan, insisting that the Chief was approachable, circulated his draft on Tuesday, June 13.

The next day Burger circulated his response to Brennan's draft to the whole conference. This was record time for him. "I have your very interesting memo on the broad problem of the above case," Burger wrote. "In the short time you have had I marvel at how you have done this job. We need more exchanges of this kind to develop our thinking."

In view of "the lateness of the season," the Chief agreed, the Court had been unable to come up with a definition that will separate protected from nonprotected "sex material."

> I think I agree that people in the commercial world are uncertain of the standards. We are, and they merely reflect our uncertainty. I confess I do not see it as a threat to genuine First Amendment values to have commercial porno-peddlers feel some unease. For me the First Amendment was made to protect commerce in *ideas*, but even at that I would go a long way concerning *ideas* on the subject that has had a high place in the human animal's consciousness for several thousand years. In short, a little "chill" will do some of the "pornos" no great harm and it might be good for the country.

Extraordinary, thought Brennan. How could even the Chief feel that the Court could act on the basis of what an individual thought was "good for the country"?

> Even accepting that the "Redrup technique" compounds uncertainty, I prefer it to a new, uncharted swamp.

So the Chief was willing to leave them in the business of reviewing, one by one, the hundreds of cases that came to them each year. But Brennan found other parts of the Chief's memo to him somewhat more encouraging:

> I strongly agree with you that there are some obscene materials not protected by the Constitution. [He also agreed that governments could] stop pandering and touting by mail or otherwise with brochures etc. that offend.

This had long been Brennan's primary concern.

> I agree (if it is your view) that all public display that goes beyond mere nudity that depicts or suggests conduct can be barred. I think if it can be barred on 14th and Constitution Avenue [in public], it can be barred in a saloon and probably theatre.
>
> In general I agree that traffic via words in print is in a different category from pictures, movies or live shows.

Burger also shared Brennan's concern about protecting children from pornography. "I consider the state free to make a serious felony out of any conduct that permits access of minors to nonprotected material," he said. Most importantly, he would be willing to extend the *Stanley* logic to permit importing pornography for private use.

Brennan was still partially encouraged but wondered what the Chief had in mind. Surely his draft was not ready for publication. He went to see Burger to talk over the situation.

The next Monday, June 19, the Chief sent around a simple note. "In the present posture of the [obscenity] cases neither Justice

Brennan nor I can make specific recommendations as to the disposition of the cases held for opinion. . . . We will discuss this at the
June 22 Conference."

Brennan reassessed the situation. White, Blackmun and Powell
seemed concerned with the need to give a publisher or seller fair
warning that he could be prosecuted; he must be told what is obscene. If that hurdle could be overcome, they might follow the
Chief's lead and permit the states to restrict obscene materials
even from consenting adults.

To keep them from voting with the Chief, Brennan wanted
them to take cases that did not involve unwilling viewers but
rather cases in which consenting adults had sought out pornography.

One involved the sale of a pornographic novel without illustra-
tions to an undercover police officer who asked to buy some
pornography. The other two involved an adult movie theater and
an adult bookstore, both plainly marked, both without offensive
advertising outside, and both of which refused to admit juveniles.
If those cases, involving only printed matter or consenting adults,
could be argued early, Brennan might be able to show that his approach was preferable to the Chief's redefinition of obscenity.

The conference on June 22 readily agreed with Brennan's suggestion to take the additional cases* and to argue them early in the
next term. They also put over the three cases before them. They
now had a package of eight cases that would present virtually every
unanswered question in obscenity law.

Brennan could see that he had his work cut out for him in the
coming year. He summoned one of Douglas's clerks and briefed
him on what to pass along to Douglas in Goose Prairie: everything
was fine; they had granted the new cases; Brennan was confident
they would prevail in the fall.

On Powell's first day at the Court, Marshall had paid a courtesy
call on his new colleague. He found Powell standing in his clerks'

---

* *Kaplan v. California; Paris Adult Theatre v. Slaton; Alexander v. Virginia.*

small office. The two men—Marshall carrying 250 pounds on a 6-foot-1 frame and Powell a skeletal 6-foot-3—stood uncomfortably for a moment.

"Do you have your capital punishment opinion written yet?" Marshall asked jovially, slapping Powell lightly on the back.

Powell smiled tentatively. Was it possible that he was expected to have mastered such a difficult and consequential area of the law so rapidly? Had the others completed their opinions, even before the Court had considered the cases or heard oral argument?

"No, I haven't had time to consider that yet," he replied.

"Well, I wish you luck," Marshall said. "My wife Cissy is after me, and thinks we should string them all up. But," he added, patting a wad of papers in the inside pocket of his coat, "you'll see what I've written."

He slipped out the door with a chuckle.

Beneath the surface humor, Marshall was very concerned. The Court had ruled only on procedural questions in capital punishment cases. In just over a week, it was going to address the central question of whether the death penalty was among the "cruel and unusual punishments" prohibited by the Eighth Amendment. There were only five cases to be argued* before the Court, but the decisions could determine the fate of about 700 prisoners across the country who were waiting on death row.

Marshall was opposed to the death penalty in any form. He considered it the most conspicuous example of the unfairness of the criminal justice system. It almost seemed a penalty designed for poor minorities and the undereducated. The rich and well-educated were rarely sentenced to death. They hired fancy lawyers. With his experience in the South, and a year spent during the Korean War investigating the cases of black GIs sentenced to death, Marshall knew very well how the system worked. The death penalty was the ultimate form of racial discrimination.

As he reviewed the situation, Marshall thought the prospects looked bleak. The only faintly positive sign was the Court's curious

* *Aikens v. California; Furman v. Georgia; Branch v. Texas; Jackson v. Georgia; Moore v. Illinois.*

handling of death cases in the last several years, which reflected a deep ambivalence among his colleagues. The Justices had taken a series of preliminary conference votes on the death penalty, each retracted without having been made public.

In the 1968 term, the Justices had secretly voted 6 to 3 to strike down the Arkansas death penalty *(Maxwell v. Bishop)*. State capital punishment laws, the conference had decided, must require, after a finding of guilty, a *separate* hearing on sentencing. This would allow a defendant to testify, and to present mitigating facts, without forcing him to take the witness stand during his trial.

Warren, Douglas, Harlan, Brennan, Fortas and Marshall had made up this 1968 majority. Black, Stewart and White had dissented. Warren had assigned the opinion to Douglas, who hurriedly drafted and circulated a sweeping opinion. Harlan had had difficulty with Douglas's opinion; it went too far, calling into question sentencing procedures, not only in death cases but in all criminal cases. Harlan had switched his vote and the comfortable 6-to-3 majority had become a very close 5-to-4. Before the opinion could be issued, Fortas had resigned, leaving the Court deadlocked, 4 to 4.

The next year, the tie vote on this case was broken when Warren's vote to strike down the law was replaced by Burger's to uphold it. But the new 5-to-3 decision was still too close for Harlan's comfort. He insisted that they put the case over again, to wait for a ninth justice.

Blackmun's vote to uphold the death penalty in the 1970 term *(McGautha v. California)* completed the shift. The 1968 secret vote of 6 to 3 to strike the law had become a 6-to-3 majority the other way.

Harlan wrote the opinion in *McGautha* that amounted to a limited procedural approval of existing death penalty laws. It held that juries did not have to be given definite standards to guide their sentencing decisions, and that the state did not have to provide the separate hearings—one for guilt and one for punishment—in capital cases.

After Harlan's opinion was announced, the conference met to determine which of the hundreds of persons on death row—whose appeals had been pending the outcome of this case—could now be executed.

Stewart balked. He pointed out they still had not decided whether the death penalty was cruel and unusual, and therefore forbidden by the Eighth Amendment. At his suggestion the conference agreed to take several cases to focus on that issue. The moratorium on executions would continue.

Douglas, however, objected. It was a phony issue. They had already decided the question by a secret vote in a 1967 case (*Boykin v. Alabama*), though the result had never been made public since the case was decided on other grounds. Only he and Marshall had voted to strike down the death penalty. Douglas had done so only because a man had been sentenced to die for armed robberies. Had it been a murder case, Douglas said, he would not have found the penalty cruel and unusual. That would be absurd. The death penalty had been around for centuries; it had been recently reaffirmed by several legislatures. It would be "frivolous" to grant a temporary reprieve while the Court pretended to consider an issue it had already settled.

Douglas circulated, and threatened to publish, a rare dissent from the *granting* of cert—as opposed to the more common practice of publishing dissents from a denial of cert. It would be cruel and unusual for the Court to raise the hopes of men on death row, only to execute them a year later. But Douglas failed to persuade his colleagues and withdrew his dissent.

Now, one year later, the Court was about to deal with the "cruel and unusual punishments" question. Marshall figured it was the final showdown. In his view, the odds that five justices would vote against the death penalty were not good; in fact, they were awful. His might be the only vote to abolish the penalty in all instances. Even if Douglas and Brennan came around, that would make only three votes. And capital punishment was now a hot political issue. Nixon had made the death penalty a foot soldier in his war on crime.

Still, Marshall thought that there was one factor working for him. Before his death, Black had predicted privately to his colleagues that the Court would eventually strike down the death penalty, not because of legal arguments, but because of the sheer numbers— 700 men and women—awaiting execution on death row.

This argument had been part of the strategy of Marshall's old law firm, the Inc. Fund. The Fund had led the battle to block executions and had created an informal moratorium on the death penalty by litigating each case in the federal courts. There hadn't been an execution since 1967. Though Black believed the death penalty was constitutional, he predicted that the Inc. Fund strategy would ultimately prevail. In the end, a majority would not want that much blood on its hands.

Marshall had two clerks research the "cruel and unusual punishments" arguments. Though the death penalty was used at the time the Eighth Amendment was adopted in 1791, so were certain other punishments—branding, butchering ears and flogging. They had since been ruled "cruel and unusual." Earl Warren had written in a 1958 opinion (*Trop v. Dulles*) that the Eighth Amendment was not "static." It changed, guided by "the evolving standards of decency that mark the progress of a maturing society." It was time, Marshall reasoned, to demonstrate that maturity.

At oral argument on January 17, Anthony Amsterdam, a young law professor, presented the Court with what Marshall considered the best arguments for the abolition of the death penalty.

First, Amsterdam argued, the death penalty was imposed most frequently against minorities and the poor; statistics showed a clear pattern of discrimination. Second, the death penalty was imposed in an arbitrary and random fashion; there were no consistent criteria for determining who was executed and who was spared. Third, the death penalty could not be an effective deterrent, since it was so infrequently imposed. Fourth, the death penalty was unacceptable to contemporary society; eleven states had entirely abandoned it, and juries with an option to impose it more often than not declined to do so. This last was the evolving standards argument.

Charles Alan Wright, a professor of law at the University of Texas, argued in favor of the death penalty law. Wright said that the legislatures had purposefully given the death penalty option to the juries. The infrequency of imposition did not defeat its purpose. "I would think that it would be cause for rejoicing that we've become increasingly selective about imposing the ultimate and most severe penalty," he declared.

White interrupted Wright to ask whether he was not bothered by the arbitrarily infrequent way juries and judges seemed to be applying the penalty. Stewart pointed out that statistics showed that the juries' imposition of the penalty discriminated against blacks.

Wright agreed. He found both points troubling, but argued that neither rendered the penalty itself cruel and unusual. In his own view there might be some procedural defects in the administration of the laws. But the Court had really settled much of this in the *McGautha* case the previous year. "The Court having decided so recently and so decisively that jury sentencing is proper, that the jury does express the conscience of the community, I would think you'd need quite a powerful showing to change the Court's mind," Wright declared.

Though Marshall and Brennan agreed with all four of Amsterdam's arguments, Douglas rejected the evolving standards argument. Individual rights and protections of the Bill of Rights were absolute. They did not change over time. Douglas had spent his career arguing that point. To give in on it would open up the Bill of Rights to judicial reinterpretation. The Court could as easily cut back on freedoms as extend them. But he was now convinced that so far as the death penalty was discriminatory it was cruel and unusual. He too would vote to strike it down.

Marshall now saw three solid votes to strike. On the other side, Burger and Rehnquist were solid votes to uphold. White, normally sympathetic to prosecutors and state legislators, was a likely third. Blackmun, Powell and Stewart would determine the future of the death penalty, Marshall believed.

Stewart's inclination was to vote to uphold the capital punishment laws. Amsterdam's arguments were seductive, but most did not bear up under close scrutiny. Were the death laws really discriminatory? More blacks received death sentences; but more blacks were convicted of capital offenses. Neither did Stewart buy the argument that capital punishment was ineffective as a deterrent. The statistics were not conclusive. The evolving-standards argument didn't wash either. A large majority of the states, at least thirty-eight, had death penalty laws. Some states, and the United

States Congress, had recently enacted new capital punishment legislation.

Stewart also saw an even larger problem. The death penalty could not *suddenly* become unacceptable, "cruel and unusual." What about all those who had been executed before the informal 1967 moratorium? Even under an evolving-standards argument, the Court would look awful. It would appear to have been mistaken the many years it had allowed people to be executed. He could never join such a flat Eighth Amendment ruling.

Still, Stewart was deeply troubled. He had been staying up nights thinking about the issue, and particularly about the issue, and particularly about those 700 individuals on death row. Amsterdam's argument that the penalty was imposed in an "arbitrary" and "random" fashion had some basis. Stewart could find no clear reason why the 700 prisoners on death row had been given the death sentence while thousands of others who had been convicted of capital crimes had received prison terms. Something was wrong. Mass murderers might get life imprisonment and rapists the death penalty. Variations in sentences perhaps could be justified when the difference was between three and ten years in prison. But the death sentence was of a different order. Could such erratic differences be justified? Was that constitutional? Stewart wasn't sure. The infrequent imposition of the death penalty—less than 20 percent of the times when it was an available option—also seemed to render it "unusual" in the dictionary sense of the word: irregular; inconsistent; rare.

This line of reasoning appeared to raise procedural questions. But the *McGautha* opinion had supposedly addressed that issue. It allowed juries the option of imposing the death penalty, even if jurors were not given any standards or rules, or any guidance in arriving at a decision. *McGautha* was a major, though not insurmountable, hurdle if Stewart was tending to vote to strike the laws.

There were also strategic considerations. Stewart could conceive of last term's 6-to-3 majority slipping to a narrow 5-to-4. If this happened—if it seemed that the Court was going to uphold the death penalty by a one-vote margin—Stewart would have a severe problem joining such a slim majority. It really would not be acceptable for 700 people to die on the basis of one vote, particularly his. If it came out 5 to 4, Stewart decided, he would have to vote to strike the laws. That would make it 5 to 4 the other way, but no one would be sent to death. He might therefore, have to find a narrow ground on which to vote against the death penalty.

White told his clerks that Amsterdam's oral presentation had been possibly the best he had ever heard. Still, he found only one argument even remotely persuasive—the contention that the infrequency of the sentence made it an ineffective deterrent. He was concerned with the state's interests, and with the benefit that the government might derive from certain punishments. There were two elements—deterrence and retribution. These interests justified the death penalty for White, even though he was willing to accept that it was inherently "cruel and unusual." If the state's goal of deterring crime and extracting retribution were met, the penalty was justified and constitutional. Certainly the prospect or the high probability of being executed for certain crimes would give a potential criminal pause. But the fact that the ultimate penalty was imposed so infrequently changed things. In fact, at the present time, the probability was that it would *not* be imposed. The deterrent value was no longer credible. On the other hand, the optional death penalties in force clearly reflected the will of the state legislatures, and White did not believe that the Court should frustrate that will unless there were overwhelming reasons. "You can't run the criminal justice system from the courthouse," he said more than once.

But the legislatures had let the death penalty laws remain on the books, and had enacted new ones, without considering the constitutional and moral questions that stemmed from the fact that juries and judges used it so seldom. The legislatures were not facing up to their jobs. White was uncertain what to do.

To Marshall, Stewart's concerns about being part of a 5-to-4 majority to uphold the death penalty made Stewart a likely *fifth* vote. Marshall still needed a *fourth*. There were two leading candidates. Blackmun, who, as Marshall knew, was tormented by the issue, seemed the more likely. As an appeals court judge, he had written the most recent federal opinions on cruel and unusual punishment in the Arkansas prisons.* He had also, while on the appellate court, expressed deep reservations about the death penalty in another case *(Maxwell v. Bishop)* and had finally voted to uphold the death penalty only because the Supreme Court had done so. Now that Blackmun was on the highest court in the land, Marshall hoped that he would vote his conscience.

Powell was the other possible vote, Marshall thought. Although Powell had not asked a single question during oral argument, Marshall could see that he was doing his homework. Powell was a product of the enlightened white establishment that Marshall had for thirty years been trying to shock into collective remorse. Marshall hoped that Powell might be able to see capital punishment as a civil rights issue. At least, he seemed open on the question. Marshall thought that, in the end, Powell's gut reaction would determine his vote.

The conference met on the death cases on January 21, 1972. The Justices agreed that all votes would be very tentative, even more tentative than usual. Marshall figured that with Blackmun and Powell speaking seventh and eighth, the preliminary outcome would not become clear until the conference had gone once around the table.

The Chief began. He observed that if he were a legislator, he would vote against the death penalty, but he was not. He would uphold. Clearly the penalty was constitutional.

Douglas and Brennan argued to strike the death penalty as Marshall had expected.

Then, there was a surprise. Instead of hanging back, waiting to see whether he might be the fifth vote to uphold, Stewart indicated that he was inclined to vote to strike the current capital punishment laws. He would not go along with a sweeping Eighth Amendment abolition of the death penalty. But the randomness

---

* *Jackson v. Bishop.*

and arbitrariness of the sentencing decisions made the laws "cruel and unusual."

Marshall was pleased. He now had four votes. But White and the three Nixon appointees had not spoken.

Then came another surprise. White said that he too was troubled by the infrequency. It had changed his perspective. Infrequency nullified the state interest in deterrence. He too was inclined to vote to strike.

Blackmun and Powell voted tentatively to uphold the laws. Rehnquist voted firmly to uphold.

Though he was delighted by White's vote, Marshall was more than a bit skeptical. White's had been an unlikely vote, and it seemed shaky.

Given the tentative nature of their expressions, and the extraordinary importance of the cases, the Justices each agreed to write a separate opinion. That would give them nine opinions to consider. The full range of views and arguments would be presented.

Burger suggested that the conference discussion and the result, since it was not really final, be kept from the clerks and all other Court personnel, as had been done in the Charlotte busing case the term before. He also requested that all draft opinions be circulated only to the Justices.

"Boys, it is a surprise to me, but the death cases seem to be coming out 5 to 4 against the death penalty," Brennan told his clerks after conference. But the situation was fluid, he added. White and Stewart were very unsure of grounds on which to base a decision to strike the death penalty. Brennan was particularly concerned about White. It was essential to hold him, but Brennan wasn't optimistic.

Worse still, both Stewart and White had to square their new positions with their opinions in the death case the year before. There might be arguments to strike down the laws, but the arguments had been settled in the *McGautha* case the term before.

Marshall, with casual glee, lost little time violating Burger's secrecy mandate. When he instructed one of his clerks to circulate his previously prepared opinion, he was asked whether the clerks in other chambers should get the usual copies. "Sure," he responded. "Why not?"

The fifty-eight-page draft was an unusually scholarly and comprehensive treatise on the history of the death penalty in America and England. Marshall argued for an absolute ban and had assembled every conceivable argument that the death penalty was discriminatory. But the draft did not speak to Stewart's or White's concerns.

A month later, the California Supreme Court decided that the state's death penalty violated the California constitution's prohibition against "cruel or unusual punishment." Douglas's chambers got advance notice of the decision, and within three days, Douglas had distributed a *per curiam* draft dismissing the one hundred California cases that were awaiting the Court's ruling.

Burger was upset by the California decision. It deprived the Court of the most brutal of the five cases that had been argued: a cold-blooded rape-murder. If there was an argument for capital punishment, it was in such a case (*Aikens v. California*). He stalled the proposed dismissal. The Chief was worried that the California decision would add weight to the argument that contemporary values were evolving toward an abolition of the death penalty. They could wait on the dismissal question until they decided the other cases, he argued.

Still unsure where the cases before them would finally come to rest, the conference agreed to wait.

When Powell finally accepted his nomination to the Court, he had never really pondered the fact that he might have to make a decision with such profound moral, ethical, almost religious implications. A light sleeper at best, he had awakened several times in recent nights, worrying about the death cases. It was not so much the emotional issues that preoccupied him, as the intellectual ones. He wanted to be sure that he did the right thing, that he had considered all the arguments. He knew that if he were the governor of a state, he would be susceptible to arguments for granting clemency in death cases.

But he was a Justice. His task was to interpret the Constitution.

Mercy might be appropriate in some cases, but he was responsible for making a rule of law for all cases. That was what bothered him most. He felt that he was in many ways ill prepared. He had practiced corporate law for nearly four decades and had never aspired to be a judge. His experience was in arguing cases, not deciding them. He directed a clerk's attention to the 403 volumes of the Court's published opinions that lined the wall of his office. "Bill Douglas, now, he knows what is in those books," Powell said. "I don't."

Powell had confidence in his legal skills, but he was not comfortable or familiar with all this material. He had always operated from solid ground, had always been as well prepared as anyone. In legal circles, he had earned a reputation for excellence. Now, for the first time in his life, Powell faced the possibility that he might not do a good job. Fear became an unarticulated motivation. There was only one way to catch up. He intensified his already grueling work schedule, resolving to read every Court opinion ever written on the death penalty. To make more time, he even gave up going to church on Sunday.

Accustomed to having law partners to consult with, dozens of junior associates to do research, and numerous secretaries to do the typing, Powell was surprised that a justice in the highest court in the nation had a staff of only five . . . three clerks, a secretary and Hugo Black's former messenger, Spencer Campbell.

As he read through the cases and the companion material, Powell sensed that his initial vote at conference had been right. Nearly every case and all of the research reinforced his position. It would be an extreme example of judicial activism to claim that the Constitution prohibited the death penalty. Since it was clear to Powell that Stewart and White were unsure, he began to feel instinctively that he could sway them. He was the most flexible among the conference minority, more in the center than Burger, Rehnquist or Blackmun. It might be possible to win another vote for his side and switch the Court. As he read on, excerpting cases, Powell discovered an unbroken line of precedents to uphold the death penalty. The specific reference to capital punishment in the Fifth Amendment of the Constitution certainly implied that it was acceptable at the time. Striking down the death penalty would mean that the Court was substituting its conclusion for the decisions of the various legislatures. It would show a basic lack of faith in democracy.

This opinion was Powell's first exercise in judicial craftsmanship. He became convinced, not only of its correctness, but of its power to persuade, though he had some difficulty initially in translating his conservative and cautious instincts into judicial pronouncements. His views as a citizen suddenly seemed less applicable than he had expected. But he found a way every time, locating precedents to support his conclusions. The greatest help came from reading Harlan. Powell knew that those who had served with Harlan—even the Justices who had bitterly disagreed with his views—had held him in great respect. Harlan had been the Court's scholar. Powell began to study his opinions more closely. They made the most sense. But if he were to win over Stewart or White, Powell felt, he had to fully understand and answer the arguments from the other side.

Powell found the one issue that seemed to be at the heart of Harlan's hesitation about the death penalty. It was one of Douglas's concerns and probably lay behind Stewart and White's willingness to strike the laws. It was racial discrimination.

Powell was willing, for the sake of argument, to accept the statistics that appeared to show a pattern of some racial discrimination in the imposition of the death penalty. He suspected that both Marshall and Brennan had hoped this consideration would touch his conscience. It was the very issue that had caused Harlan to waiver three terms before. Powell had no illusions about racial discrimination. He had been insensitive about discrimination for too long, blindly accepting the tradition of separation of races until the 1950s. But the South and Powell had come a long way.

Blacks probably had been discriminated against and more often given death sentences, just as they had been discriminated against in every other way. But these were things of the past. Juries now included blacks, or "minority group elements," as Powell referred to them. Trials were fairer. Since a defendant, white or black, was now given every imaginable protection, discriminatory punishment was much rarer. A perfectly fair trial was an illusion, Powell believed. If juries were to be allowed discretion, some discrimination might intrude. But that issue had been resolved in the prior term. The impressive body of precedent could not be ignored, Powell wrote in his draft. "No Justice of the Court, until today, has dissented from this consistent reading of the Constitution."

In order to answer Marshall's argument that the death penalty was excessive in cases not involving murder, Powell noted the facts in the two rape cases under review. "Petitioner Jackson held a scissors blade against his victim's neck. Petitioner Branch had less difficulty subduing his sixty-five-year-old victim."

Powell conceded, however, that the death sentence could be excessive and constitute a "cruel and unusual punishment" in a given case. Therefore, cases should be considered on an individual basis. This consideration, Powell felt, was important to those who worried about instances of racial discrimination. But striking all the death penalty laws was simply unnecessary.

Powell's third revision, forty-nine pages, was circulated on May 12.

Burger, Blackmun and Rehnquist immediately indicated that they would join Powell's opinion, although none had yet finished writing his own. White and Stewart also complimented Powell on his opinion, its thoroughness, the depth of the research.

Powell misread Stewart and White's polite encouragement as enthusiasm. Unfamiliar with Court protocol, he did not understand the tradition of complimenting the "learned Judge" before ripping him to shreds. The tradition helped keep disputes on an impersonal plane, or at least maintained the facade that battles were legal and not to be taken personally.

But Powell was now sure that he could get either Stewart or White to join him. A majority opinion his first term on the major case of the year would be quite an accomplishment. The prospect confirmed Powell's belief in the importance of teamwork and quiet persuasion. He had been a success in his law firm because he was cooperative. It had brought him smooth, neat, timely achievements.

Powell admired Brennan's easy manner of lobbying, his warm solicitation of views, the gentle prodding of his hand on a colleague's elbow. But it was Powell's style to be indirect. He had laid out a comprehensive view of the case. He would not patronize Stewart or White. He had no intention of overplaying his hand. He was sure that his opinion boxed them in.

The logic was overwhelming, particularly on the question of the juries' discretion to impose the death penalty that had been decided in the *McGautha* case of the previous year. It was too high a hurdle for Stewart and White to leap. They would have to overrule it, and that was an unlikely prospect only a year after a major constitutional decision. Powell was familiar with Stewart's and White's devotion to precedent, especially recent precedent. Powell told his clerks, "It looks like we'll get our Court."

The clerk who had labored over the opinion despite his personal opposition to capital punishment was sickened at the prospect.

Stewart, however, was still looking for a ground on which to base a decision striking the death penalty laws. One of his clerks drafted an opinion that came to the sweeping conclusion that the death penalty was cruel and unusual in all cases. It agreed with Brennan and Marshall's view that society had evolved beyond imposing the death penalty. Stewart rejected it. He wanted to take a smaller step, one that attacked the current administration of the laws, nothing more. Randomness, lack of uniformity, basic unfairness— those were the issues.

Brennan followed Stewart's ups and downs closely. The two talked several times. Through his back channel to Stewart's clerks, Brennan took his colleague's bearings very carefully, trying to determine Stewart's precise concern. It was soon obvious. Black had been right. The 700 people on death row—600 now after the California decision—were the issue for Stewart. It was hard for the Justices to feel removed from the pound of sodium cyanide pellets or the 2,000 volts that would extinguish those lives.

In one of its briefs, the Inc. Fund had included some eyewitness descriptions of executions. "When the executioner throws the switch that sends the electric current through the body, the prisoner cringes from torture, his flesh swells and his skin stretches to a point of breaking. He defecates, he urinates, his tongue swells and his eyes pop out. In some cases I have been told the eyeballs rest on the cheeks of the condemned. His flesh is burned and smells of cooked meat. When the autopsy is performed the liver is so hot that doctors have said that it cannot be touched by the human hand."

"Potter will not pull the switch on 600 people," Brennan told his clerks. "I know Potter is firm, but no one knows what Byron is going to do," he said. For practical purposes the case was deadlocked, 4 to 4, with White up in the air.

Stewart agreed with Brennan that White was unpredictable. White had a technique for dealing with hard cases and decisions. He would set the matter aside for a while and then take it up again, weeks or months later. The important factors often sorted out over time. "You may think you are not thinking about it, but maybe you are," he once said. White had put the death cases aside.

In early June, Stewart began writing his opinion, working in his study at his home in Northwest Washington. It was a matter of writing and reasoning. No amount of research would solve the problem now. He sought to narrow his opinion as much as possible, to emphasize that he was addressing the specific state laws that were before the Court and not whether the death penalty was "cruel and unusual."

It was still the randomness that bothered him. Stewart looked for exact words to describe the few who were selected from among the many. He chose *capriciously, wantonly* and *freakishly*. And he searched for the perfect metaphor. "These death sentences," he wrote, "are cruel and unusual in the same way that being struck by lightning is cruel and unusual." The system of rule by law had broken down. The death penalty was random justice, and random justice was injustice. Stewart was able to say all he needed to say in ten paragraphs.

On Saturday morning, June 10, White was in his office. Setting the matter aside had worked. He was going to vote to strike the specific laws, but not to abolish the death penalty altogether. Infrequency defeated the legislative will—the state's genuine interest in deterrence and retribution. "But common sense and experience tell us that seldom-enforced laws became ineffective . . ." he typed on his ancient manual typewriter, with its several missing keys. If the laws didn't work, the state's interest evaporated. The death penalty had ceased to be a "credible threat" or to serve the "social ends" or the "public purposes" of a deterrent. He too said what he had to say in ten paragraphs.

At about 11 o'clock White summoned his three clerks. He wanted them to do some research on the 125 death penalty cases on which cert petitions were pending. Did these other death penalty laws also provide the judge or juries with the option of imposing the death sentence? Or were some of them mandatory laws that automatically imposed the sentence for certain specified crimes? He also wanted more statistics on how often juries or judges imposed the death penalty when it was an option.

White's clerks left his office. They knew nothing more than what they had heard on the grapevine: that White had tentatively voted months before at conference to strike the laws. White had never told them. They had had Socratic dialogues with him, but he had never tipped his hand.

The clerks spent three frantic hours researching White's questions. The cert petitions did not indicate whether the laws in each case had provided for optional or automatic sentencing. So they had to look up each law. It was after lunch when they finished.

Only California had a mandatory death penalty provision, and fortunately, they no longer had to deal with it. In no other case that was being heard was the death penalty automatic. The laws of each state provided for discretion and therefore were similar to the Georgia and Texas laws.

White's clerks realized that this made the present cases more important. The decision in these two cases would apply to similar state laws, and every one was virtually the same.

About 3 P.M., White called his clerks in again. He was going to vote to strike the laws. The three clerks were overjoyed, but they held themselves back. White was uncomfortable with expressions of feeling.

White explained that his opinion, though it would apply to all the state laws that were now in force, was limited to the discretionary laws. Moreover, it invited the state legislatures to consider other types of laws. He said that he personally favored laws that imposed an automatic death sentence upon conviction for specific heinous crimes, such as the assassination of a President or a presidential candidate—crimes that had cost him two friends and the country two leaders, John and Robert Kennedy.

White resented the fact that the state legislators avoided the issue. It was time they dealt with it. If they wanted a death penalty, they would have to say so and enact new ones. White read the clerks his opinion.

One of them had an observation. "I think that overrules *McGautha sub-silentio*" (without explicitly saying so), he suggested.

White scowled. The other two clerks, out of White's line of vision, frantically motioned to their colleague to drop the point.

The clerks took a copy of the opinion back to their office. It was not White's usual craftsmanlike writing. There were no footnotes or citations. Their boss seemed to have no vanity about this opinion.

White's draft was more like a trick solution, the kind he was fond of using in debate. It was a short essay on the death penalty. He had taken the government's argument on the deterrent value of the death penalty and had turned it around. White had determined simply that the basis of randomly selecting a handful of people to die was irrational.

His clerks found it ironic that the decision to save all the lives on death row revolved not around any notion of unfairness, but on the practical interests of the state in putting them there. Still, the clerks were satisfied that White had reached the right result. It was more than they had expected. They took the draft, made a few small changes, and retyped it, hoping he wouldn't notice that they had altered a few words.

White had written that he did "not *at all* intimate" that every death penalty law would be unconstitutional. The clerks thought that was too explicit an invitation to the states to try again to meet his objections with new, carefully drafted laws. They tried to get White to drop the words "at all," but White refused.

Stewart thought that his opinion and White's said the same

thing. When joined with the separate opinions of Douglas, Brennan and Marshall, that made a majority to strike all the current death penalty laws.

Though technically not abolishing the death penalty, Stewart felt that the moral authority of such a Court pronouncement would end the issue. He was fairly sure that the states would not enact the barbaric mandatory laws. The Court would never again have to face the death penalty.

At a conference called to discuss the status of unresolved cases, White raised the possibility that the term's decision on the death penalty might pose a problem for an abortion decision. If the Court struck down the death penalty and at the same time allowed abortion (which they had not yet decided to put over), the public reaction would be awful. The Court would be portrayed as allowing convicted killers to live, and sentencing unborn babies to die.

The argument left Blackmun in visible pain. He had another problem too, and he directed it to White. If they struck down the laws in these states, there would be an ensuing rush to pass mandatory death sentence legislation. That would be a tragic irony. Most death penalty laws had originally been mandatory. Jury discretion was an enlightened innovation; it was more humane to consider individual circumstances. It would be a shame to throw penology back into the Middle Ages. He had thought the death penalty question was something for legislatures to decide. Now he feared what they would do.

Rehnquist also shared his concerns with White. The Court had no business reviewing any of these state laws unless there were allegations of racial discrimination. He acknowledged that human error might result in some men being sentenced to death for no particularly good reason, perhaps even for an absolutely bad one. But the human error of wrongfully depriving a man of his constitutional rights was less severe than mistakenly striking down an otherwise constitutional statute. For the Court to thwart the will of a state legislature was, in Rehnquist's view, to violate the rights of every individual in that state. That was a far greater wrong than allowing one man to die.

Burger was deeply disappointed in both Stewart's and White's opinions for still another reason. Burger made the point in his dissent; he noted that Stewart and White would seem to have no objection to the death penalty if the "rate of imposition is somehow multiplied. . . .

"It seemingly follows that the flexible sentencing system created by the legislatures, and carried out by juries and judges, has yielded more mercy than the Eighth Amendment can stand. The implications of the approach are mildly ironical."

But Burger agreed with Stewart's assessment of the decision's impact. "There will never be another execution in this country," he predicted privately.

Powell was disappointed. He had come so close, he believed, to getting the majority. He was also surprised and distressed to find the legal reasoning in the opinions of Stewart and White so shoddy. Clearly, they had switched their positions since the *McGautha* case the previous year. They were simply unwilling to say so.

As soon as the typewritten copies of the White and Stewart drafts were circulated, Douglas's clerk called his boss in Goose Prairie. Douglas also immediately caught the inconsistency with *McGautha*. He wanted to add a footnote to his own opinion laying into Stewart and White for not facing this squarely. His tone was severe, and he was not about to be dissuaded from attacking his two new allies. He was sure the footnote would not destroy the coalition.

After several days, copies of the two opinions had still not arrived in Goose Prairie, and Douglas called to berate his clerks. Somehow, he held them responsible for the slow mail. He did not want to listen to any excuses. He would deal directly with Brennan. Douglas spoke to Brennan by phone on Thursday, June 15. They agreed that Brennan should draft a short *per curiam*, summarizing the result that the majority had reached in their separate opinions. Douglas insisted that the *per curiam* include the lineup of who had voted on either side, so that the result would not be lost in the welter of opinions. He also told Brennan about the footnote he intended to write and asked that announcement of the case be postponed at least until Monday, June 26, so that the footnote could be inserted in his opinion.

Brennan tried gently to dissuade him. The coalition was not necessarily solid.

Douglas would not move.

The footnote soon followed. It was, as Brennan had feared, uncompromising. "The tension between our decision today and *McGautha* highlights, in my view, the correctness of Mr. Justice Brennan's dissent in that case, which I joined." Douglas then pointed out the similarity between Stewart's and White's opinions and Brennan's *McGautha* dissent.

Much to Brennan's relief, Stewart and White ignored the attack.

With all the votes and opinions in, Burger wanted to clarify the choices that were now available to the states. The majority, he wrote as a final addition to his opinion, had not ruled all death penalty laws unconstitutional. Mandatory or automatic sentences were still probably constitutional. State legislatures had "the opportunity, and indeed the unavoidable responsibility," to consider these alternatives.

On the morning of June 29, the last day of the term, the 5-to-4 decision was announced.

The nine separate opinions totaled 50,000 words, 243 pages— the longest decision in the Court's history.

With his long sideburns and moderately long hair, Rehnquist looked younger than forty-seven. Wearing his tortoiseshell glasses, he sat slouched in a chair with his penny loafers propped up on the mahogany conference table to the right of his office door. The informal posture reflected his easygoing approach to life at the Court. He had quickly settled into a comfortable routine.

Rehnquist watched with some amusement as the Court tackled an important antitrust case *(U.S. v. Chas. Pfizer & Co)*. Stewart, White and Marshall recused themselves, leaving only six Justices to decide the matter. The initial conference vote was 4 to 2 for the company, with Douglas and the Chief in the minority. The Justice who was assigned the majority would have to plow through briefs, exhibits and trial transcripts that filled six feet of shelf space. Brennan had made up his mind before conference that none of them should have to waste so much time. With a twinkle in his eye, he announced that on further reflection he was persuaded by the Chief's logic. He would switch and vote against the company, making it a 3-to-3 tie. Since the tie would still affirm the lower court decision for the company, his switch would have no effect on the actual outcome of this case and no one would have to write an opinion.

The liberals found it hard not to like the good-natured, thoughtful Rehnquist. They could even bring themselves to respect his crisp intellect and diligence. And they weren't surprised when Rehnquist began promptly to live up to his advance billing as a solid conservative vote, siding invariably with the prosecution in criminal cases, with business in antitrust cases, with employers in labor cases and with the government in speech cases.

His extreme legal philosophy worried the liberals. Rehnquist had a very narrow view of the Fourteenth Amendment, which was passed after the Civil War to remedy the effects of slavery and guarantee the rights of black citizens. The Court had for nearly a century used this amendment to ensure basic freedoms for all citizens. In Rehnquist's view, the amendment was misapplied when used to give rights to prisoners, women or other groups. For the first time in a half-century, a Justice was flatly stating that the Court had no business reflecting society's changing and expanding values. He seemed prepared to turn the clock back a century.

To Marshall, Rehnquist's stark revisionism often seemed crude and mean-spirited. Marshall insisted on looking beyond Rehnquist's apparently sincere literalism to the motives of the man who had nominated him to the Court. Marshall viewed Rehnquist's nomination cynically as Nixon's calculated revenge designed to curtail liberty for the less fortunate and underprivileged. The prospect of living out his remaining years on the Court with Rehnquist did not please Marshall. Marshall was particularly chilled by Rehnquist's warning that the liberals should curtail their broad interpretations of the Constitution. It was only recently that activism on the Court had become "liberal" activism, Rehnquist reminded them. Only forty years before, the Court's activists were conservatives. The balance was once again shifting back, Rehnquist said. Once it had, the liberals would be the ones calling for judicial restraint and chiding the conservatives for ignoring precedent.

Even more chilling to the liberals was Rehnquist's ideological commitment to keep the federal courts out of certain types of cases. He argued that state legislatures, state governments, and state courts should be given the benefit of the doubt when it came to defining the individual rights of their citizens. Only the most extreme abuses could be corrected, he felt. The Court had no business forcing its views on the states; it was not the voice and conscience of contemporary society.

Beneath Rehnquist's stated commitment to judicial consistency, the liberals saw his willingness to cut corners to reach a conservative result. Polished, articulate opinions seemed cleverly, sometimes deceptively, to gloss over inconsistencies of logic or fact. In one case (*Jefferson v. Hackney*), Douglas and Marshall objected that Rehnquist's majority opinion misrepresented the legislative history of the federal welfare program. Slow even to correct an outright misstatement, Rehnquist still insisted on publishing an opinion that twisted the facts. His own clerk was so embarrassed by Rehnquist's refusal to modify the opinion that he sent a personal note of apology for his role in the case to the clerks in other chambers.

Brennan had worried that Powell would become as inflexible as Rehnquist. He was also fearful that Powell might defer to Burger. As he reviewed the results of each conference with his clerks, Brennan referred frequently to whether Powell "was being taken in by the Chief" or "saw through" the Chief's antics. He hoped that the Chief would offend Powell and drive him into the arms of the liberals.

Powell had begun cautiously and to Brennan he seemed precise and fair-minded, somewhat like Harlan. Harlan and Powell had both concluded, from years of private law practice, that narrow solutions to legal problems were better than sweeping ones.

The parallel with Harlan was unmistakable when Powell became the swing vote in two cases that had been held over from the previous term (*Apodaca v. Oregon* and *Johnson v. Louisiana*). Both cases involved the question of whether juries must be unanimous in their verdicts in criminal cases. The year before, Douglas, Brennan, Stewart and Marshall had said yes. Burger, Black, White and Blackmun had said no. Harlan had staked out a unique position; he had held that juries must be unanimous in federal trials but not in state trials. Undecided, the case had been put over.

After it was reargued, and with Black and Harlan gone, Rehnquist voted as Black had. The Court was again split 4 to 4. Powell did not vote, but after studying the long draft that Harlan had had his clerks prepare the year before, Powell adopted Harlan's position, splitting his vote by voting one way for federal trials and the other on state trials.

Burger tried to get Powell to switch. White ordered one of his clerks to write a "hatchet job" on Powell's opinion that would highlight the inconsistency. Powell would not budge. Brennan was unhappy with the outcome, but he took consolation in the fact that Powell had at least chosen to follow Harlan rather than Burger. Brennan liked to tell his clerks that Harlan had been the "only real judge" on the Court in the years of Brennan's service, the only Justice who weighed the legal issues with sufficient dispassion.

Powell was to be the swing vote in three important First Amendment cases (*Branzburg v. Hayes, U.S. v. Caldwell, In re Pappas*) that dealt with the question of whether news reporters had to reveal to grand juries the identities of confidential sources. After much hesitation, Powell finally decided to give White a fifth vote for an opinion declaring that reporters, like all other citizens, had to give information to grand juries. But Powell's vote came with a separate concurrence, with qualifications that suggested that the issue might have to be reconsidered if reporters were harassed by grand juries. Again, it was reminiscent of Harlan. He had used his crucial swing vote to limit the effect of a majority opinion.

In dissent, Stewart called attention to Powell's important qualifications, which, Stewart said, "leaves room for the hope that in some future case the Court may take a less absolute position in this area."

Brennan found additional comfort during Powell's initial months as a Justice. Before coming to the Court, Powell had publicly supported the Nixon administration's claims that domestic radicals could be wiretapped without the customary warrants from a judge. But in a case that raised that very issue *(U.S. v. U.S. District Court)* Powell reassessed his views and wrote a strong majority opinion rejecting each of the administration's arguments. Burger had tried to assign the case to White, who, along with himself, wanted to duck the central constitutional question of whether the warrantless wiretap violated the Fourth Amendment.

White rejected the assignment, noting that he and the Chief were alone in their view. Douglas immediately reassigned the case to Powell, who held firm in the face of Burger's continuous pressure not to write a broad constitutional ruling.

From Brennan's perspective, the initial impact of Nixon's new appointees was not as bad as he had feared. Rehnquist was a rigid ideologue willing, even anxious, to overturn the work of the Warren Court. Yet no major Warren Court precedent had been overruled that term, and Powell was the main reason.* He seemed determined to be his own man, and he remained as flexible and reachable as Rehnquist was inflexible, unreachable. Powell had positioned himself in the center, along with Stewart and White. And since Stewart and White went in opposite directions on so many key issues, Powell was becoming the true swing vote. There was now someone else in the center who might provide a fourth or fifth vote for the liberals.

And another vote was softening up on the right. Blackmun seemed to be trying to push away from the Chief.

---

* In *Kirby v. Illinois,* Powell was again a swing vote and he took a middle course. He refused to extend a Warren Court precedent and require that the state provide lawyers at all lineups. At the same time, he refused to join an effort to overrule the Warren precedent itself.

*   *   *

The four main death penalty cases had not resolved a fifth one (*Moore v. Illinois*). Lyman A. "Slick" Moore had been sentenced to death for a shotgun murder, but his appeal raised issues other than the "cruel and unusual" nature of the death penalty. With the death penalty now struck down, the Court had to decide these other issues—or Moore was doomed to life in prison.

Moore argued that he had been unfairly convicted. The prosecution had withheld from the defense the fact that the three principal witnesses who claimed to have heard a "Slick" brag of the murder had all told police that they didn't think this Moore was the same "Slick." A judge had also permitted prosecutors to wave a sawed-off shotgun in front of the jury, though the prosecution admitted at trial that it was not the murder weapon.

At conference, the vote was 7 to 2 to uphold Moore's conviction, with Marshall and Douglas the only dissenters. Moore would not get a new trial, but the death penalty decision in the other four cases would keep him from being executed.

The Chief assigned the case to Blackmun. As usual, Blackmun was late with his circulation. Douglas expressed his exasperation over the delay at conference. "Circulations from Harry are like returns in an election from rural counties—late," Stewart once said.

When the opinion finally came around, it said the information, if withheld, did not prove Moore's innocence, but only tended to show that he was not the same man who had bragged about the murder. Waving the shotgun before the jury, Blackmun stated, was not a sufficiently significant error to justify a new trial.

Marshall was upset. During his days of criminal-law practice, he had seen many men convicted by distorted presentations of the facts. He had a clerk prepare a detailed analysis of the evidence, challenging Blackmun's reading.

The identification by eyewitnesses had been crucial to obtaining the conviction and Blackmun was ignoring many of the facts damaging to their testimony. This was a miscarriage of justice. Marshall's analysis was circulated as a dissent. Blackmun responded in a set of footnotes arguing his own version of the facts.

Powell and Stewart quickly switched their votes, and Marshall needed only one more to take away Blackmun's majority. His friend Brennan would surely provide the fifth vote. Brennan, after all, had been a moving force behind a whole series of cases that required prosecutors to turn over all exculpatory evidence to the defense.

One of Brennan's clerks thought that if Brennan had seen the facts as Marshall presented them, he would not have voted the other way. He went to talk to Brennan and, thirty minutes later, returned shaken. Brennan understood that Marshall's position was correct, but he was not going to switch sides now, the clerk said. This was not just a run-of-the-mill case for Blackmun. Blackmun had spent a lot of time on it, giving the trial record a close reading. He prided himself on his objectivity. If Brennan switched, Blackmun would be personally offended. That would be unfortunate, because Blackmun had lately seemed more assertive, more independent of the Chief. Brennan felt that if he voted against Blackmun now, it might make it more difficult to reach him in the abortion cases or even the obscenity cases.

Sure, "Slick" Moore deserved a new trial. But more likely than not, it would result in his being convicted again. After all, Moore had a long record. He was not exactly an angel. Anyway, the Court could not concern itself with correcting every injustice. They should never have taken such a case, Brennan said. He felt he had to consider the big picture.

"He won't leave Harry on this," Brennan's clerk reported to Marshall's clerk.

The clerks were shocked that such considerations would keep a man in prison. They wondered whether Brennan still would have refused to switch if the death penalty had not been struck.

Marshall's clerk asked his boss to talk to Brennan.

Marshall refused. It was not his style. He resented pressure from the Chief and he was not about to imitate his methods.

Marshall's clerk made a final appeal through Brennan's clerks.

Brennan had his priorities. His priority in this case was Harry Blackmun. There would be no new trial for "Slick" Moore.

1972 Term

HARRY BLACKMUN RETURNED to Rochester, Minnesota, for the summer of 1972 and immersed himself in research at the huge Mayo Clinic medical library. Rochester and the clinic were home to Blackmun, a safe harbor after a stormy term. He worked in a corner of the assistant librarian's office for two weeks without saying a word to anyone on the Mayo staff about the nature of his inquiry.

In his summer office in a Rochester high-rise, Blackmun began to organize the research that would bolster his abortion opinion. He talked by phone nearly every day with one of his clerks who had agreed to stay in Washington for the summer.

Blackmun pondered the relevance of the Hippocratic oath, which prohibits doctors from performing abortions. He also wanted to understand the positions of the medical organizations and to learn more about the advances in sustaining the life of a fetus outside the womb.

One by one, new elements found their way into his draft. His clerk worked each change into the text back in Washington. The language remained Blackmun's; the more rigorous analysis was the work of the clerk. For the first time, the right to privacy emerged explicitly. It was not absolute. It was limited by the state's interest in protecting the pregnant woman's health and the potential life of the fetus.

As they developed their analytic basis, Blackmun and his clerk tried to answer the crucial question: when did the state's interest in protecting the life of the fetus become overriding and outweigh the woman's right to privacy? Clearly there was such a point. The state's interest increased with time. But no definite answer could be derived from the Constitution.

Blackmun turned to medicine. Doctors often divided pregnancies into three equal stages, or trimesters, each of roughly three months. Abortions were generally safe in the first trimester and, under proper medical conditions, could be performed safely in the second. It was at about this time, at the end of the second trimester, that the fetus became *viable,* or capable of living outside the womb. That was at about twenty-four to twenty-eight weeks, six months for all practical purposes. Therefore, the two medical interests—protecting both the health of the mother and the potential life of the fetus—seemed to converge and become overriding at about this six-month point. Abortions during the first two trimesters could and should be permitted. The draft gradually emerged as a strong, liberal prescription. It would prohibit states from interfering until the third trimester.

The clerk who was working on the opinion began to worry that one of the other clerks, strongly opposed to abortions, might try to change their boss's mind. He took no chances. Each night he carefully locked up the work he had been doing for Blackmun. At the end of the summer, he carefully sealed the latest draft in an envelope, put his initials across the tape, and had it locked in Blackmun's desk. Only Blackmun's personal secretary knew where it was.

Powell also made abortion his summer research project. As a young lawyer in Richmond in the 1930s, Powell had heard tales of girls who would "go away" to Switzerland and New York, where safe abortions were available. If someone were willing to pay for it, it was possible to have an abortion.

Powell understood how doctors viewed abortion. His father-in-law had been a leading obstetrician in Richmond, and his two brothers-in-law were obstetricians. Powell had heard all the horrifying stories of unsanitary butchers and coat-hanger abortions.

Nevertheless, Powell came quickly to the conclusion that the Constitution did not provide meaningful guidance. The right to privacy was tenuous; at best it was implied. If there was no way to find an answer in the Constitution, Powell felt he would just have to vote his "gut." He had been critical of Justices for doing exactly that; but in abortion, there seemed no choice.

When he returned to Washington, he took one of his law clerks to lunch at the Monocle Restaurant on Capitol Hill. The abortion laws, Powell confided, were "atrocious." His would be a strong and unshakable vote to strike them. He needed only a rationale for his vote.

In a recent lower court case, a federal judge had struck down the Connecticut abortion law.* This opinion impressed Powell. The judge had said that moral positions on abortion "about which each side was so sure must remain a personal judgment, one that [people] may follow in their personal lives and seek to persuade others to follow, but a judgment they may not impose upon others by force of law." That was all the rationale Powell needed.

Brennan and Douglas worried that votes might have shifted since the previous spring. Blackmun remained a question mark, Stewart might defect, and they were not sure what Powell would do.

At conference on October 12, Blackmun made a long, eloquent and strongly emotional case for striking down the laws. Stewart too seemed ready to join. But the big surprise was Powell. He made it 6 to 3.

Immediately after conference, Douglas called Blackmun to tell him that his presentation had been the finest he had heard at conference in more than thirty years. He hoped the call would sustain Blackmun for the duration.

Before the end of October, Blackmun's new draft in the abortion case was circulated to the various chambers.

Brennan read it carefully. He waded through the positions of the medical professional organizations, the expanded historical section, the long-winded digest of the medical state of the art. Despite all this, Blackmun's bottom line was acceptable. The states would be prohibited from regulating abortions until "viability." That

* *Abele v. Markle.*

meant state regulation only during the third trimester. But Brennan spotted a weakness in the argument. Connecting the state's interest in the fetus to the point of viability was risky. Blackmun himself had noted that medical advances made fetuses viable increasingly early. Scientists might one day be capable of sustaining a two-week-old fetus outside the womb. Advances in medicine could undermine the thrust of the opinion.

Brennan had other concerns. Blackmun had focused on the rights of the doctor and the rights of the state. The most important party, the woman, had been largely neglected. Her rights were the ones that needed to be upheld.

Brennan found yet another analytical fault in the draft. Blackmun had discussed at length the state's dual interests in protecting the pregnant woman's health and the potential life of the fetus. Both interests were closely intertwined in Blackmun's draft. Brennan thought they were quite distinct. He handed Blackmun's draft to one of his clerks. "It doesn't do it," he said.

Brennan's clerks worked up a long memorandum. The delicate question, however, was how to communicate Brennan's thoughts to Blackmun. If Brennan phoned and said, "Harry, here are my ideas," Blackmun might be intimidated or fumble for months and still not change the draft adequately. On the other hand, if Brennan sent a printed opinion to the conference, Blackmun might think he was trying to steal the majority. The last thing Brennan wanted was to author the Court's abortion decision. He could imagine too vividly what the Catholic bishops would say.

In mid-November, Brennan took his clerks' memo and recast it as a series of casual thoughts and suggestions. It was important that it not appear to be an alternative draft. Brennan addressed a cover memo to Blackmun saying he fully agreed with his draft, but wanted to pass along some ideas. Brennan's thoughts ran forty-eight pages. Copies were sent to all the Justices.

Blackmun liked some of Brennan's suggestions. He quickly sent a memo to the Justices saying that he was incorporating them. Before he revised his draft, however, he decided that there was another set of views to be taken into account.

The Chief had made it clear to Blackmun that he would "never" join the draft as it stood, permitting unrestricted abortions up to viability, or the end of the second trimester. Blackmun wanted the Chief's vote, and he thought he saw a way to get it while still taking into account Brennan's suggestions. Instead of the one demarcation line, viability, Blackmun would create two. This would also be more medically sophisticated; it would show that the two state interests—protecting the pregnant woman's health and protecting potential life of the fetus—arose at different times. He settled on a formula.

1. First 12 weeks (first trimester); no state interest at all; abortions unrestricted and left up to the medical judgment of the doctor.
2. 12 to 24 weeks (second trimester); state interest arises and abortions can be regulated only to protect the woman's health.
3. After 24 weeks (third trimester); state interest arises to protect the potential life of the fetus.

This formula had the effect of somewhat limiting abortions in the second trimester. But eliminating viability as the dividing point, Brennan's worry, guaranteed that medical science could not keep reducing the time period during which abortions would be legally available.

Marshall was not happy with Blackmun's proposal. It was too rigid. Many women, particularly the poor and undereducated, would probably not get in touch with a doctor until some time after the first 12 weeks. A woman in a rural town might not have access to a doctor until later in pregnancy. And according to the Blackmun proposal, the states could effectively ban abortions in the 12-to-24-week period under the guise of protecting the woman's health. Marshall preferred Blackmun's original linkage to viability. If viability were the cut-off point, it would better protect the rural poor. Clearly, viability meant one thing in Boston, where there were fancy doctors and hospitals. There, a fetus might be sustained after only a few months. But in rural areas with no hospitals and few, if any, doctors, viability was probably close to full-term, or late in the third trimester.

Marshall presented all this to Blackmun in a memo.

Blackmun respected Marshall's point of view. Marshall clearly knew a lot about many real world problems that Blackmun would never see. He incorporated all of Marshall's suggestions. His new draft specified:

1. For the stage up to "approximately" the end of the first trimester, abortions would be left to the medical judgment of the doctor.
2. For the stage after "approximately" the end of the first trimester, abortion procedures could be regulated to protect the woman's health.
3. For the stage after "viability," abortions could be regulated or even prohibited, to protect the fetus.

The clerks in most chambers were surprised to see the Justices, particularly Blackmun, so openly brokering their decision like a group of legislators. There was a certain reasonableness to the draft, some of them thought, but it derived more from medical and social policy than from constitutional law. There was something embarrassing and dishonest about this whole process. It left the Court claiming that the Constitution drew certain lines at trimesters and viability. The Court was going to make a medical policy and force it on the states. As a practical matter, it was not a bad solution. As a constitutional matter, it was absurd. The draft was referred to by some clerks as "Harry's abortion."

Stewart had one more change that he insisted on before he would join the opinion. It was imperative that they say more clearly that a fetus was not—as far as the Fourteenth Amendment was concerned—a person. If the fetus were a person, it had rights protected by the Constitution, including "life, liberty and property." Then the Court would be saying that a woman's rights outweighed those of the fetus. Weighing two sets of rights would be dangerous. The Court would be far better off with only one set of rights to protect. Stewart was certain that in legal terms a fetus was not a person. No previous case had held so. States conceded that, where the mother's life was at stake, a fetus had no rights. When the Fourteenth Amendment was passed in 1868, abortions were common enough to suggest that the state legislatures that had ratified the Amendment did not consider fetuses to have rights.

Blackmun did not disagree, but he felt the point was implicit in the opinion. Why expand it and stir up trouble?

Stewart was insistent, and Blackmun finally agreed to say clearly that a fetus was not a person.

After he had joined Blackmun's opinion, Stewart still wanted to add his own concurrence. Unlike Douglas, he was not inclined to write separate opinions spelling out small, technical disagreements with the majority. Stewart often joined inadequate opinions—"junk," he once called them—believing that this was a vital part of the compromising process. It also left him more time to write his own majority opinions.

But the Blackmun opinion lacked an explicit constitutional foundation for the abortion ruling. In a middle section providing his legal reasoning, Blackmun had brought the broadest arguments against restrictive abortion laws. He had written a sweeping general conclusion that the basis for lifting the restrictions could be found in the Ninth and Fourteenth, even in the First Amendment, and that it was implied in a series of privacy cases, ranging from the 1965 Connecticut contraceptive case to the previous term's contraceptive case so carefully tailored by Brennan (*Eisenstadt v. Baird*).

"Zones of privacy," Blackmun had written, do exist "under the Constitution." Stewart could not fully accept that. It was too broad. It was precisely the cause of his dissent in the 1965 Connecticut contraceptive case and of his hesitancy the previous year in *Eisenstadt*. He wanted to identify the part of the Constitution that conferred the freedom to have abortions during the early months of pregnancy. Stewart believed that a woman's right to an abortion in the early months was a "liberty" protected under the due process clause of the Fourteenth Amendment. But that approach carried with it historical baggage that Stewart would rather avoid.

In the 1930s the Court had used the clause to strike down key New Deal legislation. Since "liberty" could be construed to mean anything that five Justices agreed should be protected, critics charged that the Court had become a superlegislature, substituting its judgment for that of elected legislators. This approach, called "substantive due process" (to differentiate it from the more common procedural rights covered by due process), had been gradually discredited.

Since Stewart felt that "substantive due process" was the real basis for the Blackmun opinion, he believed that Blackmun was hesitant to admit it in the opinion. Stewart circulated his own concurrence, joining Blackmun's opinion, but adding his observations on the real roots of the opinion.

Reading Stewart's concurrence, Douglas found it laughable that Stewart, of all people, was concerned with constitutional purity. Douglas believed that Stewart's real motive in writing a concurrence was to put some distance between himself and Blackmun's opinion, which Stewart obviously thought was poorly reasoned and written.

Douglas shot back a memo arguing that Stewart had the history all wrong. This was not "substantive due process," Douglas said. He had been one of the earliest and most vociferous critics of that doctrine. The basis for the decision was clear. The Blackmun opinion was based on the right to privacy, Douglas countered.

Blackmun wanted no part of the Stewart-Douglas debate. He was tired of compromising and dealing with everyone's gripes. This latest "sniping" was ridiculous. The important thing was that he already had six votes.

Given his gloomy expectations at the outset of the abortion debate, Douglas felt the Court had come a long way. The right to privacy was being given constitutional foundation in a major opinion. He dropped his debate with Stewart. It was a great victory, and Douglas wanted to add a concurring opinion underscoring its significance.

He decided to revise a lyrical concurrence that he had drafted the previous term about what he called the

> customary, traditional, and time-honored rights, amenities, privileges and immunities that come within the sweep of "the Blessings of Liberty."
>
> First is the autonomous control over the development and expression of one's intellect, interests, tastes and personality.

Second is freedom of choice in the basic decisions of one's life respecting marriage, divorce, procreation, contraception, and the education and upbringing of children.

Third is the freedom to care for one's health and person, freedom from bodily restraint or compulsion, freedom to walk, stroll, or loaf.

A clerk urged him to go beyond his discussion of a right to privacy and conclusively nail down a right to abortion.

Douglas responded, "I'm only writing this for me."

White shortened his dissent from the previous term. The states, not the courts, should decide the question of limits on abortion. Blackmun's trimester-and-viability scheme was pure legislation. "As an exercise of raw judicial power, the Court perhaps has authority to do what it does today," White wrote. But he expressed doubts about a constitutional sanction that would allow a woman to get rid of an unwanted child on a "whim" or out of "caprice."

"The Court," White wrote, "apparently values the convenience of the pregnant mother more than the continued existence and development of the life or potential life that she carries."

Rehnquist's dissent had little to do with abortion. As always, Rehnquist pushed his views on restricting federal court powers and the women's rights to bring these cases into court. First, he attacked the most basic element of the cases. No one had standing to bring these cases into court, he said. Assuming the women were pregnant when the suit was brought, they would be at least in their third trimester by the time the lower court decided the case. Since Blackmun's opinion held that states could deny abortions during the third trimester, there was no claim for the women to bring.

Rehnquist pointed out that in 1868, when the Fourteenth Amendment was adopted, at least thirty-six states or territories had laws on the books limiting abortions. It did not appear that the framers of the Fourteenth Amendment intended to bar the states from regulating abortions.

By early December, Blackmun's final draft had circulated. Stewart's and Douglas's concurrences were finished, and White's and Rehnquist's dissents were ready. There was still nothing from Burger.

White was particularly unhappy with the progress of the term. Dozens of cases were ready to come down except, more often than not, for the Chief's vote. He wrote a memo pointing out the bottleneck.

By early January, there was still nothing from the Chief. Blackmun grew increasingly nervous. He was worried about his reputation for being chronically late. He had not yet brought down an opinion for the term. Abortion was ready; he wanted it to come down at once. Blackmun and the others in the majority finally began pointing toward a Monday, January 15, announcement of the abortion decisions. Still there was nothing from Burger.

On January 12 at conference, Stewart put it to the Chief directly. "Vote now or let the decision come down with only eight votes," Stewart suggested.

To the majority's surprise, Burger said that he had decided to join the Blackmun opinion but, like some of the others, he wanted to add his own concurring remarks. "I'll get it to you next week," he promised.

Stewart and Brennan thought he was stalling. The Chief was scheduled to swear in Richard Nixon for his second term as President on January 20. It would undoubtedly be embarrassing for Burger to stand there, swearing in the man who had appointed him, having just supported a sweeping and politically volatile opinion that repudiated that man's views.

At the Friday, January 19, conference, the Chief said that his schedule had been busy, and he still had not gotten to the abortion decision. Stewart figure that, having manipulated a delay until after the Inaugural, Burger would acquiesce. The others wanted a Monday, January 22, announcement, three days later, and Burger said that he would have something.

Over the weekend, he wrote a three-paragraph concurrence. Ignoring the sweep of the opinion he was joining, Burger said that one law (Texas) was being struck because it did not permit abortions in instances of rape or incest, and he implied that the other law was being struck because of the "complex" steps that required hospital board certification of an abortion. He did not believe that the opinion would have the "consequences" predicted by dissenters White and Rehnquist, and he was sure that states could still control abortions. "Plainly," he concluded, "the Court today rejects any claim that the Constitution requires abortion on demand."

The day of the scheduled abortion decision the Chief sat in his chambers reading the latest edition of *Time* magazine. "Last week TIME learned that the Supreme Court has decided to strike down nearly every anti-abortion law in the land," an article said. The abortion decision had been leaked.

Burger drafted an "Eyes Only" letter to the other Justices. He wanted each Justice to question his law clerks. The responsible person must be found and fired. Burger intended to call in the F.B.I. to administer lie-detector tests if necessary.

Dutifully, Rehnquist brought up the matter with his clerks. It was harmless in this case, he said. But in a business case, a leak could affect the stock market and allow someone to make millions of dollars. None of Rehnquist's clerks knew anything about the leak, but they asked him if it were true that the Chief was thinking of lie-detector tests. "It is still up in the air," Rehnquist said. "But yes, the Chief is insisting."

Rehnquist's clerks were concerned. Such a witch-hunt would be met with resistance. Certainly, some clerks would refuse to take such a test and would probably have to resign. The Chief is mercurial, Rehnquist explained. "The rest of us will prevail on him."

Brennan summoned his clerks and read them the Chief's letter. It was another example, he said, of the Chief usurping the authority each Justice had over his own clerks. "No one will question my law clerks but me," Brennan said. Then in a softer voice, he added, "And I have no questions." The real outrage for Brennan was not the leak but the delay. If the Chief had not been intent on saving himself and Nixon some embarrassment on Inauguration day, there probably would have been no damaging leak.

Marshall asked what his clerks knew about the incident. When he was assured that they knew nothing, he told them to forget it.

Douglas treated the letter as he had treated a request from the Chief the previous term that all clerks be instructed to wear coats in the hallways. He ignored it.

Powell was out of town, so one of his clerks opened the Chief's letter. The clerk had talked to the *Time* reporter, David Beckwith, trying to give him some guidance so he could write an intelligent story when the decision came down. But the delay in announcing the decision had apparently left *Time* with a scoop, if only for half a day.

The clerk called Powell and told him about the Chief's letter and his own terrible mistake in talking to Beckwith. He volunteered to resign.

That would not be necessary, Powell said. But a personal explanation would have to be given to the Chief.

Powell called Burger and explained that one of his clerks, a brilliant and talented young lawyer, was responsible. The clerk realized his mistake and had learned his lesson. The clerk went to see the Chief.

Burger was sympathetic. Reporters were dishonest and played tricks, he said. It was a lesson everyone had to learn.

Apparently never expecting to learn so much about the little deceptions of both reporters and sources, Burger pressed for all the details. It took nearly forty-five minutes to satisfy his curiosity.

The clerk concluded that Burger understood, that he was being a saint about the matter. Burger wanted a memo detailing exactly what happened. The clerk would not have to resign.

Later, the Chief met with top editors of *Time* in an off-the-record session. He labeled Beckwith's efforts to get inside information at the Court improper, the moral equivalent of wiretapping.

Blackmun suggested to his wife, Dottie, that she come to Court to hear case announcements on Monday, January 22. He did not tell her why. As Blackmun announced the decisions, Powell sent a note of encouragement to Blackmun's wife. Powell suspected they were about to witness a public outcry, the magnitude of which he and Blackmun had not seen in their short time on the Court.

"I'm very proud of the decision you made," Dottie later told her husband.

After the abortion decision was announced, Blackmun took congratulatory calls through most of the afternoon. But former

President Lyndon Johnson died the same day, and the news of his death dominated the next morning's newspapers.

Blackmun was unhappy that the abortion decision did not get more attention. Many women, especially the poor and black, would not learn of their new rights. But the outcry quickly began, led by the Catholic Church. "How many millions of children prior to their birth will never live to see the light of day because of the shocking action of the majority of the United States Supreme Court today?" demanded New York's Terence Cardinal Cooke.

John Joseph Cardinal Krol, of Philadelphia, the president of the National Conference of Catholic Bishops, said, "It is hard to think of any decision in the two hundred years of our history which has had more disastrous implications for our stability as a civilized society."

Thousands of letters poured into the Court. The guards had to set up a special sorting area in the basement with a huge box for each Justice.

The most mail came to Blackmun, the decision's author, and to Brennan, the Court's only Catholic. Some letters compared the Justices to the Butchers of Dachau, child killers, immoral beasts and Communists. A special ring of hell would be reserved for the Justices. Whole classes from Catholic schools wrote to denounce the Justices as murderers. "I really don't want to write this letter but my teacher made me," one child said.

Minnesota Lutherans zeroed in on Blackmun. New Jersey Catholics called for Brennan's excommunication. Southern Baptists and other groups sent over a thousand bitter letters to Hugo Black, who had died sixteen months earlier. Some letters and calls were death threats.

Blackmun went through the mail piece by piece. The sisters of Saint Mary's hospital, the backbone of the Mayo Clinic, wrote outraged letters week after week. He was tormented. The medical community and even his friends at Mayo were divided. Blackmun encountered picketing for the first time in his life when he gave a speech in Iowa. He understood the position of the anti-abortion advocates, but he was deeply hurt by the personal attacks. He felt compelled to point out that there had been six other votes for the decision, besides his, that the Justices had tried to enunciate a constitutional principle, not a moral one. Law and morality overlapped but were not congruent, he insisted. Moral training should come not from the Court but from the Church, the family, the schools.

The letters continued to pour in. Every time a clergyman mentioned the decision in his sermon, the letters trickled in for a month from members of the congregation. The attack gradually wore Blackmun down. At breakfast with his clerks, when the discussion turned to the decision, Blackmun picked up his water glass reflectively, turning it slightly on edge and staring into it in silence.

The criticism also drew Blackmun and Brennan closer. Blackmun wrote Brennan a warm thank-you note: "I know it is tough for you, and I thank you for the manner in which you made your suggestions."

Brennan tried to cheer up Blackmun. Doing the right thing was not often easy, he said. The one thing in the world Brennan did not want known was his role in molding the opinion.*

Blackmun did not cheer up easily. The hysteria on each side of the issue convinced him that any decision would have been unpopular. However, the deepest cut came when the state of Texas filed a petition for rehearing that compared Blackmun's conclusion which held that a fetus was not a person, to the Court's infamous 1857 decision that said that Dred Scott, a slave, was not a citizen or person under the Constitution. Blackmun thought that comparing his opinion with the Court's darkest day of racism was terribly unfair. And, after all, it had been Stewart who had insisted on that part of the opinion.

Months later, Blackmun gave a speech at Emory Law School in Atlanta. He was chatting with students and faculty when a petite young woman with black curly hair ran up the steps to the stage. She squeezed through the group, threw her arms around

---

* When the clerks later put together bound volumes of the opinions Brennan had written that term, they included the abortion opinions, and on page 156 they wrote, "These cases are included with Justice Brennan's opinions for the October term 1972 because the opinions for the Court were substantially revised in response to suggestions made by Justice Brennan."

Blackmun and burst into tears. "I'll never be able to thank you for what you have done. I'll say no more. Thank you."

The woman turned and ran from the room.

Blackmun was shaken. He suspected that the woman was probably someone who had been able to obtain an abortion after the Court's decision. He did not know that "Mary Doe," the woman who had filed one of the original suits in Texas under a pseudonym, had just embraced him.

The Chief had begun an ambitious remodeling program during the summer of 1972 to give the Justices bigger offices to accommodate the increasing number of law clerks.

Douglas thought that giving each Justice an extra office was a waste of the taxpayers' money. He had his office moved to a smaller chamber, wedged between two marble staircases, and decided to cut back from three clerks to two. Even then he figured that two clerks would probably spend half their time talking to each other, so he would get the work of only one.

His clerk-selection committee had picked two women for the 1972–1973 term: Janet Meik, a pleasant, soft-spoken graduate from University of Southern California Law School, and Carol Bruch, an outspoken honors graduate from the University of California School of Law at Berkeley.

The previous term's clerks, who had laboriously developed a somewhat successful relationship with Douglas, were worried when Bruch announced that she planned to delay her arrival in Washington by several weeks in order to take the California bar exam. They tried to convince her that she would need the extra time to keep up with the mass of cert petitions and requests from Douglas, who called in frequently from Goose Prairie.

Bruch was stubborn. She intended to set limits on her work day. She had two children to care for in the evenings. There was only so much Douglas could ask of her. The clerks tried to warn her there was no limit to what Douglas could and would demand.

Douglas's abuses of his clerks were legend. He "fired" his clerk in the 1968 term one day before the clerk's wedding. The clerk had planned to hold his wedding reception at the Court the next day, and he went ahead, fearing that Douglas would appear and evict everyone from the building. Douglas arrived and, for the first time in an entire term, was gracious. The "firing" was never mentioned again.

The following term, Douglas told one of his two clerks that he would be fired except for the fact that he was a nice boy and that he was so incompetent that he would not be able to get another job. "I can get better legal advice from drunks in the gutter," Douglas said.

The two women clerks got quick confirmation of the Douglas legend. In an early phone conversation from Goose Prairie, Douglas said he was sending them something they would need.

It did not come.

Bruch finally called Douglas.

Douglas had no phone at Goose Prairie and was angry at the inconvenience of having to go miles to a neighboring ranch. "If this goes wrong, it's because I have a goddamn incompetent law clerk," he shouted.

"I'm sure it will work out," Bruch said.

"If you're in over your head, you can leave and I'll get someone else," he said, hanging up in a fury.

Douglas complained about his new clerks to Chuck Ayres, the head of his clerk-selection committee, the dean of the University of Arizona law school, and a former Douglas clerk himself. Ayres called Bruch and Meik to see what was wrong.

Both Meik and Bruch were upset. Bruch, determined not to let Douglas intimidate her, decided to drop him a note. "When you are displeased, I would be grateful if in the future you would let me know directly," she wrote.

Both clerks kept grinding out the cert memos. The night of Wednesday, September 6, with many hours of work left, they took a break at 8 P.M. to watch an hour-long interview Douglas had given to CBS reporter Eric Sevareid. It had been filmed in Goose Prairie.

When Sevareid asked him about the increased number of law clerks, Douglas replied, "We don't need clerks."

"Why don't you need clerks?" Sevareid asked.

"Because these are highly individual decisions. Nobody in my office can tell me or should tell me how I should vote. . . . We don't need the law clerks."

"You mean," Sevareid asked, "you'd be prepared to do all the looking up of all the precedents yourself?"

"Oh sure," Douglas said.

Meik and Bruch laughed. They went back to their office and stayed until 1 A.M. getting the next batch of cert memos ready to send to Goose Prairie.

Blackmun, whose chambers were nearby, dropped by and told the clerks not to worry. Bill Douglas was tough on him, too.

When Rehnquist heard how Douglas was treating the two women, he told his own clerks that Douglas had been the same when Rehnquist had clerked twenty years before. In those days, Douglas had only one clerk, and Rehnquist remembered that Douglas had once reduced the clerk to tears during a confrontation.

Douglas arrived back at the Court in mid-September. He seemed friendly enough on first meeting, Bruch and Meik concluded. On one case, however, Bruch was confused by a cryptic note Douglas had scrawled giving his instructions. The note appeared to ask her to apply an area of the law that had nothing to do with that case. She went to other clerks and even to the Clerk of the Court, but no one could figure it out. Finally, she went to Douglas's senior secretary, who suggested that Bruch ask Douglas because he was in a good mood.

Bruch went into his office. "Excuse me, Mr. Justice," she said. "I've been looking at this note and I'm afraid I don't understand it."

"I'm not running a damn law school," he barked.

"It seemed to me that this problem can be handled, but I wondered what you mean by this note," she tried again.

"You can read my opinions on the subject," Douglas said.

Bruch left and decided to write another note.

"I'm very sorry I made a mistake on this case. I'm sure there will be other times this year when I will make other mistakes. However, I've found that civility in professional relationships is most conducive to improved relationships. You can afford to be basically polite to me."

She left the note on Douglas's desk when he was out of the office and warned the secretaries that he would probably blow up.

Later in the day, Douglas came steaming out of his office shouting at the two secretaries because they hadn't reached someone he wanted to talk to on the phone. He said nothing to Bruch.

One morning later that week, Douglas went to the clerks' office. "I gather that you think I'm not civil," he addressed Bruch. "Nothing that I ever say is personal. This is the rough-and-tumble of the law as practiced in courtrooms daily. If my law clerks can't take it, I don't want them."

Turning on his heel, he walked out.

Stunned, Bruch took a second to recover. "I don't need unnecessary sarcasm, Mr. Justice," she blurted after him.

He did not turn.

Bruch realized her mistake immediately. Douglas had come as close to an apology as he could.

Douglas was negative about all of Bruch's work. When there was a petition that both Meik and she wanted Douglas to grant, Meik signed the recommendation alone. They both feared that Bruch's name would doom it.

Former clerks were called regularly for clues to the meaning of Douglas's notes, requests and his frequently incomplete references to old cases. The published volume of the Douglas impeachment investigation, which contained a list of all his opinions, was an excellent source. Often Bruch and Meik asked his secretaries to decipher Douglas's statements. His sentences were almost a private code, their meanings evident only to him.

"I'm going to write," he announced one day, referring to a case by docket number.

A few days later, Douglas asked Bruch for her research.

She had done nothing. Evidently, his remark was meant to be interpreted as an order to begin work on the case.

Bruch was exasperated. She told Douglas that he had not made clear what he wanted them to do.

"Get out," Douglas yelled.

"We can't read your mind," she said leaving.

From then on, Douglas ignored Bruch. He continued to rely on

Meik, but telephoned David Ginsburg, his first clerk in 1939, and asked him to find him a third clerk. A male Harvard law school graduate got the job and was able to get along with Douglas. Bruch stayed on but had little contact with Douglas.

As the term wore on, Janet Meik got to know the Court's night staff of cleaning women, maintenance men and janitors. Where most clerks had treated them as invisible, she took an interest in their problems. The picture was bleak. Employees in the lower-echelon jobs were virtually all staffed with blacks, the upper-echelon jobs were nearly all white.* Laborers and messengers were commonly asked to perform personal work for the Justices, particularly for Douglas, who insisted on using Court personnel to chauffeur him, serve at parties in his home, do grocery shopping, run personal errands, and transport his oriental rugs to storage at the Court each summer—all on their own time. Cleaning women lived in fear of being summarily dismissed for breaking something. They had to pay for all china and crystal broken while cleaning up for private dinners hosted at the Court by the Justices.

Meik was particularly concerned about work hazards at the Court. Several workers had been seriously injured falling from rickety scaffolding used to clean the marble edifice. Hydrochloric acid, outlawed as a cleansing agent in most places, was still used to clean the massive bronze entrance doors. Discipline was severe and loyalty presumed. Slight deviations were dealt with by transfer or firing. There was no appeal, since the Court was exempt from the civil service laws. As the clerk pressed the laborers' claims, she found no sympathetic ears in the Court staff hierarchy. Nor did any of the Justices seem interested.

Meik became increasingly friendly with one of the most articulate members of the all-black labor force, John Wright, the son of the Chief Justice's messenger and valet, Alvin Wright. The two began dating and then decided to live together. Wright's superior at the Court warned him that he was not to be seen with Meik at the Court. Co-workers heard supervisors criticize their "interracial"

---

* For a detailed discussion of labor problems at the Court, see Nina Totenberg, "The Supreme Court: The Last Plantation," *New Times*, July 26, 1974.

relationship. The laborers were ordered not to speak to clerks. Wright continued both to push militantly for reforms in the work-crew assignments and to date Meik.* Finally he was fired. There was no appeal. No one spoke up for him except Meik.

Shortly afterward, several black members of the Supreme Court police force began organizing a union. Told by the Court staff that no union would be recognized, the organizer went to talk with Marshall.

Not my domain, Marshall said.

When Meik advised the organizers to hire outside counsel and go to court, they explained they were intimidated. The Court was a plantation. They could do nothing.

Retired Chief Justice Earl Warren joined all the clerks for lunch late in the year. He was asked about segregation in jobs at the Court.

Warren explained that in his first term on the Court when he was ready to announce the decision in the school desegregation cases, he had looked around the Court and realized there was not one black secretary. Quickly he had ordered several hired.

Unfortunately, he said, there had not been much progress since then.

Two weeks into the term, the Court heard the first of the obscenity cases. These were three cases that Brennan wanted considered first. They posed the question of whether states could ban consenting adults from walking into a theater or store and buying or seeing what they wanted and expected to see. There was no exposure of books or movies to unwilling viewers or children.

The first case involved the Paris Adult Theater in Atlanta, whose owner had been convicted of showing the X-rated movies *Magic Mirror* and *It All Comes Out in the End*. At oral argument on October 19, the attorney for the theater noted the Chief's frequent public complaints about the Court's heavy case load. One way to reduce it, he suggested, was to permit the "controlled" sale and

---

* John Wright and Janet Meik were later married.

showing of sex-oriented films. The courtroom erupted in laughter. The Chief did not smile.

A second case involved the Peek-A-Boo Bookstore in Los Angeles. Murray Kaplan, the proprietor, had been fined $1,000 for selling a paperback, *Suite 69*, to an undercover detective seeking "any good sexy books." The third case also presented the adult-bookstore issues.

At conference, Burger and Brennan continued their maneuvering. They were still struggling for the uncertain votes—White, Powell and Blackmun. Burger indicated he would again try his hand at an opinion encompassing a grand solution to the whole problem and would wait a few weeks until the cases that had been held over from the previous term were reargued. Brennan said that he too would be circulating something.

The Chief went back to chambers to begin work. He decided to start with the Peek-A-Boo Bookstore case. It looked like the easiest, and he might be willing to pacify the liberal wing by declaring that books consisting entirely of text are protected fully by the First Amendment.

The clerk working on the case offered Burger the book *Suite 69*. Though it was a repetitive and explicit description of a series of orgies, it seemed to be comparatively well written for its genre— more trivial than obscene, Burger's clerks concluded. The Chief took the book home for the weekend. He returned to the Court on Monday morning appalled and disgusted. "Trash," he declared, tossing the paperback on his clerk's desk.

Burger's position was hardening. He hated pornography and smut peddlers. Something had to be done to suppress them. Care had to be taken, of course, to preserve legitimate First Amendment rights, but Douglas's concerns were overstated. For Burger, the issue was more than anything else a question of taste. Obscenity was vulgar; citizens had a right to be protected from it. But all this was difficult to express. The Chief needed someone who could translate his gut reaction into a tightly woven argument.

The clerk working on these cases with the Chief was uniquely compatible with him. He had studied at Oxford for three years after college and had married the former secretary to Burger's friend from England, Lord Chief Justice John Widgery. Only twenty-seven, the clerk looked years older with the balding, softened appearance of a middle-aged attorney. More importantly, this clerk was a talented translator of the Chief's visceral reactions into reasoned legal positions.

Starting with the Chief's memo from the previous year, the clerk sifted through the available literature, looking for legally sound and intellectually sophisticated reasoning to support Burger's views on censorship and obscenity. Burger recommended that he read an article that his chief clerk had found the previous year, written by conservative Yale Law professor Alexander Bickel.*

Bickel agreed with the *Stanley* decision, that willing viewers should be left to watch what they wanted in the privacy of their homes. But he turned the logic around to argue that the privacy of the home should not be extended. If it were, there would be an increased risk of invading the privacy of others.

Burger suggested that a passage from the Bickel article be used. "A man may be entitled to read an obscene book in his room, or expose himself indecently there, or masturbate, or flog himself, if that is possible, or what have you."

The Chief proposed that the sentence be cut after the words "indecently there."

"We should protect his privacy," Bickel continued. "But if he demands a right to obtain the books and pictures he wants in the market, and to foregather in public places—discreet, if you will, but accessible to all—with others who share his tastes, then to grant him his right is to affect the world about the rest of us, and to impinge on other privacies."

The Chief liked the last clause. He wanted it emphasized with italics. The article stated better than anything else Burger had read why the privacy argument could not be extended wholesale. He circulated it to his colleagues.

In November, the obscenity cases put over from the term before were reargued. Burton Marks, a flashy criminal attorney, lectured

* *The Public Interest*, No. 22, Winter 1971; On Pornography, pp. 25–28.

the Court on the realities of pornography. "We are back again before this court . . . to discuss . . . the continuing saga of life in the pits, or what goes on in the lower courts, because we don't know what, actually, this Court is saying with respect to the pornographer."

Marks explained that movies often declared obscene were advertised every day in *The Washington Post*, and were showing regularly in local theaters. He argued that his clients were businessmen. "Maybe they're in a dirty business that you don't like, but, nevertheless, they are in business," he said. "They don't want to violate the law."

But the problem was that they could not tell what the law defined as obscene, Marks said. Judges ignored previous rulings and reacted viscerally to the material before them. He had been involved in cases where judges had refused to recognize that almost exactly the same material had been ruled legally protected in other cases.

Rehnquist interrupted. "You're not talking, then, about precisely the same film, an absolute duplicate, you're talking just about similarities?"

"I'm talking about two films that if you put them back to back and took away the faces of the actors, it would be impossible to describe any difference in what was portrayed on the screen," Marks said.

"But films presumably, at least, sold under different titles or produced by different producers?" Rehnquist asked.

Marks agreed, but he contended that the materials were the same. "If I see a magazine that shows a picture of a naked woman, with her legs spread, what's known in the trade as a 'beaver shot,'" Marks continued, ignoring the startled looks of the Justices, "and this Court has said that's protected, and I see another magazine with a woman with her legs spread and a beaver shot with a different title and a different woman, I would like to be able to tell my client: 'It's all right to sell that, because it's been held protected.'"

Marks paused. He noted Rehnquist's broad grin.

"But some courts will say, 'Why, that's ridiculous, it's a different woman and it's a different camera angle and it's a different magazine, so how could the material be protected?'"

Marks fumbled in a briefcase for a *New Yorker* magazine cartoon he had brought. "It shows two gentlemen in black robes strolling along," he said, "and one of them is saying, 'If it turns me on it's smut.'"

At conference that week, it was immediately clear that the Chief had decided to reject the privacy argument in all the cases. He had one other firm vote, Rehnquist's.

Brennan reiterated his willingness to extend the privacy logic, provided that children and unwilling viewers could be protected. Stewart and Marshall were firmly with him. Douglas would never join any opinion that preserved a definition of obscenity, but he would surely concur in the judgment. White, Powell and Blackmun were inclined toward a more restrictive view of obscenity than Brennan, but they all had problems with the Chief's view.

Brennan felt he had a fighting chance with the three uncommitted votes. But the California pornographic brochures case (*Miller*), in which Burger attempted to redefine obscenity the previous term, was the wrong vehicle. The brochures had been mailed unsolicited to an unsuspecting restaurant manager and his mother. Both were clearly unwilling viewers. Revising last year's memo as a potential majority opinion, Brennan decided to concentrate on the Atlanta theater case.

The theater had no outside display advertising except signs indicating that it exhibited "Atlanta's Finest Mature Feature Films." It had a sign on the door saying: "Adult Theater—You must be 21 and able to prove it. If viewing the nude body offends you, Please Do Not Enter." Children were not allowed inside. This was the perfect case in which to extend the privacy argument allowing consenting adults to see what they chose.

Brennan decided not to wait for the Chief to circulate his opinion and got his opinion out first.

Burger circulated his drafts in the early spring, one at a time. They put to rest any hope that he might be willing to extend the privacy doctrine. While a person had a right to have what he wanted in his home, pornographic or otherwise, the Chief said, it did not follow that he had a right to import or acquire it. These steps were "seductive," leading ultimately to a result no one wanted—widely available pornography. It was time for "line drawing." Privacy in the home was where Burger drew the line.

The Chief's draft also offered the states a new set of guidelines in defining obscenity. Where the previous definition had held that a work must be "utterly without redeeming social value" to be found obscene, Burger said the courts need only find that "taken in context [it] lacks serious literary, artistic, political or scientific value." That would stop pornographers from avoiding prosecution by slipping in a passage from Shakespeare.*

Where the Court had traditionally permitted pictures of nude models without any sexual conduct, the Chief proposed that "lewd exhibition of the genitals" be banned. Similarly, the Chief shifted the Court's attention away from the traditional standard of how *explicit* the obscene material was. In the Chief's view, the sexual acts themselves were "hard-core" rather than the pornography. He would allow communities to ban any offensive portrayal of a "hard-core" sexual act, no matter how clinical, vague or even metaphorical it might be.

The full realization of how far the Chief was willing to go, however, did not sink in until he circulated his draft opinion in the Peek-A-Boo Bookstore case. Though stories of how shocked Burger had been by *Suite 69* had spread through the clerk underground, few believed that he would declare that books without pictures could be banned. But Burger had written that, from its first obscenity opinion, the Court had made no distinctions as to the medium. Even if it consisted of words alone, obscenity was not protected by the First Amendment. "For good or ill, a book has a continuing life. It is passed hand to hand, and we can take note of the tendency of widely circulated books of this category to reach the impressionable young and have a continuing impact."

---

* The Chief cited Rehnquist's *per curiam* opinion in the Wisconsin underground paper case of the year before. "A quotation from Voltaire in the flyleaf of a book will not constitutionally redeem an otherwise obscene publication . . ." What was originally to have been an opinion setting textual materials apart as intrinsically protected, was now support for the opposite thesis.

Burger's draft in the *Suite 69* case came as a particularly painful blow to Brennan. Brennan had designed his obscenity strategy years before as a way to protect books. Now, his attempt had been turned around against him.

After the Chief's shenanigans in the abortion cases, Douglas could not be more cynical. But the possibility of banning books stirred his worst fears. The stronger the censor's hand, the greater the danger. He drafted a footnote to the opinion he had completed the prior term: "What we do today is rather ominous as respects librarians. The net now designed by the Court is so finely meshed that, taken literally, it could result in *raids on libraries*. Libraries, I had always assumed, were sacrosanct, representing every part of the spectrum. If what is offensive to the most influential person or group in a community can be purged from a library, the library system would be destroyed."

The Chief had held out some faint hope of getting Stewart's vote on the obscenity cases. But Stewart was distraught over Burger's apparent willingness to allow cases to be decided on the basis of local standards. What the Chief was proposing would yield at least fifty separate First Amendments. For Stewart, there was one Constitution, and one First Amendment, and one Supreme Court that existed to protect free speech everywhere. It would be absurd, he told the conference, that what a person could see or hear would depend on where the person lived. But Stewart was fatigued. Brennan could lead the fight.

Brennan circulated another draft critical of the Chief's new restrictive definitions. There had been recurring abuses and misreadings of obscenity law by lower court judges. Juries had been vindictive toward pornographers. State legislatures might well pass new laws severely restricting free speech. "Utterly without socially redeeming value" had been the most important safeguard in the obscenity law. It was being gutted.

The Chief thought Brennan's concerns ridiculous. In his next draft he said that "these doleful anticipations assume that courts cannot distinguish commerce in ideas, protected by the First Amendment, from commercial exploitation of obscene material."

By late April, White was tired of the unproductive dialogue between Brennan and Burger. He was still unsure in which direction to go. Brennan's approach dictated too much to the states—telling them what they could and could not do in the obscenity area. It would be like ordering a neighborhood to accept the most rancid pornography as long as it was for consenting adults. He was unimpressed with Brennan's complaints that the local governments would never be able to unambiguously define obscenity. After all, in order to protect children and unwilling viewers, Brennan still retained a definition of obscenity—"explicit portrayals of ultimate sex acts," which Brennan listed.

Besides, no one could predict whether lower courts, judges, juries and state legislatures would do better under Brennan's definition than under the Chief's. For White, the Chief's approach seemed to allow more local flexibility, but his drafts had their problems. They were filled with awful ramblings, and each new version seemed to contain intemperate language. Burger's clerk delivered each successive draft to White's chambers with an apology for its tone. The clerk said he had done his best to harness and control the Chief, but Burger insisted on releasing a little venom.

Almost ritualistically, White's clerk would secure White's suggestion that certain language be dropped, and then would feed the edited version back to Burger's chambers. The omitted reference would be replaced by other, often equally intemperate language.

In one draft, the Chief compared obscenity to garbage floating in the harbor of Hong Kong. And if the people of Hong Kong are required to clean up their garbage, he wrote, then the United States should clean up its own garbage. Burger refused to delete the comparison, and only reluctantly allowed it to be rephrased by his clerk—"Nor do modern societies leave disposal of garbage and sewage up to the individual 'free will,' but impose regulation to protect both public health and the appearance of public places."

But for White there was a more troublesome problem. Some limits had to be set to say where local control ended and where First Amendment protection began. Legitimate expression had to be protected. Local communities and states could not simply be left to decide what the First Amendment meant. In that event, Stewart's fear that the First Amendment would be Balkanized into fifty separate doctrines would become a reality. Under the Chief's definition, world-famous works of art might be banned in some places. Popular literature that was objectionable in some places could be censored. The thought troubled White.

Still, White did not want to tell the states exactly what they could and could not ban. He wanted a requirement that would defend clearly protected speech and yet allow the states flexibility. He would permit the states to define obscenity as they saw fit if they specifically described exactly what acts they found to be obscene, and if the work both appealed to the prurient interest and was patently offensive "hard-core" conduct. Listing those acts would at least put pornographers on notice as to what was obscene. It would also limit the whims of local enforcement authorities. With that addition, White would join Burger's opinion.

Burger accepted White's suggestion, and added a few examples of what a statute could regulate as "hard-core" pornography: "Patently offensive representations or descriptions of ultimate sexual acts, normal or perverted, actual or simulated; patently offensive representations or descriptions of masturbation, excretory functions, and lewd exhibition of the genitals."

Burger had his third vote. There were two to go.

In Powell's chambers, his two liberal clerks kept up the pressure on their boss to join Brennan. They were concerned, however, about Powell's frequent weekend trips back to his home in Richmond. The third and most conservative clerk in the office was also from Richmond and he often drove home with him. Each time Powell returned, his attitude seemed to have become more conservative.

But the other clerks were still optimistic. Powell's initial shock, at his first glimpse of pornography the previous term, had faded. His appreciation for First Amendment values seemed to be growing.

He had written a *per curiam* opinion (*Papish v. Mo.*) overturning the conviction of a journalism graduate student for distributing an obscene underground paper that had reprinted a cartoon of policemen raping the Statue of Liberty and the Goddess of Justice above the caption " . . . with Liberty and Justice for all." The same issue reported the trial of a New York radical organization known as "Up Against the Wall, Mother Fucker" with the headline "Mother Fucker Acquitted."

Powell was sufficiently sensitive to the language that in place of the word "Fucker," he used "F—." But he expressed no doubt that this was political speech under the First Amendment.*

One of Powell's clerks became confident that his boss would ultimately join Brennan's opinion. He assured his fellow clerks that Powell would be "OK" on the subject. Toward the end of the term, the clerks from all chambers had lunch with Powell. Powell enjoyed such contact. He warmed up quickly and was soon sharing his innermost thoughts. A question came up about obscenity.

Powell told them he had decided to vote with the Chief.

Now the Chief had four votes, and Brennan had four. It was up to Blackmun.

Blackmun was fully aware that once again, a major case was waiting to be decided by his vote. He could make his new friend Brennan or his old friend the Chief author of the majority opinion.

Most of Blackmun's problems with the Chief's draft had been resolved as the year wore on. The Court had held in two other cases (*Roaden v. Kentucky* and *Heller v. New York*) that before criminal prosecutions could begin, accused pornographers must be allowed a hearing to determine whether the materials are obscene. Much of

---

* Rehnquist circulated a dissent that struck Brennan as among the most unusual he had seen since he arrived at the Court. Rather than concentrating on the obscenity question, Rehnquist instead detailed the six-year academic progress of Barbara Papish, the distributor, a graduate student in journalism. After noting she was on academic probation, Rehnquist pointed out that she distributed two publications for Students for Democratic Society using the words *fuck, bullshit* and *shits,* and one of them with a picture of two rats labeled "CIA" fornicating on the cover.

Brennan was not shocked when the Chief concurred with Rehnquist. But he was surprised and discouraged when Blackmun joined Rehnquist's dissent. Blackmun's sensibilities were still easily offended, Brennan concluded.

the Chief's offensive language had been taken out or cleaned up, and White had gotten him to require that state legislatures detail the obscene acts they would ban. Brennan's warnings of disastrous consequences and a continuing crush of cases seemed exaggerated.

Like White, Blackmun concluded that Brennan's continued willingness to retain even a limited definition of obscenity meant that one was necessary. The Chief's solution seemed as safe a bet as Brennan's.

But Blackmun had a lingering problem with the passage in Burger's draft that said materials should be "taken in context." The way Burger used the phrase, it really meant the exact opposite of "taken as a whole." Blackmun was concerned that any pornographic section, no matter how small, could get the most worthwhile work banned. "Taken in context" was a license to take material "out of context."

Burger's clerk was once again liaison between his boss and Blackmun. Blackmun asked that the old Brennan phrase—taken as a whole—be restored. The clerk added it.

Burger struck it out.

Blackmun renewed his objection. The clerk again tried to change it. Once again, Burger said no.

Burger's clerk told his boss that he did not believe Blackmun would join without the change. He would go with Brennan instead.

Burger was not accustomed to defiance from Blackmun. But the abortion decision had proved that Blackmun could not be taken for granted. Now Burger waited.

The only way for Blackmun to influence the Chief was to withhold his vote.

Finally, reluctantly, the Chief agreed to permit the change. Blackmun became his fifth vote.

Brennan was more saddened than angered by the loss. He revised his draft as a dissent. He finally was willing to renounce all definitions of obscenity, as Douglas had been beseeching him to do for sixteen years.

There was a right, Brennan said, to receive information regardless of its social worth, regardless of its obscenity.

Douglas shrugged at Brennan's belated conversion. If Brennan had seen this four years earlier, when the liberals still had a clear majority, or even the year before, when there was still a chance, it would have meant something. In the meantime, Burger had cited all Brennan's old opinions to support his position. Now, they would have to wait and see what havoc the Chief had wrought.

Burger's 5-to-4 majority decisions in the obscenity cases were scheduled to come down on June 21. While they waited for the opinions, the Burger clerk who had worked on them sat with another Burger clerk, listing questions that the opinions left unanswered. By the time they were done, they had more than two dozen.

Unanswered questions or not, Burger's clerk was relieved to have completed this task. The case would come down in a few days. At least there would be no more absurd changes by the Chief. There would be no more negotiations, no more apologies to the other clerks and Justices, no more saving Burger from his own rhetoric. The clerk had reached the end of his rope, but he was free.

Then a memo arrived from the Chief. It said to hold the opinion; the Chief had some additional last-minute changes to make.

The clerk wobbled in his office chair. Then he heard the snickers. It was a joke by his fellow clerks. He didn't think it was very funny, tampering with a man's sanity.

The opinions came down on June 21. Burger was very proud of them. He had made another important pronouncement in a troublesome area of the law. For the first time in sixteen years, he noted from the bench, "A majority of this court has agreed on concrete guidelines to isolate 'hard core' pornography from expression protected by the First Amendment."

In Washington, the local prosecutors hailed the new rules. Some adult-bookstore owners quietly removed their more explicit ware from the shelves. A few weeks later, an Albermarle County, Virginia, prosecutor announced that he would prosecute anyone selling *Playboy* magazine on local newsstands. The magazine violated community standards in Charlottesville, home of the University of Virginia.

When the Chief read a news story on the prosecutor's action, he immediately jotted a memo to the conference. He had never intended to ban *Playboy*, he insisted. His opinion was clear on that point.

On January 17, the Court heard oral arguments in a sex-discrimination case *(Frontiero v. Richardson)*. Many such cases had been building in the lower courts as women challenged laws that discriminated against them.

In this case, a female Air Force lieutenant, Sharron Frontiero, had asked the Air Force for larger quarters and allowances of several hundred dollars a month because she had married. Under federal law, these increases were automatically granted to married men. But for a woman to qualify, she had to prove that her husband was legally dependent and that he received more than half his support from her.

In previous cases, the Court had declined to treat sex discrimination as it did race discrimination—as virtually unconstitutional in all cases. The term before, the Court had unanimously struck down an Idaho law that gave automatic preference to men over women as administrators of estate *(Reed v. Reed)*. But the decision, written by Burger, had held simply that states could not pass laws treating men and women differently unless some clear reason was given for doing so.

At conference, Burger proposed that they handle the Air Force law exactly the same way. The liberals wanted to go further, but the Chief's proposal was acceptable. Only Rehnquist wanted to uphold the law.

Burger assigned the case to Brennan. He preferred not to give Brennan civil rights cases, but since they agreed on the reasoning this time, little harm seemed likely to come of it.

But as Brennan went to work on the Air Force case, his misgivings about the rationale grew. Maybe the time *had* come to treat sex discrimination cases the same way as race cases. The kind of discrimination that was practiced against women had many of the same characteristics of past treatment of blacks—denials of the right to vote, to hold office, to serve on juries.

Brennan became convinced that a clear statement was needed. Yet, he did not want to offend the conference. His mandate had been to write an opinion striking down a single law, not to make a broad constitutional rule.

Brennan circulated a draft opinion on the limited grounds, and then he sent around an alternative section that proposed a broad constitutional ban, declaring classification by sex virtually impermissible. He knew that his alternative would have the effect of enacting the Equal Rights Amendment, which had already passed Congress and was pending before the state legislatures. But Brennan was accustomed to having the Court out in front, leading any civil rights movement. There was no reason to wait several years for the states to ratify the amendment. This could be a landmark case if he could get four more votes. Douglas, Marshall and White rapidly joined his alternative. Now, he needed only one more vote.

Powell realized Brennan saw him as the possible fifth vote. But he didn't like Brennan's draft, which read at times like a Women's Liberation tract, calling sex discrimination in statutes "romantic paternalism" that put "women not on a pedestal but in a cage." More importantly, Powell was sensitive to the Equal Rights Amendment debate. With a proposed amendment before the state legislatures, the issue was clearly in the political arena. That was where it belonged. There was no need for a summary, unrestrained exercise of judicial power.

Powell circulated a short dissent to Brennan's sweeping version, trying to gather votes for the other side. Burger, Blackmun and Rehnquist joined him. That made it 4 to 4. Stewart would be the deciding vote.

Stewart felt caught between his two best friends on the Court, Powell and Brennan. Generally he didn't like equal protection decisions. They were often a kind of judicial legislation. While he disagreed with Powell's suggestion that the pending amendment precluded Court action, he did see it as a problem. This was not a matter that needed to be settled immediately. The Court should move slowly.

Stewart indicated that he favored striking individual laws as they came up and, perhaps after a number of years, doing what Brennan proposed. It would be better for the dynamics of the law—a slow evolution and then a clearly logical ultimate step. Besides, Stewart was *certain* the Equal Rights Amendment would be ratified. That would relieve the Court of the burden. The responsibility really should be assumed by legislatures.

With Brennan continuing to press him for his vote, Stewart proposed a compromise. If Brennan would go back to his first draft opinion and simply strike the one law, Stewart would probably go along with his broad constitutional rule on the next sex discrimination case. But it was important that Brennan not publish the alternative draft without his vote. If that happened, Stewart would be on record against him and it would be more difficult for Stewart to join a similar opinion in a year or two. He would look inconsistent. Outsiders might question his sudden conversion.

Brennan perceived Stewart's offer as a "deal." He rejected it and decided to publish the alternative draft, even though he had a plurality of only four. Stewart concurred simply in the part striking the one law.

Brennan felt certain that he had come within an inch of authoring a landmark ruling that would have made the Equal Rights Amendment unnecessary. If either Earl Warren or Abe Fortas had still been on the Court, he lamented to his clerks, he would have won.

When Powell first arrived on the Court the previous year and voted with Burger in a particular case, Stewart asked why. "I thought I would follow the leadership of the Court," Powell had replied.

Stewart was dumbfounded. He decided he had better explain to his new colleague something about the realities of life at the Court. The leadership was not Burger. He was Chief Justice in name only. The leadership belonged to the Justices in the center, the swing votes, those who were neither doctrinaire liberals nor conservatives. It belonged to Stewart and White and Lewis Powell if he chose.

By his second term, Powell understood. The Chief provided no intellectual leadership. In fact, when it came to legal analysis, he was grossly inadequate.

Powell was writing a majority decision *(In re Griffiths)* in which the question arose as to whether states could prohibit resident aliens from becoming members of the bar. A Dutch citizen, living in Connecticut, had challenged that state's citizenship requirement as a denial of equal protection under the Fourteenth Amendment. Powell thought it was a simple question of fundamental fairness. Resident aliens paid taxes, served in the armed forces and contributed to the country in various other ways. The Supreme Court permitted resident aliens to argue cases. Powell could see no basis for Connecticut's rule barring a whole class of people from practicing law.

As work on the opinion progressed, Burger came by for one of his frequent, unscheduled visits. He plopped down in a chair in Powell's office. Powell was annoyed at the interruption. Now he was at the Chief's mercy. There was no telling what he would want to discuss, or how long he would stay. Often the visits took two hours out of Powell's afternoon. Powell joked that the Chief was giving open-ended discussion a bad name. He had tried to stop these visits. He had told his secretary that if the Chief called to say he was coming, she was to say that Justice Powell requested that he be allowed to come see the Chief instead, since protocol demanded that a junior Justice visit the senior. That way Powell could visit Burger and leave after a few minutes, pleading an appointment or pressing work. It had seemed a good idea. But the Chief had simply stopped calling ahead.

On this visit, Burger said he had been thinking about the Connecticut lawyer's case. Maybe they should change their votes. The Fourteenth Amendment was being overworked. Wasn't this a state question, something states were empowered to regulate? Lawyers were officers of the courts. Perhaps the Court had an obligation to protect the profession.

Powell was a bit confused. Exactly how, he asked the Chief, would keeping aliens out of the bar association protect the profession? Lawyers were already subject to sanctions or disbarment or even prosecution if they did something wrong.

Well, lawyers were not held in the esteem they merited, the Chief complained. Recent disclosures in the growing Watergate scandals regularly exposed unethical and illegal behavior by lawyers. The most newsworthy lawyer of the day was White House counsel John Dean, accused of covering up the Watergate break-in.

Powell politely asked what that had to do with an alien who wanted to practice law.

Burger seemed to think that aliens might somehow contaminate the legal profession. The Chief kept referring to the image of lawyers and how this would harm that image.

Powell recoiled from Burger's conclusion. Here was the head of the American judiciary lobbying a fellow Justice, a former head of the American Bar Association, to prevent aliens from practicing law.

Powell was determined to stick to his opinion. He was ultimately joined by everyone but the Chief and Rehnquist.

It was not just the Chief's intellectual inadequacies or his inability to write coherent opinions that bothered Powell. There was something overbearing and offensive about the Chief's style. Once, after apparently spending a long time reviewing the voluminous record in one case, Burger brought the record to conference. When Powell expressed his opinion, the Chief rebuked him. "Lewis," Burger said, "you can't possibly say that. If you'd read the record, as I have, you would know that is simply not the case." He then reached back for the record. "Here, Lewis, take the record and read it," he said, handing Powell the huge file.

Powell returned to his chambers sheepishly, blaming himself and his clerk for not having been more thorough. Guiltily he read the record only to find that the Chief had either misunderstood or misrepresented it. He ultimately concluded that the Chief's heavy-handedness could not be viewed as merely a superficial trait. At the first conference in June, the Justices met to review the status of all outstanding majority opinions in order to make sure all were in circulation. Traditionally, all majority drafts were to be sent out by June 1, so there would be at least some chance that the Court could adjourn by the middle of the month.

Each Justice except Blackmun said that his majorities were in circulation or at the printer. Blackmun said that there was one case that he just couldn't get out. He had been working on it day and night, but he had been unable to complete it.

Burger showed no sympathy. As the others sat in silence, Burger chastised Blackmun.

"I really caught it at conference," Blackmun told his clerks after he returned to his chambers. He resolved to work even harder.

Powell's clerks, however, discovered that Burger also had a majority opinion outstanding. Once again, they raged to Powell about Burger's hypocrisy. For the first time, Powell did not defend the Chief.

The Chief's stunts on delaying his votes and on the assignments also irritated Powell. He had been too tolerant his first year. Now he was less indulgent about Burger's manipulations. Whatever the Chief's motives, the result was inexcusably sloppy.

Powell had also been initially skeptical about stories of Marshall's laziness and inattention. His disbelief had deepened a few days after he had circulated a thirty-two-page majority draft opinion ruling out a challenge to the use of property taxes for financing public education (*San Antonio v. Rodriguez*).

It was a monumental case, billed as promising massive educational upgrading for poor children everywhere. Marshall, White, Brennan and Douglas felt that the property taxes had to be reallocated, to even out the expenditures in different areas. Otherwise, there would never be a way to ensure equal educational opportunities, a right they felt was guaranteed by the Constitution.

The other side argued that the Constitution did not require any such reallocation.

Powell's thin five-man majority depended on Stewart's crucial fifth vote. Stewart was unwilling to get the Court embroiled in another issue of such magnitude. If the Court were to get involved, it would precipitate hundreds of cases in the federal courts as their decisions had done in desegregating schools and requiring reapportionment to meet the "one man, one vote" standard.

Moreover, Stewart felt it struck at one of the foundations of a capitalist state. People accumulated wealth in order to spend it where they chose—on their children, in their own communities.

Marshall was unhappy with Stewart's position. He assigned one of his law clerks, among the best at the Court, to prepare a devastating legal analysis of the majority opinion. For months the clerk did nothing else. Marshall circulated the forty-page dissent, responding to each of Powell's arguments and to some not even offered. It was well-reasoned, even brilliant.

How, Powell asked his clerks, did Marshall turn out such a masterpiece so quickly?

The clerks were frank. Marshall's clerk was first rate, and Marshall had given him several months to write the opinion. Depending on whom you believed, Marshall himself had spent maybe fifteen minutes to an hour going over the draft.

Powell couldn't quite believe it. "Who is the Justice down there?" he asked rhetorically.

He finally decided to see for himself. Congratulating Marshall on his fine dissent, Powell asked him a question regarding one of the major issues. "Did I say that?" Marshall cracked, brushing the question aside. Powell was not sure Marshall even understood the question.

Powell also found White an enigma. Not a particularly likable man, not genial like Brennan, White was fiercely combative. He was especially intimidating when he was struggling to hold a majority. Powell couldn't quite figure out what made White tick. His opinions, like his personality, were a constant puzzle.

Powell had a difficult time making up his mind on a Fourth Amendment search case that White was writing (*Almeida-Sanchez v. U.S.*). Powell had been counted as the tentative fifth vote in the conference majority of White, Burger, Blackmun and Rehnquist to uphold the search. Stewart, to whom Powell found himself growing closer, both personally and professionally, was dissenting with the liberals.

Federal immigration agents, acting as a roving border patrol, had stopped a car about twenty-five miles from the Mexican border in California to search for illegal aliens. The roving patrol was authorized by federal law to stop and search cars within 100 miles of the border. The agents searched the car and found no illegal aliens. But they did find 161 pounds of marijuana.

The driver of the car, convicted of illegally transporting drugs, appealed on the basis that his Fourth Amendment rights had been violated. The occupants of the car had given no consent for the search; the federal agents had no search warrant; and the agents acknowledged there was no probable cause to suspect that the particular car was carrying illegal aliens. The car, in fact, had been stopped on an east-west highway, not a north-south road that connected directly with the border.

White's draft argued that the case involved a border search: government agents were allowed to search people at the border without warrant, consent or any probable cause. The roving patrol was an extension of the border search.

Powell promised one of his clerks that he would not join White's opinion until the clerk had prepared a memo arguing the other side.

Stewart had written in dissent that if the Fourth Amendment was going to mean anything, federal agents had to obtain consent or have some probable cause to conduct a search. If neither was required, Congress could effectively legislate the Fourth Amendment out of existence.

Powell didn't agree. Immigration agents were not the same as regular police. Powell also recognized that the growing number of illegal aliens from Mexico was a major problem in the Southwest. He did not want to take another enforcement tool away from the government. He sent his join memo to White, without letting his clerk know. White now had his fifth vote.

Powell's clerk, feeling betrayed, complained heatedly. But Powell said it was late in the term and the decision could only wait so long. He was the Justice, and would make the final choice.

Reexamining White's draft, however, Powell found some troubling points. White had accepted Congress's determination that such a roving patrol search was reasonable: "Congress had long considered such inspections constitutionally permissible under the Fourth Amendment." The problem was that the Court, not the Congress, made the final rulings on what was constitutionally permissible under the Fourth Amendment. Powell decided that his clerk was right. There was no way to ignore the Fourth Amendment.

Perhaps there was some middle ground. Warrants obviously could not be required for each car search, but maybe there was a way to observe the spirit of the Fourth Amendment's warrant requirement. What if the border patrol were required to seek warrants for specified areas or roads for limited periods of time, say days or weeks? Powell settled on that as his compromise. But, since there had been no warrant in the particular case, he would join the Stewart dissent overturning the conviction and giving Stewart a majority. He would write his own concurrence. Powell notified White's chambers that he was switching sides.

White didn't like losing Powell's vote, much less the majority, but it was unlikely that Powell would switch again. For all his competitiveness, White played by the rules, and he wanted to find some humorous way of letting Powell know that he was not angry.

Several days earlier, White had been watching a baseball game on television. The Baltimore Orioles' rookie outfielder Al Bumbry, the potentially winning run, had been thrown out at home plate in a heartbreaking play.

Knowing that Powell followed baseball and liked to go to Orioles games in nearby Baltimore, White sent a memo to Powell saying that he felt like Bumbry. He had made his way around all of the bases, only to be thrown out at home plate.

White loved Denver. He had practiced law in the "Mile-High City" for nearly fifteen years. It was a city of relative racial harmony when White lived there, but recently it had become a school desegregation battleground. "Showdown in Denver," a *Wall Street Journal* headline proclaimed. The Denver school desegregation case (*Keyes v. School District No. 1*) was about to become the *Brown* case for the rest of the country outside the South.

White was not sure whether he should participate. His old law firm in Denver had once been the bond counsel for the school board. Sitting at his desk, idly mutilating paper clips and twirling them in his fingers, he told his clerks of his concerns. White normally withdrew from cases where there was any question of his impartiality. But he had been away from Denver for thirteen years, returning there only to vacation. "When can I start sitting again on these cases?" he asked rhetorically.

He wanted to participate. What's more, Rehnquist had recently argued that some of the Justices were overdoing disqualification. By recusing themselves whenever there seemed to be the slightest possibility of a conflict, Rehnquist contended, Justices were avoiding their responsibility to decide cases. Disqualifications that were likely to leave the Court in a 4-to-4 deadlock should be avoided if possible. In such ties, he noted, the "principle of law presented by the case is left unsettled."*

This argument interested White. His vote might be the key to the outcome. If he disqualified himself, it was quite possible that Powell and Rehnquist would join Burger and Blackmun in opposing the busing order in Denver. The Court would split 4 to 4. White decided to leave the question of his participation in the air, and he went to oral argument on October 12. He would ask no questions, and he could always disqualify himself later.

Unlike the South, Colorado had no history of legislated school segregation. So the black parents first had to prove that the Denver school board was responsible for separating school children by race. Then they could argue that such unconstitutional school board actions required desegregation orders.

In a series of hearings in district court, the black parents had shown that the school board had made decisions that promoted segregation—building new schools in minority neighborhoods to accommodate the size of the minority group; changing attendance boundaries to make sure the schools stayed segregated; refusing to build schools in locations that would serve minorities and whites together. District Judge William Doyle agreed with the black parents that a small, racially mixed area of Denver called Park Hill, which included only eight of the city's 119 schools, was segregated

---

* Various liberal groups had criticized Rehnquist for taking part in three cases the previous term, since he had had some contact with the cases while at the Justice Department. One case (*Laird v. Tatum*) involved Army surveillance of antiwar groups. While at the Justice Department, Rehnquist had testified before a congressional committee on the exact issue on which the case was decided. He had told a congressional panel he did not think the antiwar activists had standing to bring suits. Then, as a Justice, he had cast the deciding vote against them. Rehnquist subsequently took the unusual step of publishing a memo justifying his participation.

by school board actions. He ordered the busing of 4,000 pupils, a small fraction of the 90,000 children in the system.

In the larger, "core city" area of Denver, Judge Doyle found that, while there were no clearly deliberate acts of racial discrimination (such as the gerrymandering of attendance zones), the twenty-five schools there were still segregated. The students, mostly black and chicano, were receiving an inferior education, he found. Test scores were lower, teachers less experienced, dropout rates higher, school facilities inferior. The treatment that core-city students were receiving was separate and unequal. The separation might be legal, but the inequality was not.

So Doyle also ordered desegregation and improvement of education in core-city schools, and he ordered that another 7,000 students be bused, bringing the total to 11,000. Under Doyle's orders, most one-race schools would be eliminated. There would be some racial mixing in every school, though there would not by any means be a strict racial balance.

The Tenth Circuit Court of Appeals upheld Doyle's order for the smaller Park Hill area, but reversed him on the core-city schools. It pointed out that since the black parents had failed to show that segregation there was the clear result of any school board actions, Doyle had no power to order any remedy for the core-city schools.

The black parents, saying all schools should be desegregated, appealed to the Supreme Court.

At the conference, White took himself out of the case, and the others voted 5 to 3 in favor of the black parents, the majority consisting of Douglas, Brennan, Marshall, Stewart and a very tentative Blackmun. Blackmun said he would go along only if the opinion relied exclusively on prior decisions. And he would not go along with anything that said district judges could reach out and desegregate every school that happened to be segregated.

In particular, Blackmun did not want to go beyond the Charlotte case. He rejected Douglas's view that judges could desegregate schools regardless of the cause of the segregation. School boards must first be proved responsible for causing some of the segregation; then, and only then, was he willing to let judges correct the situation.

Douglas assigned the opinion to Brennan. The assignment lifted Brennan's spirits considerably. It was the best case he had been given since Earl Warren's retirement more than three years before. He was not unmindful of the delicacy of the task. If Blackmun switched, the 5-to-3 majority would become a 4-to-4 deadlock, leaving the appeals court's limitations on busing intact. That would be no opinion, and thus, no law would be decided. It would be impossible for a federal judge to order system-wide desegregation without proving intentional illegal state action that affected each school. Brennan certainly did not want district judges to get *that* message. It would halt desegregation efforts in cities outside the South, until the Court could find another case in which White could participate.

Brennan worked out a first draft. Taking the school system as a whole, rather than considering separate areas as Doyle had done, Brennan held that the Park Hill segregation was sufficient to declare the entire system segregated and order desegregation in every school.

Brennan took particular pleasure in relying principally on the Chief's Charlotte decision for his law. He drew especially on a long section that Marshall had insisted the Chief include two terms before. It dealt with the impact that school board decisions on the location or closing of schools had in promoting segregated neighborhoods.

By December, Brennan had sent a draft to the other Justices. The Denver school system had intentionally violated rights. For all legal purposes, it should be considered a dual school system with the obligation to desegregate every school at once.

Douglas, Marshall and Stewart indicated they would join Brennan.

Burger and Rehnquist said they would dissent. Powell, the third dissenter, said that he wanted to write his own opinion. He was particularly offended by the moralistic tone of the Brennan draft, which, he felt, extended the harsh judgment made on the South to the North.

There was no word from Blackmun.

Brennan finally sent his clerks out to see what they could learn from Blackmun's clerks.

Nothing.

Despite his decision not to take part, White was following the developments closely. One day, as White and Blackmun were talking, the case came up. Brennan's draft, Blackmun said, went way beyond what was necessary. He had reviewed the facts. Several things were beyond dispute. The district judge had found that the black parents had failed to prove that the school authorities had done anything intentionally to segregate the core-city schools. Brennan's draft ordered a remedy in these schools despite a contrary finding of fact. Maybe the actions that pertained to the Park Hill schools were isolated. Brennan was adopting a kind of domino theory. A single act in one part of town did not justify system-wide desegregation orders. Blackmun said he could not join such a sweeping proclamation.

White mentioned Blackmun's objections to one of his own clerks, who in turn passed them on to one of Brennan's. Within hours, Brennan had an account.

When the opportunity arose, Brennan asked White directly what he should do to win over Blackmun.

White told Brennan his draft went too far. He suggested toning down the sweeping language. "But don't make any changes on my account," White said. He reminded Brennan that he was, after all, out of the case.

Brennan went back to work. He softened his rhetoric and tried to spell out his reasoning so that Blackmun could see that its logic was dictated by common sense. Brennan emphasized that the constitutional violations were not isolated in one school, but were "systematic" and "substantial." He noted that there were 5,000 blacks in the Park Hill schools, where deliberate segregation had been proved. They represented nearly 38 percent of Denver's total black school population. Common sense dictated that the racially discriminatory acts of the school board had an impact beyond those schools. These acts had a ripple effect. Manipulation of attendance patterns in one group of schools clearly affected other schools.

Brennan cited one of the basic evidence texts (*Wigmore on Evidence*) which said that prior patterns of behavior can be used in measuring intent. The intentional segregation in Park Hill would establish a presumption that segregation in the core city stemmed from the same illegal intent. It was only a presumption, Brennan wrote. The school board would have a chance to challenge it, since his opinion, if it were the majority, would send the case back to the lower court to be tried again.

This time, with the burden of proof shifted, the black parents wouldn't have to prove that the board intended to segregate the core-city schools. The board would have to prove that it had nothing to do with the acknowledged segregation in the core city's schools. Shifting the burden, Brennan emphasized, was not a novel idea. His treatment of this Northern case was fully in line with, and just a logical extension of, the Court's prior rulings in Southern cases. It would make things more difficult for the school board, but it would give them another chance. And the school board could try again to prove that Park Hill was for practical purposes a separate area—a crucial point assumed, but never really decided, by the lower court. But Brennan also added a set of criteria making it difficult to prove. He circulated his revised draft.

Douglas, Stewart and Marshall were still willing to join. Blackmun was still thinking it over.

Powell's dissent in the Denver case gave him a chance to express himself on what he viewed as the major issue of the day. He decided to write his own opinion in order to elaborate views that he had developed during many years of service on school boards. Years of law practice and public service had left him with fundamental views on successful management. If society was to be well run, its own leaders must themselves do a good job. Outsiders, especially courts, could not force anyone to do a good job. No matter how correct, they inspired resentment rather than cooperation. The courts could only outline what decision makers should consider.

Powell believed that most people were well-intentioned, and the courts should capitalize on this good will. The courts had to rely on, rather than undermine, the best instincts of people. The courts should try only to regulate the extremes of behavior.

Powell sat at his desk, Dictaphone in hand, and dictated dozens and dozens of pages. It was more an essay than a Supreme Court opinion, his clerks thought.

The long draft had two contradictory strains. First, Powell vented his resentment that the South had been forced to integrate, while the North ignored its own segregation. Powell proposed that the traditional distinction between segregation by law (as in the South) and segregation resulting from residential segregation be abolished. The Court should address the condition of segregation and inequality of education, whatever its origins. It should treat the North and South the same way—get out of the business of determining who "intended" to segregate children, and deal simply with segregation wherever it was found. This potentially radical proposal—agreeing essentially with Douglas's long-sought changes—was significantly tempered by Powell's other strain, an attack on busing. He called busing "the single most disruptive element in education today."

Powell agreed with earlier court decisions that school boards must be forced to desegregate their schools, but he insisted that they be allowed to do it in their own way. Federal courts had no business forcing them to bus children. The neighborhood school was the foundation of a sound school system. He would direct school boards to adopt future policies to reduce segregation, but leave it to them to decide how. He did not imagine that many would choose busing. "Any child, white or black, who is compelled to leave his neighborhood and spend significant time each day being transported to a distant school suffers an impairment of his liberty and his privacy," he dictated.

Powell objected mainly to the busing of elementary-school children. He recalled seeing children on street corners in Richmond at 7:30 A.M., bundled up, waiting in the cold for a bus. It made him shudder. The nearest school might be two blocks away and the child was going to ride ten or twelve miles to satisfy some judge's abstract notion of racial justice and equality. Powell felt that much of this was brought on by the Charlotte decision. He would cut back on it. That decision was ambiguous and internally contradictory. "A paste-pot job," he called it.

Two of his clerks suggested extensive changes. The draft was like a long letter to Powell's friends back home in Richmond, they thought. Powell was sensitive to the problem. He did not want it to be either an antibusing or a probusing tract. He toned it down.

Brennan did not think much of Powell's dissent. He was even less enthralled, however, when Powell decided to call his twenty-page draft both a dissent and a concurrence—the latter because Powell agreed with Brennan that the case should be sent back to the district court for further hearings.

Brennan urged him not to publish, but Powell was not to be dissuaded.

Burger found little improvement in Brennan's second draft. The opinion gave the school board a theoretical but not a practical chance to prove its innocence. But he also saw another series of desegregation cases coming up to the Court presenting an equally explosive and vexing question—the power of judges to order city-suburb desegregation.

In Richmond, Virginia, a District Judge, Robert R. Merhige, Jr., issued an order merging the 70 percent black Richmond system with two adjacent, 90 percent white, suburban school systems into one huge metropolitan school system. The merger order involved relatively modest city-suburb busing, but it radically redrew school attendance zones across county lines.

Burger felt that the judge had vastly exceeded his power in creating a new school district that cut across political boundaries. In the Charlotte case the order encompassed both city and suburbs, but at least that had been one school system.

The Chief figured that he had a much better chance of winning the Richmond case than the Denver case. Blackmun was willing to join Rehnquist and him on this one. Stewart might have problems with the judge's sweeping order. That would be four votes. But Powell, who had served nineteen years on the Richmond and Virginia state school boards, would likely disqualify himself. Burger saw at least a 4-to-4 deadlock upholding the Fourth Circuit Court of Appeals which had reversed the district judge. The problem was that a 4-to-4 deadlock would leave the lower courts with no law on the subject. They would have nothing to apply to city-suburb busing plans that had been ordered or were being considered in Detroit, Boston, Dayton, Hartford and elsewhere.

Both Denver and Richmond cases posed questions about the power of federal judges to order sweeping remedies in school desegregation cases. But from the Chief's point of view, the Detroit case, which was working its way up to the Court, was preferable to both the Denver and Richmond cases. It was the best example of a judge exceeding his power.

Burger calculated that he had a much better chance of pulling in Stewart and Blackmun's votes in Detroit. And unlike the Richmond case, Powell would be able to vote in the Detroit case. Burger drafted a memo to the conference suggesting that the Denver and Richmond cases be put over until the next term, when they could be considered with the upcoming Detroit case.

"That son of a bitch," Brennan said. The Chief's memo was a blatant, last-ditch effort to stop the Denver decision, and it was a poorly disguised attempt to sabotage desegregation nationally, Brennan believed.

Blackmun was also cynical about Burger's suggestion. The Richmond and Denver cases were difficult enough, taken separately. Suggesting that the Court consider it all as one package was clearly inappropriate. Burger was trying to stall the Denver case. Blackmun circulated a memo opposing Burger's proposal, and then he sent a second memo saying that he was inclined to join the latest Brennan Denver opinion. He approved the idea of sending the case back for more fact finding, and giving the school authorities another chance.

Brennan was overjoyed. Burger had overplayed his hand.

That left the Richmond case. Powell, as expected, disqualified himself. Douglas, Brennan, Marshall and White were willing to uphold the city-suburb busing order, but on this case, Blackmun would not go along. He agreed with the Chief and Rehnquist. To extend desegregation within a city or a school district was one thing. Redesigning school districts and redrawing political boundaries was unacceptable.

It was up to Stewart. Stewart felt that no city-suburb busing could be ordered unless a violation were shown in both city and suburban school districts. Although it was a close call, he did not believe the violation in the suburban district had been proven. Stewart was also deeply affected by nonjudicial considerations. Public opinion was at stake. Just as the Warren Court decisions outlawing prayer in the public schools had eroded confidence in the Court, the busing issue was costing the Court dearly. People chose to live in certain neighborhoods because of the schools. Forced city-suburb desegregation was an attack on that freedom of choice.

The mainstream of society opposed forced integration of the schools when it meant busing. Stewart wanted the Court to keep that mainstream in mind wherever possible. To back limited city-suburban busing in Richmond could mean massive new long-distance busing in every major city in America. Stewart told his clerks that he had ridden the bus on the Charlotte and Denver decisions, but that Richmond was different. "It is where I get off," he said.

The Richmond plan looked dead unless Blackmun changed his mind.

In May, the liberal half of the Richmond decision—Douglas, Brennan, White and Marshall—tried to break the 4-to-4 deadlock. White drafted a long memorandum for Blackmun's benefit, documenting the reasonableness of the city-suburban desegregation. The judge's order in Richmond was a logical extension of the Charlotte decision, he argued.

Blackmun would not budge.

Finally, conceding the deadlock, the Court allowed the case to be announced. The equally divided Court struck down the city-suburban busing in Richmond. But the decision would not be a precedent for other cases.

"Look at this, guys," Brennan called to his clerks when Blackmun finally sent around his formal join in the Denver case. It guaranteed him five votes. With Powell's technical concurrence in the remand, he had six votes.

Rehnquist was not taken in by any of Brennan's changes to get Blackmun's vote. In his dissent, Rehnquist accused the majority of taking "a long leap in this area of constitutional law." Under Brennan's opinion a single school board action in one part of town, Rehnquist said, could be the basis for a federal judge to order system-wide desegregation. In reality, he said, the Court was putting the school district in "federal receivership," to be run by a district judge.

That left the Chief.

Brennan expected him to write his own dissent or join Rehnquist's.

In early June, a short memo from Burger arrived in Brennan's chambers.

The Chief said he was going to concur in the result.

Brennan laughed. Frequently a refusal to join an opinion was an insult. But for such a vocal dissenter at conference to suddenly join the majority in any form could only be considered humorous. "Can you believe this?" Brennan asked his clerks, slapping the memo down on a desk.

They tried to figure out whether the Chief was engaged in some subtle ploy, but they couldn't find one. Burger provided the seventh vote.

The decision was announced formally on June 21. The newspapers reported it as a 7-to-1 majority for strong desegregation and busing orders in the Northern cities. The opinion was a primer for judges outside the South. It gave them the tools to order sweeping remedies. Substantial pockets of intentional segregation in any city made it a candidate for Southern-style desegregation orders and extensive busing.

Brennan found it hard to believe that he had actually won.

Rehnquist usually voted with Burger; they agreed on many things. But Rehnquist didn't share Burger's concern with appearances and formality. He was very casual. During the nice weather, he and his clerks sometimes ate lunch in one of the two enclosed courtyards. They brought their food in paper bags and simply enjoyed the sun and the outdoors. As they were picnicking in shirtsleeves one day, Burger's messenger, Alvin Wright, set up a small table with silver service and a white linen tablecloth. Moments later, Burger came out with his clerks. Burger, his jacket on, poured the wine.

Rehnquist and his clerks chuckled a bit. But as they gazed on the solemnity at the Burger table, Rehnquist's laughter grew almost uncontrollable. He and his clerks had to dash inside.

During his first term, Rehnquist worried some about what influence his clerks might have on his opinions. He had clerked at the Court after law school and had written a magazine article in 1957 alleging that most law clerks were generally "to the 'left' of either the nation or the Court." He described the bias as "extreme solicitude for the claims of Communists and other criminal defendants, expansion of federal power at the expense of State power, great sympathy toward any government regulation of business."

He mentioned the possibility of "unconscious slanting of material by clerks" when reviewing cert petitions. And though he had written that he didn't think clerks exercised too much influence in the actual drafting of opinions, he was careful when he got to the Court to write all the first drafts himself. Midway through his first full term, he realized that he had been wrong. The legal and moral interchanges that liberal clerks thrived on were good for the Justices and for the Court. Rehnquist grew to trust his clerks; they would not be so foolish as to try putting something over on him. And there was the question of efficiency. The clerks were helpful with first drafts. It saved him time, and helped focus his own thinking.

Rehnquist was known around the Court for his friendliness toward clerks. He learned their names, and found some of them as interesting as the Justices. He suggested letting the clerks into the Justices' dining room or setting up a lounge for both clerks and Justices. Those ideas got nowhere, but he did get a Ping-Pong table for the Court.

Rehnquist's clerks occasionally took a moment out to play basketball on the court in the upstairs gym, and since there was very little time, they often overlooked the rule against playing in street shoes. One day, at oral argument, Rehnquist's clerks noticed their boss whispering with some of the other Justices. He scribbled a note and summoned a messenger who carried it to where the clerks were sitting in the audience. They felt very important.

"We have just talked it over and from now on the rule against street shoes will be strictly enforced," the note read.

As the junior Justice, Rehnquist was in charge of the annual Christmas Party. It was a noisy party, and Rehnquist found it hard to get all personnel together for the carolling. Finally, he stood on a piano bench. "Achtung!" he shouted.

One clerk thought it was too good to be true. Rehnquist, the fascist. But most thought that it showed that Rehnquist had a sense of humor.

Stewart wasn't working too hard. The joke around the Court was that he and Marshall passed each other in the corridor most days just before noon—Stewart on his way to work, Marshall on his way home. But Stewart paid close attention to what was going on, and his clerks knew that if they could engage his interest, he would swing into action.

One of Stewart's clerks took up the cause of a federal prisoner serving twenty years for bank robbery (*Fontaine v. U.S.*). The man alleged that his guilty pleas had been coerced through physical abuse while he was in the hospital suffering from a gunshot wound, heroin addiction and mental illness. The record gave some support to his claim that these factors had caused him to waive his rights for a lawyer and plead guilty. The Court was going to deny cert, until Stewart circulated a long dissent from denial of cert that his clerk had prepared. The conference later voted 8 to 1 to direct the district judge to grant the man a hearing, shaming some of the clerks in the other chambers for their failure to discover the possibility that the allegation of coercion might be valid.

But certain issues drew only scorn and indifference from Stewart. In one case, Ohio and Kentucky, divided by the Ohio River, could not agree on their common boundary. An 1820 Supreme Court case put the river in Kentucky and therefore was precedent. But Stewart, who came from Ohio, told his clerks that he had another reason for voting against his home state. "My father always told me at the breakfast table that the Ohio River was in Kentucky."

Another time, Stewart was assigned to write a Fourth Amend-

ment car search case *(Schneckloth v. Bustamonte)*. He was happy
with the assignment and wanted to write it in a way that would
avoid raising potentially troublesome questions. He assigned one
of his clerks to draft the *Schneckloth* opinion, and a long draft was
duly returned to him. Weeks passed and there was no comment
from Stewart, no instructions for rewriting, no word of approval or
disapproval. It had not been sent to the printer. Where was
Schneckloth?

Stewart's other clerks began to make jokes about the missing
opinion. "Have you seen *Schneckloth?*" became a familiar remark
around his chambers and then the Court. The clerk who had
drafted it, a meticulous and devoted lawyer, was plagued by the
missing *Schneckloth*.

He finally decided to ask Stewart. He went into his office. "Have
you seen *Schneckloth?*"

"Yes," Stewart said, pulling open his top drawer. "I can see it any
time I want."

The clerk was not sure he understood, but he concluded that
Stewart was holding the case so he could circulate it late in the
term. Caught in the spring crush, there would be little time for it to
trigger yet another grueling debate over the Fourth Amendment.

Schneckloth, one of the first cases argued, was among the last to
come down.

In spite of his victory in the Denver school case, Brennan was
unhappy about his first full term with the four Nixon appointees.
His clerks had the feeling that a sense of despair had overtaken
him. Brennan had dissented forty-seven times during the term,
more than he ever had dissented before.

It was not only that Brennan had values different from those of
the Nixon justices, but now he was often not even a part of the real
debate. Stewart and White had taken over the direction of the
Court along with the Nixon appointees, Brennan concluded. They
were the mainstream. Brennan was the outsider, and he was
pained at the direction the Court was taking.

Brennan felt that his greatest achievements on the Court were
the legislative reapportionment cases of the 1960s—the "one-man,

one-vote" cases. Those decisions required that state legislative and United States congressional districts be drawn and redrawn to include the same number of voters, so that each person's vote would count equally. Even 3 percent deviations were not permitted. Under a 1969 decision, the states were required to make a "good faith effort to achieve precise mathematical equality." Half the states had achieved variations of less than 5 percent.

Earl Warren had often called those cases the most significant decisions of the Court during his tenure, despite the fact that Brennan had written many of the key opinions. Brennan was the father of reapportionment.

But this past term, in a case involving the state of Virginia (*Mahan v. Howell*), a new majority of Burger, Rehnquist, Blackmun, Stewart and White had allowed a reapportionment scheme that included a 16.4 percent variation in the size of the districts. After conference on the case, Brennan returned to his chambers near tears. "I'll talk to you boys later," he told his clerks, leaving at once for home.

Most irritating to Brennan was that the Court was adopting a secret internal rule of thumb to use as a guide for future cases, rules that they would not publish. The new apportionment rules for state legislatures would permit variations of less than 10 percent. Variations between 10 and 20 percent would be accepted if the lines were drawn with good reason, for example to conform with city or county boundaries. Only variations over 20 percent would not be permitted. Brennan was distressed that the Court was so willing to shed its idealism. He knew local politicians. They would do anything to redraw district boundaries to ensure their reelection.

Brennan's clerks thought he might be ready to resign. He had taken to calling Burger a "usurper," and he became wistful even at the mention of Earl Warren. When he talked about Burger, he would often say, "The Chief—and I want to draw the distinction with the Super Chief." At his regular 9 A.M. coffee session with his clerks and secretary, Brennan began to dwell increasingly on the past.

The Chief was intensifying his efforts to cut back on the Court's work load, Brennan complained. Under Warren, the Court had done more for social justice than the Congress. Burger cared more about efficiency. Almost from his first day, he had been complaining about the Court's case load. He had appointed a committee of professors and well-known lawyers to study the problem, and his committee had proposed a new "National Court of Appeals" to weed out nearly 90 percent of the petitions to the Supreme Court.

While the proposal was being debated in legal circles, Burger decided to attack the problem from within. Burger thought his clerks had to spend too much time reviewing the cert petitions and preparing summations for him. Since each chamber had to review roughly 4,500 petitions each year, Burger proposed that they pool their efforts. The cert petitions would be divided equally among the clerks of all chambers, and summary memos and recommendations would be circulated to each of the Justices. Each chamber would have only one ninth of the work.

Powell liked the idea. His law firm had been vastly better organized than the Court. A cert pool would improve efficiency. Rehnquist, Blackmun and White also agreed to join. With fewer certs to prepare, the clerks would do a better job on those they were assigned. Stewart decided to leave it up to his clerks. They were the supposed beneficiaries of the new pool. His clerks said no. They didn't want other clerks making recommendations to their Justice.

Brennan was vehemently opposed. The Chief's proposal, he told his clerks, was "outright manipulation." Burger was trying to expand his empire. With control of the paper flow, he would gain control of the Court's work. And neither the Chief's clerks nor Rehnquist's could be trusted to make a neutral presentation of the facts or issues in a petition.

Brennan's appraisal was that the case load problem was a myth anyway. It had a lot to do with the Chief's intellectual insecurity. Piles of cert petitions, even with summary memos from his clerks, intimidated him. Brennan rarely used his clerks on the petitions. He did them himself. It was like separating the weeds from the flowers in the garden.

Brennan was so irritated that he made one of his few public

speeches since Fortas resigned. He described some cert petitions from the term. They posed questions such as:

"Are Negroes in fact Indians and therefore entitled to Indians' exemptions from federal income taxes?"

"Are the federal income tax laws unconstitutional insofar as they do not provide a deduction for depletion of the human body?"

"Does a ban on drivers' turning right on a red light constitute an unreasonable burden on interstate commerce?"

Brennan spent maybe ten or fifteen seconds on these petitions, and after sixteen years on the Court, he had developed a special feel for recognizing the important cases.

Douglas and Marshall also declined to join the cert pool. It was organized with the four Nixon appointees and White as members.

The Court before the resignation of Chief Justice Earl Warren. Left to right, front row: John Marshall Harlan, Hugo L. Black, Earl Warren, William O. Douglas, William J. Brennan, Jr.; second row: Abe Fortas, Potter Stewart, Byron R. White, Thurgood Marshall.

Earl Warren and Warren E. Burger.

John M. Harlan and
Thurgood Marshall.

Hugo L. Black.

William J. Brennan, Jr., in chambers.

William O. Douglas at his home in Northwest Washington.

Yoichi Okamoto

Thurgood Marshall enjoys his
own humor.

Abe Fortas.

UPI

An informal photo of the Burger Court in 1977. Left to right: John Paul
Stevens, Lewis F. Powell, Jr., Harry A. Blackmun, William H. Rehnquist,
Thurgood Marshall, William J. Brennan, Jr., Warren E. Burger, Potter
Stewart, Byron R. White.

Potter Stewart in chambers.

Byron R. White in chambers.

Harry A. Blackmun in chambers.

Warren E. Burger taking a stroll.

Lewis F. Powell, Jr. in chambers.

William H. Rehnquist in chambers.

John Paul Stevens in chambers.

William O. Douglas returns to the Court after suffering a stroke.

Thurgood Marshall with his clerks in chambers.

John Paul Stevens with his clerks—in chambers and in the Court's cafeteria.

"WE WERE TOLD THEY WERE 'STRICT CONSTRUCTIONISTS'"

The Herblock cartoon discussed on page 517.

William H. Rehnquist discussing cases with his clerks in chambers.

The Chief in chambers while lunch awaits.

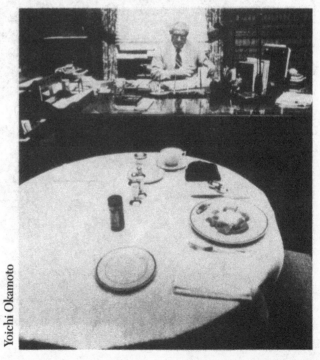

The Burger Court, 1976. Left to right, front row: Byron R. White, William J. Brennan, Jr., Warren E. Burger, Potter Stewart, Thurgood Marshall; second row: William H. Rehnquist, Harry A. Blackmun, Lewis F Powell, Jr., John Paul Stevens.

UPI

1973 Term

1973 Term

I N JULY 1973, Congresswoman Elizabeth Holtzman, a New York Democrat, and four Air Force officers asked the federal courts to stop the United States from bombing in Cambodia. A district court in New York issued an injunction halting the bombing, but the injunction was subsequently lifted by the Court of Appeals. The American Civil Liberties Union, representing Holtzman and the Air Force officers, brought an emergency appeal (*Schlesinger v. Holtzman*) to Marshall as Circuit Justice, since the Supreme Court was in recess. On July 30, 1973, Marshall held a closed-door hearing in his chambers. Although he was predisposed to stop the bombing, Marshall also thought that it would be irresponsible to do so if it were only to be reinstated by a majority who would refuse to decide the constitutionality of the war in Southeast Asia. More importantly, the matter would be resolved within two weeks when congressional appropriations financing the war would end. Marshall decided to be cautious, and he issued a short order refusing to halt the bombing.

Since the Court was not in session, the A.C.L.U. was free to take the matter to another justice. If the second justice allowed the bombing halt, it would remain in effect until the entire Court could consider it in September. Accordingly, the A.C.L.U. immediately dispatched an attorney to Goose Prairie in the hope that Douglas would give them a more sympathetic hearing. Douglas had continued to press the war issue before the Court. He had dissented from cert denials in war-related cases and had challenged the others to face up to the U.S. involvement in Southeast Asia. Now, Douglas agreed to hold a hearing on the request and traveled fifty miles down from the foothills of the Cascades to the courthouse in Yakima, Washington.

The government's attorney suggested that a confrontation should be avoided.

"We live in a world of confrontations," Douglas replied. "That's what the whole system is about. I don't enjoy these confrontations myself. I'd rather be up at Goose Prairie."

After the hearing Douglas decided to end the Court of Appeals stay. The district court could then proceed to order a bombing halt. It was already late in the afternoon, and Douglas phoned the Court in Washington to leave word that the printers should not go home. He dictated the first part of the opinion from a truck stop on the way to Goose Prairie. "Do you have that?" he asked. His secretaries struggled to hear him over the din of trucks in the background. The exchange was repeated again from another phone as he proceeded down the road. He read the last section from Whistlin' Jacks, the final rest stop, and last public telephone, before Goose Prairie.

Douglas compared the case to a capital punishment case:

> The classic capital case is whether Mr. Lew, Mr. Low, or Mr. Lucas should die. The present case involved whether Mr. X (an unknown person or persons) should die. No one knows who they are. They may be Cambodian farmers whose only "sin" is a desire for socialized medicine to alleviate the suffering of their families and neighbors. Or Mr. X may be the American pilot or navigator who drops a ton of bombs on a Cambodian village. The upshot is that we know that someone is about to die.
>
> Since denial of the application before me would catapult our airmen as well as Cambodian peasants into the death zone, I do what I think any judge would do in a capital case.

Douglas's order and opinion were filed at the Supreme Court the next morning, August 4. The government immediately went back to Marshall, asking him to prevent the district court's order halting the bombing from going into effect.

Marshall found himself in a dilemma. Normally a single Justice would never overrule another. It was one thing to act when another Justice had refused. But once an order had been issued by a Justice, it was up to the full conference to decide whether to reverse it.

Marshall called Brennan, who suggested a solution that would avert an embarrassing confrontation between the Court and the Executive Branch, and at the same time avoid overruling Douglas directly.

To protect himself against the possibility that Douglas might accuse him of unilaterally overruling another Justice, Marshall called each of the other seven Justices to secure their agreement. Then he asked his clerk to draft the complicated opinion. The clerk, who was avidly opposed to the war, and impatient with Marshall's timidity and inattention, refused. Marshall would have to write it himself, he said.

After struggling with a full opinion, Marshall gave up and drafted a simple order. He filed the nine paragraphs six hours later. Since the district court order had not yet gone into effect, the Pentagon did not miss any of its scheduled bombing sorties for the day.

A few days later, Douglas released a bitter dissent, openly rejecting Marshall's circumvention of his order and challenging the use of the telephone to poll the conference. In addition to undermining an exchange of views, it was in violation of the six-member-quorum rule, he charged.

> I do not speak of social propriety. It is a matter of law and order involving high principles . . .
>
> A Gallup poll type of inquiry of widely scattered Justices is, I think, a subversion of the regime under which I thought we lived . . .
>
> What members of the Court told Brother Marshall to do on August 4, 1973, does not, with all respect, conform with our ground rules.

Douglas was even less gracious in private. He referred to Marshall as "spaghetti spine."

Rehnquist slipped into the conference room one day and took his seat.

He pulled a magazine from his stack of papers. The *National Lampoon*, a humor magazine, had just released its February issue. The centerfold was entitled "Amicae Curiae"—Friends of the Court—and it depicted, in a color cartoon, all nine of the Justices engaged in a variety of sexual activity.

The Chief, naked except for holster and pistol, was on the floor licking the boot of an otherwise naked young woman.

Brennan was standing in front of two very young girls holding his robe open.

Stewart was measuring the throat of a young woman with a ruler, apparently in preparation for oral sex.

Rehnquist, clad in a woman's bra and red garter belt, was parading before the others cracking a black whip.

White, a blindfold partially covering his glasses, was apparently engaged in some taxing sexual activity, though the cartoon did not make it clear what that activity was.

Powell was kneeling naked, his hands bound together, while a black woman in underwear marked "Exhibit A" flogged him.

Marshall stood by the side of the bench doing nothing but looking up at Douglas, who sat alone on the bench with a naked young boy at his side.

Blackmun was sodomizing a kangaroo.

Chuckling, Rehnquist passed the issue around the table. Most of them laughed. The Chief was angered both by the cartoon and the fact that it had been brought into conference.

Afterward, Marshall sent a clerk to buy extra copies for his college-age children.

Brennan proudly told his clerks that while every other Justice was portrayed engaging in some sexual activity, *he* was pictured protecting several young children by blocking their view with his robe.

His clerks decided that they owed it to him to explain "flashing."

Blackmun told his clerks how funny the centerfold was, especially the portion depicting Rehnquist "in drag." The only problem, Blackmun said, was that he couldn't figure out what he was supposed to be doing with the kangaroo.

The clerks drew straws to see who would tell him.

*   *   *

The previous year's obscenity decisions began to bear expected fruit as juries returned convictions in erratic and unpredictable patterns. The four obscenity dissenters—Brennan, Marshall, Douglas and Stewart—continued to believe the Court should reverse such convictions, but despite their four votes they did not insist that each case be granted cert. Brennan knew they would lose and a formal decision would convert local obscenity convictions into national precedents, turn minor inequities into landmark losses. He preferred to let disparities exist in the lower courts without the Supreme Court adding its imprimatur. Instead, they regularly filed a boilerplate dissent from the cert denials. They would not push to take a case until a fifth vote to reverse a conviction seemed likely.

Powell was the most susceptible to being won over as far as Brennan was concerned. Brennan's clerks looked through the movie stills, magazines and books that poured into the Court, hoping to find one where a local jury had clearly gone too far—a case that would show the absurdity of letting local "community standards" prevail.

Each time Brennan found an outrageous conviction, he sent the material to Stewart, who would have the best sense of Powell's reaction. Generally, Stewart reviewed the exhibits on Saturdays so his secretary would not see them. But in no case had Powell gone along. He did not want to second-guess a local jury. Finally, Brennan found a case (*Jenkins v. Georgia*) that seemed a sure bet. A moviehouse operator in Albany, Georgia, had been convicted and fined $750 for showing the R-rated film *Carnal Knowledge*. Here was a movie that was clearly not obscene. It was pure Hollywood establishment and had no explicit sex. The film had been directed by the highly regarded Mike Nichols, was on many critics' "Ten Best" lists, and actress Ann-Margret had been nominated for an Oscar.

A screen was set up, and several Justices attended the special showing. As the film progressed, there was little of the usual cackling, running commentary or leg slapping.

"I thought we were going to see a dirty movie," Marshall complained at the end of the movie. "The only thing obscene about this movie is that it is obscenely boring," said White. The Chief left early. He told his clerks the camera work and the lighting had been well done. Rehnquist said he liked the music.

At conference, all nine Justices were prepared to say *Carnal Knowledge* was not obscene and to reverse the conviction. But the four First Amendment liberals wanted the Court to admit that the problem grew directly out of Burger's obscenity opinions of the previous year. The Chief wanted only to send a message to local jurisdictions that there were limits: clearly, *Carnal Knowledge* was not obscene. He did not want to pull back from his landmark opinion the year before. So he assigned Rehnquist the case along with another obscenity case *(Hamling v. U.S.)* involving *The Illustrated Presidential Report of the Commission on Obscenity and Pornography.* Rehnquist would have to explain why *The Illustrated Report* was obscene and *Carnal Knowledge* was not.

When Rehnquist returned to chambers to work on the opinion, the job looked simple. The *Report* had sex acts explicitly displayed. The movie had only simulated sex. But as he reviewed the Chief's major obscenity opinion *(Miller)* from the year before, he recognized his dilemma. The Chief had written that material could be found obscene where the sexual acts were "actual or simulated," as long as the act itself was "patently offensive." Could not the simulated fellatio in *Carnal Knowledge,* even though not explicit, be "patently offensive"?

Rehnquist decided he would have to carefully reinterpret the Chief's obscenity opinion, and declare that only explicit displays could be ruled obscene by local juries. The others in the Chief's old majority signed on the opinion.

Brennan saw that they were back in the "Redrupping" business; the Court would deal with obscenity on a case-by-case basis. "It is clear," he wrote with some relish, "that as long as the [Chief's] test remains in effect, one cannot say with certainty that material is obscene until at least five members of this Court . . . have pronounced it so." And he kept sniping about obscenity cases, claiming that the five-man majority allowed convictions to stand without even reviewing the material. Brennan spelled out his concerns in a series of published dissents.

White was irritated. Brennan was pushing too hard. He, in fact, had reviewed the materials submitted to the Court. As far as White was concerned, the obscenity decisions of the year before worked perfectly. The Justices still had to review a few cases, but by and large, communities were enforcing their own standards. The hardest-core pornography was available in major cities but not in small towns. White singled out one of Brennan's dissents: "One of the publications involved is *Sex Between Humans and Animals,*" he wrote. "Mr. Justice Brennan would apparently hold that the First Amendment prohibits government from denying consenting adults access to such materials, but I do not construe the First Amendment as preventing the States from prohibiting the distribution of a publication whose dominant theme is represented by repeated photographs of men and women performing sex acts with a variety of animals."

At the opening of the term, the press focused attention on the likelihood that the Burger Court might at last leave its imprint on the important race questions of the day. In mid-term the Court heard argument in their first reverse discrimination case *(DeFunis v. Odegaard)* which challenged the affirmative action programs designed to give minorities certain advantages. A white applicant to law school had been denied admission while blacks with lower test scores and grades had been admitted. Under the affirmative action program, a certain number of slots had been set aside for minority applicants. Since the applicant was white, he had no shot at them; he had been singled out because he was white, and that, he claimed, was racial discrimination.

At first, all nine Justices leaned toward holding that such fixed racial quotas were unconstitutional. Marshall considered special quotas an insult to minorities, but at the same time he knew better than anyone the difficulties posed by the remaining barriers for minorities in schools and in employment. Affirmative action programs—most of them only a few years old—would all be at stake. On the other hand, to uphold the fixed quota for minorities might create an unfortunate precedent which could be used eventually to exclude minorities.

At conference, several of the Justices indicated that they would not mind avoiding the issue by saying the case was moot; the law student had subsequently been admitted to the law school. The Court would have several more years before another reverse discrimination case worked its way up through the courts. In the meantime, affirmative action programs could continue to bring about more educational and employment equality. Stewart offered to write a *per curiam* declaring the case moot. Burger, Blackmun, Powell and Rehnquist agreed finally, but not before Douglas had first circulated an opinion ruling out virtually all affirmative action, withdrew it the next day, and then substituted a draft saying that race, as a factor in cultural background, could be taken into account in selecting candidates.

Even the liberals breathed a sigh of relief that the case was gone.* But there was another racial issue they could not avoid— busing. Powell had been pleased when the Court agreed to hear the Detroit busing case *(Milliken v. Bradley)* at the beginning of the term. He had been out of the Richmond case the term before because of his nineteen years of service on school boards.

The Detroit case, however, presented the same fundamental question that the Court had addressed in Richmond: could a federal judge order city-suburb school desegregation? Powell wanted to be the fifth vote to put a damper on such court-ordered busing. At conference, he had voted with the three other Nixon appointees and Stewart against the busing. Powell hoped the Chief would assign the majority opinion to him.

But it was also the Chief's first time in the majority on an impor-

---

* On July 5, 1978, the Court addressed virtually the same issues in the highly publicized case of *Regents of the University of California v. Bakke.* Its splintered decision held that rigid quotas for minorities in admissions programs were impermissible, but that race could be considered as one of many factors in admitting students. Typically, Powell was the only Justice on both sides. On one hand Powell provided a fifth vote for Burger, Stewart, Rehnquist and Stevens against rigid quotas; on the other, he was the fifth vote joining Brennan, White, Marshall and Blackmun permitting the consideration of race as one of several admission criteria in affirmative action programs.

tant school desegregation case since the Charlotte decision. Burger had seen his work subverted there. After twenty years of post-*Brown* clarifications, he believed it was time for a definitive new direction. He took the opinion for himself. To Burger, the case was simply a matter of establishing a fair and equitable remedy. The suburban school children and parents in Detroit's older suburbs had played no role in segregating Detroit's schools. It was unfair to punish them for it by involving them in any city-suburb desegregation scheme.

But Burger wanted this opinion to be precisely right. One of his clerks worked on it for several months, under closer supervision than usual. One day during its preparation, the Chief had all his clerks to lunch in the Ladies Dining Room. The Chief treated the lunch like a seminar and he talked freely. The discussion touched on the busing case, and somehow the mention of blacks in the city triggered a recollection.

Why, just recently, the Chief remarked, he had recommended to a fellow trustee at the Smithsonian Institution that unemployed blacks be trained as gardeners to work on the Mall between the Capitol and the monument grounds. Blacks would make talented gardeners, he said. They have such a great sense of color.

The subject somehow shifted to Jews. Unlike blacks, they can get mortgages, the Chief said, because Jews are generally more able and successful and trustworthy.

Oblivious to the startled glances of his clerks, the Chief turned to the subject of women. Women should not be allowed to serve as judges in rape trials, he said. They are too emotional, and incapable of fair judgment. Women judges greatly increased an accused rapist's chances of conviction.

Burger's draft in the Detroit case was finally completed in April, and circulated to the Court. Powell read it carefully. As much as Powell wanted to limit future busing, Burger had gone too far. The Chief's draft had totally foreclosed the possibility of *any* city-suburban school busing.

Powell was distressed also at the inadequate research and drafting. "If an associate in my law firm had done this," Powell told a clerk, "I'd fire him."

Stewart, too, was upset with the draft. He still wanted to stick to his basic opposition to city-suburban busing, but he found it difficult to desert the black parents who had struggled so long for equal educational opportunity for their children. Nor did he want to rule out totally any future possibility of city-suburb desegregation.

Blackmun and Rehnquist were also unhappy with the Chief's draft; all four members of Burger's majority showed no inclination to join.

Word of the universal unhappiness with the Chief's draft heartened Marshall. He had been sick about the conference vote. The decision would be the first major cutback in desegregation remedies by the Court since he had argued the *Brown* case nearly twenty years before. But Burger's draft was appalling. It was incredible, the lengths to which the Chief went to distort the facts of the case. Burger's draft claimed that the lower court had tried to use strict racial balancing of schools. In fact, the district court had done nothing more or less than Judge McMillan had done in the Charlotte case.

The majority opinion implied that local school board action had not segregated the schools. Marshall knew that to be untrue. The majority indicated also that a city-suburb plan would result in massive busing. Marshall knew that that too was a misinterpretation. He saw little hope, however, that the liberals could pull this one out. So he decided it was time to let loose. He authorized his clerk to prepare a sharp dissent. The majority was no longer concerned about the education of black children in a segregated urban school system. Its concern now was the convenience of white suburban children.

Stewart and Powell got together to discuss their problems with the Chief's draft. The problem, once again, would be to get the Chief to bow to the weight of the Court's center.

Powell suggested drafting a "ghost" opinion that they would gradually try to force on the Chief, piece by piece. Stewart agreed. Burger was disturbed at the obvious attempt to manipulate him, but he finally capitulated on the main issue. His opinion would not foreclose the possibility of city-suburban school busing in future cases, if a direct constitutional violation could be proven in both the city and suburbs.

Stewart then agreed to join. But he also prepared a concurring opinion, going further than the Chief. If state officials were involved in a discriminatory act, such as housing or zoning laws which had led to segregated school systems, he would support city-suburb busing.

Stewart's obvious attempt—as the fifth and crucial vote—to set the limits of the opinion irritated Burger even more.

Marshall continued to hold out. His dissents were not the kind to win votes, but they had their emotional impact.

Stewart had never publicly voted against school desegregation in a major case. Marshall hoped against hope that he could reach Stewart. Time and the Chief were his only allies. As Stewart struggled with the Chief throughout the term, Marshall looked for any sign that Stewart's frustration might make him reconsider his Detroit vote. If only he would agree at least to send the case back for further fact finding. Then, if the parents could show illegal acts on both sides of the city line, the revised Burger draft would permit city-suburban busing there. But Stewart would not budge. And Marshall would not pull a Hugo Black and keep the opinion from coming down altogether, no matter how strongly he felt. But he waited until the end of the year before letting it be announced.

Near the end of the previous term, on Saturday, May 12, 1973, less than two weeks after Nixon's top aides, H. R. Haldeman and John Ehrlichman, resigned because of the Watergate scandal, the Chief went to his annual reunion with his former law clerks. More than forty of them were expected at the black-tie, stag dinner in the ornate East and West Conference rooms. The Chief was edgy and tired as usual at the end of a Court term. But he loved these gatherings and he loosened up with a glass of sherry followed by a glass of white wine. Each of the clerks had paid about forty dollars for the dinner and a gift for the Chief. Essentially it was an event to remind themselves and their friends and colleagues that they had been part of the secret workings of the Court, that they had served the Chief Justice of the United States.

Some of the Chief's old Court of Appeals clerks knew him well and truly liked him. The recent clerks, who had seen Burger only in the somber and pressured atmosphere of the Supreme Court, were inclined to be less charitable toward him. Several took a few stiff drinks to get them through the evening. As the Chief circulated before dinner, he often forgot their names, much to everybody's embarrassment.

The former clerks had banded together in a group calling itself the "WEB Fete Society" and had planned an elaborate menu.* Six different wines, one for each course, had been carefully chosen, all in consultation with the Chief, a lifelong member of an international wine tasting society. Shortly after 7 P.M. the group—all white, all male, well-scrubbed and ill at ease in dinner jackets—ambled into the West Conference Room for dinner. There was no head table. An empty seat was left at each table so the Chief could move from table to table with each course, talking about whatever popped into his head—the wine, the building, the case load, travel.

After nearly three hours, the waiters cleared the tables and closed the doors behind them. A toast was proposed to the Chief Justice of the United States. As the highlight of the evening, the Chief had agreed to take questions and give his "family" his candid views.

Burger didn't have to remind them that he was speaking off the record. They all knew he considered every word he uttered confidential. They also were aware they would get nowhere with hard questions. The city was ablaze with Watergate, but the clerks, rising from their seats to ask their questions, avoided the subject.

---

* The menu listed the following wines and brandy:

Zeltinger Riesling 1970
Sherry Dry Sack
Muscadet 1970 Sèvre et Marne
   Beau Soleil
Châteauneuf-du-Pape 1971 B&G
Margaux 1966 B&G
Courvoisier V.S.O.P.

The food included:

Hors d'Oeuvres
Double Consommé au Sherry
Striped Bass Champagne Sauce
Parsleyed Potatoes
Entremets
Loin of Beef Sauce Béarnaise
Asparagus au Beurre
Assorted Cheese
Ile de France Bread
Demitasse

The Chief sat as each question was asked. Then, standing, he wandered about each topic for as much as ten minutes in a blizzard of free association.

At last someone asked a direct Watergate question: Would the upcoming Senate hearings and publicity prejudice a fair trial later?

The Chief bristled and started to skirt the issue, but suddenly he changed his tone. It all had to be put in historical perspective, he said. Nixon had been elected to change some things. That was his mandate. Watergate was a political battle, a way for certain political elements to do what they had failed to accomplish in the 1972 election. The President was doing what he was elected to do. Now, the news media were on a witch-hunt trying to tie the actions of his aides to the President himself. The newspapers had become character assassins, the Chief declared. All the innuendo, distortion, hearsay and sensational headlines were vindictive.

Burger's defense of Nixon, after so much evidence and so many resignations, startled some of the clerks. The Chief seemed to view Watergate in personal terms, as if the legitimacy of his own appointment, his own mandate, hinged on keeping Nixon free from the taint. "Apart from the morality," the Chief concluded, "I don't see what they did wrong."

The damaging news from the Senate Watergate hearings blared forth day after day from a portable black-and-white television set perched on a table in Stewart's outer office. Clerks, messengers and secretaries clustered around the set. Occasionally, another Justice would stop by to savor or deplore the latest revelation. Marshall, a frequent visitor, became the informal master of ceremonies and provided a running commentary. When White House counsel John Dean charged that Nixon himself was involved, Marshall shouted gleefully, "Right on, brother Dean." Falling into his stylized Amos-and-Andy routine, Marshall made it clear that he felt "Brother Dean" was telling the truth. "Dat de way it wuz, sho' wuz," Marshall declared. Nixon's defenders, on the other hand, were greeted with calls of "You lie, you lie."

Most of the Justices followed the news with fascination, concern and some detachment. They might well get a Watergate-related case; they might be required to rule on some legal question such as pretrial publicity, or attorney-client privilege. But for now Watergate was a problem for politicians, not for Justices.

The television in Stewart's outer office was on as usual on Monday, July 16, when the Senate committee announced a surprise witness. The clerks bunched around the set had never heard of Alexander Butterfield. His testimony was shocking. Nixon had secretly taped his White House meetings and telephone conversations.

Archibald Cox, the special prosecutor whom Nixon had been forced to appoint to investigate Watergate, immediately subpoenaed the tape recordings of nine Nixon-Dean meetings. The White House asked U.S. District Court Judge John J. Sirica to quash the subpoena on the grounds of executive privilege. Though it was often claimed by Presidents, the Court had never defined the scope of such privilege or even stated explicitly that it existed.

Sirica refused to quash the subpoena, and Nixon appealed the ruling. Anticipating that the case would soon be in the Supreme Court, White House spokesman Ron Ziegler said only that the President would obey a "definitive" decision by the Court.

At a pre-term briefing and cocktail party for new clerks in September, the Watergate tapes case was the principal topic of conversation: what did Nixon mean by "definitive"?

The Chief began with a routine welcoming speech, but quickly moved to Watergate. He said it was likely that the Court would get the tapes case. That would pose extraordinary problems, and the foremost among them would be security. Historically, outsiders had treated the Court's deliberations as sacrosanct. This time, however, reporters would be desperate for stories; they would use every trick. Burn bags, clean desks and locked files would be necessary. The Chief then introduced Justice Stewart, to describe the perils of dealing with reporters. Stiff and awkward, Stewart gave a mercifully short talk. The clerks should not talk to reporters, he said, and they should be careful in dealing with them at all.

Marshall missed the session, but later got a full report from his clerks. The Chief had made an ass of himself again, Marshall concluded. The clerks told him that the Chief had put an absolute gag on all conversation with anyone. "But if I don't tell Cissy what's going on in this one, she'll kill me," Marshall said. He told his clerks it was up to each to decide whether to discuss the case with his wife.

On October 12, just into the second week of the Supreme Court term, the Court of Appeals upheld Judge Sirica 5 to 2. Midnight, Friday, October 19, was the deadline for the President to file an appeal to the Supreme Court. Reporters and TV camera crews were massed outside the Court anticipating the arrival of the President's lawyers. A lawyer getting out of his car was engulfed by reporters who thought, incorrectly, that he was there on behalf of the President.

Shortly before midnight, the White House issued a statement declaring that the President was not going to appeal to the Supreme Court. Instead, Nixon proposed a compromise that would give the Special Prosecutor summaries verified by Senator John Stennis of Mississippi, an aging, nearly deaf Nixon supporter. The President also issued a direct order to Special Prosecutor Cox, "as an employee of the executive branch," not to seek any more tapes through the judicial process.

The next night, Saturday, October 20, Marshall had his clerks over for dinner at his suburban Falls Church, Virginia, home. As usual, television sets were on upstairs and downstairs while Marshall shot pool with the clerks. Shortly before 8:30, the regular programs were interrupted. Special Prosecutor Archibald Cox had been fired. Attorney General Elliot Richardson and his deputy had resigned rather than fire the Special Prosecutor. Solicitor General Robert Bork, the next in line, was Acting Attorney General. He had agreed to comply with the President's order to fire Cox. Soon all the networks were running special broadcasts. F.B.I. agents were shown sealing off and guarding the Special Prosecutor's office to prevent removal of files.

Marshall watched in disbelief. As a civil rights lawyer, he had often seen such raw displays of police power in the South, but never before in Washington. President Nixon had ordered the prosecutor to stay out of court, fired him, and was now probably seizing his evidence. Where would the man stop? Adding to the drama for

Marshall was the fact that all the President's actions seemed designed to keep the tapes case out of the Supreme Court.

Within the week, Nixon, reeling from the hostile public reaction to what had become known as the Saturday Night Massacre, capitulated and turned over the tapes to Sirica. The case was closed.

Brennan wondered what the Court would have done. The most prolific source and consumer of grapevine information, Brennan sifted through the intelligence his clerks brought back from their peers in the other chambers. Over lunch, or dropping by a colleague's chambers, Brennan probed. The results of his unofficial poll indicated that the vote might have been anything but "definitive." The four Nixon appointees seemed to favor the President's claim of executive privilege. Douglas, Stewart, Marshall and he were against it. Four-to-four with an inscrutable Byron White in the balance. White, as always, kept his own counsel. He seemed to enjoy keeping the others in doubt.

But if Watergate was not before the Court, it was much discussed at Brennan's morning coffee with his clerks and secretary. Was the new special prosecutor, Leon Jaworski, a Texas millionaire and former A.B.A. president, a shill for the White House? Brennan was not sure. Was the House of Representatives serious about its impeachment investigation?

On March 1, the Watergate cover-up indictment charged seven of Nixon's former aides including Haldeman, Ehrlichman and former Attorney General John Mitchell. The tapes question would not go away. Both Jaworski and John Doar, Chief Counsel to the House Judiciary Committee, wanted more tapes for their separate investigations. Jaworski subpoenaed sixty-four more tapes, and again Sirica ordered the President to surrender the tapes to the prosecutor. The Court was back at the center.

Sirica set 4 P.M. Friday, May 24, as the deadline for the President to appeal to the Court of Appeals for the District of Columbia. Nixon filed on time.

Two hours later at the Supreme Court a group of clerks were on the basketball court for their regular game, when someone raced in to say that Philip Lacovara of the Special Prosecutor's office was downstairs at the court clerk's office. The basketball players jogged down in their gym clothes—at some peril should the Chief see them—to get copies of the filing.

It was a cert petition asking for an expedited hearing. Jaworski was taking the extraordinary step of asking the Supreme Court to hear the tapes case before the Court of Appeals decision. In cases "of imperative public importance," requests to leapfrog the lower appellate courts were permissible, but had been granted only half a dozen times. The most recent had occurred when President Harry S. Truman seized the steel mills during the Korean War twenty-two years before.

It was a risky strategy. If the Supreme Court refused to grant expedited review it would be a stinging psychological defeat for Jaworski. Brennan felt strongly that cert should be granted. The President was saying that he, not the courts, should decide what, if anything, he was to turn over.

Jaworski said he wanted an expedited hearing to ensure there was no delay of the trial of the former top Nixon aides. For Brennan much more was at stake. The House Judiciary Committee's impeachment inquiry was in full swing. Without the crucial evidence, the wounds of Watergate would not heal. It was time for the truth of Watergate to surface, Brennan felt.

Five votes, rather than the normal four, were required to hear the case on an expedited basis, and Brennan knew that he could count on Douglas and Marshall. Douglas was eager to come to grips with his long-time antagonist. He regarded Richard Nixon as morally, intellectually and in every other way unfit to be President. Marshall was no less hostile. They might well be joined by Stewart. His skepticism about a President run amok had grown steadily. But this was the same Potter Stewart who once had been a possible Nixon choice for Chief Justice. Stewart toyed with progressive ideas, Brennan thought, but more often than not he fell back on the Ohio Republican principles of his past. White could be within reach. Burger was beyond hope. It was probably no accident that the White House had released, among the barrage of tape transcripts made public the previous April, a single transcript of no particular import that included a reference to the Chief's conversation with then Attorney General Richard Kleindienst. It disclosed that the Chief had forwarded his own list of candidates for the first Watergate Special Prosecutor through Kleindienst. Brennan was curious about what other references to the Chief might be on those tapes.

Blackmun was a possible cert vote. He had come a long way from his fawning alliance with the Chief. As his reservations about Burger grew, Blackmun had begun to draw his own conclusions about events outside the Court. It was difficult to tell where Powell stood. The smallest of clues would have to suffice. During the term he had dropped the prefix "President" and now generally referred only to "Nixon."

Rehnquist, though clearly troubled, was the most likely to support the President on principle. He had drafted the President's original position on executive privilege when he was at the Justice Department. And Rehnquist was against Justices disqualifying themselves unnecessarily from major cases, particularly cases in which the vote was likely to be close. But Rehnquist had worked closely with John Mitchell and John Ehrlichman. They were all under indictment, and Richard Kleindienst, Mitchell's successor, had resigned at the same time as Haldeman and Ehrlichman. Kleindienst was one of Rehnquist's closest friends in Washington.

On Tuesday, May 28, Rehnquist faced the inevitable. He could not sit with his colleagues. He would, however, announce only that he had disqualified himself, without offering a reason.

Brennan worried that the Court would not take the case on an expedited basis before adjourning for the summer. The White House had the strongest force of all going for it—the vast history of judicial inertia. Burger, Blackmun and Harlan had dissented in the Pentagon Papers case, all objecting to the haste with which the case had been propelled through the courts.

This was precisely the argument the White House made in its brief opposing the expedited hearing. "Attempts in the past by the Court to make a hurried disposition of an important case arising in the dying days of a term have not been among the proudest chapters in the history of the Court," the brief read. The Pentagon Papers case "is but the most recent example." The brief cited Burger's dissent in the case.

In Brennan's view, this argument was an insult to the Court. The White House was conspicuously wooing the Chief. The claim that expediting the case would lead to a hasty, ill-conceived decision was absurd, a phantom issue, in Brennan's words, "a bugaboo." Brennan felt that the Court should extend its term if necessary. His vacation in Nantucket could be postponed. Since most of the term's cases were already completed, the Court would have the rare opportunity to give the case its undivided attention. But the argument against expediting would probably persuade Powell who, modeling himself after Harlan, would object to the undue haste. The clerks were betting even money on whether the Court would go along with Jaworski.

The conference convened on May 31, one week after the Special Prosecutor's filing. The Chief brought a letter that had arrived that morning. Senate Majority Leader Mike Mansfield urged the Court to forgo "its four month recess . . . so that there will be no unconscionable delays in the consideration of Watergate or related matters."

The Chief's disdain was clear. The letter exhibited crude ignorance of the Court's work load during recess. Burger had never liked Mansfield. He was anti-courts, anti-lawyer, anti-judge, always leading the resistance to judicial pay raises.

Stewart was nearly as offended as the Chief. He was defensive about his summer-long vacation at Bowen Brook Farm in New Hampshire. He emphasized to callers there that he was working hard on cert petitions and other Court business. The other members of the conference all resented the occasional portrayals of them as part-time judges, racing off each summer to their fishing ponds and hammocks. The conference decided to send Mansfield a sharp, but tactfully worded, reply.

At 12:10 P.M., Rehnquist left the room, and they turned to the tapes case itself. The Justices agreed with two of the Chief's suggested ground rules. They would not tell their clerks about the discussion and to prevent leaks they would announce their decision immediately.

The Chief did not have to spend a long time presenting the case. They were all familiar with the facts. Burger said that he had problems with expediting the case. All that was at stake was a possible delay of the Watergate cover-up trial. That was hardly a matter of national emergency. But Burger hedged. He was not ready to vote either way.

Douglas spoke next. He did not hide his contempt for Nixon's position. Everyone, including a President, had to turn over evidence. The defendants in the cover-up trial would be entitled to all possible evidence. The Court could decide the issue quickly. He voted to expedite.

Brennan thought the President's claim of absolute "executive privilege" lacked even the slightest merit. The cover-up trial might survive the delay if the hearing was not expedited, but this called for decisive action. The Court had an obligation. He voted to expedite.

Stewart fidgeted. He too thought the President had a weak argument, and he worried how it might appear if the Court denied the petition. There was speculation in the press that the Court would not decide such a question because it was a classic *political* dispute between two branches of government. The Court's authority was now an issue. The President had made it one. This business about obeying only a "definitive" opinion was a challenge. Court rulings had to be obeyed, definitive or not. Compliance was not a matter for a President to decide. In any event, Nixon's challenge made the case a paramount legal issue. Now. It had to be decided. Stewart voted to expedite.

White disagreed. A few months' delay in the cover-up trial would not set back the cause of justice. Despite the other considerations, the only question was whether to grant an expedited hearing and bypass the Court of Appeals. If the Court's authority was being challenged, that should be taken in stride. There should be no hasty overreaction. White said he was inclined to deny the petition for now, let the case mature and come to the Court naturally.

Marshall cast a fourth vote to expedite. But it took five votes to grant the immediate hearing.

Blackmun wanted to be sure the Court did not act recklessly. Watergate might be a national emergency, but speeding the cover-up trial was not sufficient cause to depart from normal practice. He would vote to wait.

Powell thus emerged as the critical vote either way. He thought Watergate was a national emergency; special steps were justified. He was ready to hear the case now.

That made five votes to take the case immediately. Burger then said he too would go along, making the final vote 6 to 2. Thirty minutes later, a formal order expediting the case was signed by the Chief and released to the press. As usual, the votes on a decision to grant cert or expedite the case were not listed.

Though confident of the strength of their legal arguments, Jaworski and his staff were concerned that the Court might still rule in favor of the President. The Special Prosecutor's office needed to buttress its position with something more than legal niceties. Jaworski wanted the Court to reach the same conclusions that he and the grand jury had drawn: Richard Nixon was a crook. If he could get the Court to share that simple conclusion, the other arguments would follow naturally in turn, and they would get their tapes.

The most persuasive evidence in their possession was the first nine tapes that the President had turned over following the Saturday Night Massacre and that had been sealed by Judge Sirica. The grand jury had been strongly influenced by the tapes and other material sealed in that record. It had led them to the conclusion that there was only one reason the President had withheld the evidence, that he was protecting himself because he was guilty.

The Special Prosecutor's staff felt they had to draw the Justices' direct and personal attention to the sealed record. They knew, however, that it would not be easy. There were a half dozen former clerks on the Special Prosecutor's staff, and they knew very well that the Justices did not personally review long and detailed records, even in major cases. In an effort to pique their interest, Jaworski dropped an intentionally intriguing question at the Court's feet when he forwarded the record from Judge Sirica's court. Should his office print additional copies of the "sealed" portion for the public record?

The original of the record was locked in Court Clerk Michael Rodak's vault on Burger's instructions. Brennan at once asked to see it. The reason it had been sealed was immediately obvious. The grand jury which had indicted the seven former high-ranking Nixon aides had also secretly named several unindicted coconspirators. One was Richard Nixon himself.

Brennan immediately grasped Jaworski's message to the Justices. Jaworski's threshold problem in the case was to establish the relevance of the subpoenaed tapes. Did the taped conversations pertain to the charges against Nixon's former aides who would go on trial? In Brennan's view, the grand jury's finding against Nixon bolstered Jaworski's argument dramatically. Because the grand jury had found Nixon a full member of the conspiracy, the conversations were clearly relevant. Conversations that were part of a criminal conspiracy would not be protected by a claim of executive privilege. The Special Prosecutor also gained an important technical advantage from the fact that Nixon had been named a coconspirator. Hearsay statements of any alleged conspirator, whether indicted or unindicted, were admissible in trial. Therefore, Jaworski could get more tapes admitted into evidence.

The grand jury's action, however, did not remain secret for long. On June 6, the story broke in newspapers as the result of a leak from a defense attorney. Later that day, the White House filed a short cert petition asking the Court to determine whether a grand jury had the authority to name an incumbent President an unindicted coconspirator.

The issue as posed by the White House was a potential nightmare for the Court, Brennan thought. A judgment by the Court on the legality of the President's status, and the power of the grand jury to charge him as an unindicted coconspirator, would involve the Court in a direct judgment about Nixon's guilt or innocence, and that really was the impeachment issue. It was just the kind of *political* question the Court traditionally sought to avoid. But if they did not take the issue, the Court would appear biased against the President.

At conference the next Monday, June 10, the Justices decided to grant the White House petition, though some thought it was already before them, encompassed in the Special Prosecutor's petition that had been granted. They would just have to figure out how best to deal with it in the context of the whole case.

On Thursday, June 13, a story by Jack MacKenzie appeared on the editorial page of *The Washington Post*. "Evidence is accumulating, though it is fragmentary, that Chief Justice Warren E. Burger has skated close to the line between the branches of government." Citing material that had leaked during the Watergate disclosures, the story quoted two private letters that the Chief had sent to John Mitchell when he was Attorney General.

"The correspondence, by its tone and in its references to frequent conversations, confirms the impression long held in Washington that a confidential relationship developed early in the Nixon administration between Burger and Mitchell." The letters recommended people for judgeships or promotion to the court of appeals or even the Supreme Court.

The Chief was furious that his private letters had been leaked and at the implication that such recommendations were improper. The Attorney General had sought his opinion. Like anyone else, he had offered it. The article, coming at the moment the Court was considering the tapes case, struck the Chief as a heavy-handed attempt by the *Post* to embarrass him into disqualifying himself. It strengthened his will to stay in.

Brennan had finished all his opinions and dissents for the term and now turned his full attention to the tapes case. He read the sealed record carefully. In Brennan's opinion, the tapes showed that Nixon and his aides conspired to obstruct justice and therefore the conversations were not entitled to any constitutional claim of executive privilege.

Brennan kept abreast of developments in the other chambers. Tapping the grapevine, making his own soundings, he found that Nixon had virtually no support in any of the chambers. Some of the others had by now read the record. Nixon's position had eroded. Expecting a real dispute, Brennan found the opposite. It did not take him long to realize how close the Court was to unanimity. But he wanted not just unanimity of result, but unanimity of rationale. A "definitive" decision would require that all eight votes be solidly behind an articulate and persuasive opinion that disposed of each stated and unstated argument for not turning over the tapes.

Brennan knew that the other Justices had already invested a good deal of time in researching the case. Some were preparing memoranda or possible opinions. It would require a miracle for them all to sacrifice weeks of work and their egos for unanimity. Pride of authorship could be a barrier to a single, definitive opinion. But Brennan had a plan. Assuming his old play-maker role from the Warren Court days, Brennan retraced his clerks' route from chamber to chamber. His first call, as always, was to his old friend and the senior Justice, Douglas, the most likely of them all to scuttle a consensus with a cantankerous comment or an ill-conceived memo. Brennan found Douglas working in his chambers. Brennan reported his findings—sentiment was running strongly against Nixon in nearly all chambers. The Court had now to meet Nixon's challenge and issue a "definitive" opinion. This required spelling out the Court's reasoning in a single opinion.

Douglas agreed. A single opinion, of course, would be ideal.

There were problems, Brennan said. With an opinion prepared by a single justice—no matter who pulled what strings, who edited whose work, or who organized what portions of the opinion, even assuming the best and most deferential cooperation—the credit would go to a single author. The other seven might resent it. Brennan and Douglas knew they would be among the seven. There was no doubt who would assign this one—and to whom.

Brennan wondered aloud if it might be a good idea to have no single author but instead a single opinion, signed by all the Justices. It had been done in *Cooper v. Aaron*, a 1958 Little Rock, Arkansas, desegregation enforcement ruling issued in the face of local resistance and Governor Orval Faubus's assertion that a Supreme Court decision was not the law of the land.

Douglas listened.

In this case, all eight of them could write and sign one opinion, Brennan suggested. Nixon had effectively laid down the same challenge that Faubus had. Eight signatures on one opinion would make defiance less likely, and it would prevent the Chief from snapping the opinion up. They would take equal responsibility and equal credit.

Douglas said he liked the idea.

Buoyed by Douglas's response, Brennan continued his rounds. Marshall, who, as a civil rights advocate, had argued *Cooper v. Aaron* twenty years before, was enthusiastic about Brennan's suggestion. Stewart saw the advantages immediately. Brennan optimistically concluded that Powell and Blackmun were also receptive. White, however, was skeptical, and he came right to the point. Entering into agreements before the specifics were sorted out was not his style. It was a preemptive strike against the Chief, bad business.

Undiscouraged, Brennan turned to the Chief himself. Burger's reaction was lukewarm, but he politely told Brennan that he would consider it. Brennan thought that if nothing else, he had all of them focused on unanimity. He figured he, at least, had the votes to force the issue with the Chief.

With the Justices apparently in agreement, Brennan set out to finish preparing for oral argument. There were no surprises in the briefs. The Special Prosecutor offered three reasons why the President should be compelled to give up his tapes; two were predictable. First, the public interest in disclosure of information relevant in a criminal prosecution outweighed Nixon's generalized claim of privilege. Second, the President had already waived his privilege two months before by releasing his edited versions of some of the subpoenaed conversations. The third argument was somewhat more problematic, since it rested on the grand jury's naming Nixon as an unindicted coconspirator. The logic was simple enough. There was no executive privilege for conversations that were part of a criminal conspiracy. But Brennan was troubled. James St. Clair, the President's attorney, could too easily claim that an incumbent president could not be named an unindicted coconspirator in the first place. And thus call into question the validity of the subpoena. Brennan wanted to avoid that thicket.

Douglas had some answers. On July 5, three days before oral argument, he circulated a thirty-page printed draft opinion in memorandum form. The early entry allowed Douglas to help his colleagues focus on his issues.

In the past, however, Brennan had found Douglas's pre-argument memos less than helpful. They were often spun off in a single sitting and sometimes they unintentionally gave the other side effective ammunition. He approached Douglas's memo with some dread. It was satisfactory on several technical questions, but he found the central point inadequate. Rather than call attention to the Special Prosecutor's demonstrated need for the tapes in order to try his case against the defendants, Douglas focused on the needs of the defendants. He argued correctly that previous Court decisions had firmly established that criminal defendants were entitled to all potentially exculpatory information, and that since the defendants would be entitled to tapes that might exonerate one or all of them, so too was the prosecutor. But that was backward, as far as Brennan was concerned. The Court had to address the prosecutor's demand; it was his subpoena.

But Brennan was most shocked by Douglas's endless penchant for raising issues that were likely to derail consensus. In his concluding section, Douglas considered whether the grand jury could constitutionally name the President as an unindicted coconspirator. He dug an even deeper hole for the Court by dealing in such depth with the issue that St. Clair had raised. The lawyer had asked the Court to hold that the evidence shown to the grand jury was insufficient to justify the conclusion that the President was a coconspirator.

Rather than dismiss the request as absurd—the Court should not second-guess the grand jury—Douglas had written:

> It is obvious from the history of this grand jury that the finding was made for the benefit of the House Judiciary Committee which now has before it the impeachment question. So what in substance we are being asked to do is to rule that a certain bit of evidence produced by the grand jury and sent to the House Judiciary Committee is not competent evidence in impeachment proceedings. I think that beyond question that issue is a "political" issue . . .

and therefore not one to be decided by the Court.

Douglas had effectively said the Special Prosecutor's use of the secret grand jury report was a *political* action designed to foster the President's impeachment in the House of Representatives. As weak and inelegant as the President's position had become, he had one powerful historical ally: more than anything else, the Court was always reluctant to take on *political* questions involving the ultimate workings and the limits of the other branches of government. Douglas was raising issues that did not need to be addressed. Brennan found the section bizarre. Any such statement by the Court, Brennan reasoned, would be just what Nixon needed to discredit the Special Prosecutor, his grand jury and the House impeachment inquiry. Of course the grand jury had supplied evidence and some of the early tapes to the House Committee. But the Supreme Court should not comment. They should not provide Nixon with an argument to keep them out.

Brennan was sure that most of the other Justices, with the possible exception of Powell, did not want to deal with the grand jury question. He had heard through the clerk grapevine that Powell wanted to rely heavily on the uniqueness of the grand jury's finding.

Powell wanted the President to lose on the narrowest possible ground, and that would be an order to the President to hand over the tapes precisely *because* he had been named a coconspirator. Powell felt that a ruling such as that would be rarely applicable in the future. But as he thought about it, Powell realized that if the Court based its decision on the grand jury's finding, it would be endorsing it, thrusting itself into the impeachment issue. So he backed off.

Powell's clerks were generally pleased with the way his thinking was going, but they wanted him to assert himself in the case. He could expand his role if he were willing to be aggressive. But Powell still did not want to see the Court alter the fundamental power relationships among the branches of government. A President, like a Justice, needed confidentiality with assistants. Powell agreed with Stewart, who often remarked, "Government cannot function in a goldfish bowl." He did not wish to see the Court damage the principle of confidentiality. Powell wanted this President to lose, while providing every edge in the language to protect future Presidents from unwarranted intrusion into their decision making. Finally, Powell decided to circulate a memo summarizing his position on the main questions. It might, perhaps, provide the skeleton of an opinion. Powell's clerks were unhappy with the final product, which was circulated July 6. It still gave away too much. Nonetheless, they still believed they could change his position.

Brennan, just back from Nantucket, was worried and unsure of what to expect. It was unlike Powell to circulate an opinion before oral argument. But reading quickly, Brennan saw that Powell wanted to rule against the President and not, Brennan thanked God, on the basis of the grand jury finding. Instead, Powell had stated that the particular and demonstrated need for the evidence—the tapes—clearly outweighed the general claim of privilege. Brennan's relief faded when he read that "the ultimate authority" for deciding claims of executive privilege resides in the branch of government "whose constitutional responsibilities are more gravely affected."

That single idea, published as a Court opinion, could wipe out a lot of constitutional law, Brennan realized. The first full definition of the Court's authority—*Marbury v. Madison* in 1803—had established that it "is emphatically the province and duty of the judicial department to say what the law is."

Powell's position was more dangerous than the White House's, Brennan believed. In their briefs the President's lawyers said that the President had "an absolute privilege" and absolute authority to decide. Powell now was suggesting that while the Court had a *right* to consider the claim, it should *not*, but rather should back off and let the Executive Branch decide, if its responsibilities were "more gravely affected."

Douglas had said the President was trying to usurp judicial responsibility, and here Powell was giving away part of the judiciary's responsibility. It was the use of the phrase "ultimate authority" that Brennan found so objectionable. The courts, not the executive, had the "ultimate authority" to interpret the law. Brennan was deeply concerned. Powell was advocating balancing Article II (the constitutional power of the President) against Article III (the power of the courts). There were none of the absolutes that Brennan preferred.

But overall, the draft provided a starting point. Despite the narrow definition, it was a broad-brush treatment, which Brennan was sure he could remold without offending Powell.

Brennan thought Part IV of Powell's draft was even more mischievous. The subpoena to the President had been issued by the Special Prosecutor under the rules of criminal procedure set up for federal courts. These rules had the force of law. Rule 17(c), allowing the federal courts to subpoena any person to produce evidence, provided that the material sought had to be both potentially relevant to the case and admissible in a trial. One of the remaining questions in the tapes case was whether this standard had been met. Powell had written that the Rule 17(c) standard of relevance and admissibility was insufficient for a subpoena to be served on a President. A higher standard had to be met, Powell had concluded. Setting a new standard for presidential subpoenas, Powell had written that "necessity" or a "compelling need" had to be shown. That language was right out of the White House brief.

Though Powell went on to assert that this higher standard of "necessity" had been met by Jaworski in the tapes case, Brennan was not so sure. He found Powell's proposed terms vague and disturbing. Since the Nixon aides had already been indicted on other evidence that was previously available, the Special Prosecutor might have a tough time meeting someone else's definition of "necessity."

Brennan finished reading Powell's memo. A unanimity of rationale was going to be hard to achieve, but there was some consolation. If Powell's view was indicative of the other key votes, Richard Nixon would soon be yielding some tapes.

Brennan spent the Sunday before oral argument conferring with his clerks. Outside the Court, hundreds of spectators were already lined up, each hoping for one of the 120 seats reserved for the public.

The next morning, just before oral argument began, Brennan drafted a cover memo for a four-page proposal responding to Powell's standards for issuing a subpoena to the President. "I am greatly impressed by Lewis' analysis in his memorandum, particularly by his Part III. I think, however, that his Part IV requires some expansion and I am taking the liberty of circulating the attached in the hope that it may serve to focus that problem in our conference discussion."

Brennan's proposal substituted Rule 17(c)—the federal rule for subpoenas that applied to every American—for Powell's higher standard, saying that it was "adequate to protect the President from unnecessary interference or harassment." Brennan would only concede that the courts should be "particularly meticulous" to see that the rule was applied correctly in cases involving the President.

Brennan then went on to address the procedures under which Nixon would turn over the tapes. "Our decision is that the President shall transmit all of the subpoenaed materials to the District Court, excepting those portions for which he interposes a specific claim of privilege limited to national defense, foreign affairs or internal security. With respect to those portions, the President may initially decline production to the District Court." After a hearing on the specific claims, "production" could be ordered, but only after the President's lawyer had been heard. And the President, Brennan suggested, should be able to appeal an unfavorable result, *before* producing the tapes.

Across town, in the White House, President Nixon was dictating his oral diary. If he lost the tapes case, he hoped the Court would provide a method to exempt national security material. He had recently listened to the tapes of three June 23, 1972, meetings that were held six days after the Watergate break-in. The tapes were filled with discussions of the White House efforts to have the C.I.A. ask the F.B.I. to halt its investigation of Watergate for bogus national security reasons. If those tapes, which unfortunately were among those subpoenaed by Jaworski, were turned over, his defense could be destroyed. If Nixon could make that national security claim without turning over the tapes or perhaps could delay proceedings with another battle in the courts, he could gain some room to maneuver.

*   *   *

Blackmun breakfasted with his clerks as usual the morning of oral arguments, July 8. He had told them that he anticipated voting against Nixon. Why would an innocent man with nothing to hide not turn over his tapes? That common sense view determined the issue for him. The clerks warned Blackmun that the Chief would try to take the opinion for himself. Blackmun thought they were right, but he told them he was going to insist that the Chief not write it. Burger was already burdened with the only remaining opinion of the term, the Detroit busing case.

Blackmun had in fact already privately urged the Chief not to assign the tapes case to himself for another reason. The Constitution said that the Chief Justice would preside at an impeachment trial. It would be unseemly for the Court if the author of the tapes opinion later had to preside at the impeachment trial of Nixon in the Senate. Since the House seemed likely to send the case to the Senate for trial, the Chief had to consider that possibility.

Blackmun had also told Burger that the tapes decision would carry more weight in the public's eyes if the author was both a Republican and a Nixon appointee. Rehnquist was out of the case, Powell was a Democrat, Stewart was a Republican but he had been appointed by Eisenhower, and the Chief was the prospective presiding officer in the President's impeachment trial. That left only Blackmun.

In Stewart's chambers there had also been talk about who should write the opinion. His clerks felt the author should be a Republican, but not a Nixon appointee. That eliminated everyone but Stewart.

Stewart brooded about the best way for the Court to handle this great case. He worried that Nixon was intending some subterfuge with which to ultimately defy the Court. Everything must be considered. The opinion had to be written forcefully, with exacting care; every sentence and word analyzed. A course had to be charted between dangerous extremes, one that would cripple the presidency, the other that would leave this President unchecked. All this suggested that the best writer should be assigned the opinion. Stewart was not one to seek it overtly. He would not circulate a memo as Powell and Douglas had done. His bid would be more subtle. He decided to circulate, in raw form, copies of the long research memos his clerks had prepared. The memos would suggest various approaches, foreclose a few options and focus the discussion, all without risk to Stewart.

Stewart arrived at his chambers the morning of oral arguments with little time to spare. His clerks were waiting, full of questions and answers. They filed into his office and tried to brief him. But Stewart was nervous. He paced around, distracted, and brushed off their ideas. The clerks realized that he was not interested in a last-minute briefing. One of the clerks mentioned that his favorite baseball team, the Cincinnati Reds, had swept a Sunday doubleheader from the Cardinals.

Stewart perked up.* He recalled his last conversation with Nixon, at a White House reception the previous fall. The Reds' star ballplayer, Pete Rose, had played brilliantly in an important game. Nixon and Stewart had chatted about his great performance. Rose was a man of average natural ability who excelled through sheer will power. Nixon had compared himself and Rose. "I want to call and congratulate Rose," he told Stewart. "But if I did it for one, I would have to call all the players. Call Pete Rose for me and congratulate him for the President."

Stewart had been baffled. Certainly Rose was one of baseball's great players, a candidate for a contemporary list of Blackmun's superstars. In fact, Stewart had been called the Pete Rose of the Court—steady, always hustling, the ultimate team player, never one to let his teammates down. But a Supreme Court Justice could

---

* Stewart kept a dog-eared piece of newspaper in his wallet, with the mathematical probabilities of scoring runs in each inning of a baseball game. The previous fall, he had requested that his clerks send him inning-by-inning scores of the Reds-Mets playoff games while he heard oral arguments on the bench. Before the final game began, he asked for scores "every half-inning." And as it was played, he wanted a report on *each batter.* At 2:35 P.M., the game was interrupted by the surprising news of Vice-President Agnew's resignation. The clerks dutifully sent Stewart a note: Kranepool flies to right. Agnew resigns.

no more call a baseball player and congratulate him than a President could.

The President's quirks always made Stewart uncomfortable. Once, after Nixon had delivered the annual State of the Union address to a joint session of Congress, he walked up the aisle and recognized Stewart standing with his colleagues. Nixon reached out and shook hands with him alone. Stewart had felt conspicuously identified with this odd, clumsy man. Beyond such social gaffes Nixon gave a bad name to moderate Republican middle-of-the-road principles. Stewart had long ago given up on the President. He had voted for liberal Democrat Senator George McGovern in 1972. He had recently concluded that Nixon was guilty as hell, a criminal fighting to retain his presidency. Stewart was planning to challenge Nixon lawyer St. Clair at orals on the question of whether the courts had the power to decide this case. He was not sure how far to push St. Clair, but he felt it essential to extract a commitment that the President would comply with a Court decision. That was the core. Whatever the outcome, important as it might be, it would not mark the end of constitutional law. But if the President were to defy the Supreme Court, that would cripple the Court, perhaps forever.

Marshall got an oral briefing from his clerks. He did not require a research memo. Certain that he would not be writing the opinion, Marshall thought he knew enough about the case. He favored a strong opinion that would direct Nixon to turn over the tapes. Nonetheless, he too was sensitive to the need for executive privilege. Marshall would never have wanted to see tapes of his conversations with Lyndon Johnson get into anyone's hands. Presidential meetings were not tea parties. Both Johnson and he had talked openly, free of inhibitions—"Cocksucker this and cocksucker that."

At 10:02 A.M., the eight Justices emerged from behind the thick burgundy drapes. The Chief surveyed his seated colleagues, looked out over the jammed courtroom and finally nodded to Special Prosecutor Jaworski, who sat at the government's table. "You may proceed whenever you are ready," the Chief said.

Occasionally glancing at a large black notebook, Jaworski recited the history of the case and the naming of the President as an unindicted coconspirator.

Douglas was the first to interrupt. What relevance did the grand jury's finding have to the President's duty to deliver subpoenaed material? "I thought that was primarily just for the knowledge, information, of the House Judiciary Committee," Douglas said.

"No, sir, that is not correct, sir," Jaworski replied.

Stewart wanted to get the argument off this track. "You would be here, Mr. Jaworski," Stewart asked, "whether or not the President had been named as an unindicted coconspirator. But that simply gives you another string to your bow—isn't that about it?"

Jaworski agreed, but he did not drop the subject. He was sure it added considerable weight to his argument that he get access to the tapes.

Brennan felt that the grand jury question had to be buried. "You don't suggest that your right to this evidence depends upon the President having been named (by the grand jury) as an indicted coconspirator," he asked.

"No, sir," Jaworski replied.

Brennan underlined his point. "And so, for the purposes of our decision, we could lay that fact aside, could we?"

Jaworski offered a reluctant yes. After several interruptions and another flirtation with the grand jury question by Powell, Jaworski attempted to summarize. "Now enmeshed in almost five hundred pages of briefs, when boiled down, this case really presents one fundamental issue. Who is to be the arbiter of what the constitution says? . . . Now, the President may be right in how he reads the Constitution. But he may also be wrong. And if he is wrong, who is there to tell him so? . . . This nation's constitutional form of government is in serious jeopardy if the President, *any president,* is to say that the Constitution means what *he* says it does, and that there is no one, not even the Supreme Court, to tell him otherwise."

Stewart saw an opening to show that the President was subject to the Court's authority. Since the President had gone to district court to quash the subpoena and had filed his cross petition in the Supreme Court, "he has himself invoked the judicial process. And he has submitted to it," Stewart said.

Well, that was not quite right, Jaworski replied, because the President had argued that the Special Prosecutor had no standing to sue him. In the President's view, the matter was an internal Executive Branch dispute, and not something that lay within the Court's power to solve.

Nonetheless, Stewart said, the President is making that argument as a matter of constitutional law. " . . . His position is that he is the sole judge. And he's asking this Court to agree with that proposition, as a matter of constitutional law."

Jaworski was still not ready to agree. "What I'm saying is, if he is the sole judge . . . and if he is in error in his interpretation, then he goes on being in error in his interpretation," he insisted.

"Then this Court will tell him so," Stewart said. "That's what this case is about, isn't it?"

The Chief chimed in. He, too, was very concerned about the Court's authority. "[The President] is submitting himself to the judicial process in the same sense that you are, is that not so, Mr. Jaworski?"

Jaworski was not sure. The President had insisted that "he and he alone is the proper one to interpret the Constitution."

" . . . Each of you is submitting for a decision to this Court," the Chief said.

"That may be, sir," Jaworski said, but he had personal reservations about Nixon's willingness to abide by the Court's decision. Like the Justices, he had read the President's elusive statements about complying with a Court decision.

Jaworski came back to the grand jury question in spite of the attempts by Brennan and Stewart to warn him off.

White interrupted testily. "I thought we had put that issue aside. I just don't understand what the relevance of that is to this case," he said.

Jaworski fumbled, pointing out that St. Clair had raised one side of the question.

"I am just wondering, Mr. Jaworski, why you aren't content . . . it is irrelevant . . ."

As Jaworski stumbled further down the path, his staff sat grimacing. Their boss had apparently forgotten the first rule of oral advocacy—get a sense of the Court and go where it wants to go. Be helpful, don't argue.

Stewart finally cut him off. It was now St. Clair's turn.

The Justices had joked that in order to emphasize his claim that the prosecutor had no standing, St. Clair might not show up for oral argument. St. Clair opened by arguing that the Court's decision and the House impeachment proceedings were intimately connected.

"Well, those are none of our problems, are they?" asked Douglas, who three days before had suggested in his draft opinion that the two might overlap. That morning, Douglas had dropped the argument and circulated a redraft of his opinion without it.

St. Clair insisted that the two were related. The Court was embroiled in impeachment politics, he said. The tapes which the Special Prosecutor wanted, if they were turned over, would be passed on to the House impeachment inquiry, St. Clair insisted. "So this fusion is going to continue," he added. "No one could stand here and argue with any candor that a decision of this Court would have no impact whatsoever on the pending inquiry before the House of Representatives concerning the impeachment of the President."

Stewart suggested a hypothetical murder to which the President was one of the few eyewitnesses. Would he be unavailable to the courts because of an impeachment inquiry?

This was different, St. Clair responded. The subject matter of the two Watergate inquiries was identical. He insisted repeatedly that the Court was entering into impeachment questions. It was not the Special Prosecutor who would ultimately use the tapes, but the House impeachment inquiry. That made it a *political* question.

Marshall cut in. "So that the House can get [the tapes], the President can get them, and the only people I know that cannot get them is the Courts," Marshall said, drawing appreciative laughs from the courtroom.

"You have not convinced me that we're drawn into it by deciding this case," Brennan said.

"The impact of a decision in this case undeniably, Mr. Justice Brennan, in my view, cannot have—it will not be overlooked," St. Clair said.

"Any number of decisions of this Court has ripples," Brennan responded.

Burger reentered the debate, "Mr. St. Clair, you left me in a little bit of doubt about this mechanical problem. I think perhaps we diverted you from it," the Chief said, raising an issue that St. Clair had mentioned in passing. "Are you suggesting that on a given tape, which is a reel type of thing, having an hour or more of material or maybe several hours—"

"Two or three days," St. Clair helped.

"Two or three days—Oh, I see," the Chief said. He had spoken many times with the President at the White House or on the phone. He was surely on some of these additional tapes. "That the first three hours might be the material which has already been transcribed and released," the Chief continued, "the next three or four hours might be a conference with the Joint Chiefs of Staff or the Chairman of the Atomic Energy Commission . . . matters totally irrelevant but confidential . . . and you want some mechanism set up so that these things can be screened out?"

St. Clair indicated that would be his position if he lost.

Marshall decided this would be a good time to make an effort at establishing the Court's authority. When presented with the subpoena, he asked facetiously, "you just ignored it, didn't you?"

"No sir, we did not," St. Clair responded. "We filed a motion to quash it."

"The difference between ignoring and filing a motion to quash is what?" Marshall closed the trap.

"Well, if your Honor please, we are submitting the matter—"

"You are submitting the matter to this Court." Marshall finished St. Clair's sentence for him.

"To this Court under a special showing on behalf of the President . . ." St. Clair said, again trying to finish the sentence.

"You're still leaving it up to this Court to decide it," Marshall tried to slam the door shut.

"Well, yes," St. Clair admitted, but added in qualification, "in a sense."

"Well, in what sense?" Marshall asked impatiently.

St. Clair hedged.

Marshall badgered him.

St. Clair acknowledged they were submitting a legal question to the Court. "This is being submitted to this Court for its guidance and judgment with respect to the law," St. Clair said, gripping the lectern. "The President, on the other hand, has his obligations under the Constitution."

The President's lawyer was suggesting that the Court's opinion would be advisory, not binding on his client. The President would be looking for a loophole, some convenient language in the opinion that would suit him. Then he would decide how to apply its decision. St. Clair was saying that the Court could decide the law, but that the President would apply it. Nixon was telling the Court that it could tell him what criteria to use in his decision, but it could not decide for him whether to turn over the tapes.

"Are you submitting it to this Court for this Court's decision?" Marshall demanded to know.

"As to what the law is, yes," St. Clair said.

The challenge to the Court's authority was now clear.

White took his turn. "Would you automatically say every conversation about Watergate is in the course of the performance of the duties of the President of the United States?"

"I would think it would be, yes sir," St. Clair answered.

"Why is that, Mr. St. Clair?" White asked, letting out a little more rope.

The Watergate conversations were part of Nixon's role as President, insuring that the allegations were fully investigated and prosecuted, St. Clair said.

White let the answer hang in the air. He and the others had read the transcripts of the early tapes. Nixon had not acted as an investigator or a prosecutor.

Powell was still concerned that the President be given an extra measure of protection from harassment by subpoena. "Mr. St. Clair, may I get back to what seems rather fundamental to me," he said, leaning forward. "Let us assume that it had been established that the conversations we're talking about here today did involve a criminal conspiracy, would you still be asserting an absolute privilege?"

"Yes, quite clearly," St. Clair declared.

"What public interest is there in preserving secrecy with respect to a criminal conspiracy?" Powell inquired.

"The answer, sir, is that a criminal conspiracy is criminal only after it's proven to be criminal," St. Clair responded, smiling.

"But my—," Powell tried to begin.

"And we're not at that point yet," St. Clair added.

"My question was based on the assumption that it had been established that the conversation did relate to a criminal conspiracy," Powell insisted.

St. Clair insisted that the claim of privilege remained absolute since no one had been found guilty. The tentative allegation that there was a conspiracy was not enough to subpoena the evidence.

Powell listened to all this in disbelief. Reduced to its essentials, St. Clair's argument was that the President was immune from criminal investigation. The only remedy that would reach him was impeachment. Powell determined more than ever to vote against this seemingly unlimited assertion of power.

Marshall viewed St. Clair's absolutist position as absurd. He posed a hypothetical question involving an "about-to-be-appointed" judge who pays off the President.

"How are you going to impeach him if you don't know about it?" Marshall asked.

"Well, if you know about it, then you can state the case," St. Clair offered logically. "If you don't know about it, you don't have it," he said.

"So there you are," Marshall began, warming to the task. "You're on the prongs of a dilemma, huh?"

"No, I don't think so," St. Clair responded.

"If you know the President is doing something wrong, you can impeach him," Marshall said, gloating, his eyebrows arching. "But if the only way you can find out is this way [a subpoena], you can't impeach him, so you don't impeach him. . . . You lose me some place along there."

The courtroom filled with laughter.

" . . . Very few things forever are hidden," St. Clair said lamely. "This is not a case where there is no information. If anything, there is more than enough."

Jaworski's counsel, Philip Lacovara, stepped up to finish the Special Prosecutor's argument.

The Chief returned to the subject that seemed to concern him the most. "Mr. Lacovara, I wanted to get to this mechanical question that Mr. St. Clair brought up," he said. Burger launched into one of the day's longest questions about how Judge Sirica could review the relevant Watergate conversations without listening to other presidential meetings.

Lacovara assured him there was a mechanism to protect these other conversations.

"Then," the Chief asked, " . . . there is, you suggest, no disagreement between you and Mr. St. Clair?"

None, Lacovara assured him. And he closed carefully.

" . . . We submit that this Court should fully, explicitly, and decisively," Lacovara paused, "and *definitively* uphold Judge Sirica's decision."

St. Clair provided a short rebuttal, and the Chief ended the session at 1:04. "The case is submitted," he said.

In the robing room afterward, the consensus was that the arguments for both sides had been generally uninspired. There was a good deal of head shaking and grumbling about St. Clair's absolutist position—a position that had not been made fully clear in his brief. It seemed more extraordinary now than ever.

The next morning the eight Justices met in conference to vote on the case. Everyone was well prepared. The memos from the chambers of Douglas, Powell, Brennan and Stewart had defined the scope of the case. Dealing first with the technical questions, they all agreed that the Sirica ruling on the subpoena was of sufficient constitutional significance to be appealed to the Supreme Court. It was properly before them.

The first disagreement arose when Powell held firm to the position he had expressed in his memo on Rule 17(c), that there was a need for a higher standard of evidence for Presidents than for other people.

White disagreed completely. The Court should ensure that the President was treated like any citizen, no more, no less. There was no suggestion in the Constitution or elsewhere that a President was entitled to any higher standard. Moreover, if some such higher standard—whether it be "necessity," "compelling need," or whatever—were established, White did not believe the Special Prosecutor had met it. He had met only the normal standard. Thus, White said, he would be forced to dissent on that point if the others supported Powell's position.

The discussion was sharp and heated. The question of the standard was only one possible sticking point. The difficult questions revolving around the grand jury's naming of the President as an unindicted coconspirator should be sidestepped, they all agreed.

On the central question of executive privilege, the Justices agreed that the judiciary's specific need for sixty-four particular tapes for a criminal trial outweighed the President's generalized claim of confidentiality. At the same time, they all acknowledged that some form of executive privilege existed, at least implicitly.

Brennan saw the consensus immediately. The President did not have a single vote. Even more encouraging, there was reason to believe that the gaps among the Justices could be bridged. A single opinion seemed within reach. That would be the greatest deterrent to a defiant President. Brennan decided to float again his suggestion of a single opinion, authored by, and signed by, all eight. Someone had to steer a middle ground between Powell and White—the emerging antagonists on the question of standards for Presidents and other citizens. The Court could erupt into a confusing mixture of opinions, concurrences and dissents. Without reconciliation, Richard Nixon might find a loophole. The Chief was not capable of preventing that, Brennan believed.

Brennan spoke up. The Nixon challenge had to be met in the strongest way possible. An eight-signature opinion would do it. With the memos now in circulation, they could bang out an opinion in a week of concentrated effort. Each Justice might be given a section to work on, and they could convene in a few days to measure progress. Brennan reminded them of the impact of nine signatures on the Little Rock school opinion. It had been one of the Court's finest moments. The country would benefit from such a show of strength now.

Having laid the groundwork carefully with each Justice, Brennan sat back anticipating quick seconds. Instead there was an uneasy silence, not a word of support from anyone. Brennan felt betrayed, figuring he was like one of the Watergate figures, left to twist slowly in the wind.

The Chief broke the silence. He would take the opinion. The decision was similar to the Court's famous *Brown* school desegregation opinion; it required the Chief Justice. Burger hoped that he would be able to have it out in a week, perhaps by the next Monday. Brennan made a final appeal for a joint opinion. The Chief replied that he would consider the assignment decision further and give his final decision tomorrow. But Brennan knew the course was set.

The clerks turned to humor to kill time as they waited to learn what was going on. One of Powell's clerks, disturbed by his boss's memo the day before, drafted a phony opinion and gave it very limited circulation to the clerks' dining room. "We believe the principle of executive privilege is important. . . . This case is different from all others that will come before the Court. The Court should be guided by a solicitous concern for the effective discharge of the President's duties and the dignity of his high office.

"However, we're deciding this case differently, because Nixon is a crook and somebody ought to throw the son of a bitch in jail."

Marshall laughed heartily when his clerks showed him a copy. The copies were destroyed for fear that one might fall into the wrong hands.

Marshall was afraid a single opinion would never attract all eight votes. The Justices were agreed on the result, but not on the reasoning. The discussion in conference had been odd. Conversation at conference normally focused on a case in light of the Constitution. This discussion had centered more on the Court's role and power than on the case.

The Chief got right to work with two of his clerks. This would be his most historic opinion, perhaps the Court's most momentous opinion. This was an opinion that would establish the Chief's independence from Richard Nixon. And, like Earl Warren before him, he would pull together and hold a unanimous Court on an extraordinarily divisive issue.

The Court could, to his mind, deal with no more sensitive a topic than the subtle relationships among the three branches of government. He had a passionate interest in the Aaron Burr case, the first case of a subpoena being issued to a President—in that instance, Thomas Jefferson. A still life he had painted of a two-volume study written about the Burr case hung above the desk in his working office. He had tried his hand at a dramatic play about the case, but never finished it.

This would be the opinion that would give the Chief a chance to draw on his legal knowledge about the separation of powers, an expertise he had refined in the Adam Clayton Powell case, when he was on the Court of Appeals, and which had been reversed by the Warren Court.

Burger knew that the possibility of a Senate impeachment trial was growing more likely each day. Trusted clerks were assigned to gather background information on impeachment, on Senate trial procedures, and to review the trial of President Andrew Johnson, the only President to be impeached and brought to trial in the Senate. The clerks were instructed to maintain the utmost discretion. The discovery that such research was underway would trigger unwelcome news stories and headlines—"Chief Justice Expects Impeachment and Senate Trial; Staff Busily at Work."

The Chief dreaded the prospect. His every ruling, as presiding officer, would be debated and criticized, every action measured as pro- or anti-Nixon. The Senators were unaccustomed to outsiders. All this publicity—the Chief Justice as trial judge in the spectacle of the century—would be bad for the Court and all courts. The judiciary would be thrust into a political storm. However much Burger might enjoy the limelight, a trial of Richard Nixon was disturbing. It could shatter the Court's general aloofness and distance from political events. Congress might retaliate.

The Chief's clerks were well aware that their boss had never been a trial judge. That was a problem in itself. More troublesome was his tendency to fly off the handle when pressed. A Senate trial of the President might last weeks, even months. Television cameras would be focused on him. The Chief was not equipped for such an ordeal. His first impulses were too often wrong. His hasty reactions, in his memos and opinion drafts and, they had heard indirectly, at conference, were generally filtered out by the Court process without ever becoming public. Some of the Chief's clerks feared that he would flounder. Perhaps a man like Powell could keep things on an even keel, but the Chief was sure to blunder. Worse still, he was smart enough to realize it, and that would take a heavy toll on his self-esteem.

The problems of a Senate trial could be put aside; they were speculative. For the time being, Burger and his clerks focused on the work at hand. Seated at the ceremonial desk in the conference room, the Chief told his clerks to pull up the two black leather chairs. They would work right there. He jotted down an outline in large block letters. Each of them would take one section and begin drafting. Then they would reconvene, read through the work line by line, and correct as they went. It was a tedious approach, but it was the Chief's style. He worked best talking out the question, with someone to keep him company.

They would begin with the facts section, Burger instructed. As always, the draft should be perfectly fair, there should be no slant, no clue as to the outcome. The briefs and internal Court memoranda had summarized the history and background of the case. The three men worked late into the night.

Frustrated and gloomy, Brennan went to the Georgetown University Hospital to visit Earl Warren on Tuesday afternoon, July 9. The former Chief was recuperating from a mild heart attack he had suffered the week before. It was his third hospitalization for heart trouble in a year.

Warren was eager to know what was happening in the Nixon case.

Brennan delivered the good news: Nixon had lost, and it was unanimous. Predictably, the Chief had taken the opinion for himself.

The irony was not lost on either man. The remnants of the Warren Court, so hated by Nixon, and the emerging Nixon Court, so hated by both Warren and Brennan, had banded together. Brennan left at about 5:30 P.M., glad that he had been able to give his old, dear friend a needed lift.

Later that night Brennan learned by telephone that Warren had suffered a cardiac arrest at 8:10 P.M. and died. When he heard the news, Brennan wept.

The Chief quickly released a statement praising his predecessor. Warren had been "constantly available for consultation on the growing problem of the federal courts. . . ." Burger accepted the suggestion of one of his staff members that Warren's body lie in state in the Great Hall of the Court—an unusual honor.

Marshall, deeply grieved at the loss of the one white man who had done the most for black people in the twentieth century, also issued a public statement. "When history is written, he'll go down as one of the greatest Chief Justices the country has ever been blessed with. I think he is irreplaceable."

Brennan did not allow himself to spend too much time grieving. The Nixon case had to be kept on track. Brennan had already written a memo on the standing question. He decided that it should now go to the Chief. Calling on his surface charm, he wrote a cover memo and sent it Wednesday morning, July 10.

DEAR CHIEF,

I think the analysis tracks your oral analysis yesterday of the issue. Needless to say insofar as its incorporation, or any part of it, furthers your preparation of the opinion I freely deed it to you in fee simple absolute.

I don't think I presume in saying that that is also the thought of the brethren who have sent you memos on this and other issues. I think Lewis, Potter and Bill Douglas (I borrowed some of the attached from Bill's memo) have written out some particularly persuasive views.

I repeat that I enthusiastically share the view expressed I think by all yesterday that we should announce our decision in this case as promptly as the preparation of a thoughtful and comprehensive opinion will permit. To the extent you find useful what others of us have written out, that objective is of course furthered.

When the Chief got the memo, he didn't think it offered much help. Only Brennan would be so presumptuous. Of course, no decision should wait beyond the time necessary to prepare "a thoughtful and comprehensive opinion."

To Douglas, Richard Nixon was, and had been for nearly thirty years, the enemy. The Nixon presidency had all the earmarks of a hostile takeover of government. Nixon was "the other side." Douglas told friends how Nixon had once reminded him of a speech Douglas had given more than thirty years before to Nixon's law-school class at Duke University. Nixon said the speech had been so impressive that it inspired his own political career. Hearing that, Douglas said, was the most upsetting moment of his life, the only time he actually felt "suicidal."

Douglas was overjoyed that the case was going against Nixon. He wanted to keep the Chief happy and see to it that Burger's opinion was as solidly anti-Nixon as possible. But Douglas was worried about the timing. If he had been assigned to write the opinion, it would have been out in a day or two. The work was already done and the quickest denial of Nixon's claim was in order. The House Judiciary Committee had just released its own transcripts of eight of the Nixon tapes that had been turned over earlier. In an elaborate 131-page, side-by-side comparison the Committee had demonstrated that Nixon's version was hopelessly incomplete, that it had twisted meanings and had omitted damaging portions.

Nixon's former aide John Ehrlichman, meanwhile, was on trial at the Federal District Courthouse for approving the break-in at the office of Daniel Ellsberg's psychiatrist. That outrageous crime typified Nixon and his administration as far as Douglas was concerned. Douglas had long suspected that the White House had broken into his office and stolen a copy of his memoirs, and had bugged the conference room. He was sure, although he had no proof.

Since Nixon's strategy was delay, the opinion writing must be speeded up. Late in the morning of July 10, Douglas phoned Brennan. Would Brennan join in another attempt to persuade the

Chief to divide the opinion among all eight Justices? Warren's death had changed things, Douglas said. Burger would have the funeral preparations to worry about. The opinion could not be allowed to drag on all summer. Without a joint effort, it might do just that.

Brennan found Douglas's request amazing. Why hadn't he spoken during conference? He needed only to have seconded Brennan's motion. This was unforgivable. The time to speak up had passed. Brennan would not lead a charge up that hill again.

But Douglas pushed him, and Brennan agreed finally to accompany Douglas to the Chief's office to discuss the matter. When they arrived, the Chief seemed more relaxed than usual. He was conciliatory. He was aware of their feelings, he said, but this was one of those cases that would be better if written by a Chief Justice. Of course he would welcome the assistance of all the others. He sounded sincere to Brennan.

Brennan could not help but feel that Warren's death had sobered the Chief. An outpouring of national praise for Warren as a great leader, healer and compromiser might have prompted Burger to reassess his relations with his colleagues. Perhaps Burger would adopt Warren's willingness to lead through compromise.

The Chief said that he would circulate each section of his opinion as soon as he finished it. Something would be ready in a day or so, and he would welcome suggestions.

Douglas and Brennan knew the Chief had closed his mind on the subject. It was unlikely that he would turn the opinion over to the others, now that he had begun work. They left, concluding that it might have been worse. Perhaps a unanimous opinion was still possible—even from the Chief's chambers, Brennan said.

The Chief felt pressured. He had spent hours at his desk with his two clerks. The work was going smoothly. Honoring his promise, he decided that the first two sections of the draft were ready to circulate. One dealt with the facts, the other with the technical, though uncontroversial, question of appealability. Just over a week had passed since conference. Perhaps now he would convince the skeptics of his ability to turn out an opinion in timely fashion. Burger read the material over and decided to add a brief cover memo.

MEMORANDUM TO THE CONFERENCE

The enclosed material is not intended to be final, and I will wel-come—indeed I invite—your suggestions. Regards, WEB.

Though the job had eluded him, or he it, Potter Stewart knew what it meant to be a Chief Justice. A Chief must be a statesman, a master of the Court's internal protocols, able to inspire, cajole and compromise, a man of integrity, who commanded the respect of his colleagues. But, most of all, a Chief Justice had to be a student of the nation's capital, able to see the politically inevitable, willing to weigh the Court's destiny against other Washington institutions. A Chief Justice, Stewart believed, should be a man not unlike him-self.

Warren Burger was none of these things. He was a product of Richard Nixon's tasteless White House, distinguished in appear-ance and bearing, but without substance or integrity. Burger was abrasive to his colleagues, persistent in ignorance, and, worst of all, intellectually dishonest. "On ocean liners," Stewart told his clerks, "they used to have two captains. One for show, to take the women to dinner. The other to pilot the ship safely. The Chief is the show captain. All we need now is a real captain." Stewart was convinced that the Chief could never lead them to a safe, dignified opinion befitting one of the most important cases in the Court's history.

When the Chief's first two sections came in, Stewart read them carefully. The facts section was poorly written, dashed off with lit-tle care. There was not enough attention to the sequence of events or to the key issues.

The section on appealability was not much better. It offered no cogent response to St. Clair's argument that Sirica should first have held Nixon in contempt before the case could be brought to the Court. This should not have become a complicated section to draft. Douglas's draft had already included two simple reasons why the Court could and had to intervene: the risk of a constitutional confrontation between the two branches of government; and the protracted litigation that might result if normal contempt proce-dures were followed.

The next afternoon, July 11, Stewart and Powell talked about what should be done with the Chief's sections. The two men agreed that they were awful. If they were not vastly improved, the sections would be an embarrassment to the Court. Even worse, if they foreshadowed the quality of what was to come, the opinion not only would hurt the Court's reputation, but could damage its future relations with the other branches of the government. This opinion would be analyzed and dissected for years to come.

All of the eight Justices seemed to be in general agreement on the basic outline. It would be a shame not to produce the best possible piece of legal work, which the Chief could not conceivably do alone. Despite what he said about welcoming comments from the rest, they knew Burger rarely incorporated individual suggestions unless he saw a risk of losing his majority.

Stewart and Powell talked strategy. Brennan's suggestion of a joint opinion could be implemented, but they would have to work behind the Chief's back. Each of the other Justices would systematically propose alternative drafts to various of the Chief's sections. They all could then express their preference for the substitute sections. Seeing that he was outnumbered, the Chief would be forced to capitulate. They would have to gauge White's thinking and see if he could be brought along. Blackmun would have to be won over at once. Although he had broken with Burger in the past and was disgusted by Watergate, Blackmun might support Burger here. They would have to enlist him quickly, tactfully, somewhat indirectly. They knew that Blackmun enjoyed preparing the detailed facts sections in cases. If he could be persuaded to redo the facts section, the others could praise it, suggest it be incorporated, in reality substituted. That would cement an alliance with Blackmun. In turn, he would support the alternative drafts on the other sections. Once committed, Blackmun could oppose the Chief as forcefully as any of them. Stewart left the discussion convinced that the center could once again control the outcome, though it would not be easy.

In addition, Stewart was as concerned with Powell as with any of the others. His proposed section on executive privilege had been Powell both at his best and at his worst. By trying to steer a middle course, Powell had accepted too much of the claim of executive privilege. On Powell's bottom line, the President lost and would have to turn over his tapes, but his language was hat-in-hand. It might provide the President with a rationale for defiance.*

Powell saw it differently. He was sure that his memorandum would set the style and tone of the final opinion. Brennan had already told him he was "greatly impressed," and Brennan could bring his liberal colleagues, Marshall and Douglas, on board. Stewart was in agreement. Blackmun could be persuaded. White, of course, had to be convinced, perhaps with Stewart's help.

That left the Chief. Powell believed that his approach would appeal to Burger. Powell was sure that the Chief wanted to push Nixon off the cliff at the point where the fall was the shortest. Powell's memorandum gave weight to executive privilege, recognizing each of the President's arguments. His was the only proposal that solved the delicate problem of issuing an order to another branch of the government in a manner least likely to provoke defiance.

Later that afternoon, Powell and Stewart approached Blackmun. The Chief's facts were inadequate. Only Blackmun could repair the damage, they said. Blackmun readily agreed. He would do his best with the facts. He certainly could do better than the Chief had done. He gathered all the relevant material and headed for the Justices' library.

When Brennan heard of the Stewart-Powell plan, he thought it was magnificent. He was also delighted to learn that Blackmun had so enthusiastically expressed his independence. Brennan agreed that Blackmun should handle the facts. He thought the rest of the lineup equally obvious. Douglas should take on appealability; he himself standing; White the 17(c) rule on admissibility and rele-

---

* Powell's proposal said that in deciding the case "a court should be guided by a solicitous concern for the effective discharge of [the President's] duties and the dignity of his high office." Powell had said that there was a "public interest in preserving the confidentiality of the Oval Office and in avoiding vexatious harassment of an incumbent President. . . ." Protecting the confidentiality of the President "is of an entirely different order of importance" than protecting that of an ordinary citizen.

vance; and Powell and Stewart, together, the extremely sensitive executive privilege section. Marshall, the Court's least productive worker, could be mollified without giving him a section.

Stewart took the first step. "Dear Chief," he wrote, "Responding to your circulation of yesterday, I think, with all due respect, that Bill Douglas's draft on appealability is entirely adequate . . ."

Brennan quickly followed with a similar memo to the Chief praising Douglas's section.

Powell dictated a single cautious sentence: "Dear Chief: Potter's suggestion as to Bill Douglas's draft on appealability is entirely acceptable to me. Sincerely, Lewis."

Douglas sent his own "Dear Chief" memo saying Brennan had shown him a proposal on the standing section: " . . . It seems to me to be adequate and might put us quickly another rung up the ladder if the other Brethren agree."

When a copy of Douglas's memo arrived in his chambers, Brennan was afraid that it might appear that he was circulating sections privately. He immediately sent his standing section, previously given only to the Chief and Douglas, to all the others.

The four memos from Stewart, Powell, Brennan and Douglas were greeted by the Chief with some consternation. He had hardly begun and four of his colleagues were already criticizing his work. Everyone seemed to be in such a hurry. Deciding to meet what he thought they saw as the major problem—a possible delay of the opinion—Burger gathered together his drafts of the standing and 17 (c) sections for circulation. In a cover memo, he said: "I believe we have encountered no insoluble problems to this point."

The Chief then decided to confront the others' concern about delay in a second memo:

MEMORANDUM TO THE CONFERENCE

I have received various memos in response to preliminary and partial sections circulated.

With the sad intervention of Chief Justice Warren's death, the schedules of all of us have been altered. I intend to work without interruption (except for some sleep) until I have the "privilege" section complete and the final honing complete on all parts.

I think it is unrealistic to consider a Monday, July 15, announcement. This case is too important to "rush" unduly although it is in fact receiving priority treatment.

I would hope we could meet an end-of-the-week announcement, i.e., July 19 or thereabouts.

Brennan was extremely frustrated by the Chief's memo. Certainly there was agreement that July 15 was not a realistic announcement date, but not for the reasons Burger gave. The Chief simply did not perceive the problem: all of his sections needed major rewriting.

The next morning, Friday, July 12, Douglas was appalled at the Chief's standing section which dealt with the question of whether Jaworski could sue the President. It borrowed from the Brennan draft, but contained neither a satisfactory explanation of the regulations governing the prosecutor's office nor the fact that those regulations had the force of law. In Douglas's view, the Chief had failed to fully and conclusively establish that the courts often resolved disputes within other branches of government. Obviously the Chief didn't really believe the courts should get involved in such disputes. Burger still believed he was right and Warren wrong in the Adam Clayton Powell case.

The day before, Douglas had told the Chief that Brennan's standing section was "adequate." Now Douglas decided to be more explicit. Putting his felt-tip pen to paper again, he wrote to Burger that he had just reread Brennan's suggestions and "would, with all respect, prefer it over the version which you circulated this morning."

Stewart thought Douglas's memo was too harsh. If they appeared to be running over the Chief, he would get his back up and they would win nothing. It was pointless to provoke him. Stewart was sure they had to join at least one of the four sections the Chief had already circulated. Since his standing section was the least offensive, and in some respects, one of the least important, provided it said the Special Prosecutor had standing, it was the section to join. A join at this point would also put some distance between himself and Brennan; generally that was valuable strategy when dealing with the Chief.

Stewart drafted a memo saying that with a minor change—substituting "the President's" for "an executive"—he could go along with the Chief's standing section. "If that change is made, I could subscribe to this draft as part of the opinion," Stewart wrote. He also added, both to prod the Chief and to conciliate Brennan, "I could equally cheerfully subscribe to Bill Brennan's version."

One of Stewart's clerks was given the memo to forward to the Chief and to the other chambers. Reading it over, the clerk thought his boss was being too conciliatory to the Chief. Burger's standing section was not good enough. The opinion was more important than the Chief's ego. Since Stewart had left for Earl Warren's funeral and was not likely to be back that day, the clerk took matters into his own hands and slipped the original and all copies of the memo into his desk drawer. He would raise the subject with Stewart the next day. He hoped Stewart would be glad the memo had not been sent.

Earl Warren's funeral at Washington's National Cathedral provided a moment for reflection for the Justices.

President and Mrs. Nixon were there, and the Justices had agreed it would only be proper that they avoid any exchange or contact with the President. After the service, however, Nixon stepped forward to escort Mrs. Warren out of the Cathedral. The Justices moved aside and kept their distance.

The car ride across the Potomac River to Arlington National Cemetery seemed to take an eternity. At the grave site, taps sounded, the Army band played "America the Beautiful," and the flag draped over the coffin was removed and handed to Burger, who in turn, gave it to Mrs. Warren.

Back at the Court, Douglas went over the Chief's proposed section on the 17 (c) standard. It recited the contentions of each side and described the governing case law.*

Burger said the Court could not conclude that Judge Sirica was in

---

* One case (*Bowman Dairy Co. v. United States*) established that such subpoenaed material had to be produced *before* trial, while another (*United States v. Iozia*) prohibited "fishing expeditions" to gather more evidence for a criminal trial.

error in finding that Jaworski had met the 17(c) standard. By putting it negatively, the Chief left the distinct implication that a higher standard than routine application of Rule 17(c) had to be met.

Douglas was furious. This was not the sense of the conference. He wrote a memo to the Chief declaring that he would not join the Chief's proposed section.

For three days, White had said little, lying in wait. He saw the Rule 17(c) section as the key. That was what the case was about. Would the existing rules and law be applied to the President in the same manner as they would be to any other citizen? The Chief's answer was ambiguous. He had tilted toward raising the standard. So White rewrote the section to enhance the importance of Rule 17(c) as a simple application of *existing law.*

Since the President had claimed the standards of 17(c) had not been met, White wrote, the Court must first overcome this barrier before deciding any other questions. Quoting from the rule, White noted that the subpoena may be quashed if it is found to be "unreasonable or oppressive." But, White said, the Special Prosecutor had—through the sealed record of grand-jury proceedings—shown in most instances that one or more participants in the subpoenaed conversations had testified that Watergate was discussed.

"As we see it there is a sufficient likelihood that each of the tapes contains conversations relevant to the Watergate case . . ." White wrote. Not only were the tapes relevant, but it was "sufficiently likely" that the tapes would be admissible as evidence at trial. No "cogent" objection to their introduction as proper evidence could be lodged. The only possible objection was that the statements were hearsay. But, White wrote, under court decisions the hearsay rule does not apply to a defendant's recorded out-of-court conversations with a coconspirator. They would be admissible at least against the defendant. And if a conspiracy was shown, the statements were admissible against all defendants, whether present or not, if made in furtherance of the conspiracy. Addressing the question of statements by unindicted coconspirator Nixon, White wrote, "The same is true of declarations of coconspirators who are not defendants in the case on trial."

White had his suggestions retyped and took them to Stewart,

who liked the approach. It answered questions that the White House could raise in order to keep the tapes from being used at trial.

With that, White decided to circulate his proposal. "DEAR CHIEF," he wrote, "The attached is the bare bones of an alternative treatment which I am now embellishing to some extent. Sincerely, BYRON."

Douglas got his copy and pounced at once. He agreed with White's proposed 17(c) section, he declared in a memo to the Chief. Brennan was also pleased with White's proposal. It seemed wholly in line with his own suggestions on Rule 17(c) that had circulated the day of orals. In order to preserve his position with Powell, he decided not to endorse White's memo formally.

Powell was distressed at White's memo; the President was getting nothing, no extra consideration. Even Brennan had said the courts should be "particularly meticulous" to insure that Rule 17(c) had been correctly applied. Desiring to reach a middle ground, Powell circulated his own revised memo. He dropped his "necessity" standard and substituted a requirement that a "special showing" be made to establish that the material was essential. At the bottom of Brennan's copy, Powell wrote in his own hand, "I have tried to move fairly close to your original memo on this point, as I understand it, and what you said at conference. LEWIS."

Brennan was confused by the personal note. In his own memo, Brennan had purposely steered clear of endorsing a higher standard, particularly a "special showing"—whatever that might be.

The Chief, who had at first been mildly bewildered by the sudden activity, was now angry. Brennan, Douglas, Powell, Stewart and now White—of all people—were sabotaging his work. Marshall had been silent, but he would certainly follow Brennan. Burger had an insurrection on his hands. He decided to waste no time in getting to Blackmun, his one remaining ally.

Blackmun had just finished his crash project of revising the statement of facts in the case when the Chief appeared at the door to his chambers. It was an awkward moment. Burger had no idea what Blackmun was preparing.

The Chief entered Blackmun's office and began complaining bitterly about the criticism he was getting on nearly all fronts. Ten critical memos had flown back and forth in the past two days. He could barely get a rough draft out of his typewriter before someone was circulating a counterdraft, suggestions or alternatives. It was amazing, he said. He could not get the counterdraft read before a barrage of memos arrived approving everyone's work but his own.

Blackmun listened.

Didn't the other Justices realize that he had been busy with the Warren funeral, the Chief said? He had his always-growing administrative duties, managing the building, the 600 federal judges. "It's my opinion," he finally asserted, "they are trying to take it away from me."

Blackmun hated scenes, and he disliked crossing the Chief. But it was time to tell the Chief where he stood.

"Before you go on, I think you should see this," Blackmun said, handing the Chief his revision of the facts section.

"What's this, Harry, a few suggested changes you'd like?"

"No," Blackmun said. "It's an entirely new section which I think you should substitute for your initial draft."

"Well," said the Chief, flustered, "it's too late now for such major revisions."

"Would you at least please read the new draft?" Blackmun asked.

Burger's eyes flashed. He turned and stormed out the door without a word.

Blackmun wanted to calm the Chief. He picked up one of his perfectly sharpened pencils on his desk and wrote a cover memo for his facts section.

"DEAR CHIEF, With your letter of July 10 you recommended and invited suggestions. Accordingly, I take the liberty of suggesting herewith a revised statement of facts and submit it for your consideration."

He continued in a more personal vein. "Please believe me when I say that I do this in a spirit of cooperation and not of criticism. I am fully aware of the pressures that presently beset all of us." The draft was circulated. The tone of the cover memo signaled to several of the Justices that something had happened. Blackmun told them about his encounter with the Chief. The incident became known as the "Et Tu Harry" story.

When the clerk network passed word that Blackmun had agreed to draft a counterstatement of the facts, several clerks joked that Blackmun would write it like his *Flood v. Kuhn* baseball antitrust opinion. He would begin the facts, "There have been many great Presidents," and then list thirty-six Presidents, leaving out the thirty-seventh, Richard Nixon.

Brennan was elated both by the revised Facts section and by word that Blackmun had stood up to the Chief. He wrote a memo that rubbed salt in the wound. "DEAR CHIEF: I think that Harry's suggested revision of the Statement of Facts is excellent and I hope you could incorporate it in the opinion."

Stewart, too, was quite happy to see the Blackmun section. To one degree or another, all seven Justices were now confronting the Chief. But Burger's position could harden in the face of such pressure. Stewart had three minor points he wanted to add to Blackmun's section, to show that he was not just criticizing the Chief's work. He wrote Burger: "I think Harry Blackmun's revision of the statement of facts is a fine job, and I would join it as part of the Court opinion, with a couple of minor additions."

Brennan went to the Court on Saturday, July 13. It was unusual for him to come in on a Saturday, but to preserve the momentum he felt he must stay on top of developments. He checked to see who else was there. Douglas had returned to Goose Prairie; Blackmun was attending a conference in New York City; Powell was in Richmond; Marshall was at home. Only Stewart and White were in the building. The three discussed the situation. It was nearly noon. White, accustomed to an early lunch, suggested they go out to eat. He preferred a quiet place near the Court, where they would probably not be recognized on a Saturday.

White and Stewart each invited two of their clerks. The three Justices and four clerks piled into White's car and drove to the Market Inn, a dimly lit restaurant on the other side of the Capitol. They sat in a dark corner of the almost empty restaurant, near the bar. A motley assortment of pinups, etchings and paintings of nude women covered the walls.

"Bill, you're the guy who likes nudes. What do you think of these?" White joked.

Brennan laughed. Then he quickly got down to business.

The Chief's drafts had invited anarchy. The Court had fractionalized at each new circulation by the Chief. In addition to the objections everyone had noted, the Chief's work was sloppy and ungrammatical. The Chief, Brennan declared, was going to embarrass the Court.

Stewart agreed. The Chief was, once again, not doing his homework. The delay he proposed was absurd.

A clerk suggested that perhaps the Chief wanted to scuttle the opinion.

He would if he could, the Justices seemed to agree.

Brennan criticized the Chief's work—its general imprecision, its aimless rhetoric, its lack of analysis.

"I don't know what it says or what it means," Stewart agreed.

Exactly, Brennan said. The vague language floating out there was very "dangerous."

The Justices found themselves entering the clerks' longstanding debate: Was the Chief evil or stupid?

Finally, Brennan declared that he for one favored firmer action. Since the Chief had not responded to any of the many suggestions they had supplied, they should put together an entire alternative draft from their work to date. They could no longer just make piecemeal suggestions and propose alternatives and hope the Chief would incorporate them, Brennan said. There was enough material in circulation to fashion a solid opinion, a composite counterdraft. Acting in concert, no single Justice would be out on a limb challenging the Chief.

Stewart, however, noted that he had sent out a memo the day before essentially going along with the Chief's standing section. Even though Brennan's section was better, Stewart argued that they had to go along with one of the Chief's sections. If they did eventually force through an alternative draft, Stewart said, they would still want and need the Chief's vote for unanimity. It was important to demonstrate support for at least one part of his work.

Stewart's clerk, the one who had impounded his memo, sat feeling very uneasy. With a troubled look, he told Stewart that the memo backing Burger's standing section had not been circulated.

"Why?" Stewart asked.

"Because it is in my desk drawer," the clerk replied.

"You'll deliver that after lunch," Stewart said sharply.

White again raised the 17(c) question. He repeated his strong opposition to any requirement, even hint of a need, for a higher standard for presidential subpoenas.

Stewart also felt they should not fashion a higher standard, but said he thought such presidential material should be treated differently. The district court judge should inspect it in private before it was turned over to the prosecutor.

Brennan agreed with Stewart. He suggested that White include in his rewrite of 17(c) something along the lines of Brennan's own suggestion that the courts be "particularly meticulous" in applying the 17(c) standard to presidential subpoenas.

White said that would be possible. He would circulate by late afternoon a fuller version of his section on the 17(c) standard.

You know Lewis feels quite differently? Brennan said.

Yes, White replied.

But the question remained. How far could the Chief be pushed? What were his limits on this case? The discussion went around the table. How dangerous was the Chief's opinion really? If it did nothing truly damaging to the law and was just his usual sloppy work, bad grammar, and memorable lapses in language usage— what, then, was their responsibility? This was not a case, they agreed, in which they could just concur in the result.

What sort of counterweight was a rump majority against a Chief Justice who had assigned the formal opinion to himself? Theoretically, they could take the opinion from him. But practically, Stewart pointed out, they might make more trouble for themselves than was necessary. After all, they had not seen the guts of the case—the Chief's section on executive privilege.

There were nods around the table. White too preferred a middle ground that would avoid a head-on collision with the Chief.

They paid for their lunches, Dutch treat. In the car on the way back, someone mentioned the Ehrlichman trial. He had been found guilty the day before. Stewart said that, as a white man, he would not want to be tried in the District of Columbia, where the juries were predominantly black.

"You bet your ass," Brennan agreed.

The clerks quickly dubbed the meeting "the conspiracy lunch." It was unusual for them to meet with Justices other than their own, especially to plot strategy. As they saw it, the Justices were preparing a coup.

Back in his office, White decided to accommodate Brennan. He took his own six long paragraphs and added a seventh, at the end, lifted almost verbatim from Brennan's own suggestions on the 17(c) standard. It included the "particularly meticulous" language. He made only one change. Where Brennan had said in conclusion that Judge Sirica's refusal to quash Jaworski's subpoena was "amply justified," White substituted "consistent with Rule 17(c)," the regular standard. That made it clear that this case really was being handled under the normal standard.

White ordered his section typed. It was virtually the same as his "bare bones" memo of the day before.

The next morning, Sunday, July 14, Brennan redrafted Powell's section on the standard for presidential subpoenas, trying to get it closer to White's 17(c) position. But he retained Powell's sentence that "the District Court did not rest on satisfaction of Rule 17(c) alone." Still convinced that there had to be a national security exception, Brennan reworked his section on instructions to the judge, again stating that claims could be accepted for "national defense, foreign affairs or internal security." But, he wrote, the legitimacy of those claims rested finally with the judgment of the District Court. After hearing the President's arguments, it could still order both *in camera* inspection and eventual delivery to the Special Prosecutor. It was much stronger than his own earlier draft.

Monday morning, July 15, Brennan, White and Stewart met again to pick up where they had left off at Saturday's lunch. White said he had read through Brennan's revision of Powell's 17(c) section and did not like it. He and Powell were on very different tracks. White would not buy even a suggestion of higher standards for a president.

Stewart saw that White had dug in on 17(c). White could be as inflexible as the Chief. In addition to his original reservations about the other Justices developing substitute opinions and trying to force them on the Chief, White now had second thoughts about substituting sections one at a time. Even that might be going too far. He left the meeting quite concerned and went back to his chambers. The cabal was out of control. Brennan was pushing too hard. The Chief would see Brennan's hand in this if he hadn't seen it already. White was loath to have it appear that he had drifted under Brennan's influence. He had to prove his independence both to the Chief and to Brennan.

White swiveled to the right for his typewriter.

> DEAR CHIEF: Your statement of the facts and your drafts on appealability and (standing) are satisfactory to me, although I could subscribe to most of what is said in other versions that have been submitted to you.
>
> My views on the Rule 17(c) issue you already have.
>
> With respect to the existence and extent of executive privilege . . . I cannot fathom why the President should be permitted to withhold the out-of-court statements of a defendant in a criminal case . . . For me, the interest in sustaining confidentiality disappears when it is shown that the President is in possession of out-of-court declarations of those, such as [Charles W.] Colson and Dean, who have been sufficiently shown to be co-conspirators. . . . Shielding such a conspiracy in the making or in the process of execution carries the privilege too far.

White had the memo retyped and sent simultaneously to the Chief and to all the other Justices. When Brennan received it, he decided that the weekend's work had been wasted. White had gone at least halfway over to the Chief's side. Without a unified front, the Chief would never accept the other Justices' revisions.

Brennan had to get White back in the fold. He jotted out a

memo: "DEAR BYRON: I fully agree with your expanded Sec. 17(c) treatment, recirculated July 13, 1974, and hope it can serve to cover that issue in the Court's opinion." He specified that copies be sent to all the others, including the Chief. Maybe that would appease White.

Stewart followed with a similar memo to the Chief.

"I agree with Byron's revision of the discussion of the Rule 17(c) issues," Stewart said.

Trouble had surfaced, however, on another front. Marshall's clerks were miffed that they and their boss had not been included in Saturday's "conspiracy lunch." They told Marshall about the lunch, and he was mildly put off. Somewhat overstating Marshall's reaction, they then told Brennan's clerks that Marshall was quite upset that the others would meet without telling him. Marshall was so displeased, they said, that he might not even join the effort to force an alternative draft or sections on the Chief, even if he were invited.

When Brennan heard of the hurt feelings in Marshall's chambers, he was out the door at once.

He reminded Marshall that he had not been in the building on Saturday. Otherwise he would, of course, have been invited to the lunch. Brennan then undertook in some detail to bring Marshall up to date. His support was crucial, particularly given the widening difficulties with White and Powell. Douglas had deserted to Goose Prairie. And you could never tell when Blackmun would bolt to the Chief. Perhaps White had already done so.

Marshall said that he would go along. His clerks drafted a short memo for him to sign. It was the coldest prose they could fashion.

DEAR CHIEF:

1. I agree with Byron's recirculation . . . of the section on 17(c).
2. I agree with Harry's Statement of Facts.
3. I agree with Bill Brennan's treatment of the section on [Standing].
4. I agree with Potter's memorandum on the question of appealability.

Sincerely,
T.M.

Brennan was relieved. The memo was more direct than he expected. TM was back on the team.

Marshall's memo went off like a grenade in the Chief's chambers. Of all the memos this was the most combative. It obviously reflected the sentiments of Marshall's clerks, and the fact that Marshall was giving them free rein. It would be hard to budge that chambers.

It wasn't only Marshall's chambers. The Chief's clerks could see the hands of their fellow clerks in other chambers in all the various alternative drafts and supporting memos. They realized that because the seven other Justices had no other cases to work on, their clerks had little to do. So the Justices and the clerks spent their time cutting the Chief's rough, preliminary drafts to ribbons.

Burger was calmer. Idle hands do the devil's work, he advised his clerks. The others were nitpicking and trying to spoon-feed him, he said, but it wouldn't work. He had never responded to that kind of pressure. Their job was to keep working and take the opinion a step at a time.

But the Chief was also beginning to feel more insulted and less bemused by the patronizing approach of his colleagues. He resented the challenge to his authority and competence. It was different in the English legal system he loved so much. Once when he was in England for a judicial meeting, everyone was talking and the senior English judge had just lifted his finger. The others had stopped in midsentence. The senior judge did not even have to speak to obtain silence. Unfortunately, the Chief Justice of the United States did not command the same respect.

But the Chief decided to fight back with a memo to the conference on the nature of his prerogatives as the designated author.

> My effort to accommodate everyone by sending out "first drafts" is not working out.
>
> I do not contemplate sending out any more material until it is *ready*. This will take longer than I had anticipated and you should each make plans on an assumption that no more material will be circulated for at least one week.

The Chief had been getting support, meanwhile, from an unexpected quarter. Douglas had been shuttling down to one of the telephones near Goose Prairie and calling the Chief with words of encouragement.

Yes, it was a Chief Justice opinion, Douglas had reassured Burger. The sections looked good. Douglas requested that Burger keep him informed and let him see the rough of the privilege section as soon as possible.

The Chief knew that Douglas's zeal in the tapes case somehow went beyond the legal issues. Nevertheless he appreciated Douglas's support. To ensure that his reclusive colleague in Goose Prairie would stay with him, he immediately dispatched a copy of his privilege section. Then he drafted another memo to the conference.

> In my earlier memo today on our "timetable" I should have mentioned that at Bill Douglas's urgent request I mailed him a very rough draft of what I had worked up on the weekend on the "privilege" section. On reviewing it Sunday I came to the conclusion that while it may be useful to Bill at his distance to show my "direction" it was far too rough and incomplete for circulation and I will not circulate it generally. Regards, WEB.

The Chief knew that as the senior Associate Justice and the symbolic liberal, Douglas had great influence. More importantly, if the end product suited him, Douglas would not quibble over a paragraph or a word. A tacit acceptance of the draft by Douglas could turn the tide.

At the "conspiracy luncheon," Stewart had offered to redraft Powell's section on executive privilege, and now he got down to work. Altering Powell's deferential language, Stewart wrote that confidentiality in government was important, but he stated firmly that in every case, the Courts, never the executive, would make a final determination. Stewart chose a simpler argument than Powell. He adapted and enlarged upon the argument already made by Douglas, that due process would be denied everyone—prosecutors, defendants, witnesses, the public at large—if all the evidence was not turned over.

More importantly, on the sticky issue of the Rule 17(c) standard, Stewart lowered Powell's standard from "compelling justification" to a milder "sufficient justification." That might safely allow him to walk the line between Powell and White.

On Tuesday, July 16, Stewart privately sent his redraft to Powell, and Powell said it was acceptable. Stewart concluded that Powell had given up on the higher standard. Buttressed by Powell's support, Stewart sent copies to White, Brennan and Marshall. Those three then met to review Stewart's section and passed word to Stewart that it was acceptable. White and Powell had finally found a point of agreement, Stewart hoped.

As best he could tell, Stewart now had five votes for the section. Rather than further aggravate the Chief, Stewart decided not to send his own substitute draft to the Chief but to wait for the Chief's circulation on the privilege section.

Of all the Justices, Stewart was at once the most desirous of confrontation and the most committed to compromise. The tension between the two impulses at times seemed to exhilarate him.

The Chief spent the day grinding out his privilege section. The work went faster than he had expected. He tried to borrow generously from some of the ideas provided by Powell, Douglas, and even Brennan, and the pieces fell together nicely. The Chief found Brennan's suggestions surprisingly deferential to the President. Brennan's "national defense, foreign affairs and internal security" exception to what would be initially submitted to Sirica's court was extraordinarily broad. It certainly presented the White House with many opportunities to withhold evidence from Sirica.

Since the White House had not claimed any such exemptions, the Chief did not want to invite them. "Absent a claim of need to protect military, diplomatic or sensitive national-security secrets," the Chief wrote, "the White House's invocation of executive privilege hardly suffers in this case from an *in camera* inspection of the subpoenaed tapes."

By early evening, the Chief had what he felt was a satisfactory draft. He resolved to make an appeal to perhaps the most obviously conspirational of the Justices. He reached Brennan by phone at home.

Burger told Brennan he had finished a draft of the privilege section and would like him to have a copy before Brennan left for Nantucket for the weekend.

Brennan said he would be delighted to see it.

Telling him that things were moving faster than he had indicated the day before, the Chief hinted that the opinion could come down shortly after the weekend—perhaps on Monday, July 22.

That indeed would be good, Brennan said. The Chief was obviously in an excellent mood. They fell into an animated discussion of non-Watergate matters.

Early the next morning, Wednesday, July 17, Brennan received his copy, of the executive privilege section. On initial reading, Brennan thought it was in better shape than the Chief's other sections. There were, however, some problems. First, the Chief was not emphatic in meeting the White House challenge by restating the ultimate responsibility of the courts to decide all such constitutional disputes. Second, the Chief talked of the "competing demands" of the executive and judicial branches, which had to be weighed in order to determine which would prevail. That determination turned on the extent to which each branch's "core functions" were involved. Such functions for the executive included war powers, the conduct of foreign relations, and the veto power. On the other hand, one of the "core functions" of the judiciary was ensuring that all evidence was available for a criminal trial.

The Chief then reasoned that in the tapes case a "core function" of the judiciary was clearly involved, whereas none was for the President. Under that reasoning the President lost. The Chief had also sidestepped Powell's demand for a higher standard by simply saying that the Special Prosecutor had shown "a sufficiently compelling need" for the material to be inspected by Judge Sirica.

Brennan assumed that the core functions formulation—a potentially vague and expandable creation—could probably be rendered harmless by limiting its meaning to foreign affairs, military or state secrets. It was doubtful, he felt, that the Chief would balk at that.

Though it was rough, Brennan felt that the draft was adequate and immediately told the Chief so. He recommended that Burger circulate it.

Encouraged by this response, Burger sent the section around. A full opinion draft, he told the others, would be ready by the end of the week.

The other Justices were not happy with the Chief's privilege section. Stewart didn't trust it. He particularly did not like the core functions analysis. Even if more narrowly defined than in the Chief's draft, the term implied that a President had an absolute constitutional prerogative over his core functions. These "core" functions were very loosely outlined as the Chief named them—war, foreign relations, the veto power or, as the Chief had written, whatever was implied when the President was "performing duties at the very core of his constitutional role."

That was precisely Nixon's claim. He was fighting the subpoena on the basis of just such broad definitions. Language like that could arm Nixon's defense. There were dangerous sentences in the Chief's draft, such as:

" . . . The courts must follow standards and implement procedures that will adequately protect the undoubted need to preserve the legitimate confidentiality of that office."

or

"The courts have shown the utmost deference to presidential acts in the performance of Article II core functions."

or

"In the present case, however, the reason for the claim is somewhat removed from the central or core functions of the Chief Executive."

Not only did the analysis present problems for the current case—in some areas almost inviting a Nixon rebuttal—but a phrase like "core functions" could invite future chaos. The Court could find itself with years of work defining what was and wasn't a core function. The expression could exclude the Court from intervening in future disputes.

Powell agreed with Stewart. When they met with Brennan and Marshall, Stewart made his case, and Powell supported him. Marshall agreed.

Brennan, however, disagreed. The term could be rendered harmless by narrowing the definition. It was more important to keep the Chief on track.

No, Stewart argued. The Chief had moved into dangerous territory.

Brennan saw the others were flatly opposed and was embarrassed by his initial enthusiasm. They might well be right about core functions. Brennan, holding out for a compromise, said he was sure the Chief was not wedded to the term or the analysis.

The four decided to nibble at the Chief's privilege section a subsection at a time. Stewart should circulate only the portions of his substitute section that might be added to the Chief's, particularly the *Marbury v. Madison* restatement—the portion that forthrightly and definitively ruled that the courts had absolute authority to resolve the dispute. They would wait until the Chief circulated his full opinion, all sections from facts to privilege, to attack the concept of *core functions*.

Before leaving for Nantucket on Thursday, July 18, Brennan dictated a memo to Burger.

> DEAR CHIEF,
>
> This will formally confirm that your "working draft" circulated July 17, of "The Claim of Executive Privilege" reflects for me a generally satisfactory approach . . . I do however agree with Potter, that St. Clair's argument, that the President alone has the power to decide the question of privilege, must be dealt with. Potter's suggested way is satisfactory to me.

Brennan closed by saying that he expected to have some more suggestions and would pass them on.

Marshall's memo to the Chief was even fainter in its praise of Burger's draft. "I agree with its basic structure, and believe that it provides a good starting point with which we can work." But, he added, he agreed with Stewart that the White House position that the President should ultimately decide what is privileged should be "firmly and unequivocally" rejected.

Marshall also objected to two footnotes. Number five in the Chief's privilege draft said that the Constitution does not mention executive privilege. "There is similarly nothing said in the Constitution authorizing the very subpoena at issue in this case," Marshall said. This footnote should be dropped, Marshall said, adding that he saw "no reason to raise any doubt on this score or to discuss the question at all."

Footnote number seven distressed Marshall even more. Leaving open the question of specific claims of privilege on foreign policy or national security matters, the Chief had written that "deference" was also due "discussion of highly sensitive domestic policies, for example, devaluation of the currency, imposition or lifting of wage and price controls . . ." These discussions were " . . . entitled to a very high order of privilege, since the economic consequences of disclosure of such discussions could well be as pervasive and momentous as the disclosure of military secrets."

Marshall thought that was outrageous. Conspiracies, such as the alleged administration deal to raise milk prices in return for campaign contributions, might be reasoned privileged.

White did not like what he had seen. The Chief was creating too much law to dispose of the case. He sat down at his typewriter and composed another message.

DEAR CHIEF:

I am in the process of considering your draft on executive privilege.

I am reluctant to complicate a difficult task or to increase your labors, of which I am highly appreciative, but I submit the following comments for your consideration.

First, he said, "I do not object to Potter's suggestion . . ." Then came the real message. There was too much discussion of executive privilege and a construction of newly defined power for the courts to decide these issues. Too little was being made of Rule 17(c). All citizens, Presidents among them, were obligated equally to cooperate in criminal trials. That was the heart of the case. In this case,

> The courts are playing their neutral role of enforcing the law already provided them, either by rule, statute, or Constitution . . . I doubt, therefore, that we need discover or fashion any inherent powers in the judiciary to overcome an executive privilege which is not expressly provided for but which we also fashion today.

He repeated his perennial point that *Marbury v. Madison* did not create judicial review; the Constitution did. "I always wince when it is inferred that the Court created the power . . ." To underscore his point, White wrote, "Perhaps none of these matters is of earth-shaking importance, *but it is likely that I shall write separately if your draft becomes the opinion of the Court.*" (Emphasis added.)

As the latest wave of memos arrived at his desk, Burger saw that large accommodations would be necessary. He decided first to add four long paragraphs at the front end of the privilege section, incorporating Stewart's suggestion. *Marbury v. Madison* (despite White's point) was cited at the beginning and the end—"It is emphatically the province and duty of the judicial department to say what the law is." It was rather obvious, but if Stewart, Brennan and Marshall thought it was important, so be it.

Now for White. White's multiple memos on one subject were clear. Rule 17(c) was what concerned him. The Chief took his own 17(c) section, cast it aside, rearranged some of the paragraphs in White's 17(c) proposal, and incorporated it almost verbatim. Keeping only three of his own sentences on the admissibility of recorded conversations and one of his own footnotes, the Chief dropped only one of White's sentences, one that he deemed redundant, given what would follow in the executive privilege section. Several of White's footnotes were dropped as unnecessary. The Chief was now certain that each of White's major points was included in some form. White would have to join. And with White neutralized, and the others accommodated on the *Marbury v. Madison* issue, the Chief decided to phone Nantucket and talk to Brennan.

Brennan was surprised to get the call.

Burger said the entire opinion would be circulated in draft form by the weekend; sufficient revisions had been made to meet White's objections. He was hopeful that the opinion might come down by the next Wednesday. It would be helpful if Brennan could return to Washington by Monday to help finish work.

Brennan agreed and hung up. He was both pleased and disappointed. At last there would be a complete draft from which to work. But Brennan did not see how White could have been so easily accommodated. He also thought the Chief did not yet understand how profound were the disagreements. White's draft represented a full-fledged renewal of his debate with Powell over the standards applicable to a presidential subpoena. Skeptical, Brennan made arrangements to return to Washington.

The Chief also talked to Douglas in Goose Prairie. He told him his timetable. He said he was thinking of using White's 17(c), but only if Douglas approved. Many of Douglas's thoughts had also been used, the Chief said. His memo had been invaluable.

Douglas encouraged the Chief again. Then he called his chambers and had a memo sent to the Chief and to the conference declaring simply that White's 17(c) section "is O.K. with me."

The Chief spent the next day, Friday, July 19, in his chambers, working with his clerks to pull the opinion together for the first time. Though he tried to incorporate any reasonable suggestion from the memos of the other Justices, the Chief still had to modify the language in several of the memos. Powell's proposal that the courts show "solicitous concern" was changed to "great deference."

Brennan's repeated invitation to the White House to withhold national security material as privileged was also altered.

In the last ten days the Chief had tried to accommodate nearly all the others. He used some of Powell's language on the importance of confidentiality, and the need for deference and restraint by the courts. He simply incorporated Stewart's *Marbury v. Madison* section. He inserted almost verbatim White's section on Rule 17(c). He picked up some ideas from Douglas, particularly his appealability section. He used some of Brennan's standing section. And he tried to accommodate Marshall's objection to two footnotes: one was deleted completely, the other was modified.

That left Blackmun. The Chief used large parts of his statement of the facts. What difference did it make anyway? When he took his completed draft to Blackmun, he told him that no one had seen it yet. Before he circulated it, he wanted the benefit of his friend's editing skills.

Blackmun agreed happily.

It was a small price to pay. Burger had endured Blackmun's nit-picking before and would again. Most probably Blackmun's suggestions would be small and meaningless. It was not likely that he would want conceptual changes.

Blackmun made a few stylistic suggestions and corrected some grammar and spelling errors before he returned the draft with his approval.

The next morning, Saturday, July 20, *The New York Times* carried a front-page story on the tapes case: "The Supreme Court may be unable or unwilling to hand down a decision in the Nixon tapes case until after the House Judiciary Committee has voted late next week whether to recommend the impeachment of President Nixon."

The story, citing unnamed sources, said that six Justices had tentatively held against Nixon but that the Chief joined by Blackmun was writing a dissent that was delaying the announcement of the decision.

The Chief was in his chambers early Saturday. He was in an excellent mood. He read over the draft one last time and was proud of the work. Though the others had tried to pick the opinion to death, it was solid, complete, straightforward and well reasoned. The rest of them had gone over every word he had written, demanding changes. But they had essentially acceded to what he felt sure would be the most important part of the case—the part with the most far-reaching implications. The key sentence was still there. "The protection of the confidentiality of presidential communications has . . . constitutional underpinnings." Nixon was going to lose the case, but the larger principle he claimed to be fighting to protect would be upheld.

The Chief finally sent the draft down to the printer. With nothing more to do, he proposed that his clerks join him for lunch. One could not go because out-of-town friends had stopped by his house. The Chief offered to drive him home before he went off to lunch with his other clerk.

Since the chauffeur was off, the Chief got behind the wheel of a Ford—the Court's car since the beginning of the energy crisis—and headed out of the basement garage. They drove to the clerk's house, dropped him off and then went on to lunch. Afterward, they would return to the Court to measure the reactions of the other Justices. The Chief had noticed that some of them were in the building.

Stewart had arrived at the Court that Saturday morning thinking that the first official full draft would come around. When it was brought to him, he read the twenty-nine pages slowly. As he had expected, the core functions analysis was there, the central part of the section on executive privilege that the Chief had labeled Part C. Stewart was uneasy. As inelegant as the writing was, something else worried him. The tone was odd, the references somehow stilted, the citations of cases slightly off the mark. Could there be some subtle meaning beneath the words that he was missing? Could the Chief be slipping something in to sabotage the opinion? Could he be omitting something to create a loophole?

Nixon was desperate. Surely he would look for any ambiguity or favorable point on which to base a last-ditch defense. He might accept the Court's judgment on the law but reinterpret some obscure reference in the opinion. Could there be a bubble of imprecision that would give the President the "air" he needed?

Stewart realized he might be getting too suspicious or paranoid, but the simple fact was that he just didn't trust the Chief, particularly on this case. He recalled a Sherlock Holmes mystery, *The Silver Blaze*, in which Holmes discovered a clue in something that *didn't* exist, a watchdog that *didn't* bark. By recognizing this seemingly trivial anomaly, Holmes deduced that the dog's owner, the apparent victim, was actually the perpetrator of the crime. The notion of the "dog that didn't bark" began to haunt Stewart. Was the Chief purposely leaving unanswered some crucial, but hidden, question? Stewart's instinct was to drop as much as possible from the Chief's draft and substitute his own analysis and language. If Stewart could not locate the loopholes, at least he might remove some of them, if only accidentally, by putting the argument in his own words. The best way to get the Chief to adopt changes was to go slowly, item by item. Once the Chief accepted a change, he generally forgot where it had come from and became certain it had been his idea.

But now there was not much time. The Chief was talking about an announcement in four days, and Stewart had not even told Burger his major complaint about the core functions analysis. An early announcement looked impossible. However awkward, there was no choice but to move a step at a time even if the deadline had to be pushed back. Stewart could at least count on support from the others who had approved his version; at a minimum that included Powell, Brennan and Marshall.

Then there was the matter of control. Since Burger had come to the Court, the major opinions had been the achievement of the center coalition. There was no reason that this opinion should be any different. To a great degree it was rightfully theirs. The Chief had to be reminded of this fact of life. It was not the Chief's Court, or a Nixon Court.

White had come to the Court unsure of what the day would bring. Marshall, having missed the previous Saturday, also came to his chambers. After the Chief's draft had circulated, they stopped by Stewart's chambers. Stewart was sitting at his desk in a polo shirt. White was still pleased that the Chief had adopted his 17(c) section. He and Marshall sat at the left end of the desk, and a small group of clerks hovered at the front and right side.

They went through the draft line by line. Stewart made his case against the core functions analysis, restating every argument. White and Marshall agreed that it would be better to substitute Stewart's simpler alternative. Powell and Brennan also agreed, Stewart reminded them, so they had five votes. There were other minor problems. *President* should be capitalized. Then they decided to list their nonnegotiable demands.

The door to Stewart's inner office was open, and they heard someone come into the outer office. There was a second of silence, and Marshall turned toward the door. "Hi, Chief," he boomed.

Burger hesitated in the doorway. He just wanted to make sure that everyone had received a copy of the full draft, he said. The printers, he said apologetically, had forgotten to heat the lead to set type that morning so the draft had been delayed until midday.

It was obvious what Stewart, White and Marshall were doing.

It looks good, Stewart said. His hands working furiously, he picked up a rubber band, put it in his mouth and began to chew it—an old nervous habit.

White was more direct. He said there were still some problems and they were trying to isolate the main ones.

Yeah, the Chief responded. He appeared tense, but he was gracious. Well, he said, he was still shooting for a Wednesday announcement. He said goodbye and left.

The group waited in silence as Burger closed the outer door behind him.

"Jesus," Marshall said, "it's like getting caught with the goods by the cops."

Stewart was visibly distressed. This could make the Chief more intractable.

In any event, they told each other, the Chief's little visit had changed things. Their small intrigue, or what remained of it, was no more. Before the Chief put a more sinister interpretation on the meeting than was warranted, they had to do something, and at once. They had to lay out their demands clearly.

Stewart said maybe they could turn the incident to their advantage. The Chief's discovery had given their convocation legitimacy. Burger would be expecting them to come to him with suggestions. It was important to find a way to present their demands with the force but not the appearance of an ultimatum.

With Stewart orchestrating, they singled out the necessary modifications. It boiled down to some changes in wording and the core functions problem.

"Well, Potter," White remarked, "I'm going home. You go tell him."

Everyone laughed.

"I'm not going by myself," Stewart said to more laughter.

"Oh yes," White replied. Stewart was definitely the man for the job. Given his close relationship with the Chief, he would be most effective.

After some more moments of teasing, White agreed to go with Stewart and Marshall. They walked down the hall to Burger's office.

The Chief greeted them. They outlined their suggestions.

It all sounds fine with me, the Chief responded, except the elimination of the core functions analysis.

But that was the biggest problem they had, Stewart said.

Well, the Chief replied, he preferred his core functions section, and he was going to keep it. In fact, this was the part of the opinion that offered the most explicit reason for why the President had to lose—an essential core function of the judiciary was pitted against a general need for confidentiality.

Stewart could see that the Chief was growing increasingly adamant. Instead of debating it right now, Stewart suggested that perhaps he should go back to his office and draft an alternative subsection C along the lines that he and the others had been talking about. He would have it ready for the Chief's consideration by Monday.

The Chief had little choice but to agree. He would look over Stewart's proposal.

After the three Justices left, the Chief vowed to his clerks that he would hold his ground. He could see that Stewart was the leader. His suggestions were the most sweeping and unacceptable; Stewart was not going to carry it off. No way, the Chief said.

Back in his chambers, Stewart got out his uncirculated version of the privilege section. Brennan, Marshall and Powell had already approved it.

The fault in the Chief's reasoning lay in his effort to balance the President's interests against those of the courts. On one side, the Chief put the Article II powers of the President, which he said contained executive privilege. On the other side of the scale, the Chief put the Article III power of the courts. Since there was a specific demonstrated need for evidence in a criminal trial, the weight was on the Judiciary's side of the scale. Burger's conclusion in this case was that there was an imbalance. Little or nothing of weight on Nixon's side, and great weight on the Court's.

Stewart was opposed to creating new constitutional concepts such as core functions, but he had other important problems with this section as well. The definition of executive core functions was too broad and too vague. The term was an open door for a defiant reinterpretation by the President. And the definition of judicial core functions was apologetic. The judicial interest seemed manufactured. The Chief's opinion smacked of judicial legislation, as if the Court were conjuring new constitutional grounds for compelling the production of evidence as a special indulgence for fellow judges. Burger had dismissed Stewart's constitutional due process basis for the need for evidence in a footnote rather than in the text.

Also, Burger's effort to balance the needs of one branch of the federal government against the interests of another, raised the separation-of-powers question. Since such questions were generally left to the head of the affected branch rather than the courts, the Chief was simply asking for trouble.

Perhaps there was an easy way of handling this, Stewart thought. The Chief had balanced the needs of the President against those of the Court. Why not balance them against the Constitution? The Fifth and Sixth Amendments guaranteed due process and a fair trial with all the evidence. Taking some language from the memos of Douglas and White to develop a constitutional foundation for a subpoena, Stewart wrote that "the needs of due process of law in the fair administration of criminal justice" required the evidence. This line of argument would force Nixon to pit his claims against the Bill of Rights, the commitment to the rule of law, and the concept of due process.

The case came down not just to the question of a subpoena, the courts' technical requirement, but to the future of the constitutional system. The Chief's version missed the central point, dismissing it in footnote 16. The central feature of Burger's section, four pages in his draft, was two long citations from twenty-year-old civil cases (*C. & S. Air Lines v. Waterman Steamship Corp.* and *U.S. v. Reynolds*). Stewart thought the Chief's draft reflected an obsession with the technical administration of justice and an utter lack of concern about fundamental constitutional questions.

Now that he had his foundation, Stewart began tinkering with both drafts, trying to develop an alternative that would change the thrust of the opinion but least challenge the Chief. He kept the Chief's first two paragraphs, and the next long paragraph except for the last sentence, which said the courts must have standards and procedures to ensure that the "legitimate confidentiality" of the executive is preserved. That sentence had originally come from Powell's pre-argument memo. Stewart then substituted a new line of reasoning for the Chief's core functions analysis. He wrote seven paragraphs in place of the Chief's final four, keeping only Burger's last sentence, which summarized the decision. Stewart had his clerks come in on Sunday, July 21, to type the new version, twelve pages, triple-spaced.

Early Monday morning, July 22, Stewart went over the draft. He was satisfied that it gave the tapes subpoena a firm constitutional basis while giving executive privilege a very limited constitutional status. He then went to White and Marshall and went over it with them in detail. They agreed that they would join the Chief only if he accepted Stewart's substitute. Afterward, Stewart sent a copy to the Chief. That still left four Justices out of the picture—Douglas, Brennan, Blackmun and Powell.

Stewart decided to make sure that everyone understood they were on a one-way street; there was no turning around. He wrote:

RE: Nixon cases

MEMORANDUM TO: Mr. Justice Douglas
                            Mr. Justice Brennan
                            Mr. Justice Blackmun
                            Mr. Justice Powell

Byron, Thurgood, and I were here in the building on Saturday afternoon when the printed draft of the tentative proposed opinion was circulated. After individually going over the circulation, we collected our joint and several specific suggestions and met with the Chief Justice in order to convey these suggestions to him.

. . . our joint suggestions were too extensive to be drafted on

Saturday afternoon, and I was accordingly delegated to try my hand at a draft over the weekend. The enclosed draft embodies the views of Byron, Thurgood, and me, and we have submitted it to the Chief Justice this morning.

As of now, Byron, Thurgood, and I are prepared to join the proposed opinion, if the recasting of [the section] is acceptable to the Chief Justice . . .

At this late stage it seems essential to me that there be full intramural communication in the interest of a cooperative effort, and it is for this reason that I send you this memorandum bringing you up to date so far as I am concerned.

P.S.

Copies to: The Chief Justice
          Mr. Justice White
          Mr. Justice Marshall

P.S. As you will observe, the enclosed draft borrows generously from the draft of the Chief Justice as well as Lewis Powell's earlier memorandum.

Blackmun was pleased to see someone stand up to the Chief. Stewart's proposal was far superior, if for no other reason than the weight and authority of the language. Blackmun made it known that he was now prepared to join if the substitution were made.

Powell also found Stewart's version preferable and gave his tentative approval. But he was not deluded. Very little had been taken from his early memo.

Brennan flew in from Nantucket later that afternoon and read the proposal. Though he thought it overly generous in its use of the Chief's language, there were no apparent major changes from the first version he had approved. He quickly called Stewart to say that he agreed strongly that the substitution was essential.

Douglas was scheduled to return from Goose Prairie that afternoon. The Chief sent a messenger to the airport to give Douglas a copy of the full draft he had circulated two days earlier. If Douglas ratified his version, it could puncture the counterdraft movement. Brennan, however, made sure that a copy of Stewart's proposal was also at the airport. He also took the precaution of sounding out Douglas before the Chief could get to him. Douglas agreed that the substitution should be made. That was seven votes, according to Brennan's count. The Chief was the only holdout to his own opinion.

Burger was exhausted. In addition to closing a Court term and attending his official functions, he had worked for more than two straight weeks without a day off. Burger felt the others had been merciless. And Stewart's memo calling for future "full intramural communication" was a joke, after the way he had operated behind his back for weeks. This was all particularly ironic given the Saturday meeting. The Chief didn't think the little gathering in Stewart's chambers he had wandered into on Saturday was in the spirit of "full intramural communication." Each of them had taken a section of his draft and chewed it to bits. If he had written only an eighth of the opinion, he too could have fussed over every word and each comma.

But what would the others do? The Chief had talked to some of them. All, to one degree or another, seemed sympathetic to Stewart's proposal. Burger felt he had been sandbagged; he needed time to consider his options. He dashed off a quick "Personal" memo to the conference.

> Potter's memo of July 22, 1974, enclosing a revision of Part "C" prompts me to assure you that I will work on it promptly with the hope to accommodate those who wish to get away this week.
>
> The two versions can be accommodated and harmonized and, indeed, I do not assume it was intended that I cast aside several weeks work and take this circulation as a total substitute.
>
> I will have a new draft of Part "C" along as soon as possible. I take it for granted voting will be deferred until the revised opinion is recirculated.

Once again, Brennan saw, Burger had not even understood the vast difference between the two approaches. The two simply could not be "accommodated and harmonized" as the Chief had proposed. Any attempt by the Chief to accomplish that would inevitably result in another half-baked, paste-up job.

At least the Chief finally perceived that he was up against the wall. For Burger to plead that any vote be deferred meant that they were gaining some ground.

Burger knew that he faced a tough choice. There was no "give" in Stewart's posture, and Stewart seemed to have lined up all the others. Burger read through the alternative drafts. They were really two different ways of saying the same thing; the approaches were different but the bottom line was the same. The President would have to turn over his tapes. Whichever version they used would not make any difference to history or constitutional law. Burger was sure his version was better, but the others thought differently. What was the big deal? It came down to three pages out of a thirty-page opinion. All of them, living day and night with the case for weeks, had become wrapped up in each word and phrase. Did the difference have any substance? Burger could find none. It would all seem silly in a few weeks. But the Chief knew that making concessions was part of holding the Court together. The main thing was to get the opinion delivered. He wanted it unanimous. They were on the final leg. The only thing holding them up seemed to be this section. Stewart had left the first two paragraphs the same. That was settled. The Chief then took Stewart's next two paragraphs about the rule of law and compressed them, shifting some of the sentences around, dropping others.

Next, Stewart had reduced the Chief's citation of one case to a passing reference. But, of course, Stewart had dissented in that case. The Chief decided to restore the full citation (*Branzburg v. Hayes*).

Stewart also made only offhand references to the twenty-year-old cases the Chief had cited. Burger wanted those back in. He then switched around and condensed some of the next four Stewart paragraphs—the central basis of Stewart's argument that due process and the fair administration of justice required the President's relevant evidence.

Burger did not find it particularly painful to make the alterations.

Stewart's draft didn't really say anything he would not have written himself. The core functions approach was just one of several possible lines of reasoning. Also, he had improved on Stewart's prose.

Late in the day, Burger had a rough of this amalgamation typed, and took it to Douglas, who now seemed the most reasonable of his colleagues. Douglas was happy with the new section and told the Chief it would win quick approval from the others.

Meanwhile Brennan had gone to dinner and returned to the Court. Having initially expressed fairly strong support for the Chief's privilege section, including the analysis of core functions, he felt guilty now. Perhaps the Chief didn't understand that Stewart's version was a necessary improvement. With his clerk, Brennan had begun writing a detailed letter to the Chief spelling out why Stewart's constitutionally based approach was better.

Fortified by Douglas's support, the Chief walked over to Brennan's chambers about 9 P.M. Burger was in an effusive mood. The last problem surely was solved. He told Brennan he had revised the "C" section and had just shown it to Douglas, who liked it.

Brennan was alarmed. The first vote for a draft was often the most important psychologically. Douglas's vote could make the other six appear to be the holdouts.

The effort of harmonizing the two versions, the Chief said, had been very difficult. Stewart's draft proposal could not be accepted as a substitute because it was so poorly written.

This remark struck Brennan as almost comic, but he decided that the time was ripe to step forward. He preferred Stewart's version, he said, and had just drafted a note explaining why. The core functions argument would not do.

Burger was surprised. *That* has been dropped in the new harmonized version, he said.

What was *that?* Brennan asked incredulously.

Core functions was dumped, Burger replied.

But of course, Brennan said, *that* was the dispute.

That, Burger said, was nothing more than "the little word discrepancies" between the two versions.

Brennan was skeptical. He asked to see the latest revision.

Sure, Burger said. They returned to Burger's chambers to get a copy.

Brennan read it quickly. Though still in rough form, the new version made no mention whatsoever of core functions. The whole notion had been jettisoned. Even more intriguing, Brennan thought he recognized whole sections, apparently verbatim, from Stewart's draft.

Though Burger's new version was not perfect, Brennan thought it was acceptable.

Brennan told the Chief he was delighted. If *this* is it, he would go along.

That is my compromise, the Chief said.

Brennan bid him a very pleasant goodnight and walked out. He reread the draft to make sure there were no hidden meanings, and he compared it carefully with Stewart's. He did not want to rush to accept something the others would oppose; it had been, after all, his initial encouragement of the Chief on the core functions argument that had slowed down the efforts to win concessions from Burger.

Brennan went to see Douglas. Was he right? It seemed like a capitulation by the Chief.

Douglas agreed.

Brennan was amazed. There were nine paragraphs in the section, some of them long. Only two, the introductory and least important paragraphs, were from the original. The other seven were from Stewart's draft. More than three quarters of the language was Stewart's. Most importantly, the basis was due process and not core functions. And all four footnotes in the section were Stewart's.

Brennan and Douglas decided that Brennan should phone the others that night. Brennan called Stewart first to tell him of the victory.

Stewart was dubious.

Brennan read every word of that section of the modified draft to Stewart.

If *that* was it, Stewart agreed, the Chief had caved in. Of course, he would join.

Unable to contain his enthusiasm, Brennan phoned White, then

Marshall and finally Blackmun. It was a victory both in principle and for their strategy. They all three agreed that they could join if it turned out to be final.

Brennan could not reach Powell by telephone, but he conveyed the outcome of the calls to Douglas, who phoned the Chief to suggest a conference the next day in order to ensure that they were all on track.

The Chief agreed. His coalition was building.

By 10 A.M. the next morning, Tuesday, July 23, the Chief had formally circulated his revised section C as seven double-spaced pages.

Brennan read over Burger's cover memo. "As I view this revised Section 'C,' it does not differ in substance from the original circulation." Incredible, Brennan thought. Was it a face-saving rationalization, or did the Chief not comprehend what had been forced on him?

Stewart went over the new draft line by line, word by word, to make sure that nothing had been slipped in from the night before. His own language had been clearer and more forceful, more eloquent, but enough language and basics were there. They had beaten the Chief this time.

The Chief followed with a memo saying there would be a conference at 1:30. At 1:25, the conference bell rang. The tension was more pronounced than ever. Various pieces of the opinion draft had been okayed, but this was really their first look at the whole. It was now virtually impossible to trace the turns and twists the opinion had taken: ideas articulated by Douglas and Powell, modified by Brennan, quickly sketched by the Chief; a section substituted by White; a footnote dropped for Marshall; Blackmun's facts embroidered over the Chief's; Stewart's constant tinkering and his ultimatum. Still hanging over them all was the possibility that the President of the United States might ignore them.

Since the printed draft was not yet ready, they sat down and made sure that each had a complete typed draft. They discussed a few minor changes. All seemed to agree that they could join the Chief's opinion.

The eight Justices were exhausted. Summer was slipping away.

As they proceeded, the tensions were replaced by a slightly self-conscious notetaking, as if they were preparing for some further drafts.

Douglas, just back from Goose Prairie, suddenly spoke up from his end of the table. There were too many changes that he had not seen or approved. The opinion had drifted in too many directions. Many elements were not derived from their original conference discussion, or from the Chief's initial work. If all these changes were left in, Douglas said, he would file a separate opinion, a concurrence.

Brennan felt helpless. It had been settled, but now, as in hundreds of cases over the years, Douglas was going to do his own thing. Before Brennan could say anything, Powell said that he too was considering a separate opinion. Through many small subtle changes, the Chief's opinion had shifted from the middle course he thought they had agreed upon. The notion of deference to presidential confidentiality, and the need for a higher standard to be applied for subpoenas to an incumbent president, had not been given real consideration in the opinion. They were ruling that any grand jury could subpoena material from the President in a criminal investigation. That was too sweeping. They could, and they should, rule more narrowly, fitting the circumstances to this unique case. Their job was, in part, to ensure that the presidency and the chief executive's decision making were protected from unwarranted intrusions. This opinion failed to do so.

The room erupted. The tentative unanimity that had prevailed only a few minutes before had evaporated.

White was sitting quietly for the moment, but Brennan thought he would probably be next. A separate opinion by Powell would likely touch him off and compel him to respond.

Brennan made an impassioned plea for unanimity. Everyone had problems with the opinion, he said. He too had problems. But it was a compromise document and it was essential both to the Court and to the nation. They might not be able to imagine what was at stake in this case, nor could they predict the consequences of their action. The Court must speak with one voice. He turned to Powell and Douglas. The opinion is fine, he pleaded. Please let it go, he beseeched them.

Brennan betrayed no hint of his real feelings—that, had the opinion been in the hands of a more capable man, this would never have happened. But he made as strong an entreaty as he had ever made at conference.

The Chief watched, happy to have Brennan's support for his opinion. From the Chief's perspective, Powell was acting like a spoiled child.

As Powell listened to Brennan's appeal, he could see that, like the others, Brennan was overwrought and frantic. Brennan spoke with a tremor in his voice. He was not expressing an ordinary argument, but a conviction. Powell had a nearly inflexible rule: If at all possible, never let a separate opinion or concurrence jeopardize personal relations. Brennan might be right. The need for one voice possibly outweighed the need to precisely state and limit the opinion. Certainly it was not an outrageous opinion. The corporate product was bland enough; and it would not be an embarrassment. Powell might have fought Brennan alone, but Brennan had support. Most significantly he had the Chief's.

Okay, Powell said, he would go along. He withdrew his threat graciously. He would accede to the majority.

Douglas also backed off, and the room itself seemed to cool.

Powell had another suggestion. The formal announcement should be delayed for at least five days. In that way the opinion would come down after the House Judiciary Committee was scheduled to begin its formal vote on impeachment. It was uncertain whether the Committee would vote to impeach, but Powell worried that the Court decision would hand the pro-Nixon Republicans a strong argument for delaying any vote until they had obtained the additional tapes. It would take months for the tapes to make their way from Judge Sirica's courtroom to the Committee members. Those opposed to impeaching could make the point that without the tapes they would be now authorized to have, the Committee would be acting prematurely in judging Nixon.

Brennan, Stewart and Douglas pounced hard on Powell. Many of the Court's decisions, perhaps all of them, had political repercussions of one kind or another. In the past they had always rejected suggestions that they delay cases for political reasons, they told Powell. The Court could not, it must not, ever get in the business of selecting which secondary effects it preferred and adjust its timetable to suit them.

Brennan was astonished that Powell could express such a political motive, even though it seemed contrary to the interests of the man who had appointed him. Brennan actually believed that no matter what the Judiciary Committee did, delaying the decision would play into Nixon's strategy of delay.

Powell's suggestion was dropped as quickly as it had come up. There was nothing left to debate except a few technical matters. Since they had not decided the grand jury question—whether an incumbent President could be named an unindicted coconspirator—they would dismiss that issue in a footnote, as one improvidently granted—that is, "DIGGED."

Still the conference dragged on. The case was so important that the Justices kept going over the same ground, repeating themselves. It could not be as simple as it now seemed. They finally adjourned until the Chief's printed opinion was ready.

It came around to all the chambers at 5:30 P.M.

Stewart checked to make sure that all his changes had been retained. Stylistic and other minor changes were phoned in to the Chief. Another conference was not needed.

The Chief took the final vote. It was *8 to 0—unanimous for his opinion.*

Burger ordered a press release saying only that the Court would convene the next morning at some time between 10 and 11 A.M.

That evening Douglas decided to have a get-acquainted meeting with the new clerks he had hired for the next term.

He sent his messenger, Harry Datcher, to get the clerks, whom he barely knew. "He wants you guys to come in for drinks," Datcher told the three young attorneys. Datcher got the liquor and the glasses, and brought them into Douglas's office.

Douglas had an apéritif wine. It was about all he could drink; he had an allergic reaction to other liquors. The Nixon case would be coming down tomorrow, he told them. Nixon had lost, 8 to 0.

One of the clerks wondered about the latest draft of Douglas's opinion, which they had seen.

"It seems a good idea to have only one opinion and have the Chief do it," Douglas replied. The President was not special. The matter was a straight criminal subpoena case. Everyone had privacy interests, but the President had no greater privacy interests than anyone else.

Douglas sipped his wine. There was no gloating, but the fact that he had invited the clerks for a drink made it clear that he was very happy.

The next morning, July 24, the Court convened at 11 A.M. Rehnquist was not present. Once on the bench, the Chief took a few moments to pay tribute to Earl Warren, since there had been no meeting of the Court since his death two weeks before. Then Burger announced the case and began reading a summary of its major points in his best, most forceful voice. A silent, unanimous Court sat on either side of him.

Finally it was over, and the reporters raced from the courtroom.

Jaworski, who had fallen into a depression and had talked privately of resigning as Special Prosecutor, emerged from the Court to cheers and applause. "If I had to write it myself," he said, "I couldn't have written it any better."

After leaving the bench, the Chief took two copies of his work and wrote on each, "With thanks for long hours together, Warren E. Burger." He handed them to his two clerks. "Thanks again," he said.

Stewart told his clerks that the Chief's initial draft of the decision would have got a grade of *D* in law school. It had been raised to a *B*.

In San Clemente, California, President Nixon picked up his bedside phone. His Chief of Staff, Alexander M. Haig, told him that the Supreme Court decision had just come down. Nixon had seriously contemplated not complying if he lost, or merely turning over excerpts of the tapes or edited transcripts. He had counted on there being some exception for national security matters, and at least one dissent. He had hoped there would be some "air" in the opinion.

"Unanimous?" Nixon guessed.

"Unanimous," Haig said. "There is no air in it at all."

"None at all?" Nixon asked.

"It's tight as a drum."*

After a few hours spent complaining to his aides about the Court and the Justices, Nixon decided that he had no choice but to comply.

Seventeen days later, he resigned.

---

* See *RN: The Memoirs of Richard Nixon*, pp. 1051–52.

1974 Term

AFTER THE ANNOUNCEMENT of the Detroit busing case, the Chief adjourned the Court until the first Monday in October. He was jubilant. Two of the Court's most important decisions had been handed down in two days, and both were his. But stories soon began to appear in newspapers suggesting that the Nixon tapes opinion was not the Chief's work, that it bore his name only as a matter of protocol. These stories were not detailed, but they all implied that Stewart and White had authored the opinion. The Chief had no intention of having his effort belittled. The rumors were lies.

Barrett McGurn, the Court's press officer, called in reporters on August 5. He told them that the Chief had worked forty-one straight days at the Court drafting the Nixon case. His days had often begun at 8 A.M., and he had worked until midnight, taking time out only to eat a meal at his desk. Cleaning crews had been allowed in the Chief's office once a week, only after all his papers and notes were locked away. There had only been one conference during the whole interval. It was obvious, therefore, that the Chief had not changed his vote, as some rumors had suggested.

McGurn's defense of Burger was buried inside the papers the next day, as front-page headlines reported on the contents of new Nixon tapes. This time they showed clearly that the President had plotted to cover up the Watergate scandal.

That same day, the Chief and his wife, traveling under the pseudonyms of Mr. and Mrs. Grant Cannon, left for a European vacation. The Chief disliked traveling in Europe during the summer. It was too hot, and there were too many tourists. But the summer recess was the only time he could get away.

The Burgers had been in the Netherlands only a few days when the Chief was summoned to an overseas phone call. It was Philip Buchen, a close friend of Vice-President Gerald R. Ford. President Nixon was resigning, Buchen said. Ford wanted the Chief Justice back the next day to swear him in as President.

Burger told Buchen he would have to speak directly to the Vice-President. Ford called him. It was true; Nixon was resigning. Could Burger see his way to return?

"Oh, I have to be there," Burger said, "I *want* to be there." Ford would be the first unelected President in United States history. It was essential, as a symbol of legitimacy, that the Chief Justice be present at his swearing-in.

An Air Force Boeing 707 was dispatched from Andrews Air Force Base to pick up Burger and his wife. It landed in Washington on August 9, just in time for Burger to make it to the White House for the noon ceremony.

Government leaders and friends and relatives of the Vice-President had gathered in the formal East Room and applauded as Burger and Ford entered.

"Mr. Vice-President," Burger said, "are you prepared to take the oath of office of the President of the United States."

"I am, sir," Ford replied.

In less than a minute it was done.

"Congratulations, Mr. President," Burger said, shaking Ford's hand. He was the first to address Ford by his new title.

Burger stayed in Washington to attend President Ford's first address to a joint session of Congress the next week. He felt obliged to show the flag.

On August 12, he and his wife flew back to the Netherlands. As guests of the United States ambassador in The Hague, the Burgers found their schedule crowded with appointments, dinners, interviews. In a discussion with the Dutch Prime Minister, Burger defended the tapes decision, saying that it "had not by any means weakened the presidency and on the contrary had strengthened it, since the Court's decision made reference for the first time to the doctrine of presidential privilege." The orderly transfer of power showed the resilience of the American constitutional system. This was "in substantial part due to the tone set by President Nixon in his excellent, statesmanlike address of resignation," Burger said.

The Chief returned to the Court in September. This was a time for him to get his bearings, catch up on administrative work, and take a look at the coming term.

Kenneth Ripple, called "the Rip" by other clerks, would be Burger's chief clerk for a second year. Ripple exercised the Chief's authority on matters of format, paper flow, red tape, appearance, security and bureaucratic procedure. His memos were referred to as "Ripplegrams."

Ripple told the new clerks who were to work for the Chief that they were absolutely forbidden to speak with reporters. If a clerk was ever seen in the presence of a reporter, he would be fired. There would be no questions asked, nor any explanations accepted.

Ripple ran the cert pool like a drill sergeant for the five Justices who participated. Cert pool memos were only rarely given to the Chief directly. His copy was reviewed by one of his clerks and further condensed. A pool memo that ran longer than three pages was honed down to one. Important parts of the one-page summary and of the supporting documents were emphasized with yellow highlighter pen.

Once, the stenographic pool accidentally circulated photocopies of the highlighted summaries to the other chambers and the Chief's clerks panicked. The summary mark-ups, as they were called, were supposed to be a secret. The clerks tried to retrieve the photocopies, but it was too late. Clerks around the Court hooted when they saw how Burger's memos were prepared. It confirmed what they had suspected. The Chief had neither the capacity nor the interest to digest even the simplest cert memo.

The other Justices still found Burger's preoccupation with administrative detail hard to take. When one of his memorandums on security arrived, Powell picked it up, tore it into shreds and flipped it into his wastebasket without comment.

On Friday evening, September 20, Burger tried out a new bicycle his family had given him for his sixty-seventh birthday. After practicing a few figure-eights in his drive-way, he set out on the darkened streets of Arlington, Virginia. Not far from his home, a car forced him off the road. His front wheel struck a high curb, and he was catapulted onto the sidewalk. He spent six days at Bethesda Naval Hospital recovering from a deep cut over his eye which required six stitches, a dislocated shoulder and five fractured ribs.

By the end of September the Chief was back at the Court, roaming the building as usual, suggesting a clean-up here, paint or polish there. But he looked drawn and ill. He had lost weight, his eyes were puffy, his skin was more wrinkled. He now looked his sixty-seven years.

Powell and his wife, Jo, returned to Washington right after Labor Day and went about getting settled for the new term in their Harbour Square apartment, which overlooked the Potomac River. Jo had made Powell give up smoking—not an easy step for a man who had long represented tobacco companies and who loved the smell of smoke. Powell was determined to stay in good physical shape. He walked one of two measured distances near his apartment every day. The first was a mile course that ran south along the river to Fort McNair; the other ran 1.3 miles northwest along the river to Hogate's Seafood Restaurant. He had measured each route carefully in his car.

At his chambers, Powell would change from his street shoes into more comfortable Hush Puppies. His chambers were previously the office of the Clerk of the Court. He had gotten a peek at the re-modeling plans before he moved in, and he sent a letter to the Architect of the Capitol. He preferred bookcases, he wrote, to the planned fake fireplace and chimney on the south wall.

The architect answered that it was "customary" for each Justice to have a fireplace, real or not.

Powell would knock on the hollow wooden chimney and tell visitors how even a Supreme Court Justice was impotent before government bureaucracy.

Part of these September mornings was devoted to answering mail—a letter to an old friend, a note to a former clerk, an order to his tailor for new suits. One task was the hiring of another law

clerk, since each Justice was now authorized to have four. The
choice was important to him. Powell was fond of noting that
he spent more time with the other eight Justices than with his
wife. Actually, he spent more time with his clerks. They became his
family.

Powell thought it was important to find clerks who could write
refined opinions, talented aides who would enhance his growing
reputation as the closest approximation the Court had to another
John Harlan. Unlike some other Justices, Powell did not have a
clerk-selection committee. He met the two dozen top applicants
himself. Spencer Campbell served tea during the interviews.
"Spencer," Powell would explain to his visitors, had been Hugo
Black's messenger and "had been at the Court for nearly forty
years—longer than anyone."

Powell had in mind a candidate for the current opening, but he
sought his clerks' advice. They urged him to select a young lawyer,
Joel Klein, with whom one of them had clerked the previous year
for Burger's old archrival on the Court of Appeals, Judge David
Bazelon.

Klein, bearded, anti-establishment, a Harvard Law School graduate *magna cum laude,* had made psychiatry and the law his field.
While still at Harvard, he had worked at McLean, an exclusive
mental hospital outside Boston. After Harvard, he flirted with the
idea of medical school. Instead, he chose to spend a year as research assistant to Professor Alan Dershowitz, another former
Bazelon clerk, at Stanford's Center for the Advanced Study of the
Behavioral Sciences. He had worked there on a book on the legal
theories of civil commitment, the involuntary hospitalization of
those believed mentally ill. He was now working in Washington at
the A.C.L.U.-sponsored Mental Health Law Project.

Powell quickly grasped that Klein's brash, outspoken style would
be a perfect counterpoint to his own genteel Southern background.
He prided himself on hiring liberal clerks. He would tell his clerks
that the conservative side of the issues came to him naturally. Their
job was to present the other side, to challenge him. He would
rather encounter a compelling argument for another position in
the privacy of his own chambers, than to meet it unexpectedly at

conference or in a dissent. Klein became Powell's fourth clerk, and Powell soon decided it had been a wise choice. He was pleased with his new clerk's fervent social concerns. Klein's raised voice and his wild gesticulations became part of chambers life.

Powell's clerks, in their turn, were struck by their boss's tender manner. He seemed to have a thousand friends. The clerks referred to him affectionately behind his back as "Lew."

Powell felt fiercely competitive with the other Justices. The last place he would go for assistance with a sticky legal problem was down the hall to another chambers. He either consulted the law books himself or worked it out with his clerks.

After two and a half years on the Court, Powell remained ambivalent about life as a Justice. "You don't get a sense of power here," he confided once. He found no dramatic moments, no emotional highs like those in a trial courtroom. At the Supreme Court, no cannons went off. Even the Nixon tapes, a monumental case, had not given him the moment of emotional release normally associated with great tasks.

As a young student studying history, Powell had learned that military men and lawyers ran the world. He had no desire to be a military man, so he became a lawyer. Once, Powell invited Washington Redskins football star Larry Brown to lunch at the Court.

Brown asked Powell if he preferred being a lawyer to being a judge.

"Would you rather be a player or a referee?" Powell replied.

As the beginning of the term approached, the Chief scheduled the regular start-of-the-term cocktail party and get-acquainted session for the new clerks. There were more women clerks at the Court this term than ever before—Brennan, Blackmun and Powell had each chosen one for the first time. All three of Bazelon's clerks from the previous year were at the Court; eleven of the twenty-nine clerks had clerked at the U.S. Court of Appeals for the District of Columbia; and an overwhelming majority of the new clerks were liberals, products of the antiwar Watergate period. Many were already friends and all were busy forming their own version of an old-boy network. Cynical as they might wish to seem, however, many of them were taken aback by the irreverence of the clerks of the previous year toward the Justices and the Court.

The party provided the first glimpse of Douglas, already a legend. White still looked like a football halfback. Rehnquist was young and jolly, flaunting his informality. Soon the Chief took the floor, welcoming everyone and expounding on the history and traditions of the Court. He was, several clerks reluctantly admitted, impressive.

Burger turned the floor over to Brennan, a true hero to many of the clerks. A gentle man, smiling ear to ear, the great civil libertarian began slowly. There is one responsibility that all of them— Justices and clerks—shared, Brennan said. That was to preserve, at all cost, the confidential nature of the internal workings of the Court. The Justices, Brennan said, trust that the confidences shared with the clerks will be respected. A hush fell over the room.

Never, Brennan said, has any news story that leaked from the Court been traced to a clerk. Should anything ever leak, that bond of trust would be broken. Justices would never again be able to enjoy the same confidence with clerks. Remember, he lectured, reporters use the same public cafeteria as the clerks would be using this term, and they had been known to follow clerks through the line to eavesdrop. He had already informed his own clerks not to talk to reporters under any circumstances; even a "no comment" could be misconstrued by a reporter. "I do not talk to reporters at any time, at any place, on any subject," said Brennan. Finally, he stepped aside and the party continued, subdued, for another half-hour.

Some clerks were stunned. Was the author of so many important First Amendment opinions so paranoid and contemptuous of the press? The clerks could believe that Brennan was sincere about the need for confidentiality. But why turn a simple ground rule into a rebuke?

Brennan later told his clerks that the conference had insisted that he, as senior Justice, give the briefing since the Chief had delivered a diatribe on security during the previous term which had been too severe. Brennan said that he had felt obliged to overstate his case; but his clerks knew that Brennan *was* paranoid about the press.

The term got off to a relatively good start for Douglas. Relations were better with two of the perennial irritants in his life—his clerks and the Chief.

In an early immigration case *(Saxbe v. Bustos)*, the conference was deadlocked 4 to 4, with the Chief reserving his vote. Douglas drafted an opinion that allowed an increase in immigration of day workers from Canada and Mexico. Despite a disinclination to beg for votes, he walked over to Burger's chambers and left not long after with the Chief's join memo in hand.

Douglas's three clerks were working day and night to answer his queries as fast as humanly possible. At least once they brought sleeping bags to the office and spent the night to meet a deadline.

No clerk was fired in the first months, though early in the fall one of them had committed the *faux pas* of substantially reorganizing one of Douglas's drafts. When he had seen the changes, Douglas leaned on his buzzer summoning the clerk. Sitting quietly at his desk, Douglas said only: "I can see you've done a lot of work, but you are off base here. If and when you get appointed to the Supreme Court you can write opinions as you choose."

The clerk was surprised by the lack of severity.

On Tuesday, December 31, Douglas came to his chambers wearing a tweed hat with a wide brim. He was off that afternoon to Nassau for a New Year's vacation break. Though he loved to travel, Douglas didn't really want to go south at this time. He preferred cooler climates, and because he had a bronchial infection his doctor had recommended that he not travel at all. But his wife, Cathy, had wanted the trip.

Douglas called in his clerks. The next few days would be a slack period, he said. They could take some time off if they wanted.

The clerks were flabbergasted. The clerk-selection committee had warned that Douglas granted no vacations whatsoever. But Douglas was clearly in a holiday mood. He packed his briefcase, put aside a popular novel, James Michener's *The Drifters*, and after wishing his secretaries a Happy New Year, went to meet his driver for the ride to National Airport.

They arrived in balmy Nassau in the early evening. Once they had settled in their hotel room, Cathy went to the lobby to buy something and returned a few minutes later. She found her seventy-six-year-old husband collapsed on the floor. Dazed but still conscious, Douglas was having trouble moving his left arm and leg. He was taken to a hospital, and American diplomatic officials in Nassau were informed.

The Chief was at a New Year's Eve party when he received word that Douglas had been stricken. He could learn only two details. It looked like a stroke, and Douglas was in serious condition. The Chief reached President Ford by phone about 10:30 P.M. in Vail, Colorado, where the President was on his annual skiing vacation with his family. Within an hour, at the President's direction, a jet transporting Douglas's personal physician, Dr. Thomas Connally, was on its way to Nassau. The doctor quickly decided that it would be best to get Douglas back to the United States, where he could receive better care.

As they prepared Douglas for the flight to Washington, Cathy told him that President Ford had sent the plane for his trip back. "My God," Douglas said groggily, "you know they'll drop us in Havana."

When Douglas finally arrived at Walter Reed Army Hospital, he was immediately put into intensive care. Douglas's staff at the Court received scant information. Abe Fortas, the former Justice and one of Douglas's closest friends, visited Douglas at the hospital and stopped by his chambers on Thursday. Fortas told Douglas's clerks that their boss might be back in three to four weeks.

The following Monday, Cathy called Marty Bagby, Douglas's senior secretary. The Justice, she said, was "hollering for Mrs. Bagby." Traffic was snarled because of a snowstorm, and it took Bagby some time to reach Walter Reed. When she entered Douglas's room, he was sitting up in a wheelchair, wearing a checked shirt he had packed for the Nassau trip. "What took you so long?" he asked.

*   *   *

That Monday, January 6, the eight other Justices gathered for a special conference. What action, if any, should they take in Douglas's absence?

There were no formal rules on the participation of a disabled Justice. Technically, he could vote on all cases. A Justice did not have to attend oral argument or listen to a tape of it. He did not even have to attend conference. He could send his conference vote by memo, or through another Justice. But a sick Justice was a handicap. The really tough cases, cases on which the Court was closely divided, could not be decided if one Justice was unable to vote, or if there was a chance that he might die or retire before the decision came down. Brennan had once said that a disabled Justice was almost as bad as one you disagreed with.

The Justices approached the situation carefully. There was nothing more delicate. Each man was implicitly threatened by the very notion of the others determining the fate or power of one of them. Worst of all was the uncertainty. Douglas might recover quickly and be back soon. They agreed to delay arguments in five cases in which Douglas was likely to be the swing fifth vote, rescheduling them for later in the term.

On January 27, Douglas was removed from the seriously ill list at Walter Reed and his condition was listed as satisfactory. One of his clerks and a secretary spent most of each day at the hospital with him. At least superficially, Douglas kept his hand in the affairs of the Court.

But when Brennan visited his friend at Walter Reed in late January, he saw that the fire and passion and energy were gone. Douglas's speech was impaired; he had difficulty enunciating certain words. Cooped up, he was confused about the time; waking in the middle of the day, he often thought it was morning. It was clear to Brennan that Douglas's return was not imminent.

On Thursday, January 30, the Court released its February argument calendar. Some of the cases postponed from January were now to be rescheduled. Brennan was nervous; the conference could wait no longer. Then, on February 11, six weeks after Douglas's stroke, Marshall fell ill with pneumonia and was sent to

Bethesda Hospital for treatment. With his two liberal colleagues now hospitalized, Brennan had serious cause for worry.

Douglas's prospects were not good, and who could tell about Marshall—a sixty-six-year-old man who was overweight, smoked heavily, at times drank too much, and had soured on his work. But Brennan was determined to appear upbeat. He gathered the law clerks of both Douglas and Marshall in his office with his own clerks. He was nurturing, confident and open. They would keep things going, he told them. The nine clerks, working together, would help him keep on top of any developments at the Court. His own clerks knew that Brennan was less than confident. Each time the Chief passed at conference, each time he changed his vote, each time he circulated a stupid memo, Brennan's irritation grew. His clerks thought that every time he looked at Burger, Brennan was reminded of how much he missed Warren.

One day, Brennan was giving a detailed conference briefing to his clerks. He began a review of the vote in a particular case. He explained how White voted, holding up his thumb. Then, with his index finger, he indicated Powell's vote. Skipping his middle finger, he continued to count. He saved the Chief for last. "And the Chief . . ." Brennan smiled wryly and raised his middle finger in an obscene gesture.

Brennan felt that he got terrible assignments from the Chief. One decision he was assigned to write (*Antoine v. Washington*) addressed the question of whether Indians in Washington state could hunt and fish in the off season. The answer turned on an interpretation of an executive order issued by President Ulysses S. Grant 102 years before. Brennan seethed at having to write this "chickenshit case." He had a solid majority of six, including the Chief, but typically, the Chief had not sent in his join memo, even though Brennan's draft had been in circulation for several weeks.

Late one afternoon at about four o'clock, just before Brennan planned to leave for home to see his ailing wife, the phone rang. The Chief wanted to see Brennan on the Indian case. Brennan went down and waited. The Chief was tied up with other business, his secretary said. Brennan returned to his office, only to receive another call an hour later. "Dummy wants me," Brennan told his clerks in disgust as he walked out the door.

At Burger's chambers, Burger showed Brennan several words he wanted added to a long paragraph in the draft. Brennan said he would consider the addition. Then he stomped back to his chambers and summoned his clerks. They had never seen him so angry. "Here is his change," Brennan said. "What the fuck does it mean?"

The clerks and Brennan examined the paragraph. It made no sense. Brennan concluded that it was just another of the Chief's niggling and arbitrary changes, made perhaps only to prove that he had read the draft. He was also suspicious of the Chief's timing. Burger knew Brennan left at 4:30. Brennan resented the Chief's apparent insensitivity to his wife's illness, but he was determined not to be provoked into matching the Chief's pettiness. Swallowing his resentment, he told the Chief that he would be happy to make the addition. Then he left the Court wondering: Why did he still care?

At the hospital, Douglas was impatient. Each day, he spent hours in arduous physical therapy for his arm and leg. The paralysis in the leg showed some signs of improvement; that in the arm did not. Once, he took several steps with a leg brace. But he could not, or would not, walk outside the therapy room. For Douglas, who had always overcome his problems through sheer determination, the frustration was excruciating. As a child, he had conquered polio after the doctors had said he would never walk again. He had missed most of the 1949 term when a horse fell on him and cracked twenty-three of his ribs and punctured a lung. But, as he later joked, the horse died and he lived.

Douglas's secretaries and clerks visited daily, and he dictated to them. But with his left arm immobilized, the difficulty he had turning pages slowed him immensely. As he realized that his body no longer responded to his mind, he became increasingly confused and depressed. His doctors feared that he had lost his drive to walk again. He would drift off, shifting from one subject to the next. Now he concluded that it was the hospital and not his illness that was the barrier. He had to get out.

Blackmun stopped by. Douglas pleaded, only half joking, asking

Blackmun to become his guardian: "Will you be my *best friend**
and swear out a writ to get me out of the place?" Finally, he announced to one of his secretaries and his messenger, Datcher, that
he was going to escape. The doctors got wind of the plan and
stopped it. But Douglas persisted. The doctors at last agreed to let
him spend one night at home. An overnight pass was granted for
Wednesday, March 19.

Once out of the hospital, Douglas ordered Datcher to drive him
to the Court. He arrived about 5:30 P.M. and was wheeled to his
desk. He had been away seventy-eight days. Working there for several hours was taxing. His wife, Cathy, called, upset. The overnight
pass was so he could come *home*, not *work*, she said. He was in a
good mood, and said he would be there shortly.

The following day, Douglas refused to check back into the hospital. It was not unexpected. The doctors got him to agree to come in
at least three times a week for physical therapy.

Reporters saw Douglas around the Court and asked Barrett
McGurn about the sling on his left arm. Douglas wanted the press
office to say that his arm had been injured in his "fall," as Douglas
referred to his stroke.

McGurn consulted with the Chief. Burger didn't want to dispute
Douglas; he told McGurn to issue the misstatement about the
"fall" in Douglas's name, rather than as a statement from the Court.
No more information about Douglas was to be given out, the Chief
ordered. To make Douglas's return easier, Burger had the Court
carpenter build a ramp so his wheelchair could be rolled up to the
back of the elevated bench.

On Monday, March 24, Douglas, drawn and pale, was wheeled in
for oral argument. His eyes had a haunted, wild look. At the afternoon session, he had to leave in the middle because of intense pain
in his left side. The next morning, Douglas called reporters to his
office shortly before the 10 A.M. oral argument began. Sitting at his
cluttered desk, he tried to appear casual.

A reporter asked what he was going to do.

* *A variant of the usual term* next friend, *meaning guardian.*

Douglas said he was going to listen to the tapes of all the January and February cases. He would be able to cast his vote in each one.

Had he considered resigning?

"Never entered my mind," Douglas said.

Was he staying on, waiting for a Democratic President to replace Gerald Ford, so that Ford would not name his successor?

"That is not a factor in any of my calculations," he stuttered.

When he was asked how he felt, Douglas was more frank; "I have been through a considerable ordeal; there is not the same energy I had beforehand."

Slurring his words, he conceded that he was walking only in therapy sessions at the hospital, but added: "Walking has very little to do with the work of the Court." He maintained that he would walk soon, however, and invited the reporters to go hiking with him the next month.

Had he left Walter Reed the week before without his doctor's permission? one reporter asked. Douglas just sat with his pale, glassy-blue eyes staring at his desk. Someone mercifully cut short the embarrassing silence with another question.

When the Chief got word of Douglas's pathetic performance, he was upset. Far from settling anything, Douglas's press conference only raised more questions about his health.

Burger believed Douglas was developing the paranoid qualities of many stroke victims. Douglas complained that there were plots to kill him and to remove him from the bench. Once he was wheeled into the Chief's chambers and maintained it was his. Rumors circulated among the staff that Douglas thought he was the Chief Justice. Douglas could sit in one position comfortably for only a short period, and he often fell asleep at oral arguments. When Court sessions were gaveled to a close, the other Justices disappeared quickly behind the red curtains. The audience was left standing, their eyes naturally on Douglas, who sat alone waiting to be helped out.

After working part-time at the Court for about three weeks, Douglas acknowledged that he had not been ready to return. On April 10, he checked back into Walter Reed with a bad cold. The Court still had the problem of a disabled Justice, and there was no clue to the future, only the certainty of more uncertainty.

*   *   *

Brennan was at his desk one afternoon when Blackmun called with a question about a sticky legal technicality. Did Brennan have any ideas?

"Harry, I'll be right over," Brennan said. Dropping his own work, he hurried down the hall to Blackmun's chambers.

A clerk passing by Blackmun's office observed the two Justices a short time later. Blackmun was at his desk and Brennan stood behind him, one arm on Blackmun's shoulder, the other extended to some memo or law book. It was part of Brennan's "cultivation of Harry project," as one clerk called it.

Brennan thought that Blackmun was continuing to drift away, not only from the Chief's influence but from his own conservatism, and he was determined to encourage it. He had no hope that Blackmun would ever be a regular liberal vote. But Blackmun at least took each case as it came, with a minimum of prejudice. Keenly aware that Blackmun was always fearful that his language in opinions might someday come back to haunt him or the Court, Brennan showed him how narrow decisions were possible in several cases.

The clerks in the Chief's chambers joked that after Blackmun circulated certain opinions, Brennan would take him to lunch out of gratitude. Once, the Chief's clerks were sure that Brennan had joined a Blackmun draft even before he had read it. Even on the tax cases, which Brennan hated, he gave extra consideration to them because they were Blackmun's area of expertise. "This is a tax case. Deny." That was Brennan's normal reaction to a cert request in a tax case. But when Blackmun circulated a tax opinion, Brennan responded with a florid note, praising the work and scholarship. On a major securities case *(Blue Chip Stamps v. Manor Drug Stores)* Blackmun had charged that the majority opinion "graves into stone" with "three blunt chisels" certain arbitrary principles, exhibiting "a preternatural solicitousness for corporate well-being." Brennan readily joined the overwritten dissent.

In another case, the question was whether the city of Chattanooga, Tennessee, could prohibit the production of the controversial rock musical *Hair* in its civic auditorium *(Southeastern*

Promotions, Ltd. v. Conrad). Onstage nudity, simulated sex, four-letter words, pro-drug and antiwar themes marked it as a distinctively 1960s protest. Religious and historical figures were mocked, and interracial love was hailed.

One of the street people in the play was called Burger. The insult was not intentional, since the Chief had not been on the Court when the script was written in 1967. Nonetheless, no play could have been more designed to offend the Chief.

Burger wanted to uphold a decision not to allow the play in a city-owned auditorium. He assumed that his five-man majority in the 1973 obscenity cases, including Blackmun, would stand firm. But Brennan felt that, because the city had banned the play before seeing it or even its script, the question was really one of prior restraint. He bombarded Blackmun with memos and other material and spoke with him at length about the application of prior-restraint law to the case. The issue was not the right of the local community to define or ban obscenity, but the banning of something *before* it appeared. This was a denial of the very sort of hearing that in the 1973 obscenity cases Blackmun had insisted each pornographer be given before anything could be declared obscene.

Blackmun finally voted with Brennan at conference, making Brennan the senior member of the majority present. Brennan assigned the case to Blackmun, and Blackmun agreed to undertake the opinion on the condition that he would not be breaking new ground. He wrote an odd opinion, saying that such a play could be banned only if there was a "clear and present danger." Brennan was so anxious to nail down Blackmun's vote that he joined before talking with his clerks. What was the possible "clear and present danger"? they asked. Nudity? Rape? Brennan got Blackmun to drop the phrase.

Burger was aghast. He remarked several times to his clerks that he didn't understand what Blackmun was doing. It had to be the influence of Stewart and Brennan. The Chief gave no credit to Blackmun.

Burger was also having more and more trouble with Powell, who seemed to constantly flirt with the Court's left wing. At times

Burger found Powell unreachable, willing to listen but seemingly unable to understand his points. When the conference considered a Jacksonville, Florida, law banning the showing of films with any nudity at drive-in movie theaters, Powell voted to uphold the ban (*Erznoznik v. City of Jacksonville*). Despite some nudity the movie, *Class of '74*, rated R, was not obscene in Powell's view, but the local law regulating its showing was a reasonable and permissible exercise of police power. Not only could the movie screen be seen from nearby highways, but also from a church parking lot.

The conference was deadlocked 4 to 4, with Douglas back in the hospital. After the conference, Powell's clerks besieged him. Even his most conservative clerk argued that since the movie was not obscene, its showing at the drive-in was protected by the First Amendment. Ordinarily his vote ended the chambers debate, but this time he seemed to encourage it, even though he had already voted. His clerks knew which arguments to push. It was really a matter of balancing the privacy interests of those offended by the drive-in with the First Amendment rights of the theater owner and customers. Could not the passersby readily avert their eyes?

Powell disagreed. Moreover, the case just wasn't that important.

But the principle was, the clerks insisted. Clearly the government could not regulate expression simply because it was offensive to the majority. Could a billboard erected by an unpopular political candidate be banned because it was offensive to a majority and could be seen from the street, or a church parking lot?

The clerks also raised the matter of economic consequences. They had come to realize, as they got to know Powell, that his business bias was even greater than it appeared to be in his final written opinions. The clerks called it "Lew's corporate dignity doctrine." He seemed convinced that business did little or no wrong. They joked that cert petitions in business cases might well be addressed, "Dear Lew."

Now in this case, they pointed out that a theater owner in a similar instance had had to spend nearly $250,000 to construct a barrier to block the view. The result was an unfair burden, almost a tax, on theater owners who wanted to show R-rated movies that were, after all, protected by the Constitution. It wasn't exactly the corporate dignity argument they were making, but a corporate survival argument.

The clerks finally turned to the sort of hairsplitting, literal-minded argument that appealed to the lawyer in Powell, to his legal fastidiousness. The Jacksonville regulation prohibited the showing of "the human male or female bare buttocks." As Blackmun had said earlier at oral argument, that meant a ban on all backsides, even those of a newborn baby. It was absurd.

By now, even Sally Smith, Powell's jovial, fiercely loyal secretary, had joined the discussion. Powell often found Smith a kind of good-sense barometer. They asked for her opinion. There was nothing wrong with a baby's backside on an outdoor movie screen, she said.

After further reflection, Powell decided to change his vote. The ban should be struck down on First Amendment grounds. He actually felt good about the switch. It had been the right kind of family conference. Everyone had had his say, and he—the pater familias, the senior partner, the corporate president, the school board head—had made the final decision.

Burger was surprised at Powell's vote switch, but he was alarmed when he saw Powell's first draft. It was a powerful opinion reasserting the prohibition of government regulation of aesthetic, political and moral expression. And before Burger knew it, Blackmun, and Douglas of course, had joined it, making it a 6-to-3 decision.

"What the hell is going on in Powell's chambers?" the Chief grumbled.

Burger announced that he intended to write a dissent, but for weeks failed to circulate it. Although Powell was angered that Burger would hold up a decision just because he disliked the result, he could do nothing without confronting the Chief, and he was not yet ready for that. In fact, Powell was determined to bend over backward to maintain good personal relations with all the other Justices. Burger finally let the case be announced.

Early in the term, Douglas had sent a memo to White suggesting that the Justices confine themselves to the simple and traditional phrase, "Please join me," when they notified a colleague of their willingness to vote for his opinion. Douglas had found the effusive praise in some recent memos distasteful. But Powell knew they all had their pride. In a December 4 join memo to Brennan's opinion on the Regional Railroad Reorganization Act cases, Powell dictated:

> DEAR BILL, Mindful of the reasons advanced by Bill Douglas in his letter to Byron, I reluctantly limit my comments on your fine opinion to "Please Join Me." Perhaps Bill [Douglas] will not mind if I add that I also admire his fine dissenting opinion. Sincerely, LEWIS.

Powell's clerks surmised that "Lew" wanted to have it both ways: the majority opinion and the dissent were both "fine." It seemed to be his way of saying that the dispute was not personal, but only a matter of different legal reasoning.

Powell's effort to build ties with his colleagues seemed to pay off when he was assigned to write a group of border search cases (*U.S. v. Brignoni-Ponce; U.S. v. Ortiz;* and *Bowen v. U.S.*). Over a long lunch with Rehnquist, Powell became well aware that his opinion was not Rehnquist's natural position, but that Rehnquist had decided to go along to give Powell a solid majority. Powell really appreciated this "team playing." He often praised Rehnquist's flexibility.

Brennan was disturbed that Powell seemed indifferent to the Warren Court tradition of protecting low-income and minority groups. For over a decade, activist lawyers had been using the federal courts to attack social inequities that they could rarely address in the state courts or through the political process. Poor people had a nearly impossible time proving in federal court that a specific financial loss was caused by state or local government action. So, with the Warren Court's blessing, lawyers brought an increasing number of class actions that alleged violations of basic constitutional rights of entire groups without having to establish any one specific financial damage; all were damaged.

In one case (*Warth v. Seldin*) civil rights activists in Rochester, New York, had challenged a nearby suburb's zoning law. The ordinance required all homes to be single-family units on large lots, in effect barring low-income minorities. The challengers sued to overturn the ordinance as discriminatory. Two lower courts had denied them standing and refused to hold a hearing on their claims. Powell was assigned the majority opinion for his fellow Nixon appointees and Stewart, who agreed with the lower courts that the activists didn't have standing to sue in federal court. His opinion said the challengers had failed to allege and prove that they could not buy a particular residence; the case was hypothetical; the alleged injuries were intangible and speculative.

Powell's clerks were upset. They believed the case had less to do with fine legal definitions of standing than with something more basic. "My daughter can't find a decent place to live in Richmond any more," Powell said in response to their arguments. His instinct was to protect neighborhoods, and zoning was the traditional method.

As Stewart explained it to his clerks, the case called for a value judgment, not a legal one. The challengers were asking the courts ultimately to rule on economic differences that kept low-income minorities from living near affluent whites. "What they are really asking us to do is to overrule the capitalist system," Stewart said.

Powell's and Stewart's clerks tried to persuade their Justices to break from what one clerk called the "suburban majority" of the Nixon appointees and Stewart who seemed obsessed with protecting property rights. Neither would budge. Powell's clerks were particularly dismayed. They would have expected Rehnquist to deny disadvantaged minorities an opportunity to be heard in federal court, but not Powell. They agreed with Brennan, who had written in dissent that the whole issue of standing—keeping the case from being argued in court—was a ruse for the conservatives to avoid expressing their real feelings. Powell had written that the poor minorities were victims, not of the zoning law, but of the economics of the housing market, something the courts could do nothing about.

Brennan's dissent argued that Powell was using legal technicalities to prevent the disenfranchised groups from pressing their claims. And there was a Catch 22. In order to have the standing to sue, you had to have the money to begin building a low-income housing project and be willing to go to the inconvenience of filing a plan so the local zoning board could reject it. In order for the poor to sue, they had to be rich. Brennan found the whole idea absurd and deceitful. It was the ordinance being challenged—not neutral economic factors—that insured that the housing market would never change. Even worse, Powell's opinion barred virtually everyone else from raising a claim on behalf of the poor. But Brennan couldn't break a single vote away from the majority.

Brennan saw this as an extension of a disastrous trend. The lower courts would get the message that the poor must prove precisely how they were affected before they would even have standing to bring suit in federal court. The Court would no longer be the final protector of rights, the guarantor of fair play.

With Douglas in and out of the hospital, the term's main cases continued to back up. There were many discussions at conference about what to do. Cases would be heard and decided, Douglas would participate and vote as he was able, the conference decided.* But there was a point at which the welfare, prestige and authority of the Court might come into play. As it became increasingly obvious that Douglas was physically and mentally disabled, a consensus began to develop. They would hold up on any 5-to-4 decisions that had Douglas in the majority to see if someone in the minority would be willing to switch and make it 6 to 3. If that did not happen, those 5-to-4 cases would be treated as if they were 4-to-4 ties, and they would be put over for reargument the next term.

This strategy had the practical effect of nullifying Douglas's vote. It would be counted only when it did not matter. Douglas would not be allowed to affect the outcome of a single case. But uneasy as they were over taking this step, the Justices felt that it was necessary to protect the long-range interests of the Court. Douglas was

---

* Normally, during indefinite illnesses Justices did not try to participate in cases argued while they were gone. Douglas himself had not participated in many of the 1949 term cases when he suffered his horseback riding accident.

almost certainly on the way out, and each of them realized that Gerald Ford was not likely to replace him with another liberal. If the new Justice was a conservative, all the recent 5-to-4 votes might easily go the other way. They were all horrified at the prospect of half a dozen major decisions being reversed in a year's time. The Court would appear to be a political institution, its decision less rooted in the law than in the personalities and politics of the individual Justices.

The Justices also decided that they would no longer permit Douglas to be the fourth vote to grant cert. The decision to cut Douglas out was informal, and it was treated as a deep family secret. But Burger nevertheless worried; if anyone ever learned about it, he would be remembered as the Chief who had let the conference take away a sick Justice's vote. To avoid the problem, Brennan several times cast his own vote as the fifth (provided he was not already one of the four) when Douglas indicated from the hospital that he wanted the Court to hear a certain case. Burger went one day to see Brennan to discuss the situation. "You are Douglas's best friend," Burger said. "Will you speak to him about resigning for the sake of the Court and his own health?"

Brennan was amazed. Douglas would never take that from anyone, including Brennan, he told the Chief. Douglas would get out of his bed and kick him out of the room.

But someone had to do it, the Chief said. Something had to be done.

Brennan explained that he did not have that type of relationship with Douglas. Douglas was very much his senior. When Brennan had come to the court, Douglas had already been there eighteen years. If anyone had that sort of influence with Douglas—and it was by no means clear that anyone did—it would be Abe Fortas or Clark Clifford. Perhaps the Chief should speak with them.

Afterward, Brennan related the story of Burger's visit to his clerks; he cited it as a further demonstration of the Chief's stupidity and insensitivity. The Chief had served nearly six full terms with Douglas. He should know that no one pushed Douglas around. Any encouragement or advice often had the opposite effect. And Douglas's illness had made him even more recalcitrant and unreachable. Moreover, it was the Chief who was holding up the Court with his slow votes, late circulations and delayed joins.

Brennan found it painful to visit Douglas in the hospital. Once Brennan had asked Douglas about his visitors.

Douglas had trouble articulating the name, but he said a "black man" had come to see him.

Who? Brennan asked.

A black man, Douglas said, straining to get the words out clearly. The black man that was on the Court with them.

My God, wondered Brennan, had Douglas forgotten Marshall's name? "Oh, you mean TM?" Brennan asked.

No, said Douglas impatiently, a "black man" and he spells his name with a "u."

Blackmun, Brennan realized. You mean Harry Blackmun.

Yes, Douglas replied.

Brennan left, saddened beyond belief.

Douglas realized after months at Walter Reed Hospital that he was not making much progress; he decided that he wanted specialized treatment. After investigating several hospitals, he settled on New York University Medical Center and its famed Rusk Institute of Rehabilitation Medicine, known for its successes in rehabilitating stroke victims. But he would not go until he finished one piece of business at the Court.

On Monday, April 21, Douglas was wheeled to the bench to hear oral argument. The case was *Fowler v. North Carolina*, the only death penalty case the Court had scheduled for the term. His presence there, straight out from the hospital, heightened an already electric atmosphere. The fact that the Court's leading liberal had dragged himself from his hospital bed was of enormous symbolic value to the foes of capital punishment. In the nearly three years since the 1972 decision, thirty-one states had passed laws restoring the death penalty. Two hundred fifty-three people in twenty-three states had been sentenced to death and were on death row awaiting the Court's decision.

Douglas sat through the ninety-minute session without asking a question. Then he returned to Walter Reed and left for the Rusk Institute the next morning. When he missed the death penalty conference, the other Justices, although avoiding a formal vote, were deadlocked 4 to 4. They finally decided that the case should be put over for reargument the next term.

By May 11, less than two months from the end of term, the Court had decided only half its cases. Douglas was holding things up. But there was one case (O'Connor v. Donaldson) that the Court could decide. It was the biggest of the term, as far as Burger was concerned. The case provided an opportunity to settle an old score with his archenemy, David Bazelon. In the 1960s, on the Court of Appeals, one of the bitterest Burger-Bazelon feuds had been waged over the application of psychiatry to criminal law. For years, in memos and in published opinions with Burger usually in dissent, the two judges had battled over the handling of insanity pleas in criminal cases.

Bazelon, who had at first taken a broad view of mental illness as a defense in criminal cases, later partially recanted. But Burger's triumph ended there. Bazelon had remained determined to free as many involuntarily confined mental patients ("those nuts," as Burger called them privately) as could safely be released.*

One of Bazelon's worst opinions in Burger's view, was a 1966 case (Rouse v. Cameron) in which he became the first appellate judge to suggest that civilly committed mental patients had a "right to treatment"—that the government, when holding people involuntarily, had an obligation to provide some kind of psychiatric care. Burger thought that this was dangerous nonsense, judicial activism at its worst. But Bazelon's decision had spurred a growing effort to

---

* In one appeals court case (Lake v. Cameron) in 1966, Bazelon suggested that a senile, sixty-year-old woman be released from the notorious St. Elizabeth's mental hospital in Washington, D.C. He wrote that the woman might be given an identification tag, so that if she were found wandering in the streets of Washington she could be returned to her home.

"This city is hardly a safe place for able-bodied men," Burger retorted in a harsh dissent mocking Bazelon's majority opinion. If "she should be allowed to wander again, all of her problems might well be rendered moot either by natural causes or violence."

establish such a right to treatment. It had not yet been ruled on by the Supreme Court. But in the fall of 1974, the Chief and one of his clerks spotted a cert petition that provided a test of the issue.

Kenneth Donaldson, a former carpenter, had been involuntarily confined in a Florida mental institution for fifteen years until his release in 1971. Alleging that his constitutional rights had been violated, Donaldson had sued the doctors under the civil rights statutes and had won $38,500 in damages. More incredible to the Chief was that on appeal the Fifth Circuit not only had upheld the damages but also had written a sweeping opinion that said there was a "right to treatment" and firmly established a constitutional basis for it. Quoting extensively from Bazelon, the Fifth Circuit opinion was another of those omnibus opinions that established new rights the Chief was unable to find in his copy of the Constitution. It was another new legal fiction created out of the Fourteenth Amendment.

The Chief had little use for the groups who were supporting Donaldson's claim—a collection of do-good organizations headed by the Mental Health Law Project. He looked forward to reversing this Fifth Circuit decision. It would be a substantial victory over a number of old opponents.

From the day the Court agreed to take the *Donaldson* case, Powell's clerk Joel Klein, who had worked at the Mental Health Law Project before coming to the Court, was a man with a mission. Klein felt the Court should uphold Donaldson's claim. Klein gathered the academic, medical and legal literature on the subject of right to treatment, including thirty law review articles, and saw to it that they got wide circulation within the Court. He missed no opportunity to drum up sympathy for Donaldson—whom, he told other clerks, he knew personally—and for the mentally ill in general. Donaldson was one of society's true victims, he said. The whole absurd system of civil commitment could be seen in this case. It was a classic instance of warehousing people who were thought to be mentally ill.

In 1957, when Donaldson was forty-eight years old, his parents had him declared incompetent because they thought he had a "persecution complex" and exhibited signs of "paranoid delusions." The judge said Donaldson would be back from the mental institution in "a few weeks." He had stayed there, a prisoner of the state, for nearly fifteen years. Although he was not dangerous to himself or others, Donaldson was kept in a ward where a third of the inmates were criminals. During the first ten years of confinement, he regularly requested both grounds privileges and occupational therapy. Both were denied.

Donaldson's attending physician and chief tormentor was Dr. J. B. O'Connor. O'Connor had become clinical director and finally superintendent at the Florida State Hospital at Chattahoochee during the years of Donaldson's confinement there. O'Connor had blocked efforts by a Minnesota halfway house and by a college friend of Donaldson's to obtain his release. The Supreme Court had denied review of Donaldson's previous appeals for freedom in 1960, 1962, 1968 and 1970.

Bruce J. Ennis, Jr., Donaldson's A.C.L.U. lawyer, didn't hold out much hope for the case. But Ennis was joined in the appeal by one of Stewart's former clerks from the 1971–72 term, Benjamin W. Heineman, Jr., who was working at the Mental Health Law Project. Heineman helped Ennis develop his strategy. It looked as if the Chief, Rehnquist, and probably White, would be against them, since they were the most reluctant to put restrictions on state power or to intrude judicially on behalf of individual rights. Brennan, Marshall and Douglas were surely with them. Blackmun, who had written an opinion (*Jackson v. Indiana*) sympathetic to a right to treatment, seemed a likely vote.

Ennis presumed Klein was working on Powell, but Powell could not be counted as a vote. That left Stewart. Heineman, one of Stewart's favorite former clerks, was to provide a window on Stewart's thinking. They could argue that Donaldson had been the victim of cruel and unusual punishment, but Heineman said Stewart would be more comfortable with a specific argument that Donaldson had been deprived of a fundamental human right, the right to liberty. In round-the-clock marathon sessions for ten days, Ennis drafted sections and Heineman rewrote them with an eye on Stewart's vote. The brief was submitted on January 4, 1975.

Ennis took Heineman to the oral argument on January 15. He

wanted Stewart to know that the case meant a lot to his former clerk. Ennis went to the podium and began to stress that the case posed a "narrow" question. The Chief interrupted at once. Ennis was wrong; the right to treatment was in question. The trial judge had claimed there was such a right when he instructed the jury, and the jury had awarded damages on that basis. The Fifth Circuit Court of Appeals had then upheld this. Wasn't Ennis asking that the Court affirm the Fifth Circuit opinion?

Well, yes. But Ennis indicated that the Court did not have to go that far. Since Donaldson was not committed for any crime, he was needlessly deprived of a basic "right to liberty." If the Court decided only that, they need not deal with the broad right-to-treatment question.

But the record was "undisputed" on the fact that Donaldson had refused the offered treatment, Burger interjected.

Just the opposite, Ennis said. His client, a Christian Scientist, had said that he preferred not to have electric shock treatment, but he had accepted medication until it was terminated by a hospital doctor. "We've tried to show this is a narrow case and properly understood does not raise any novel rights," Ennis said in conclusion.

At conference later that week, the Chief argued that they must decide the right-to-treatment question. The Fifth Circuit opinion should be written out of existence; the Court should not allow this nonsense to continue floating around in the lower courts.

Since Douglas was gone, Brennan spoke next. The main question was the award of damages, and Donaldson should certainly win there. Being locked away for fifteen years was a Kafkaesque nightmare. Brennan was not overly worried about what theory was used.

Stewart too felt great sympathy for Donaldson. But the doctors were not necessarily the ones who should be held liable. He was for reversing the award of damages against the doctors.

White was in accord with the Chief that the right of a mental patient to have treatment was the central issue. White said that he too felt there was no such right. Moreover, even if there were such a right, the doctors in this case had no way of knowing that it existed.

He was greatly sympathetic to Donaldson, but saw no case against the doctors. Nonetheless, White wanted to limit the power of the state to confine nondangerous people for treatment. That was unconstitutional. Instead of creating a new right for patients, the Court should let the states know they had no right to confine nondangerous persons.

Marshall agreed with Brennan that Donaldson had been wronged and should get his damages. Blackmun was also in favor of the damages, but he was definitely not ready to buy a right to treatment. Powell too leaned toward affirming the damages award, but they had to identify a specific constitutional right that had been violated. Since he did not believe there was a right to treatment, the decision still needed a basis, and he hadn't found one. Rehnquist was for damages, but against a right to treatment.

When it came to assigning, Burger saw the essence of the case as the right-to-treatment question. The tally on his vote sheet showed five votes—White, Powell, Rehnquist, a shaky Blackmun and himself opposed to establishing it. There was also a majority for upholding the damages award—all but Stewart, White and himself—but the Chief thought a technical way could be found to write around that. The award for damages was hardly the issue. So Burger assigned the case to himself. He was sure that he could put together something that would satisfy everybody with the possible exception of Brennan and Marshall.

Brennan was astonished. It seemed that the Chief had missed the drift of the conference. The majority had upheld the damages award to Donaldson. The chief's intention was clearly to beat the right-to-treatment concept to a bloody pulp. No one at conference had agreed to that. Still, the conference had been so confused that Brennan thought there was little he could do. His hands were tied until the Chief's opinion circulated.

The Chief designated a clerk to start work on a draft. The research must be particularly thorough. Every possible argument, every case citation and reference should be used to counter the right to treatment. The lawyer for the doctors had made a good point. If the Court let the right stand, who would determine what was treatment? Or what was adequate treatment? Those questions would haunt the Court for years. The courts would soon have to manage mental hospitals as well as school districts.

The Chief's clerk worked for nearly three and a half months on the opinion, and Burger spent many hours honing it. Finally, in mid-May, when he circulated a twenty-page printed draft, it was greeted with great interest throughout the Court. The introduction stated that the Court had granted cert "to decide whether there is a Constitutional right to treatment. . . ." Burger rejected Donaldson's broad claim that he was unconstitutionally confined—"We need not and do not decide whether [Donaldson's] confinement comported with the Constitution in every respect."

Burger then moved quickly to assault the right-to-treatment doctrine. Traditionally, he wrote, the states had power to care for the mentally ill. The first mental hospitals "were concerned primarily with providing a more humane place of confinement." This was necessary because there was

> a large range of mental illness for which no known "cure" existed.
>
> It remains a stubborn fact that there are many forms of mental illness which are not understood, some which are untreatable in the sense that no effective therapy has yet been discovered for them, and that rates of "cure" are generally low.
>
> There can be little doubt that in the exercise of its police power a State may confine individuals solely to protect society from the dangers of significant antisocial acts or communicable disease.

Citing the classic British legal historian Sir William Blackstone, Burger said the states also had the power to act as "the general guardian of all infants, idiots and lunatics." To limit this state power would be to read our "private notions of public policy or public health into the Constitution."

Burger had tailored a section to satisfy the majority who wanted to give Donaldson the $38,500 without setting a precedent. In instructing the jury, the trial judge had said Donaldson had a constitutional right to treatment, and that without treatment there was no justification for continued confinement. It was a clearly erroneous instruction, but the doctor's attorneys had failed to object.

Under Rule 51 of the Federal Rules of Civil Procedure, the failure to object during trial was fatal. Thus, the improper instructions would have to stand. Donaldson would get his $38,500, but the opinion would make it clear that there was no right to treatment, and no precedent would be set for damages in such cases.

Throughout most of the Court this section of the Chief's draft was read with a mixture of laughter and dismay. Who had ever heard of the Supreme Court deciding a major constitutional case on Rule 51? Besides, an award of damages had no basis unless there was some specific constitutional violation.

Since Stewart was away that day, a few clerks gathered in his chambers to discuss the case. Within an hour, all the chambers except the Chief's and Rehnquist's were represented. The Chief was trying to screw the mentally ill, the clerks feared, and he just might succeed. With about fifty cases still to be resolved before the term closed in six weeks, the Justices would be busy with their own work. Burger might push this one through in the last-minute crush.

This was a fascist opinion, Joel Klein argued. The Chief, with his law-and-order mentality, had gone wild—anything to protect society, and to hell with individual rights. By stating that people could be confined for "significant antisocial acts," the Chief was up to something sinister. The others did not buy all of Klein's argument, but they thought something had to be done. They would have to mobilize. The central point on which the Justices would agree was that the Chief's draft did not reflect the conference discussion or, for that matter, the vote.

The first step was to insure that no Justice impulsively signed onto the Chief's draft. Burger had to be denied any momentum. One join and a bandwagon could follow. Next, a Justice would have to write a dissent to turn the Court around and create a majority for another point of view. The clerks felt strongly that a Court opinion had to emerge that gave mental patients constitutionally protected rights. Since few such cases were decided by the Court, this opinion would have an impact far beyond this one case. Ideally, someone from the center—Powell, Stewart, perhaps White—should write the opinion. Blackmun was also a possibility.

Since White and Blackmun were not prepared to establish such a right, the clerks hoped that Powell or Stewart would be willing to write it. Powell, however, had already had several bruising battles with the Chief. Klein thought his boss would probably join a dissent but would be reluctant to lead a charge. On the other hand, Stewart had suffered through a series of poor assignments from the Chief and had recently been making more than the usual number of pointed anti-Chief comments. His clerks felt he might be ready for battle.

The Stewart clerks agreed to make a strong case to their boss for an alternative opinion.

Klein went to try out the clerks' strategy on Brennan. It was important that Brennan not leap into the fray with a stinging dissent. Brennan's dissents rarely won the support of the Justices in the center. Clerks called it "killing it from the left." Brennan approved of the clerks' strategy and said he would not write anything. He would also try to keep Marshall and Douglas from writing at this point.

When Stewart returned to his chambers, his clerks were waiting to inform him that the Chief's circulation on *Donaldson* had arrived.

How does it look? Stewart asked.

"Disaster," one clerk replied. It was worse than expected.

Stewart took a copy. He was weary when he finished. It was, as usual, an untamed piece of work. Burger was straining to decide issues that didn't have to be resolved in this case, using it to write a treatise on law and psychiatry that would preclude the courts from a role in protecting those confined in mental institutions. The Chief had either misinterpreted or intentionally ignored the conference majority. There was a majority opposed to establishing, as the Fifth Circuit had done, a broad right to treatment, but there was certainly no majority ready to deny all protections for the mentally ill.

Stewart told his clerks that he agreed with them. Some response was necessary.

"You have to do this," one of Stewart's clerks said. His clerks told him the Chief's draft did not seem to have any backers. Stewart's clerks were his first constituency. Their appeals to use his place and his influence on the Court moved him more often than their legal arguments. He said that he would try.

Stewart knew who counted. Since the three liberals would be no problem, Stewart went first to see White. He asked White if he had seen the Chief's draft yet.

"No," White said.

"Well, you better sit down before you do," Stewart said.

White agreed that the Chief's draft was unacceptable. White had been the only Justice other than the Chief and Stewart to oppose the $38,500 damage award, and he distrusted psychiatry as much as the Chief did, but locking up a person like Donaldson without good reason was repugnant, and the Court should clearly say so.

Stewart told White he was going to try a dissent.

White was noncommittal, but he emphasized that he did not want to uphold the damage award.

As was his practice, Stewart sent a short memo to the other Justices letting them know he would soon circulate a dissent. Stewart considered the memo a courtesy, but it would also discourage the others from signing onto the Chief's opinion before they saw his dissent.

The Chief was surprised when he received the memo. He did not think his position had been uncompromising. Why didn't Stewart first try to offer some suggestions? Why was he leaping in with a dissent? It just didn't make sense.

Stewart told his clerks that he wanted his dissent kept short. The key was simplicity. Since he did not want to write any new rules, one possibility struck him almost immediately. The Chief referred only to the "right to treatment." But Donaldson's lawyers had argued that he had "a right to be restored to liberty by treatment or else by release." This suggested a simpler focus; the issue was not treatment, but something more fundamental: liberty.

A ruling could be narrowly confined to Donaldson and others like him, persons who were not dangerous to others or to themselves and who were capable of surviving in society by themselves or with the help of friends or family. Such a person had a right to one thing—not treatment, but liberty. Moreover, ensuring liberty was the Court's traditional business.

Stewart's clerks went to work gleefully, buttressing the opinion with everything they could find favorable to Donaldson. Much of this had been suggested by Donaldson's lawyers, Ennis and Heineman. The dissent was laced with references to the "narrow" issue before the Court. It focused on "release," the liberty question, and referred to treatment only in a footnote. "A finding of 'mental illness,'" it stated, "cannot justify the extinguishment of personal liberty."

Yet, with all their care, Stewart's clerks could not resist addressing the Chief's apparent concern with those who are guilty of "significant antisocial acts," whatever that might mean. Their final section read:

> May the State fence in the harmless mentally ill solely to save its citizens from exposure to those whose ways are different? One might as well ask if the State, to avoid public unease, could incarcerate all who are physically handicapped or socially eccentric. Mere public intolerance or animosity cannot constitutionally justify the deprivation of a person's physical liberty.

The opinion would not grant a right to treatment, but the language would show the Court's sensitivity to the interests of those confined in mental institutions. It could not help but have a positive psychological impact in the field of mental health. That left only the question of damages.

Stewart decided the best solution was to send the case back to the lower court and let it reconsider the award of damages. The clerks thought it likely that the lower court would again award damages, but at least there would be no sweeping precedent. This solution could also satisfy White and Stewart—who opposed damages—as well as those who favored damages.

As the Stewart clerks finished the draft, Klein reviewed it to be sure there was nothing offensive to Powell. The Stewart clerks had tried to give some general definition to mental illness. Klein was pretty sure that Powell would not buy an attempt to define such a complex term, so the definition was discarded.

When Stewart had edited the draft, a typed version was photo-copied for Brennan, Marshall, Douglas and Blackmun. Sections of the tentative draft were shown to clerks in the chambers of White, Powell and Rehnquist. Since Stewart's opinion—only ten pages long, and seven of them devoted to a recitation of facts—broke so little legal ground, it appeared likely to receive broad support.

Powell was troubled. He did not like the Chief's *Donaldson* draft. All term, however, it seemed that he had been challenging Burger. The Chief's response had taken an ugly turn. In February, Powell had circulated a significant labor opinion (*Connell Con-struction Company v. Plumbers & Steamfitters Local Union #100*) for a five-man majority including the Chief. Powell's draft broad-ened the government's power to use federal antitrust restrictions against unions, and immediately drew joins from the other mem-bers of the majority except the Chief. Since Stewart's dissent had four votes, Powell was anxious to have the Chief's formal join memo, the crucial fifth vote. Burger was certain to join, Powell felt, because the opinion had an anti-union flavor. At a conference in April, Powell tried to get Burger to act. "All the votes in *Connell* are in except yours, Chief," Powell said.

The Chief stared at Powell and moved on to the next item of business.

Powell's clerk on the case then made some minor typographical changes in the draft and had it reprinted and recirculated. That way a new draft would circulate and remind Burger that the case was awaiting only his vote.

The Chief sent back a memo requesting that something men-tioned in a footnote be moved to the text.

Powell did it at once, sure that the Chief's vote could not be far behind. Another week passed. At the next conference, Powell men-tioned the *Connell* case; only the Chief's vote remained to be counted.

Burger acted as if he hadn't heard.

Powell concluded sadly that the Chief was pressuring him. Burger knew that Powell held a key vote in a number of other cases, including *Donaldson*. It was just short of blackmail. But

Powell decided that he might be overreacting. At the next conference, he again raised the Connell case.

"I'm thinking," Burger replied.

Powell had rarely been so stymied. Some things were clear. The Chief's attitude toward unions was never in doubt. Powell's clerk jokingly suggested that they send another copy of the draft to the Chief with the postscript: "P.S. Chief, the unions lose." Powell was positive that Burger could have no real objections to his draft. But there had been about half a dozen conferences now.

In late May, the Chief finally sent his join. Powell was relieved, but the experience left a sour taste. Perhaps he had been wrong, but he could find no way to get over his suspicions.

Now, on the *Donaldson* case, Powell was relieved that it was Stewart who had taken on the Chief. He liked Stewart's draft a lot better; it was narrow, short and direct. Still he wanted to see what the others did.

After the Chief's circulation and Stewart's dissent, Klein conducted a campaign against the Chief's approach, giving every phrase and sentence the worst possible interpretation, particularly the "antisocial acts" language. The debate turned not on what the Chief had said or intended, but on what Klein and some other clerks said it might mean. The isolation of the Chief and his clerks from the flow of Court gossip left the negative interpretation unrebutted, yet Klein was still unable to persuade Powell to vote for Stewart's draft.

Meanwhile, Burger was frustrated. His draft had been in circulation for two weeks, and he had not received a single join. The Chief tried to nudge Blackmun. "I think I'm going to get my Court on the case," the Chief told him. Blackmun knew differently. The Chief tried White and Powell, but got nowhere. He had expected at least Rehnquist to join right away. Maybe the join memo had been lost in the interoffice mail. A clerk checked. It hadn't. The Chief sounded out Rehnquist, who replied that he had a real problem with what had been done to Donaldson.

Now, the Chief found Stewart's dissent in his mail. And it was no ordinary dissent. Since seven of the ten pages were facts, it was clear that Stewart was trying to steal the opinion. It was a clever effort, avoiding the difficult issue of a right to treatment. Such a narrow opinion, the Chief feared, would appeal to Blackmun and Powell.

The case had simply come to the Court in an unfortunate form, Burger reasoned. The lawyers for the doctors had done a terrible job. The Chief wanted to respond to Stewart's dissent, but he had to attend a judicial conference in Williamsburg, Virginia. He complained there about some of the attorneys who appeared before the Supreme Court. "The quality is far below what it could be," he told a discussion panel. Bazelon too was on the panel, and he praised the Chief Justice for speaking up about attorney incompetence. Bazelon agreed that it was "the most serious threat to the administration of justice." Privately, Bazelon thought the most serious threat to justice was probably Burger.

In Washington the next day, June 4, the Chief tried to figure out how to gather some votes for his draft. About all he could do was try to revive the debate and let everyone know that he was still waiting. In a short memo, he proposed a new footnote to his draft and stated his view of the conference's intention on right to treatment. "I believe a majority were of the view that no such right existed."

There was still no response the next day. Burger was angry now. The right-to-treatment issue could not be left up in the air. He decided to send a sharper memo. Any opinion without a firm assertion that no such right exists, he wrote, would be a serious mistake. Anything less "will bring us quite a volume of business as 'jackleg' lawyers begin to look for new fields to conquer. The Constitutional issue is fairly presented and ought to be met."

Stewart thought Burger's "jackleg lawyers" memo was a new low. He suspected that *jackleg,* an archaic word meaning "unscrupulous," was aimed at Heineman, his former clerk. Stewart decided, however, to respond indirectly. He circulated some revisions to his "dissent" along with a short memo saying that in the area of mental illness, "the Court should proceed cautiously and deliberately. . . . The Court of Appeals used the case as a vehicle for an expansive essay on the constitutional law on civil commitment. This was unnecessary, and perhaps we should say so. But surely we should not make the same mistake."

*   *   *

On Monday, June 9, Burger sent around a new, three-page memo. He wanted mainly to insure that the Fifth Circuit opinion was "washed out." "I am perfectly willing to consider alternatives so long as they make clear that the Court of Appeals' opinion is not to be considered precedent or the law of this case," Burger said.

Stewart heard a faint cry of desperation in the final sentence. The Chief was close to beaten. He had gone from insisting on a strong statement against a right to treatment to a willingness to accept "alternatives." It reminded Stewart of the Nixon tapes case. This time, however, the Chief was not going to expropriate his work. Stewart figured this was now his opinion.

Stewart was perfectly willing to state that the Fifth Circuit opinion was not to be considered the law. He drafted a short memo proposing an additional footnote to his opinion.

On June 10, White announced in a long memo his intention to vote with Stewart. First, he had a few kind words for the Chief's draft; the Chief's concerns were not altogether unreasonable. He wished Stewart's draft had gone farther. "I would thus prefer to decide one of the questions Potter leaves open, namely, whether a State may confine a nondangerous person solely for therapy. My vote at the Conference was that the state may not do so. Otherwise, I shall remain where Brother Stewart has left me. B.R.W."

With White's memo and sure joins from Brennan and Marshall, the clerks turned to the only remaining problem: how to enable Powell to join without being the fifth and deciding vote. Klein had finally concluded that Powell did not want to be the one to tip the balance. That would be, for this term, one slap too many at the Chief. The logistics received an extraordinary amount of attention, but in the end the solution proved easy. Join memos from White, Douglas and Blackmun entered the interoffice mail system at about the same time as Powell's. So none of the Justices could be identified as the fifth and deciding vote. The dissent draft now had seven votes. Only Rehnquist had not yet voted.

In Powell's chambers the clerks broke out the liquor. The case had been snatched right out from under the Chief. Stewart's dissent would surely become a majority opinion for the Court.

Brennan, however, was still wary. Stewart had the votes, but there was no telling what the Chief might try. He might pull some stunt like reassigning the case to someone else. Conceivably, as a last-ditch effort, he could try to hold it over for reargument. It would be prudent to move fast. As Douglas was now the senior Justice in the majority, Brennan decided, Douglas should make a reassignment. Brennan called him at the Rusk Institute in New York and Douglas quickly agreed to reassign to Stewart.

Douglas's clerks wanted to be sure that Douglas's action would not be questioned. At a lunch with Stewart a few days earlier, Stewart had started talking about the last year of Woodrow Wilson's presidency. Wilson was physically and mentally incapacitated, Stewart had said, and Wilson's wife had become a surrogate President. She would visit the President and emerge with a series of orders. "The President wants this, and the President wants that." No one could be certain whether the desires were the President's or Mrs. Wilson's.

Douglas's clerks pondered Stewart's message. Did he suspect them of usurping? Was he warning them to avoid the temptation? It had all been very friendly. They decided to act cautiously on the *Donaldson* reassignment memo. They had the memo typed, signed by a clerk and sent around, but they followed immediately with a memo to Douglas securing his written authorization.

Meanwhile, the Chief retreated to his office. He had few options left. There was only one thing that would allow him a semblance of dignity. Burger picked up the phone and called Stewart. "Potter, it looks like you clearly have the votes," he said graciously. Of course, Stewart should go ahead and change his dissent to a majority opinion.

Burger immediately sent out a memo telling the conference that Stewart was writing for the majority. The reassignment memos from Douglas and Burger crossed in the mail. There was no dispute.

For the Chief, the battle was over and lost. He had maintained his poise, but when one of his clerks came in, he could hold it in no longer. What had happened? he asked, stalking about his office.

Just what the hell was going on? A major defeat on a major case, and to Potter Stewart of all people?

The clerk agreed with the Chief that his opinion had been fine, had been excellent in every respect.

It made no sense. His colleagues were out to embarrass him, Burger raged. They wanted to hurt the office he held. The clerk had never seen the Chief so angry.

His opinion, the Chief said, had been an important piece of sound legal work. When he got right down to it, the movement against him had started right after he had circulated his first draft nearly a month before. His draft might have proved unpopular, but it said what needed saying. The others had neither the foresight nor the courage to join him. Stewart's draft was not all that bad. But it just did not do enough to put to rest forever the notion of the right to treatment. The question now was how to salvage the most from a bad situation. Was a reasoned dissent in order?

The Chief looked over his twenty-one-page draft. It represented so much work; if he could use it, he had a chance to get something into the law books on the right-to-treatment issue. The more the Chief examined Stewart's majority, the more he saw an opportunity. To win his majority, Stewart had said nothing. He had written bland and evasive nonsense.

A dissent would be quickly forgotten, but a strong concurrence, addressing the issue Stewart had dodged, could have a pronounced practical effect on the lower courts. The right-to-treatment concept needed to be choked off. If it were well done, a concurrence that took no issue with the majority opinion, would appear, but for technical reasons, to have commanded the others' votes.

So the Chief began. "Although I join the Court's opinion and judgment in this case, it seems to me that several factors merit more emphasis than it gives them." His twenty-one pages were easily juggled and trimmed, his attack on the Fifth Circuit opinion sharpened, and the "significant antisocial acts" passage retained.

The Chief's final version was about half as long as the original. It was, in his view, an effective deterrent to those who might try to press new rights for mental patients. His clerk pointed out that the concurrence would look better if no one else joined. If Rehnquist signed on, it would look like a right-wing hatchet job. Standing alone, the concurrence seemed like an important message from the Chief Justice. The Chief got his wish. Rehnquist, still concerned about Donaldson's fate, decided that Stewart's approach was reasonable and gave Donaldson a fair chance to get his damage award. He was the last Justice to join the Stewart opinion.

The conference decided to announce the decision on Thursday, June 26, the next-to-last decision day before the Court was to adjourn for summer recess. Burger announced in court that Stewart would deliver the decision in *O'Connor v. Donaldson*. Stewart flicked on his reading light and turned his head toward the Chief. For a tense moment, the two men looked at each other sternly across Douglas's empty chair. Only the Justices and the clerks realized the significance. Stewart then turned to his papers. With his glasses on, in his familiar hunched pose, he read. The Chief gazed distractedly around the courtroom and toyed with his glasses.

For Stewart, it was bittersweet. It was a victory, but not the kind he had imagined when he came to the Court seventeen years ago. He had merely put out a small brush fire.

Stewart realized the risk he had run taking this case from the Chief. A few days earlier, the Chief had done something that revealed the depth of his anger.

In a case called *U.S. v. American Building Maintenance Industries*, Stewart had circulated a pro-business majority draft that would limit application of the federal antitrust laws. He had received five votes at conference, including the Chief's, and Burger had assigned the case to him. Stewart had gotten joins from all in the majority except the Chief.

White had circulated a one-sentence statement saying that, although he agreed with the result and joined part of Stewart's opinion, he was dissenting from the last part of it. Then, right after it became clear that Stewart was going to win on *Donaldson*, Burger circulated a memo saying he had rethought his position in *American Building Maintenance* and was going to join White. It was incredible to the other Justices. White had written one sentence; there was really nothing to join. And White and the Chief rarely agreed on antitrust cases.

White howled with laughter at the Chief's memo. Stewart and he both concluded that it was revenge for the *Donaldson* case. The Chief was switching from a basic position. But hilarious as it might be, White figured he had better expand his one-sentence statement. If the Chief was serious, it might be a chance to get him on record for stiffer antitrust enforcement. White added three more sentences.

Stewart was finally rescued by Rehnquist, who went to Burger and urged him to stick with the Stewart majority. Burger sent a memo saying he had once again reconsidered, and was joining Stewart's majority.

As the end of the term drew near, the last of the outstanding majority opinions began circulating. Powell had written three out of a series of four cases involving border searches. Although Rehnquist did not fully subscribe to Powell's approach, he provided a fifth vote so that Powell would have a majority.

The Chief had assigned the fourth border search case (*U.S. v. Peltier*) to Rehnquist. The conference had treated it as simply a question of whether to apply the Court's two-year-old decision (*Almeida-Sanchez v. U.S.*) retroactively. That decision had prohibited roving border patrol searches for illegal aliens without a warrant.

The conference had voted 5 to 4 that border patrol agents should not be held responsible for a standard that was not in force at the time of search. The majority felt it would be silly to exclude as evidence the 270 pounds of marijuana the agents had found, just because the search was later declared technically illegal.

When Rehnquist's draft came around there was virtually no comment or reaction to the routine retroactivity question. Then a Douglas clerk noticed an unusual twist of logic and several seemingly inappropriate citations. After reading these other cases, he came to an astounding realization. Rehnquist was drastically changing the entire exclusionary rule without explicitly saying so. Rehnquist held that evidence could only be excluded from prosecutions when the police used methods they knew to be illegal.

Since Douglas was in the hospital, the clerk took his finding to Brennan. Brennan was incredulous. The clear consensus of the conference had been to decide only the question of retroactivity. Here was an underhanded attempt to slip through a major policy shift. And Brennan was even more aggravated when he heard through the clerk grapevine that White had also been an accomplice.

Incensed at the subterfuge, Brennan instructed one of his clerks to prepare a no-holds-barred dissent pointing out the duplicity.

Powell and Blackmun immediately held up their join memos. In an effort to get things back on track, Burger sent a series of notes to them urging them to join.

Rehnquist finally agreed to drop several of the citations, but retained other references that tended to undermine the exclusionary rule.

In return Brennan dropped several of his own specific sections accusing Rehnquist of duplicity. But he retained others. " . . . if the vague contours outlined today are filled in as I fear they will be, [the Rehnquist opinion] forecasts the complete demise of the exclusionary rule . . . ," Brennan's dissent said. "This business of slow strangulation of the rule, with no opportunity afforded parties most concerned to be heard, would be indefensible in any circumstances. But to attempt covertly the erosion of an important principle over 61 years in the making . . . clearly demeans the adjudicatory function, and the institutional integrity of this Court."

Brennan told his own clerks and those from Douglas and Marshall's chambers to recheck the last few Rehnquist opinions for similarly disguised tricks. They found none. Brennan solemnly resolved to be more vigilant.

The Court adjourned June 30 with the announcement of the last cases.

The most important piece of unsettled business was William O. Douglas, who was still at the Rusk Institute. Despite four hours of vigorous daily exercise to strengthen his left side, after two months Douglas was able to take only a few steps with assistance. His left arm remained in bad shape.

The doctors asked Douglas not to leave the rehabilitation center. It was to no avail. He went shopping at Abercrombie and Fitch, dined at the Drake, Sardi's, and the Algonquin Hotel. He attended the fiftieth reunion of his Columbia Law School class, received visiting dignitaries and reporters, and completed the first volume of his memoirs. He decorated his room with "Save the Whale" posters sent him by an environmental group. Accepting an award from the Sierra Club, Douglas gave a halting fifteen-minute speech and then led the way to the hotel bar. Douglas supplemented his diet with homemade bread and peach jam sent to him by the Chief. Burger had attached a label to the jam reading "fortified," meaning he had added brandy.

It didn't take long for the doctors to realize that there was no way the rambunctious Justice would sit long without work. He was cantankerous with the hospital personnel. He borrowed the office of a medical school professor and at other times worked at the Foley Square Court House. Though he arranged to have his secretaries fly to New York on a rotating basis so he could keep up with Court business, Douglas worked only a few hours each day, because the rigorous therapy tired him out. Still on medication, he would get drowsy.

On July 11, Douglas had a visitor, the writer Sidney Zion, who asked him how his leg was progressing.

"I've been kicking forty-yard field goals with it in the exercise room," Douglas said. "Dr. Rusk wants me to call George Allen and sign up with the Redskins. They could use a field-goal kicker, and hell, if George Blanda can play, why not me?"

The visitor feigned astonishment. Although the oldest professional football player in the league, Blanda was nearly thirty years Douglas's junior.

"Yes, but you ought to see how I'm arching them," Douglas said, laughing.

The conversation turned serious. What about the future?

"There's no chance I'll retire," Douglas promised. "I'll be there in October positively."

1975 Term

1975 Term

On Thursday, July 24, the Chief went to New York to visit Douglas at the Rusk Institute. In a statement released through a hospital spokesman, Burger said he was "extremely pleased about the progress Justice Douglas has made."

Burger had actually reached a quite different conclusion: Douglas had to quit. The Chief told friends in Washington and at an A.B.A. gathering that the Court was "limping along" with a terrible backlog of cases because of Douglas's illness. There were already too many cases held over from the previous term.

On August 7, against the advice of friends, Douglas and Cathy left for Goose Prairie. They stayed there through August and early September. A radio telephone was installed in the house. In early September, Douglas decided to hear oral argument at the old Yakima Courthouse on an emergency request to prevent disclosure of grand-jury records. On his instructions, Douglas's son phoned a local newspaper to say that the Justice would be coming down the next morning. It was a showcase appearance to prove he could still function.

When he arrived in Yakima on Thursday morning, September 11, Douglas appeared tired and frail. Once he was lifted to the bench, the lawyers argued for about an hour. Douglas then announced that the Court would recess for lunch at 12:30. It was already 1 P.M.

After lunch, the lawyers finished their arguments. Douglas seemed to have understood, but he said nothing. The audience waited, puzzled, shifting in their seats. Occasionally Douglas shuffled papers, picked up his water glass, stared at the ceiling. Five minutes went by and then ten. After thirteen minutes, he broke the silence. He thanked the lawyers for their "spirited" and "helpful" argument. The spectators and the attorneys, relieved that Douglas had snapped back, awaited his decision. But Douglas began to talk about federalism. He rambled on, comparing the governments of the United States and Australia. Tension again began to rise in the courtroom. Finally, he paused and said he would issue the emergency stay. He turned to the winning attorney who had driven him to the court that morning. "I hope you will again come to Goose Prairie to visit us," Douglas said. "It is a lovely place with a salubrious climate. There are some who would like to change that, but most of us are pretty opposed."

Douglas then recessed the hearing. His public appearance had backfired. The news stories described a Justice who was clearly incapacitated.

Cathy Douglas finally decided to call Charles Reich, a former Yale professor, a former law clerk for Hugo Black, and the author of the best-selling book *The Greening of America*. She hoped that Reich, an outspoken libertarian and an old friend of Douglas, could convince him to resign. Reich said he would not dare come to Goose Prairie until Douglas invited him.

Later that day, Reich received a call from Douglas. "Charlie, can you get up here this afternoon?" he asked.

Reich said he would be there as quickly as possible. It was shortly after eight when he arrived at Douglas's cabin. Cathy greeted him. "Bill's lying down in the bedroom," she said.

Reich hesitated. The Douglas he knew would never receive a visitor in his bedroom. But Reich was told to go ahead. He entered the darkened room. He was shocked at Douglas's appearance. His face was drawn and gaunt. His son, Bill Jr., raised Douglas to a sitting position. Douglas's voice, always low, was so soft that Reich could barely hear him. They began to talk. One moment, Douglas was lucid, his old caustic, witty self. Then without warning, he broke off in midsentence, his eyes glazing. He reminisced, then suddenly returned to the present. His hands shook uncontrollably.

Several times an hour, Cathy or Bill Jr. took him out of the room because he was incontinent. Douglas summoned them like servants, with eye or hand signals. And every half-hour or so he needed to be transferred from the bed to a chair and then back.

"Bill, you must resign," Reich told him.

No, Douglas replied. "There will be no one on the Court who cares for blacks, Chicanos, defendants, and the environment." Even half functioning, he said, he would be better than no one. If he were to resign, Ford would name his replacement. That person would obviously be on the wrong side. Better to hang on, he said. "Even if I'm half dead, maybe it will make a difference about someone getting an education."

Reich responded softly. "Why do you want to be there with all those people you despise?" he asked. Staying on would eventually bring out many of the "jackals." "There are so many of your enemies lying in wait just to see you fold," Reich said. "Why spoil a perfect record? Isn't thirty-six years enough?"

Douglas did not answer.

Reich asked him whether he was going to try to hold on until a Democratic President could appoint his successor.

It didn't matter who was President, or from what party, Douglas said. Whoever it was would be someone who would not care. Powell, Black's replacement, was a Democrat. It was a dismal choice, a country-club lawyer to replace a populist. Douglas was sure that Burger wanted to get him off the Court. But he wouldn't leave. If he did, there would be no one on the Court to blow the whistle.

They went back and forth. Douglas skillfully parried each argument, though he slipped away at times, wondering aloud what he would do if he retired, whether he could do environmental work.

Reich paused. He became more explicit. Black had hung in stubbornly, but he knew when it was finally time to go. "You can't even sit on the bench," he said. What would he do if he were in pain during oral argument?

"I could leave the bench. I'll try it and see," Douglas responded. "The Court is my life. What will I do if I leave?" He paused. "I will be committing suicide."

Exasperated, Reich got tougher. "You can't even read. How are you going to decide cases?"

"I'll listen and see how the Chief votes and vote the other way," Douglas snapped.

It was nearly midnight when Reich left. He returned the following day to renew his plea. Cathy joined in. There were mail sacks of cert petitions in the cabin. "You haven't even read them," she said. Douglas said he had. "They aren't even opened," she rejoined. Douglas waved her off.

Reich could see it was useless.

On Saturday, September 27, Douglas said he would go back to Washington to see if he could handle it. They could not expect him to decide now. "I'm not quite ready to commit suicide," he told Reich.

Douglas's new clerks had no hint about what to expect when he returned. Reports from Yakima had not been encouraging.

Douglas arrived at the Court very late the morning of Monday, September 29, minutes before the week long cert conference to deal with the hundreds of petitions that had come in during the summer recess was scheduled to begin. He was unprepared, and he demanded that the files on every case, even those which were not going to be discussed, be brought with him to conference. His clerks loaded up ten carts and off they went, Douglas leading the procession in his wheelchair, his secretary pushing and spraying Lysol on the wheels to mask the odor from the bag for his incontinence.

The other Justices had been waiting in the conference room for sometime. Blackmun's jaw dropped when he saw the train of carts being pushed behind Douglas. The unpleasant odor filled the room. Douglas was wheeled to his place at the end of the conference table. His clerk opened one of his notebooks to the memo on the first case on the discuss list.

"We're not starting there," Brennan said, indicating the first case.

It took several moments for the clerks to locate the right notebook.

White seethed with impatience. He had expected Douglas to retire. Douglas's clerks shouldn't even be in the conference room. Finally, they located the case and left.

Burger was polite and helpful. Brennan sat beside Douglas, assisting him with the files and papers. The conference ended at 3:45, earlier than usual.

The rest of the week was torture for the other Justices. Douglas was in constant pain and barely had the energy to make his voice audible. He was wheeled in and out of conference, never staying the entire session, leaving his votes with Brennan to cast. Powell counted the number of times Douglas fell asleep. Brennan woke him gently when it came time to vote.

As always, Douglas demanded that the Court grant cert in about three times the number of cases there was time to hear. The tension grew. "Get him out of here," White once told Datcher, who had been summoned to wheel the sleeping Douglas from the conference room. Datcher was now more nurse than messenger.

On Monday, October 6, the first day of argument of the new term, everyone wondered how Douglas would cope. As the lawyers who were arguing the first case proceeded, Douglas's head sank to his chest. Because of his paralyzed hand, he had trouble ripping paper from his pad. He flapped the pad about with his good hand. Finally a messenger held the pad so that Douglas could tear the paper off.

After the lunch break, Douglas was more animated, chatting with Stewart, gesturing with his right arm, keeping the messengers busy with notes and requests for books. The next day he was back to dozing. A pattern was evident. Douglas had moments of lucidity and energy followed by near incoherence and sleep. His absences increased. He could barely function on the bench. He needed help to get his glasses from his coat pocket under his robe. His pills made him drowsy. Often he left the bench midway through oral arguments because of the unbearable pain.

Douglas's entrances and exits were virtually ignored by the other Justices. Marshall watched, however, and when Douglas fell asleep, he signaled a messenger to wake him.

A worried messenger once asked Burger what to do. "The best thing," Burger said, "is to do nothing."

In his chambers, Douglas lay down after the morning arguments to ease the pain, and he sometimes slept for hours. Eventually a small bed was brought down from storage. Some days Douglas was in so much pain that Cathy kept him home. Other times, he came in disheveled and unkempt. The clerks asked Cathy what was going on. "He's doing fine," was all she said. Douglas still spoke only of his "little fall." He became angry reading a draft dissent prepared by one of his clerks (*Matthews v. Eldridge*). Who did the clerk think he was, "insulting the Court"? Douglas asked. The clerk was dumbfounded. He went to Brennan, who assured him there was nothing wrong with the draft. Finally, the clerk realized what had happened. The stroke had also affected Douglas's vision. He tended to skip lines while reading. Douglas had skipped several lines.

The clerk took the opinion back to Douglas and read it to him aloud.

"Yes, that's what I want," Douglas said.

In late October, Burger circulated the first assignment sheet of the term. At the minimum, the Chief usually gave each Justice at least one or two cases to write. Douglas got none. In each of the three cases where Douglas technically had the prerogative to assign the opinion, Brennan and Burger had consulted on the assignments. Brennan, White and Marshall would each take one. Brennan was pained to find himself conspiring with Burger on assignments. The others viewed it as the surest signal that Douglas was finished.

On Wednesday, October 28, the doctors at Walter Reed told Douglas his condition would not improve. He would always be paralyzed, unable to walk, and in nearly constant pain.

Douglas was back on the bench for oral arguments the next Wednesday, November 5. At about 10:45 A.M., he passed a note to a messenger—"Tell Datcher I need to return to my office."

As Douglas was taken from the bench, Burger passed a note of his own to a messenger, underlining the first word: "*Discreetly* find out when Justice Douglas is returning." Fifteen minutes later, the messenger reported back that Douglas was resting and would not return until the afternoon. Burger interrupted the attorney who was arguing the case before them and postponed argument until Douglas returned.

After lunch, Douglas was back on the bench. He asked a messenger to get the volume of the federal statutes that included a section on the retirement of federal judges. Then, as he began getting drowsy again, he asked for some tea and his pain pills. The Marshal of the Court signaled the police to carry Douglas out.

The next day, Douglas and Cathy went to the Rusk Institute in New York. Douglas wanted a second opinion. The doctors at the Rusk Institute agreed with the Walter Reed doctors and added that with rest his condition might improve. Determined to continue, Douglas rushed back to Washington in time for the Friday conference. Again, the pain became unbearable and he had to be wheeled back to his chambers. The next Monday night, he told Cathy he was quitting.

On Tuesday, Douglas met with his friends Clark Clifford and Abe Fortas. They prepared a letter of resignation to send to President Ford. Douglas returned to the bench that afternoon with the letter folded in a coat pocket beneath his robe.

He informed Burger of his decision the next day before lunch. At noon, the Justices gathered in their private dining room to celebrate Blackmun's birthday. After they sang Happy Birthday, the Chief broke the news. "Bill wants me to tell you he's written a letter to the President."

Douglas sat quietly in his wheelchair next to the Chief. With tears in their eyes, each Justice shook Douglas's hand.

Gripping the resignation letter, Blackmun returned to his chambers still in tears. He sat and drafted a tribute to Douglas: "He was in a nice sense, a lone eagle but a strong and soaring one. . . . Decisional life was never dull when William O. Douglas was participating. His like probably will not appear again for a long, long while."

Douglas wrote a letter to the Justices in response to their tributes.

> MY DEAR BRETHREN, Your message . . . filled my heart with over-flowing emotion . . . I am reminded of many canoe trips I have taken in my lifetime. Those who start down a water course may be strangers at the beginning but almost invariably are close friends at

the end . . . The greatest journey I've made has been with you, my
Brethren, who were strangers at the start but warm and fast friends at
the end . . . The value of our achievements will be for others to ap-
praise. Other like journeys will be made by those who follow us, and
we trust that they will leave these wilderness water courses as pure
and unpolluted as we left those which we traversed.

Shortly after Douglas's resignation, the Chief invited Douglas's
clerks to tea to discuss their future. As a retired Justice, Douglas
would still have an office at the Court, and one clerk. His clerks
wanted to play an active role, and Burger agreed to reassign them
to other chambers—one to Stewart, another to Brennan, the third
to White. One would remain available in case the retired Justice,
who had flown to Portland, Oregon, and had entered a hospital
there, returned to the Court.

On Monday, November 17, the seven Associate Justices changed
their seats at the bench, in order of seniority. Brennan moved to
Douglas's empty chair on Burger's right. Blackmun found himself
near the press section for the first time. "God, now I can't sleep
anymore," he joked.

Court was called to session, and Burger read the statement the
Justices had written to Douglas. "Only when you made your decision known did we fully sense what that meant to us and to the
Court," Burger read. "It goes without saying that we shall expect
you to share our table as usual, for you remain our senior Justice
emeritus."

That afternoon, the Justices met for conference. Ordinarily, they
did not hold formal meetings on Monday, but because of Douglas's
retirement there were administrative matters to clear up and cases
left over from the previous week.

The Justices took their seats around the conference table. A chair
had been placed at the opposite end of the table from the Chief
where Douglas's wheelchair had been. As the senior Associate
Justice, Brennan took it.

Everything was still a little tense.

Rehnquist, as junior Justice for four years and therefore technically the errand boy for the conference, would soon be messenger no longer.

The Justices had all read news reports that President Ford was being lobbied by his wife, Betty, to appoint a woman to the Court vacancy. Ford's Housing secretary, Carla Hills, was mentioned most frequently.

"Bill," one of the Justices now joked to Rehnquist, "when Carla comes you should be a gentleman and continue to answer the door."

"No way," Rehnquist shot back, adding a mild obscenity for emphasis. "Carla can answer the door for herself."

They all laughed. The tension eased.

They finally turned to the cases scheduled. One was a tax case that had been argued the morning Douglas retired (*Foster Lumber Co. v. United States*). After Burger spoke, one of the Justices told Brennan that, because he was now in Douglas's seat, Brennan would have to vote for the taxpayer as Douglas always had. Smiling, Brennan did exactly that.

Also pending was a challenge to the massive federal campaign law, which had been enacted in 1974 to reduce the influence of big money and large contributions in political campaigns (*Buckley v. Valeo*). The law had four major provisions. It provided for the financing of presidential campaigns from federal tax revenue; imposed elaborate contribution and campaign-expenditure reporting in which contributors were publicly named; limited individual campaign contributions to $1,000; and set strict limits on campaign spending by candidates.

Senator James. L. Buckley, a conservative Republican from New York, and Eugene McCarthy, a liberal Democrat from Minnesota, had led the legal challenge, arguing that the limitations abridged free speech. The case presented more than twenty constitutional questions.

At conference, Burger accepted the challenger's arguments that the law, masquerading as a reform, really struck at the heart of First Amendment freedoms. To limit contributions and expenditures was to curtail political activity and speech. To force disclosure of contributors' names was a violation of their privacy and their right of political association. Public financing of presidential campaigns would open the door to governmental interference in the political process. Burger said he would vote to strike the entire law.

The other seven Justices seemed generally to favor major portions of the law, though each had a reservation about one or more of the provisions. But the majority upheld most of the law including the section on public financing of presidential campaigns.

The complexity of the case presented the Court with a major problem. The first disbursement of public money to the presidential candidates, about $6 million, was scheduled to take place January 2, only about six weeks away. Several candidates, including Jimmy Carter, might have to drop out of the race if the Court did not act by then.

Given the urgency, Stewart suggested that a committee of Justices be formed to draft a *per curiam* opinion. At first hesitant, Burger finally agreed to let Stewart, Powell and White handle the case; they could assign sections to others as they saw fit.

Stewart liked the prospect of a management team controlling the opinion. In his view, that was already how the Court's business was, in fact, handled. It soon became clear, however, that White, a loner, was uncomfortable on the committee. Stewart and Powell wanted to strike the spending limits. White disagreed and withdrew from the committee. Brennan joined in his place.

Stewart, Powell and Brennan divided the work. Stewart took the two longest sections of the opinion, upholding the limits on individual contributions, but striking the limits on what candidates could spend. Powell took the section upholding the public-disclosure and reporting requirements. Brennan took the part upholding the public financing of presidential campaigns. Though he was writing his own opinion on the case, Rehnquist agreed to write a section on the commission created to enforce the law. Despite his stated desire to strike the entire law, Burger was given the preamble and statement of facts.

Douglas returned to Washington at the end of November. When he came to his chambers, he buzzed for one of his clerks. No one came. He pushed the buzzer again. Still no one. It was strange.

They always came running. He pushed longer and harder on the buzzer.

Marty Bagby, Douglas's senior secretary, finally appeared at the door.

"Where are the clerks?" Douglas angrily demanded.

"There are no clerks," she stammered. The Chief Justice had reassigned his clerks while he was gone.

Douglas glared at her. No clerks? He was a Justice. He had work to do.

When he learned where one of the clerks had been assigned, Douglas summoned him to his office. He demanded that the clerk get to work for him right away.

Douglas began coming to work at the Court nearly every day. He circulated memorandums and tried to stay in the flow of Court business. He knew that there were provisions in the law for a retired Justice like himself to still work on lower court cases. Tom Clark, who had retired in 1967, had become a valuable Court utility man, pinch-hitting as a district court and appeals court judge.

Douglas had been a full member of the Court when oral argument was heard on the campaign finance law. He saw no reason not to participate in the decision, since his replacement would not be able to take part. He decided to write an opinion.

The other Justices were embarrassed by Douglas's attempt to remain a full member of the Court. Blackmun seemed to avert his eyes as he passed Douglas's open office door. When any of the others paid their rare visits, Douglas invariably inquired about the campaign finance case. What progress was being made?

Other times Douglas appeared disoriented. Once Datcher left him sitting in his wheelchair in the middle of the hallway. He sat alone, quiet, helpless. White passed by and said hello. There was no response. White moved closer to Douglas. "It's me, Byron," White said, bringing his face close to Douglas's. Still Douglas gave no reply.

Burger suggested in a memo to Douglas that he would find Earl Warren's old chambers more "commodious" than his own. But in Douglas's view Warren's chambers were largely ceremonial. The two tiny rooms adjoining the main room were not large enough to house a full staff, much less a working Justice. Douglas replied in a memo to the Chief. The chambers he currently occupied were sufficiently "commodious," he said, repeating the word "commodious" several times. "This will let him know I'm still around," he told a clerk.

Douglas had the law on retired Justices researched. When Franklin Roosevelt tried to pack the Supreme Court in 1937, he proposed a law allowing the President to appoint a new member to the Supreme Court whenever a sitting Justice reached the age of seventy. The plan failed, but a law passed providing for the retirement of Justices. It specified that any Justice who had served ten years or more and had reached the age of seventy "may retain his office but retire from regular active service." A retired Justice could continue to receive his salary and, under the law, might be given judicial duties by the Chief Justice "when designated and assigned."

Douglas decided to designate and assign himself.

By the end of December, the committee *per curiam* opinion in the campaign finance case was almost ready to come down, but Burger had still not completed the preamble.

Powell was concerned about the delay. Both *The New York Times* and *The Washington Post,* which Powell followed closely, had pointed out editorially the need for a decision before the $6 million was due to be paid. Burger was just as unhappy. The committee *per curiam* was terrible. The Chief circulated a memo saying the Court would regret the decision to uphold three of the four major parts of the act. Eventually, he watered down the memo into a dissent. Nevertheless, the Chief had drafted a preamble for the committee, though his own negative conclusions about the law dominated his discussion.

When Brennan received the preamble, he had a clerk edit it extensively. There was little time, but Brennan realized he could not return the revised version to Burger with corrections and edits in the clerk's handwriting. So he reworked them in his own handwriting.

Although Douglas also continued work on the campaign finance case, he found that he was being ignored. In the past, the other Justices had treated his memos and drafts with respect, and had sent him their drafts and memos. Now they were acting as if he weren't there. He wrote a memorandum to the conference from "Mr. Justice Douglas." He began, "I discuss in this memorandum the merits of the Federal Election Campaign Act cases. I also discuss aspects of the status of a retired justice. . . ."

Douglas recounted the history of the law that provided for retired Justices, and branded the effort to exclude him "much more mischievous [sic] than the Roosevelt [Court packing] plan. It tends to denigrate Associate Justices who 'retire,'" Douglas said. "Beyond that is the mischief in selecting the occasion when a Justice will be allowed to hear and decide cases." Calling his exclusion "a practice in politics," Douglas said, "The Court is the last place for political maneuvering."

He contended that by trying to participate in the campaign finance case, he was just doing his job, proposing nothing new or radical. "The break with tradition would come if for some reason, best known to a conference, a justice who had participated in bringing a case here and had done all the work on the case, including hearing oral argument, could be eased out of a final and ultimate action on the case."

Turning to the case, Douglas argued that a campaign finance law that provided public money to candidates with large popular support helped to preserve the party in power. He had substantial doubts about both the spending and contribution limits.

> History shows that financial power and political power eventually merge and unite to do their work together. . . . The federal bureaucracy at the present time is effectively under the control of the corporate and moneyed interests of the nation. A new party formed to oust the hold that the corporate and financial interests have is presently by the terms of this act unqualified to get a dime.

The memo ran thirteen pages. Douglas told his part-time clerk that he intended to publish it as a dissent when the campaign finance case was announced. The clerk alerted Stewart, White and

Brennan. Finally Brennan agreed to speak with Douglas. Fortas also came to talk to him. Later Fortas told a clerk that if he were Chief Justice and Douglas tried to come back and sit on a case, he would send Douglas a memo saying: "Dear Bill, You're off the Court so forget about it."

But Douglas would not listen to anyone. He ordered his clerk to take the draft opinion to the printer and circulate it to the other Justices. The clerk stalled, but Douglas insisted and got it printed.

The clerk later took one copy around to each chamber.

Stewart read the memo. It was classic Douglas—blowing the whistle on the "mischief" of his colleagues and on the "corporate and moneyed interests." But it had none of the polish or punch of the old Douglas dissents, only the frenzy.

"Bill is like an old firehouse dog," Burger told a clerk, "too old to run along with the trucks, but his ears prick up just the same."

The conference finally set January 30 for the announcement of the decision. Learning of the date, Douglas summoned his clerk and told him to get the opinion out.

"I won't do it," the clerk replied.

Red-faced, Douglas stared at him. "You are a traitor," he said, his pale-blue eyes rendering an icy judgment. "I will get it down there myself."

The clerk left the room and sent a note to White: "The tenth member of the Court wants to release his opinion."

Reluctantly, the conference knew it must mobilize immediately. Court officials were told to ignore Douglas's requests for help.

Thwarted at every turn, Douglas finally gave up.

The Court opinion, with separate concurrences and dissents by everyone except Brennan, Stewart and Powell was a book-length 237 pages. Brennan could not recall a single opinion that had been longer or heavier, and he joked with Burger in the robing room about who should carry it out. The official summary reported the decision as the work of an eight-man court.

After the decision was announced, White got a call from Ethel Kennedy, the widow of Senator Robert Kennedy. She was very upset over the decision and claimed that it would ruin the political parties, ruin reform, ruin everything.

"But Ethel," White said, "you don't understand what this really means." He joked that if the majority had done what he had wanted, the expenditure limits would have been upheld. That would have made it impossible for wealthy individuals or families such as the Kennedys to spend virtually unlimited amounts on their campaigns, as they had done in the past.

President Ford and his White House advisers realized that the selection of a successor for Douglas would be a very delicate matter, given Ford's role as leader of the unsuccessful move to impeach Douglas six years earlier. And, since he was the only unelected President in history, the Democrats on the Senate Judiciary Committee might make any nomination by Ford a political issue. He had to find someone quickly and get the person confirmed before the 1976 presidential primary campaigns.

Ford knew he could not replace the Court's greatest liberal with a political crony or a notorious conservative. But despite speculation about the appointment of Carla Hills, Ford's list of possible nominees grew to ten names—the others all men—including Solicitor General Robert Bork and an old Ford friend from Michigan, Republican Senator Robert Griffin. Burger sent a name to the White House—J. Clifford Wallace, a well-known conservative judge from the West Coast.

Ford ruled out Senator Griffin. He would not leave himself open to charges of cronyism. Similarly, Hills, his Secretary of Housing and Urban Development, would look too much like a political appointment. Bork would have been ideal, but his role in firing the first Watergate Special Prosecutor, Archibald Cox, in 1973 made him too controversial.

Ford finally concluded the best choice would be a sitting judge, someone virtually unknown who had worked with distinction for years on the federal bench. The list narrowed to two.

Judge Arlin M. Adams of the Third Circuit Court of Appeals in Philadelphia had nearly been nominated for the seat Rehnquist got in 1971. Nixon, in fact, had promised him a Court appointment, but Attorney General Mitchell had vetoed it because of Adams's handling of the case of Catholic antiwar activist Daniel Berrigan.

The other prospect was John Paul Stevens, a fifty-five-year-old judge on the Seventh Circuit in Chicago. Ford's Attorney General, Edward Levi, a former dean of the University of Chicago Law School, was enthusiastic about Stevens. The Bar Association committee had given both the highest recommendation. Ford had recently met both men at a White House reception and had read some of their opinions. Adams was probably the more intelligent and more self-confident, at times flashy. Stevens was a small, modest man from the Midwest, more workmanlike, solid, a man of subtle humor.

While Stevens was in private practice, before his nomination to the Court of Appeals in 1970, an opposing attorney noticed that Stevens always wore bow ties and implied that lawyers who wore clip-on bow ties could not be trusted. Stevens quietly stood up, slowly untied his regular bow tie, and retied it, all without saying a word.

A former law partner considered Stevens a lawyer's lawyer, and on the appeals court Stevens had been thought of as a judge's judge. He was noted both for thoroughness and for his sophisticated arguments.

On the basis of a few moments of small talk, Ford had preferred Stevens. Stevens also seemed to have no partisan politics, no strict ideology. His anonymity would ensure a quick confirmation.

Stevens was working in his twenty-sixth-floor office in the Federal Courthouse in Chicago when the phone rang. He had told his clerks that he would take no telephone calls. He was trying to focus on a complicated patent case. "You might want to take this one," the clerk said. "It's the White House."

Stevens picked up the phone. President Ford greeted him warmly.

"How are you?" Stevens asked.

Ford said he was fine. He asked how Stevens was.

"To tell you the truth, I'm a little nervous talking to you."

Ford mentioned their meeting at the White House reception. "Unless you have some objection, I intend to nominate you for the Supreme Court."

Stevens was overwhelmed. He thanked Ford. While he hoped it didn't appear rash or incautious, he accepted.

Ford said he would announce the nomination that afternoon from the White House.

After saying goodbye, Stevens took a walk alone and then went to see his mother. He was pleased to be nominated to succeed Douglas. After graduating first in his class from Northwestern Law School, Stevens had clerked at the Supreme Court for Justice Wiley Rutledge in 1947. Douglas had, at that point, already been a Supreme Court Justice for eight years. Stevens greatly admired Douglas.

Stevens's nomination was well received in Washington. The Senate Judiciary Committee quickly requested voluminous information about his personal, financial, academic, legal and judicial background. "I've gone through discovery in antitrust hearings," Stevens told his clerks as he compiled his records, "but never anything like this."

His net worth was $171,000, including a $125,000 house, two cars and one airplane.

The hearings on his nomination opened uneventfully on December 8. The Committee consensus held that Stevens was an obscure, scholarly, thoughtful lawyer and judge. Two days later, he was confirmed by the full Senate 98 to 0.

At the Court, Burger began preparations for Stevens's arrival. President Ford had said he would attend the swearing-in ceremony. The Chief wanted it to go perfectly. When the Court carpenter told him the new chair being prepared for Stevens wouldn't be ready on time, Burger said, "I have ruled that it will be done on time."

On December 19, Ford stood in the courtroom to announce the appointment. As he spoke, there was a commotion to one side. Douglas was being wheeled in to see his replacement take the oath. After the ceremony, Ford walked up to Douglas, who sat in his wheelchair. "Good to see you, Mr. Justice," Ford said to his old opponent.

"Yeah. It's really nice seeing you," Douglas said sarcastically. "We've got to get together more often."

With that, Douglas nodded to Datcher, who pivoted the wheelchair and pushed him out.

*   *   *

On Stevens's first day on the bench for oral argument, the Court heard a case (*Hampton v. Mow Sun Wong*) that had been held over from the previous term. It involved the constitutionality of a Civil Service Commission regulation that barred resident aliens from holding most federal jobs. At conference, the Court split 4 to 4, along the same lines as it had the previous term. That left it up to Stevens, who turned out to have a singular position. He thought the discrimination against aliens was unconstitutional if it was based only on a Civil Service Commission regulation, as it was in this situation. But, he said, it might well be constitutional for Congress or the President to ban aliens from federal jobs. That meant the vote was 5 to 4 to declare the particular regulation in the case unconstitutional. Though technically no one fully agreed with Stevens, Brennan assigned him to write for the majority. Stevens held his first majority.

Stevens also quickly asserted himself on a number of other cases. In one (*Alexandria Scrap Co. v. Hughes*), he was on the minority side of a 6-to-3 vote. The majority opinion, requiring a highly technical application of interstate commerce laws to junked automobiles, was assigned to Powell. Stevens sent Powell a personal note with a legal memorandum attached arguing his minority view. Persuaded by the Stevens memo, Powell switched his vote. Two others, including the Chief, also switched, making the final outcome 6 to 3 the other way. In Brennan's chambers, the case became the "Powell, a/k/a (also known as) Stevens, opinion."

The next month, Burger assigned a criminal case (*Henderson v. Morgan*) to Stevens. The majority had voted to uphold a second-degree murder plea, even though the defendant maintained he had not been aware that he was pleading guilty to intentional murder for which he might receive a long prison sentence. After researching the case, Stevens decided that he had been wrong to join the majority. A defendant's failure to comprehend fully the nature of the plea bargain was a denial of due process. He switched and eventually brought with him a majority of seven, all but Burger and Rehnquist.

In an obscenity case (*Liles v. Oregon*), Brennan, Marshall and

Stewart issued their standard boiler-plate dissent from the denial
of cert, objecting for the public record to the majority's refusal to
hear and overturn obscenity convictions. Though Stevens was inclined to join Brennan, Marshall and Stewart on obscenity questions, he nonetheless wrote a short opinion *concurring* in the
denial of cert, rare compared with the more common *dissent* from
denial. Since the five-man 1973 majority *(Miller)* upholding obscenity convictions was still "adamant," he said, it was "pointless"
to grant cert only to have the majority reaffirm its well-known view.
He would not be—nor did the three dissenters want him to be—
the fourth cert vote. Rejecting Brennan's policy of issuing stock
dissents, he said, "In the interest of conserving scarce law library
space, I shall not repeat this explanation every time I cast such a
vote."

Brennan was worried about several pending civil rights cases.
They involved suits brought under federal civil rights laws, seeking
monetary damages from state officials accused of violating the due
process clause of the Fourteenth Amendment, which states that no
state shall "deprive any person of life, liberty, or property, without
due process of law."

For Brennan, those thirteen words ensured basic rights. He believed in an expansive view of the clause. He interpreted the
phrase "life, liberty or property" to mean very broadly that state
power cannot be used against an individual without due process,
without a hearing or guaranteed procedure to ensure fairness. In
Brennan's view, this included protection against damaging a
person's good name.

A case *(Paul v. Davis)* involving a Louisville, Kentucky, newspaper photographer named Edward Davis, posed the question
squarely. Davis had been arrested for shoplifting. Before his guilt
or innocence was determined, the local police circulated a five-
page flier of names and mug shots of those "known to be active"
shoplifters. Davis's name and picture were included.

Shortly after the flier was circulated, the shoplifting charges
against Davis were dismissed. But the flier came to the attention of
his employer, who warned Davis that he "had best not find himself

in a similar situation" in the future. Davis sued the police chief for damages in federal court and won on appeal.

The Sixth Circuit had cited a 1971 Douglas opinion *(Wisconsin v. Constantineau)* that held that "reputation" was a protected interest under the Fourteenth Amendment. Brennan agreed with the appellate court decision, but he was concerned that his colleagues would not agree that the precedent was correct.

Stewart thought application of the due process clause had gotten out of hand. Too many things were being brought under the umbrella of protected "liberty" or "property." Not every objectionable act by a state official should be taken to federal court as a civil rights violation. It was an outrage that the police had circulated Davis's name and picture as a known shoplifter, but Davis had not lost his job as a result. Stewart felt that the proper remedy for Davis would have been to sue under a state law for libel and defamation. Since there was no such Kentucky law under which he could sue, he was simply out of luck. The issue still did not belong in federal court.

Moreover, Stewart felt trapped by a phrase that Rehnquist had convinced him to add to a 1972 opinion *(Bd. of Regents v. Roth)*. Though it had seemed harmless to Stewart at the time, the phrase said that due process should be invoked only for those property interests specifically created by governments. The Court should not be in the business of creating new interests. Stewart was bound by his own precedent.

At conference, Stewart joined Burger, Blackmun, Rehnquist and Powell in voting against Davis's claim. In one case they could narrow the opportunities for civil rights suits, cut back on the scope of Fourteenth Amendment protections, reduce the federal case load and support states' rights.

Brennan, Marshall and White were in the minority. Since Stevens had not arrived in time for oral arguments, he did not participate.

Brennan was disgusted. Such an opinion would mean that police would be free to label anyone who was arrested a criminal, whether or not he was ultimately convicted. It meant that the Constitution did not protect an individual from being wrongly stigmatized. Brennan couldn't believe that all five in the majority would stick with a decision that was so clearly unjust.

Burger assigned Rehnquist to write. Rehnquist saw the 1971 Wisconsin case that the Court of Appeals had cited as precedent as the major hurdle that he would have to clear. In that case, a Wisconsin law prohibited the sale of liquor to anyone who was adjudged, because of his excessive drinking, to be a hazard to himself, to his family, or to the community. As a result, a woman's name had been publicly posted in all local liquor stores as a habitual drunkard. Douglas's majority opinion ruled that due process was violated by posting the woman's name without procedural safeguards, such as notice and a chance to rebut the charges at a hearing.

Rehnquist believed that he saw a way to circumvent the Wisconsin decision. The posting of the woman's name, he argued, not only harmed her reputation but deprived her of a right created by the state—the right to purchase and obtain liquor. The woman had lost more than her reputation. She had lost reputation plus the right to buy liquor. The latter was a right established by state law; reputation was not. In the present case, Davis had not lost his job. Reputation "standing alone," Rehnquist wrote, was not sufficient to require an additional hearing to meet the standards of due process.

At the beginning of the term, Brennan had told his clerks to scrutinize, word by word, all drafts circulated by either Rehnquist or Burger. Anything from Burger had to be gone over carefully both because there was no telling what to expect and because the quality of the work was usually substandard. Rehnquist, Brennan explained, often twisted the meaning of prior cases, or baldly ignored them when they supported the other side.

When Brennan received Rehnquist's draft in the Davis case, he quickly spotted his trick. Rehnquist's interpretation that due process could be invoked only when the issue involved "reputation *plus*" some additional right was a deception. In the Wisconsin opinion, Douglas had made it clear that the reputation issue was "the *only* issue present." A Rehnquist clerk admitted the draft was "the worst Rehnquist opinion ever." A Burger clerk agreed it was "terrible."

In a scathing dissent, Brennan attacked Rehnquist's "dissembling" and the "saddening denigration of our majestic Bill of Rights." But Burger, Powell, Stewart and finally Blackmun joined Rehnquist's opinion. The conference vote had held. Brennan's worst fears were realized.

Rehnquist was not through with his efforts to cut back on civil rights suits and broad interpretations of the Fourteenth Amendment. In another case *(Belcher v. Stengel)*, in which a policeman had shot and killed two people, Rehnquist contended that this was not a civil rights case, but simply an accidental death. There were no Fourteenth Amendment—"life, liberty or property"—interests involved, he said. Stevens quickly sent a memo to the conference decrying Rehnquist's suggestion. It was absurd to say that there had been no deprivation of "life" when two people had been killed. After endless, esoteric discussion of what constituted "life, liberty or property," his memo was a breath of fresh air to the liberal wing. Eventually, the conference voted not to decide the case and dismissed it without an opinion.

Rehnquist was also convinced that the Court had helped the federal government usurp too much power from the states. Unhappily, there was little he could do about it since most of the states' rights issues had been settled by the Court a century or decades earlier. An important impediment to limiting the federal government's power was a 1968 Court decision *(Maryland v. Wirtz)* that upheld application of a federal minimum wage law to nearly 3 million employees of state hospitals and schools. In the previous term, Rehnquist had argued, without much luck *(Fry v. U.S.)*, that the Court should consider overruling *Wirtz*. He had wound up alone in dissent. He thought there was now another chance. The Court had before it a potentially more important case, *National League of Cities v. Usery*. Twenty-one states had challenged a 1974 federal law that extended minimum-wage coverage to another 3.4 million policemen, firemen and other public workers. The conference had deadlocked 4 to 4 in the previous term, since Douglas's vote had not been counted. The case had been reargued.

Rehnquist felt that if he could win this case, it would once and for all break the forty-year chain of decisions that allowed

Congress to do virtually anything in the name of regulating interstate commerce. While this was a power expressly granted
Congress by the Constitution, the federal regulatory bureaucracy
had grown to staggering numbers under an increasingly expansive
reading of the clause. Over the previous twenty years, the Court
had held that much of the activist federal legislation governing labor relations, civil rights, environmentalism had been properly enacted under the clause.

Although he had dissented from the 1968 *Maryland v. Wirtz* decision, Stewart felt bound by it as precedent. Moreover, he had no
intention of departing from his policy of not providing the fifth vote
to overrule a Warren Court precedent. Precedent was precedent.
Once a case like *Wirtz* was decided and announced, it was the law.
And Stewart felt it was important that he should not be the fifth
vote, particularly by joining the four Nixon justices, to overrule
Warren Court decisions.

So with the four Nixon appointees presumably ready, Stevens,
the new Justice, would be the key.

At the Friday, March 5, conference, the Chief turned to the
National League of Cities case. For the time being, he said, he
would pass. Brennan stuck by his vote of the previous term. They
were clearly bound by the *Wirtz* precedent, which dealt with the
same issue.

Stewart announced that he, too, would stay with his vote of the
previous term upholding *Wirtz*. He didn't like it any more now
than he did when he dissented in 1968, he said. "But if I'm the fifth
vote, I have to go the other way. . . ." If Stevens voted to overrule
Wirtz, Stewart was prepared to be the sixth vote. White and
Marshall agreed that the *Wirtz* precedent controlled this case. That
made four votes. Blackmun wondered if there was some way to
distinguish this case from *Wirtz* so that they could avoid the precedent. Powell and Rehnquist took up where Blackmun left off. If
they could get around *Wirtz* without explicitly overruling it, so as
not to offend Stewart's strict sense of precedent, they could strike
down this particular law.

Stevens, however, stated that he felt compelled to uphold the
Wirtz precedent. The only distinction between the two cases was

that *Wirtz* involved minimum wages for hospital and school employees whereas *National League of Cities* concerned policemen
and firemen. He could see no constitutional difference between
hospital workers and firemen. Since Stevens would not be the fifth
vote to strike, Stewart would not strike either. That was five votes
to uphold.

Burger told Brennan, as the senior Justice in the majority, to go
ahead and assign the case. Suddenly, White interrupted. He was
on the winning side, but he was not satisfied. He said he counted
five votes—including Stewart's—for striking the statute.

"I understand why you're voting that way, Potter," White began
in the softest of whispers, addressing Stewart, "but I think it is
kind of a chickenshit position. It keeps the jurisprudence of the
Court tied up for reasons that are not on the public record."

Flustered and irritated, Stewart considered White's challenge. "I
think you are right, I'll vote the other way," he said. But he was not
going to vote for some underhanded formula that overruled *Wirtz*
without really saying so. It would have to be done explicitly.

That was fine with Rehnquist. Powell and the Chief agreed.
Blackmun was hesitant, but he said he might vote to overrule *Wirtz*
if the opinion was carefully written.

With the vote now 5 to 4 the other way, Burger took back the assignment from Brennan and assigned the case to Rehnquist.

Brennan was beside himself. Before his eyes, the clash of two legal machismos, White's and Stewart's, had produced a major reversal of the thirty-five years of law. What was White trying to do?
Brennan wondered. How could Stewart be so susceptible to that
kind of challenge? Brennan left the conference in a rage. "White
should have kept his mouth shut!" he fumed to his clerks.

Rehnquist circulated his first draft by the end of March. He had
found a footnote in the majority opinion on the *Fry* decision, the
case in which he had been the lone dissenter the year before, that
said "Congress may not exercise power in a fashion that impairs
the states' integrity or their ability to function effectively. . . ."

Citing this footnote, Rehnquist wrote that the increased burden
of paying the minimum wage to the 3.4 million additional state employees might threaten the survival or sovereignty of the states.

Rehnquist's home state of Arizona, for example, estimated that the added cost would be $2.5 million. Other states, claiming that they would be hard pressed to meet the added financial burden, said they would have to curtail affirmative action programs and summer employment for teenagers.

When Stevens received his copy of Rehnquist's draft, he took it home and went over it carefully. Rarely, in five years on the appeals court, had he seen such a misuse of precedents. Rehnquist "can't do this," he told a clerk the next morning.

Stevens liked Rehnquist, but he saw it as his job to challenge Rehnquist's disingenuous scholarship. He drafted a long "Dear Bill" memo at his desk. Unsure whether the memo ought to be a dissent or just a personal note, Stevens finally decided to circulate it to the conference. He had not consulted Brennan, the senior dissenter, and he was a little apprehensive that his memo was premature. But when Brennan received it, he was elated. The memo proved conclusively that Stevens was no slouch. He had raised more questions about Rehnquist's draft than even Brennan's most suspicious clerk had. Nevertheless, Brennan decided to write a dissent of his own. Each of his three clerks was so anxious to prepare the first draft that they held a lottery to see who would write it.

Stewart's clerks were crestfallen at his 180-degree flip, which seemed to be the result of White's dare at conference. When they received Stevens's memo, all four went into Stewart's office. If the federal-state conflict was to be confronted, they argued, this surely was not the case. This sort of states' rights argument had been discarded years before.

Stewart disagreed.

The clerks returned to their office and took the Rehnquist draft apart line by line. They returned to their boss. He appreciated their work, Stewart told them. Their arguments were powerful and well presented. But he was not going to change his mind. "I'm still going to vote with Rehnquist," he said.

Rehnquist feared, however, that Stevens's memo was having an impact in other chambers. His draft had not yet been joined by a single other Justice. Most ominously, it seemed that Blackmun was still very much up in the air. Rehnquist circulated another, slightly altered draft. Although he refused to back down on a single major point, he revised his citations of precedents.

Brennan saw the case as an important test of Rehnquist's influence in the Court. If the Court was to begin diminishing federal power, it would be a blow to liberalism. State power was almost invariably conservative.

Brennan focused on the two weakest votes, Blackmun and Stewart. He talked to Stewart's clerks, who made another run at their boss. Once more, Stewart's clerks told him, his long-standing reluctance to be the fifth vote in overruling precedent was sound. This important tenet should not be sacrificed; it was part of his strength on the Court. Stewart, however, seemed no longer worried about being the fifth vote. In fact, he contended, this actually worked to his advantage. Rehnquist could extend states' rights only as far as Stewart would let him. The clerks gave up. Stewart was behaving as if he were a one-man Congress, they felt.

Brennan had not given up. He had his most acerbic clerk retouch his dissent, charging that Rehnquist's draft was a "patent usurpation" of congressional power. The author had manufactured an "abstraction" with a "pernicious" consequence. The legal reasoning and scholarship were "awkward" and "out of context." The opinion was "devoid of meaningful content," "alarming," "startling," "cavalier," "ominous," "mischievous," and a "catastrophic judicial body blow at Congress's power." And he added: "I cannot recall another instance in the Court's history when the reasoning of so many decisions covering so long a span of time had been discarded roughshod."

Brennan gave the dissent a final perusal and circulated it to the other chambers. On Blackmun's copy, he wrote a personal note asking if there was anything that he could do to get his vote.

Stevens was amazed at the strident tone of Brennan's dissent. It was both a legal and personal assault, and it was altogether too much for Stevens. There was no way he could join, particularly as a Justice so new to the Court. Stevens wanted to build relationships with all factions, not impair them permanently. Further,

Brennan was drawing more attention to the case than it might naturally receive. Rehnquist wasn't claiming an earthshaking victory. Why announce one for him?

Stevens wrote Brennan a personal note, explaining in a congratulatory tone that while his dissent was *"powerful"*—underlining the word—he just wasn't going to be able to join. He did not state his reasons. He thought Brennan would understand.

Marshall and White joined the Brennan dissent.

By June, Rehnquist had four votes including his own, and Blackmun remained the question mark. Blackmun had read both Rehnquist's and Brennan's efforts. Overwritten sarcasm seldom appealed to him and, in his view, Brennan was once again crying wolf. Blackmun did not think this opinion was a "body blow" to the power of Congress. But he was still unhappy at the idea of overruling the *Wirtz* case. On June 10, at a case status conference, Blackmun announced that he was "terribly troubled" by the case. He was going to attend his daughter's graduation and would not think about the case until he got back. A week later, on June 17, he told his clerk that he had still not made a decision. "It is impossible for me to look at it in depth, with all the other things I have to do," he said.

After ruminating on it, Blackmun toyed with concurring in the result only, thus denying Rehnquist his fifth vote to make it a binding precedent. He finally decided to join Rehnquist's opinion, but to limit its effect by publishing his own separate opinion. It turned out to be a single paragraph: "Although I am not untroubled by certain possible implications of the Court's opinion—some of them suggested by the dissents—I do not read the opinion so despairingly as does my Brother Brennan." Although Rehnquist's opinion flatly forbade any federal intervention, Blackmun said, in future cases, such as environmental law, where the federal government had a greater interest, federal intervention would be constitutional. But since Blackmun's one-paragraph clarification gave the Rehnquist opinion full precedental value, it was extremely disappointing to each of the dissenters. Stevens, in part, blamed Brennan, whose shrill dissent, he felt, had pushed Blackmun into the majority. Brennan and Marshall blamed White for the whole fiasco, since it was his challenge to Stewart that had triggered the switch.

As the term progressed, Rehnquist and Stewart continued to grow closer, both personally and professionally. Their relationship affected the alignment of the Court. "Excellent," was the way Stewart frequently described Rehnquist. Stewart believed in meritocracy, and Rehnquist clearly had proved that he belonged on the Court.

During the term, Rehnquist finally seemed to have reached cruising speed. At fifty-one he was still the youngest member of the Court; his energy level was at its peak. As in previous years, Rehnquist assumed more than his share of routine work and research for the conference, volunteering to take on extra tasks, doing nearly a dozen unsigned *per curiams*. But more significantly, Rehnquist seemed, in the view of several clerks, to have made a conscious decision to become a more effective Justice. No longer a loner, he frequently appeared able to influence Powell, White and Stewart.

Stewart viewed Rehnquist as a "team player," a part of the group in the center of the Court, even though he usually wound up with the conservative bloc. The Justices in the center looked to Rehnquist for his analyses more than for his votes. His analyses were at times important, well-reasoned and sophisticated. His dissents sometimes forced the majority to address new issues or to narrow its focus.

Stewart knew that Rehnquist was a clever tactician. He often drafted extreme overstatements and then gladly cut out a lot in negotiation, winding up with the core of his position intact. Rehnquist could leave the others with a sense that they had won more than they had lost. In an employment discrimination case (*Fitzpatrick v. Bitzer*), Rehnquist had the assignment for a nearly unanimous Court. His first draft spelled out his most extreme view of the Fourteenth Amendment. It was, he said, meant only as a solution to the problems of slavery, not as a license to the Court to right every wrong.

One of Stewart's clerks remarked that Rehnquist was "going for the home run."

Stewart went to Rehnquist. Nice try, Stewart told him, but the breadth of the Fourteenth Amendment had been settled more than fifty years before.

Rehnquist took the offending section out and won every vote.

Stewart's clerks were not entirely happy about the way their boss seemed to have fallen under Rehnquist's spell. In one case upholding a ban on political campaigning on a military base (*Greer v. Spock*), Stewart obliterated his own 1972 precedent (*Flower v. U.S.*) with the words: "Flower . . . looks in precisely the opposite direction."

Such a declaration that two very similar cases were different was a typical Rehnquist maneuver. Afterward, when some of Rehnquist's more inexplicable decisions came down, Stewart's clerks would snipe: "Flower looks the other way."

Rehnquist was in turn contemptuous of Brennan's opinions. "Brennan's done another pretzel job," he once remarked after reading what he considered to be a standard Brennan opinion, bending the facts or law to suit his purposes. Brennan was not, in his view, a significant force on the Court, and Marshall was even less so. In a prison case (*Kerr v. United States District Court for the Northern District of California*), Burger asked Rehnquist and Marshall to work out a mutual position. Technically, Marshall had the assignment, but Rehnquist spoke with Burger's authority in negotiating a draft. When Marshall resisted Rehnquist's suggestions, Rehnquist bluntly spelled out the realities of the situation to one of Marshall's clerks. "Tell Thurgood that this is my opinion and not his, but just coming out under his name," he said.

Rehnquist realized the importance of his relationship with Burger. Though they agreed on basic principles, Rehnquist took extra steps to ensure that he stayed on the Chief's good side. He joined all but one of Burger's majority opinions during the term, even though he disagreed with several.

Rehnquist was aware of Burger's faults, his technical carelessness and his frequent mistakes. In the important cases, Rehnquist tried to straighten him out. It was a delicate undertaking. Phoning Burger, or approaching him personally, he made it a point to couch his correction as a new footnote, or a specific addition or deletion—something that would improve Burger's work. "Hey, Chief, don't you think this makes more sense if . . . ?" Rehnquist would ask, implying that the original was cogent even when it was not. That was as confrontational as Rehnquist wanted to get.

Once, one of Rehnquist's clerks brought him a particularly unworkmanlike Burger opinion. "Look what he's done," the clerk remarked sarcastically. Rehnquist read it, shook his head, frowned, sighed and fretted. Careful to pick his shots, he was reluctant to call Burger on another opinion.

Rehnquist was remarkably unstuffy. He thought it funny that there was a Rehnquist Club at Harvard Law School in which the leader was called the "Grand Rehnquisitor," and a weekly discussion called the "Rehnquisition." As the junior Justice during the first half of the term, he was in charge of the Court's annual Christmas Party. He approved a skit his clerks had prepared for the party; it was entitled, *The Making of a Justice 1976*. It was supposed to deal with President Ford's dilemma in choosing a successor to Douglas. A clerk wearing a football helmet played Ford listening to the lobbying of various political interest groups. A chorus of five clerks sang the parts of the interest groups.

> POLITICIANS. Pack the Court with hacks and cronies
> CONSERVATIVES. Weed out all the liberal phonies
> LIBERALS. Save Miranda, save Miranda, save Miranda from the Nixon Four!

Burger did not share the others' laughter.

The next day, December 16, Burger sent Rehnquist a note: "The performance of 'The Supreme Court Choral Group' at our Christmas Party was excellent and on behalf of the justices, I thank you. Happy New Year."

The skit was not mentioned. But in January, when the next assignment sheet came around, Rehnquist got only one case from Burger—an insignificant Indian tax dispute in Montana (*Moe v. Tribes of the Flathead Reservation*).

Rehnquist had nothing but contempt for Indian cases. Traditionally, Douglas had done more than his share. He had been the Court's expert. With his own Arizona background, Rehnquist was the logical replacement, but, he suspected that the assignment was Burger's way of telling him what he really thought of the Christmas party. Never one to let an opportunity pass, Rehnquist turned an opinion that was in favor of the Indians into an opinion that indicated that in most cases they would lose. It wiped away decades of Douglas's opinions.

Stewart appreciated Rehnquist's sense of humor. At one particularly dull moment at conference, after Burger and Blackmun had performed predictably, Stewart passed a note to Rehnquist on which he had drawn two tombstones. On Burger's tombstone, Stewart had inscribed: "I'll Pass for The Moment." On Blackmun's, he had written: "I Hope The Opinion Can Be Narrowly Written." Rehnquist laughed out loud.

Ignoring tradition, Rehnquist attended one conference in a Court softball team T-shirt. He also did little to dispel the impression that he was drinking straight Scotch or bourbon at his desk, even though the amber liquid in the glass was really his favorite beverage, apple juice.

Rehnquist's affability did not stop with his colleagues. He paid attention to all the Court personnel, addressing even the humblest by name. When the police at the Court had their chairs taken away from their duty stations as punishment for letting a tourist wander into a restricted area, a delegation came to Rehnquist for help. The chairs were soon returned to the posts.

He had an equally easy relationship with his clerks. By the end of the term, Rehnquist's clerks felt comfortable speaking openly about Burger's faults. Rehnquist listened and occasionally defended the Chief. He called the bad mouthing a "sport for law clerks," but it was clear that the subject was not off limits. He once asked a group of clerks what surprised them the most about the Court.

"The Chief's asinine memos," one clerk answered.

Rehnquist laughed heartily.

The Right to Life movement had developed tremendous momentum since Blackmun's 1973 abortion decision. Anti-abortion demonstrators gathered periodically at the Court, and some sent Blackmun roses on the anniversary of the decision. Blackmun, puzzled, nervous and grim, stood by his office window and watched the demonstrations. He felt that so much of the opposition reflected a misunderstanding of the Court's opinion and purpose.

Blackmun publicly defended the abortion decision, telling one audience that people "forget that the Court functions only on constitutional principles. All we were deciding was a constitutional issue, not a philosophical one . . .

"A lot of people have personalized this, thinking it's the work of the devil, to wit, me—forgetting there were seven votes for that opinion."

Yet, Blackmun knew there was considerable unhappiness with the abortion decision within the Court. The original dissenters, Rehnquist and White, kept up a steady drumbeat. In one memo for the cert pool prepared by one of White's clerks, the doctor in an abortion case was called a "fetus killer." Blackmun was furious. Rehnquist told college audiences that the Court might some day overturn the decision.

Since the 1973 decision, Burger had gone back to his original anti-abortion position, and Powell seemed shaky. While Douglas was on the Court, Blackmun was virtually certain in new abortion cases to have five solid votes to follow the 1973 decision. Douglas's resignation left the abortion issue in doubt. Blackmun did not believe that the decision would be overruled. But the 1973 decision had left some major questions open. Many states had enacted new laws that had the practical effect of restricting abortions.

A 1974 Missouri law put a number of limitations on abortions including requirements that:

- an unmarried woman under the age of eighteen obtain her parents' consent before an abortion.
- a married woman obtain her husband's written consent.
- saline amniocentesis, the most common abortion method, not be used after twelve weeks of pregnancy.*

---

* The method involves inserting a needle into the womb and injecting a saline solution, which induces labor and a miscarriage.

In the previous term, the Court had considered a case *(Planned Parenthood v. Danforth)* that challenged these provisions of the Missouri law. At first, Blackmun had insisted that the Court summarily—without oral argument—reverse the lower court opinion upholding the Missouri law. A summary reversal would be the fastest and most conclusive way to tell the lower court that its decision was wrong, and that prior decisions clearly predetermined the opposite result. Summary reversal was to tell the lower court that it had clearly misread a Supreme Court opinion. A summary opinion merely called the lower court's attention to the previous, controlling opinion.

Blackmun had written a thirty-page *per curiam* summary reversal that said that the states could do little to regulate abortions. But when it circulated, Burger, Powell, Rehnquist and White refused to join. With Douglas's illness, and the informal agreement nullifying his vote when it was the fifth, Blackmun had only four votes. That meant the case would have to be heard during the 1975–76 term. But if the Court announced that it was going to hear oral argument, the anti-abortion forces would mobilize. Blackmun and Brennan, in particular, did not want to give those forces the summer to mount an attack. They devised a plan. The Court would not announce that it would hear the case until the beginning of the next term. The announcement that the case would be heard had been made on October 6, 1975.

Later in the year, at conference on the case, Blackmun got five votes to strike each of the controversial provisions of the Missouri law.* Stewart was unhappy about going along with what he felt were further analytical errors, but since he had voted for the original 1973 decision, he saw no alternative on this one. "This is one of those cases where I'll have to hold my nose and jump," he told his clerks.

---

* Powell voted with Blackmun, Brennan, Marshall and Stewart to strike the requirement of parental consent and the ban on the saline abortion method. Stevens joined Rehnquist, White and Burger in dissent on those issues. But Stevens joined the liberals as a sixth vote on striking the provision requiring the husband's consent.

The conference also considered another abortion case *(Singleton v. Wulff)* that raised the question of whether doctors had standing to bring suit challenging a Missouri state law that prevented poor women from obtaining federally funded abortions. The first vote at conference was 5 to 4 to grant doctors standing for such lawsuits. The majority was an unusual combination of Brennan, Marshall, White, Stevens and, to nearly everyone's surprise, Burger. But again to everyone's surprise, Blackmun voted to deny standing. He told others that he was bothered by law journal articles criticizing his 1973 decision for conferring more rights on doctors performing abortions than on women receiving them. Burger then decided to switch his vote, making it 5 to 4 to deny standing to doctors.

Stewart, who had voted to deny standing at first, said he now wanted to change his vote to grant standing. That made it 5 to 4 again in favor of standing.

At that point Burger said he was not sure of his position. However, he told Brennan, the senior member of the latest majority, to assign the opinion. Brennan also was to assign a third abortion case *(Belloti v. Baird)*, which involved a remand to a lower court. It gave him three abortion cases, his most important assignment opportunity of the term. His clerks urged him to give all three cases to Marshall. Brennan balked. Important bridges had been built to Blackmun, and they were based more on the abortion issue than on any other. Blackmun would surely want the two cases in which he was in the majority. The problem remained that Blackmun was in the minority on the third dealing with doctors' standing. Clearly he could not write the majority opinion on that one. Brennan telephoned Blackmun to explain that he would have wanted to give him all three abortion cases, but that his minority position on doctors' standing made it impossible.

"I can write it that way," Blackmun replied.

Brennan was startled, but he was not about to question Blackmun's decision to switch his vote. Without hesitation, Brennan assigned him all three cases, hoping that he would remain a solid vote in future abortion fights.

Blackmun took months before circulating his first drafts in the three cases. Brennan went through the drafts thoroughly and had his clerks list dozens of suggested changes. But, before he proposed them, he joined Blackmun's drafts.

White thought the Blackmun drafts were dreadful. Blackmun's 1973 abortion opinion had subjected the Court to a great deal of ridicule. It was as if Blackmun had developed a special constitutional rule for handling medical questions. White dubbed it Blackmun's "medical question doctrine." It seemed to hold that, under the Constitution, doctors, rather than the Court, had the final authority on certain medical-legal questions. White found that notion ludicrous. Blackmun had created another "political questions" doctrine. The notion that the Court couldn't meddle in the internal affairs of the other branches of government had been broadened to include the medical profession.

White was particularly incensed about the section of the Blackmun draft on saline abortions. Blackmun had written that there was no "evidence" that the method was unsafe. What Blackmun meant, White felt, was that he had found no "medical evidence," based on his own independent research of medical texts and journals. However, "evidence" *had* been introduced in the lower court showing that saline abortions were less safe than other methods of abortion. That, White felt, was the "evidence" on which the Supreme Court should make its decision.

Blackmun appeared to have appointed himself—and, in turn, the Court—an unofficial medical board. To White, it was ridiculous. The normal rules of law and procedure had been abandoned. The Court could not go around making determinations on medical "facts," and substituting those facts for the ones that had been properly developed in the trial court. White wrote a strong dissent.

For his part, Blackmun was edgy about the abortion cases. He dropped a load of books on a desk one day and blurted out: "Fetuses!" Though he finally got five votes for each major part of his opinions, only Brennan and Marshall joined him in all the cases.

Blackmun's confidence was growing, however, in other ways. In a civil rights suit against the Philadelphia police department alleging police brutality (*Rizzo v. Goode*), Rehnquist held together a five-man majority including Stewart, White, Powell and Burger. His majority opinion said that the lower federal court had improperly intervened to control the handling of citizen complaints against police. But Blackmun, normally a states' rights regular, was struck by how well the alleged pattern of police abuse had been documented in the suit and voted with Brennan and Marshall. Brennan was pleased, and assigned Blackmun to write a dissent for all three of them. When Blackmun sent his draft to Brennan, Brennan pronounced it "splendid."

Shortly thereafter, Blackmun found himself on an airplane flight with William Kunstler, a leading radical activist lawyer. Kunstler threw his arms around the Justice, welcoming him to the company of the "liberals and the enlightened." Though it was only a vote with the minority in *Rizzo*, Kunstler congratulated him, expressing the hope that Blackmun would free himself from Burger's influence more regularly.

Blackmun replied that he hoped to join Brennan and Marshall even more often in the future.

Blackmun later told his clerks of Kunstler's big "bear hug," and recalled that a conservative woman judge was with them at the time. "I don't know what she thought," he mused. The clerks were struck by Blackmun's delight at praise from the radical left.

As far as Brennan was concerned, the term had begun on a bad note and had gone down hill. At the first regular Friday conference, Burger presented a relatively insignificant case *(Thermtron Products Inc. v. Hermansdorfer)* in which a federal judge with a crowded docket of cases had sent this particular case back to state courts because he had no time to hear it. Burger agreed with the judge's action but only Stewart and Rehnquist were on his side. As senior Justice in the majority, Brennan decided to assign the case to White, who had shown a particular interest in it. "Byron, why don't you take this one," he said.

"No," Burger interrupted, "I haven't voted. I said, 'I *would* vote to affirm.'" White challenged him. Burger had voted. But that was not his official, final vote, Burger said. He noted that the formal conference procedure was to speak in order from senior to junior, but then to vote in the opposite order, junior to senior. The vote sheets proved his point, he said, since the Justices were listed from junior to senior. He was listed last and would vote last.

Brennan realized that the Chief was technically correct. That *had* been the tradition. But the formality had been discarded years before. Each Justice stated his argument and position, saying "I would vote . . ." as he finished to avoid the necessity of a separate voting round.

The other Justices agreed. The formality had long been abandoned. Burger had voted in this case.

Okay, the Chief said. But he could still change his vote after discussion.

No one disagreed with that. Tradition held that votes could change right up to the moment a decision was announced. So Burger changed his vote and assigned the case to White anyhow. Eventually, he changed again and joined Rehnquist's dissent.

Brennan had always resented Burger's maneuvering. Now, as the senior Associate Justice, Brennan was the most directly affected by the Chief's abuses of assignment power. He estimated that Burger tried to manipulate an assignment once in each conference. The Chief would pass, which he called "reserving" his vote, or he would switch his vote after the other Justices had cast theirs. Brennan called these "phony votes." Sometimes Burger just withheld his vote and then later assigned the case.

Brennan told his clerks that when Earl Warren was Chief, on the few occasions he passed on a case he usually asked the senior Justice in the majority to assign it. Warren, Brennan said, played fair.

As Brennan became more upset about Burger and the general direction of the Court's decisions, his clerks became a force of their own. Brennan infected them with suspicion, and they, in turn, fed Brennan's distrust of the Chief. The clerks also began waging a private, rear-guard war against the Chief. With Douglas gone, they understood that Brennan would have to be the whistle blower. They became a pocket of underground resistance with strong ties to the clerks in most of the other chambers. They constantly ridiculed Burger, even at morning coffee in Brennan's presence.

Burger was "His Eminence," or "the donut," a name that grew out of a joke the previous term: What is white on top and empty in the center? Brennan's clerks worked in blue jeans, knowing Burger preferred coats and ties, and filled the halls with cigar smoke, hoping it would filter into Burger's chambers. They made fun of his memoranda, mocked his style, and placed cardboard signs on their desks with outrageous quotes from his memos and opinions in hopes that the Chief would notice them when he visited Brennan's chambers.

A Burger draft opinion once mistakenly referred to the Chief's old foe, United States Court of Appeals Chief Judge David Bazelon, as "Chief Justice." A memo quickly came around from Burger's chambers blaming the mistake on a printer's error. Subsequently, whenever a Burger opinion arrived which Brennan's clerks found particularly egregious they would call a Burger clerk to ask whether it was a printer's error.

For Brennan's clerks, each lost case was the falling of the citadel, a catastrophe. One Brennan clerk was frequently directed to use what Brennan called his "acid pen." As a result, Brennan's dissents were often written in scathing and petulant prose. Many of the Justices and clerks believed that Brennan was overplaying his hand. Increasingly, his opinions seemed designed not to persuade others but to irritate Burger. Brennan appeared to have given up trying to do a careful, scholarly job.

Near the end of the term, the Court heard a case (*Sakraida v. Ag Pro, Inc.*) involving a patent dispute over a water flush system designed to remove cow manure from the floor of dairy barns. Referred to around the Court as the "cow shit case," it was of no significance, not even posing interesting questions in the arcane field of patent law. The conference was unanimous that there was no patent violation. The case would ordinarily go to the most junior Justice, Stevens. Instead, Burger assigned the "cow shit case" to Brennan.

Brennan was insulted, but he refused to pass along the humiliation to his clerks. He did all the work on the five-page opinion himself.

Later, when an insignificant Court of Claims case (*United States v. Hopkins)* was argued, Brennan decided to vote whichever way would leave him in the minority, "so that bastard can't give me cases like this."

At conference on Friday, March 5, Burger summed up the facts in a case *(Chandler v. Roudebush)* involving Jewell Chandler, a seventeen-year-old black woman employed by the Veterans Administration, who alleged that she had been denied a promotion because of racial and sexual discrimination. After exhausting standard complaint procedures in the Veterans Administration and the Civil Service Commission with no success, Chandler had filed suit in federal court. The district court dismissed her suit, relying exclusively on the evidence developed at the agency hearings. Chandler appealed, claiming that she should be able to introduce new evidence at a federal trial.

Burger noted that four appeals courts had ruled that federal employees in such suits were entitled to a full trial while three others had said they were not. Unsure of his position, the Chief passed.

Brennan sided with Chandler. Federal employees were entitled by the same recourse as those from private industry. He was joined by three others.

Powell wasn't sure that Congress had ever intended to allow a completely new federal court trial. He and three other Justices voted against Chandler, creating a 4-to-4 standoff.

The Chief finally decided to cast his vote with Powell, tipping the balance 5 to 4 against Chandler. The next morning, the clerk in Powell's chambers who was working on the case examined the record. It was clear from the legislative history that Congress had not intended to deny Chandler or any federal employee access to federal courts. The clerk typed a memo for Powell, and Powell decided to change his vote. He wanted to inform Burger immediately, since it would change the outcome, so he called the Chief that morning. On Monday, he informed the rest of the conference, attaching his clerk's memo.

When he learned of Powell's switch, Burger reconsidered his own position. With the vote now 5 to 4 the other way, he was now in the minority and unable to assign. He decided to switch, and within hours of Powell's memo, sent a memo of his own to the conference. "Lewis's memo convinces me, however irrational it was, that Congress provided" this access to the federal courts. Now the new majority was 6 to 3 in favor of Chandler. The Chief promptly assigned the case to Stewart.

The following day the Chief sent around another memo. He was switching again. He had found new information that caused him to return to his original position. Brennan was free to assign the case. Brennan felt, however, that since Burger had already assigned the majority to Stewart, he could not reassign it to someone else.

Powell read the Burger memo and wondered why the Chief was constantly changing his positions. "I don't understand this," he said, shaking his head.

Within weeks, all the other Justices, except Burger, were persuaded by Stewart's draft and joined his opinion. It was now 8 to 1 in favor of Chandler. Burger was alone in the minority. Before the case was announced, he switched again, joining Stewart's majority. On June 1, the Court announced a unanimous decision in favor of Chandler. Burger had voted five times—a pass, twice against Chandler and twice for her.

Brennan was very concerned about how the Court would handle the highly publicized case (*Nebraska Press Association v. Stuart*) in which a Nebraska state judge had issued a "gag" order, curbing press reports about a sensational murder trial. Brennan considered the order an impermissible prior restraint, much as in the case of the Pentagon Papers. In the Nebraska case, hallowed judicial interests, rather than the national security, were at stake. The judge had issued the order to ensure that the defendant would get the fair trial guaranteed him by the Sixth Amendment.

The defendant was an unemployed handyman accused of raping a ten-year-old child, murdering her and five other members of her family, and then raping some of the dead children. It would have been a notorious trial anywhere, but the judge concluded that in Sutherland, Nebraska, population 850, only a gag order would offer the chance of finding an unbiased jury.

The media had billed the case as a confrontation between the

First and Sixth Amendments, but while sympathetic to the judge, Brennan saw better ways to reduce pretrial publicity: the trial could be delayed; potential jurors could be questioned more rigorously to weed out those whose views had been prejudiced by news coverage; and, as an extreme measure, the location of the trial could be changed. These steps, Brennan believed, would guarantee a fair trial while leaving the press unfettered by judicial orders. He believed that prior restraint might be permissible in extreme cases that involved national security during wartime, but never in coverage of judicial proceedings or reporting about crimes. This case was not a legitimate exception to the First Amendment. The Nebraska judge's order banned publication even of statements made in open court at a pretrial hearing. It was absurd. Spectators in the courtroom could discuss what was said, but the press could not report it.

The case was heard in late April. At conference, Burger said he was willing to vote to reverse the Nebraska gag order because the judge in this case had failed to demonstrate that other alternatives would not have ensured a fair trial. But he could conceive of situations in which gag orders would be permissible and he would not ban them altogether.

Brennan said he would go further. The Court not only should hold the gag order impermissible in this case, but should flatly rule them out in all criminal trials. Without such a strict rule, judges would continue to issue gag orders.

Only Rehnquist disagreed that this particular order should be overturned. But Brennan felt there were five solid votes for an absolute ban on *all* gag orders—Marshall, Stewart and himself, as he had expected, and in addition Stevens and White. The latter two had indicated that they could foresee no situation where gag orders were the only means of ensuring a fair trial. White wanted to resolve the issue now, rather than hear each case as it came up. But Burger, viewing himself as the senior Justice in a majority to overturn the Nebraska gag order, assigned the opinion to himself.

When the Chief's assignment sheet came around, Brennan exploded. The case should have been given to one of the five Justices in the mainstream, someone who favored an absolute ban.

Brennan's clerks were equally disappointed. They had hoped to have at least one major case that term. The Nebraska case, the most significant press case in years, was their last hope. It would fit nicely into the long line of important First Amendment opinions by Brennan. The clerks pushed Brennan to draft a counter-opinion expressing the views of the real majority. Since it was getting toward the end of the term, they should have it ready to circulate immediately after Burger circulated his opinion. Burger would have no time to alter his draft to express the majority's will, and Brennan would win the votes. Brennan, although unenthusiastic, told his clerks to go ahead if they had time. One clerk started immediately. The existence of the alternative "counter-draft" was kept secret from the other chambers.

Burger had taken no major cases for himself during the term until this one. He worked harder on it than on any other opinion. As he read the prior cases, he became increasingly convinced that his position at conference had been right. The judge in Nebraska had not explored the alternatives, and his gag order was unjustifiable. But there was no reason to go further. This was the Court's first such case. Circumstances might alter the Court's general predisposition against such prior restraints. It was more prudent to develop the law slowly, case by case. After all, the Court had never held the First Amendment absolute but had, in such cases as that of the Pentagon Papers, consistently left open the permissibility of prior restraint.

Burger anticipated Brennan's reaction. "Bill," he said, taking Brennan aside one day at a conference to discuss the status of unfinished cases, "you're not going to like what I've written on the *Nebraska* case."

Brennan said nothing. Though his clerks urged him to circulate the counterdraft first to get a jump on the Chief, Brennan told them to wait. He could not break protocol so blatantly. "I have to live with him next year," he said. "You don't." He did, however, allow the counterdraft to be printed so it would be ready when Burger circulated his opinion.

Late on Monday, June 7, Burger's draft circulated with a short cover memo saying that he was willing to accommodate everyone but would not give in on one point: there could be no absolute ban on all gag orders.

Brennan had already left for the day and his clerks called him at home to say that Burger's draft had come. It was exactly as expected. Could they circulate the counterdraft? Fearing the Burger draft would probably be acceptable to enough of the others, Brennan agreed. Burger was, after all, overturning the gag order, the bare minimum of consensus. Brennan knew he would have to remind the others that they had agreed to go further. The next day, Brennan prepared a cover memo explaining that his draft banned all gag orders, as the conference majority had voted.

Burger was insulted by Brennan's draft and infuriated by the cover memo. Brennan's long, polished draft, complete with the facts of the case, was a premeditated attempt to steal the majority. The direct challenge—the insinuation that his own draft did not reflect the view of the conference—was open warfare. Burger shot back a short memo to the conference taking up the challenge: If the absolute ban had been the conference consensus, he said, he would have written it that way.

Marshall and Stewart joined Brennan's opinion almost immediately. Rehnquist, Blackmun and Powell joined the Burger draft, giving him four votes. Brennan remained hopeful—White and Stevens had been with him at conference.

White knew how important the case was to Burger. He decided to give him the fifth vote. Even without the ban, Burger's opinion was a strong First Amendment statement. It said that "prior restraints on speech and publication are the most serious and least tolerable infringement on First Amendment rights." But White added a one-paragraph concurrence saying that he had "grave doubt" that such gag orders would "ever be justifiable."

Stevens did not want to offend either Burger or Brennan. He decided to concur in the judgment and join neither opinion. But in a one-paragraph opinion of his own, he wrote: Brennan's opinion was "eloquent," but he would not buy it. "I do, however, subscribe to most of what Mr. Justice Brennan says and, if ever required to face the issue squarely, may well accept his ultimate conclusion."

Brennan concluded that he had the majority in principle. White and Stevens had literally said they were with him in their opinions. But the Chief had bucked the majority will and won.

Brennan instructed his clerk to leave the facts of the case as they were written in his opinion, hinting that it had once been, and perhaps still was, the view of the majority. "Let the public speculate," he said, publishing the full opinion as a concurrence.

On Friday April 30, the conference considered the cases that were argued during the final week of orals. In one (Burrell v. McCray), the Fourth Circuit Court of Appeals had ruled that state prisoners could sue in federal court over violations of their constitutional rights without first exhausting every available state grievance procedure.

Burger, Powell and Rehnquist voted to grant cert, hoping to reverse the Fourth Circuit and deny state prisoners direct access to federal courts until they had gone through all state procedures first. In a 1970 series of cases, a conservative majority had successfully limited federal court involvement in state criminal trials. Now Burger, Powell and Rehnquist wanted to further reduce the federal courts' involvement in state proceedings. But to do this it might be necessary to overrule a 1961 precedent.

White was the fourth vote to grant cert, but for the opposite reason. He thought it was an important civil rights case, and he wanted to uphold the Fourth Circuit in it.

At conference, Burger, Powell and Rehnquist could not muster any other votes for their position.

Brennan was preparing to assign the case when Burger said he had decided to switch his vote to the majority.

"Jesus Christ," White bellowed, throwing his pencil on the table and pushing his chair back in disgust. "Here we go again."

Stewart interrupted with a suggestion. He preferred to see the Court simply rule in favor of the prisoners but without handing down an opinion. In addition to the question of access to the federal courts, there was a second question—whether the prisoners' deprivation constituted cruel and unusual punishment. Stewart felt there was more dramatic evidence of cruel and unusual punishment in other cases. This case was pale by comparison; it was not the case in which to decide that issue. It should, perhaps, be "DIGGED"—"dismissed as improvidently granted"—without a decision, he suggested. That way the Fourth Circuit opinion, favorable to the prisoners, would stand. Powell agreed with Stewart, and Burger suggested to Stewart that he research the question.

Brennan was furious. Stewart might have had some legitimate questions about the evidence of cruel and unusual punishment in the case, but it seemed clear that Powell had supported a "DIG" only as more desirable than a complete loss. If the case were to be dismissed as improvidently granted, the Fourth Circuit's opinion would be precedent only in that circuit, and not nationally, as it would be if the Supreme Court explicitly affirmed it.

One of the risks of voting to grant cert and hear a case was the possibility that the decision might not come out the way one wanted. But that was how the game was played. Brennan had himself lost many cases that way. A Justice could not be allowed to effectively withdraw his cert vote by supporting a dismissal when it seemed likely that the conference decision was going against him. That was exactly what Powell was doing. According to the Court's own rules, dismissals were permitted only when precise technical defects were discovered after cert was granted.

At the minimum, Brennan felt that all four Justices who had voted to grant cert had to favor dismissal before anyone else should be allowed to provide the necessary fifth vote. Otherwise, five Justices who did not want to vote cert in a particular case could wait until after oral argument and then vote to dismiss, destroying the Rule of Four to grant cert.

Powell did not wish to seem as if he were voting to dismiss the case because he had lost. So he decided not to vote to "DIG" unless and until there were four other votes. He promised Burger he would join as a fifth vote if there were four votes by May 20. Meanwhile, Stewart managed to get the four—himself, Burger, Rehnquist and Blackmun. On Thursday, May 20, Powell dictated a memo to Burger: "As the sun is almost down (as I promised) I join four" to dismiss. He added that it was a "shaky rule" and that "under normal standards it would be difficult to justify."

Brennan wrote a two-page dissent in which he charged that the five-man majority "plainly flouts the settled principles."

While he had not voted for dismissal, Stevens thought Brennan was wrong. Although unusual for a new Justice to take any of his colleagues publicly to task, Stevens defended the dismissal in a three-paragraph opinion. As long as one member of those voting to grant cert joined in the dismissal, "the action of the Court does not impair the integrity of the Rule of Four." When the dismissal was announced, Brennan and Stevens published their short opinions. Only the most perceptive of Court watchers got a glimpse of the real nature of the internal conflict.

Brennan and Marshall were worried about a case (*Doe v. Commonwealth's Attorney*) that had come on direct appeal from a three-judge district panel in Virginia. The panel had upheld a Virginia anti-sodomy law that outlawed homosexual acts, including those performed in private by consenting adults. Since federal law required the Court to accept appeals from three-judge panels, the Court would have to decide the case. But Brennan and Marshall could get only Stevens to vote with them to grant oral arguments. The others wanted to affirm the lower court decision summarily. "The judgment is affirmed," would be the Court's only statement.

Marshall was outraged. Privacy interests acknowledged explicitly in earlier opinions, particularly in the 1973 abortion decision, should protect consenting adults in such matters. The Virginia law that had been upheld also banned heterosexual oral sex. Marshall found it ridiculous that the state should exercise such police power. Worse, in Marshall's eyes, was the majority's unwillingness to face the issue squarely—to accept the case for argument and to write an opinion spelling out its reasoning. It was cowardly. The Court's authority rested, in part, on its ability and willingness to offer its reasons for any decision. Where were the other votes—Blackmun, Stewart and Powell—that had extended the concept of privacy as a basis for the right to have an abortion?

The four-word summary affirmance of the lower court judgment was greeted with harsh criticism from legal scholars. The Court's failure to explain itself, conservative Texas Law Professor Charles

Alan Wright said, made its decision making appear to be a "lottery." Stanford Law professor Gerald Gunther called the Court's summary affirmance "irresponsible" and "lawless."

Brennan's clerks obtained a copy of a Herblock newspaper cartoon and gave it to Brennan for his seventieth birthday on April 25. The cartoon showed a couple in bed in their brick house which was labeled "Rights of Individuals." The house was being torn down as they woke up. The wrecking crew was headed by a judge called Nixon-Burger Court, who looked very much like the Chief. A smiling Rehnquist was hauling away the bricks and plumbing in a wheelbarrow. The startled man in the bed was saying, "We were told they were 'strict constructionists.'" Brennan put the cartoon up in his chambers and promised to keep it there until the Chief saw it.

Two days after Douglas's retirement, the Court turned to the lingering dilemma of school desegregation (*Carr v. Montgomery County Board of Education*). In Montgomery, Alabama, Frank Johnson, one of the most liberal federal judges in the South, and often mentioned as a possible nominee to the Supreme Court,* had ruled that busing was not necessary there. As a result of the decision, a number of virtually all-black schools would not be desegregated. Neither the conservative nor the liberal Justices were quite sure what to do. The conservatives worried that Brennan, Marshall and White wanted to grant cert in hopes of picking up votes from Stewart or Blackmun and Douglas's replacement to direct Johnson to order busing.

The liberals were concerned that the conservatives might seize the opportunity of Douglas's departure to establish once and for all that lower courts need not order so much busing. Johnson had tied his opinion to the specific facts of the case masterfully and had carefully interpreted them in terms of the Court's recent opinions. An opinion so carefully tied to the facts was difficult to overrule.

---

* Johnson was later nominated by President Jimmy Carter to be Director of the Federal Bureau of Investigation but withdrew because of illness.

Burger passed at conference, waiting to see what Brennan would do. Disposed to take the case but fearing what the conservatives would do, Brennan paused. "Deny," he said. Surprised, Stewart hesitated a moment and then said, "Deny." When all the rest had voted to deny, Burger changed his pass to deny.

Later in the term, Powell was happy to see there were six votes for a Pasadena, California, school case to restrict federal court judges' authority (*Pasadena City Board of Education v. Spangler*); he hoped for even greater restrictions in the next case. The perfect case seemed to be in Boston, where a district judge, W. Arthur Garrity, Jr., had ordered the crosstown busing of 21,000 public school pupils, desegregating several all-white and all-black areas of the city for the first time. Violent resistance by militant whites to the order had thrust the case into the national spotlight.

When the Boston school board, and white parent groups opposed to busing, appealed the case to the Court, there were reports that the Ford administration would come out against busing. But when these reports were followed by more violence, the White House decided not to intervene. Attorney General Edward Levi announced that they would wait and see how the Supreme Court ruled.

In June, Brennan, Marshall and White met to discuss the case. Each feared that the conservatives would want to take the case in order to further limit busing. Fortunately, as Judge Johnson had done in Montgomery, Garrity had grafted his opinion to the facts, making it difficult to overturn without directly overruling several precedents.

The conservatives also caucused. Powell and Burger were anxious to take the case. Garrity had clearly exceeded the proper limits for busing. But Rehnquist surprised them by strongly opposing a cert grant. Since oral argument could not take place until the next fall, there would be another round of violence in Boston when the next school year began. This was a case to let pass even if it was in blatant conflict with the Montgomery case.

At conference, Burger led off with a terse "I would vote to deny." Unsure as to what was up, Brennan said simply, "Deny." Around the table there was not a single vote to take the case. In one minute the Court had disposed of the term's potentially most controversial case.

By letting two conflicting lower court decisions on busing stand, the Court revealed its uncertainty on the issue.

Stevens's first half-term on the Court left him disappointed and frustrated. He was distressed by the amount of paperwork. For the first month he tried to read every cert petition himself, as Brennan did. Then he gave in and accepted his clerks' cert memos. At conference, he spoke as forcefully and persuasively as he could. But as the junior Justice, he spoke last, the least effective position to be in. Burger always seemed impatient by the time discussion got around to Stevens, and the others had usually made up their minds. Stevens therefore spoke up more during oral argument, trying to get his points across before conference. He also circulated detailed memos and presented each of the others with his theories.

Stewart, in particular, welcomed Stevens's fresh approach, his intelligence and his willingness to work. He termed Stevens "first rate." Stevens did not argue grand theory or react with knee-jerk positions. His positions and his votes were as unpredictable as Douglas's had been predictable. Stevens was as meticulous as Blackmun, but not as insecure. He was as exuberant and outgoing as Rehnquist, but Stewart found his views more acceptable. He was as ready to debate as White, but not belligerent. There was no telling where he would go, nor was he afraid of changing his mind. Stewart began calling him the "wild card." He was an available vote for anyone from Brennan to Rehnquist. Stewart welcomed him as a member of the center—"the group," as he called it.

White took a less charitable view of Stevens. He felt, at times, that Stevens was erratic. Picking on Stewart's nickname for Stevens, he began referring to him as "the one-eyed Jack." Stevens's legal views were downright eccentric. After conference, White would tell his clerks that the vote was 5 to 3 to 1, or 6 to 2 to 1. He would smile when he mentioned the "1." None of his clerks had to ask which Justice was alone.

White wondered when the law reviews would come to realize that Stevens was not the imaginative new Justice he was depicted to be, but rather a man with a limited regard for precedent, a judge willing to start each issue from scratch. Stevens approached each case as a puzzle; it seemed he was looking for trick solutions. Still, White admired Stevens's confidence in his crazy ideas. "It's four to four, and we're down to the 'wild card,'" was a common refrain among the Justices when they were vying for Stevens's vote.

At one conference, Brennan expressed a strong view on the liberal side, and Rehnquist rejoined with an equally lengthy and strong conservative statement. "I agree with Bill," Stevens said smiling, and he got a roaring laugh from the others.

But as the year went on, Stevens grew increasingly disenchanted. In a complicated labor picketing case (*Buffalo Forge v. United Steelworkers*), he was in a five-man majority at conference with Burger. The Chief assigned him the case. Stevens circulated his first draft, and his other votes appeared solid until he got word that Burger was not happy with it. At conference, Stevens tried to find out what was wrong but Burger appeared uninterested. Trying to surmise what the Chief wanted, Stevens sent a new draft around. When he got no response he tried yet another redraft. One of Stevens's law clerks learned from one of Burger's clerks that the Chief was not even reading Stevens's drafts, but the clerk couldn't bear to tell Stevens. Nevertheless, Stevens suspected that Burger wasn't paying much attention to his drafts.

At the last minute Burger joined White's opinion, giving him the majority; Stevens was forced to change his opinion to a dissent. The incident had a lasting impact on Stevens. Burger had not been frank. Not only was Burger inept, Stevens concluded, but he wasn't even trying. The relationship between the two men deteriorated as Stevens's cynicism grew.

At times, it seemed to Stevens that the Justices communicated only on paper; there was not enough informal discussion. When he did talk with one of his colleagues, more often than not he came away disillusioned. He asked Marshall about one opinion that Marshall was writing, and he concluded that Marshall did not really understand the issues in it. Stevens was sure that Marshall was capable of being a good lawyer, but he had not done his homework and was relying entirely on a clerk.

*   *   *

Six years after becoming Chief, Burger was still searching for cases that would provide an occasion for striking down or drastically modifying the exclusionary rule, the rule that said illegally seized evidence had to be excluded from a trial. Two cases (*Stone v. Powell* and *Wolff v. Rice)* involved state prisoners who claimed that the evidence used to convict them had been illegally obtained in violation of the Fourth Amendment. To Burger, these seemed perfect cases: two murderers were trying to overturn their convictions by raising technical Fourth Amendment claims. After the highest state courts had rejected their claims, the men had appealed to the federal courts. Under the Constitution, any state prisoner has a right to petition the federal courts for a writ of *habeas corpus,* which required the state to show that the imprisonment did not violate the federal Constitution.

Burger had long wanted to cut off *habeas* petitions on Fourth Amendment claims. He believed they were almost always frivolous, and they clogged the federal courts. To preclude such petitions—and to overrule an important Warren Court precedent *(Kaufman v. U.S.)*—would be a major victory.

But Burger wanted more. He still wanted either to overrule the 1961 Mapp case, which applied the federal exclusionary rule to the states or, at least, to modify the federal rule to exclude evidence only in instances of flagrant, bad faith police violations of the Fourth Amendment.

After conference, Burger assessed the complex voting. There were at least five votes to cut back on *habeas* petitions. There were also four votes, White, Blackmun, Rehnquist and himself, willing to cut back on the exclusionary rule itself. Powell had voted only to cut back on the *habeas* petitions. Burger could only get his dramatic double victory if Powell were to shift and were willing to modify the exclusionary rule itself. But Burger held out hope that Powell was still open on the subject. Burger used his most potent enticement to lure Powell and assigned him the cases.

When Burger got Powell's draft opinion, however, he felt betrayed. Powell was limiting the *habeas* petitions, but he still refused to modify the exclusionary rule in any way. Burger angrily decided to apply some pressure. He let Powell know he would not join unless Powell went further. But Powell still had hopes for five votes, even without the Chief's. Stewart seemed to be a possible fifth vote though he was shaky. Powell knew his opinion amounted to overruling the Warren Court's precedent on the *habeas* petitions, and providing the fifth vote to overrule a Warren Court precedent was something Stewart was generally loath to do. Whether it would be the Chief or Stewart who provided it, Powell needed that fifth vote.

Stewart recognized Powell's precarious position. Though he was uncomfortable with Powell's opinion, Stewart knew this was not the time to leave him in the lurch. Stewart joined. The Chief's vote was unnecessary. Burger was left without any leverage; reluctantly he finally agreed to join Powell's opinion.

Stevens had hardly taken his seat on the Court when he found himself the man in the middle on the death penalty. The 5-to-4 ruling in the 1972 death penalty cases was known by the lead case, *Furman v. Georgia.* The rulings, which had struck the laws in thirty-five states, ducked the ultimate constitutional question: Does the penalty itself—as opposed to the manner of sentencing—constitute "cruel and unusual" punishment?

About thirty-five states had enacted new death penalty laws deliberately designed to avoid the restrictions of the 1972 ruling (*Furman*). No one had yet been executed under these new laws, but hundreds were once again waiting on death row.

Douglas had been in the 5-to-4 majority in the *Furman* case. That left the Court divided 4 to 4 when Stevens arrived. Stevens's position was a particularly big question mark, since he had never dealt with the death penalty issue on the Seventh Circuit Court of Appeals. Working according to a long-established pattern, Stevens prepared to take on the fifty pending death cases. After a full day in his chambers, he was home by about 8 P.M. and in bed by 10. At 2 A.M., he rose for a few hours of uninterrupted reading and work before returning to bed. These night hours were often his best and most productive.

As he worked his way through briefs and previous death penalty decisions, Stevens saw that the Court had boxed itself in with its previous rulings. The 1971 *McGautha* case said that state laws did not have to provide sentencing guidelines for a jury considering the imposition of the death penalty. Nor were separate sentencing hearings after trials necessary. The effect was an endorsement of jury discretion in sentencing. But the 1972 *Furman* decision had gone against unlimited jury discretion, finding the death penalty unconstitutional because it was imposed arbitrarily, randomly and too infrequently.

Stevens reviewed the nine separate opinions in the *Furman* case again and again. It was clear what the Chief, Blackmun, Powell and Rehnquist were saying. They did not find the death penalty unconstitutional. At the other pole were Brennan and Marshall. They opposed the death penalty as inherently "cruel and unusual" under all circumstances. The opinions of White and Stewart were baffling. Stewart's objection to the randomness, the capriciousness, the arbitrariness, and the lack of uniformity in the imposition of the penalty had been met by about fifteen states, which had passed laws requiring juries to consider all mitigating factors. White's objection, that the penalty was not an effective deterrent since it was imposed so infrequently, had been met by about twenty states that had passed laws making the death penalty mandatory upon conviction for certain crimes.

In mid-January—less than one month after Stevens had arrived—the Justices held a special Saturday conference to consider the fifty death penalty cert petitions. They generally agreed that the nine separate opinions had left people confused in 1972. They agreed they should select a group of cases to answer the Eighth Amendment cruel-and-unusual-punishment question. The Justices decided to take only murder cases. Burger wanted to hear the most brutal among the fifty petitions, a torture murder involving razorblade mutilation (*McCorquodale v. Georgia*), but he could not get three other votes. They decided to select a case from each of the states with one of the five types of laws that had been passed. A consensus emerged that the Court should take only relatively straightforward cases where the facts were clear and presented no side issues, such as racial prejudice. Since Texas had a unique law and few available cases they had no choice but to take a grisly murder from there.

The cases the conference chose presented the full spectrum and came from five states:

- North Carolina, which had a mandatory death penalty for all premeditated murder or murder in the course of committing a felony *(Woodson)*.
- Louisiana, which required the death penalty for all first-degree murder convictions, but allowed the jury to impose lesser sentences by finding the accused guilty of second-degree murder or manslaughter *(Roberts)*.
- Texas, which permitted the death penalty only for those convicted of murder in certain situations—such as murder for hire, or killing a prison employee—and where other aggravating factors were present, such as the murder being deliberate and unprovoked, or there being a "probability" that the defendant would commit future violent crimes *(Jurek)*.
- Florida, which required a separate sentencing hearing after a person had been convicted of first-degree murder, at which the jury could consider eight possible aggravating factors and seven mitigating factors. A jury's recommendation of a death sentence could then be overruled by the judge, who imposed the final sentence, or by the state supreme court *(Proffitt)*.
- Georgia, which specified that a jury had to find one of ten specific aggravating circumstances in order to impose the death penalty and then required that the Georgia supreme court review and agree with the sentence *(Gregg)*.

Powell was convinced that the Court was going to strike down the death penalty once and for all. He could see his colleagues' frustration as these cases arrived year after year. There was so much pressure—the abolitionists, the nine-year moratorium, those hundreds of people on death row. He thought either Stevens or Blackmun would join the four Justices left from the *Furman* majority to dispose of the issue. Powell thought that Stewart and White would have to hold to their previous votes and opinions. They were in the majority in both the *McGautha* and *Furman* opinions. Since those two cases were contradictory, the only logical next step was total abolition, perhaps in an opinion with a vague constitutional grounding like Blackmun's abortion decision.

Powell remained convinced, however, that he had been right in 1972. The death penalty was constitutional. Powell also viewed the thirty-five new state laws as convincing evidence that the people wanted a death penalty. Somehow the Court had to accommodate this trend without appearing to simply follow election returns. Surely there were crimes so repugnant that they warranted capital punishment. But if the Court reinstated the death penalty, Powell worried about the hundreds on death row. A wholesale slaughter would be just as awful as a sweeping annulment of the recent acts passed by thirty-five legislatures. He was grateful that he had been personally spared from looking a real live defendant in the eye and pronouncing the death sentence on him. The names of those in the cases—Gregg, Proffitt, Jurek, Woodson and Roberts—were remote and unreal to him.

Powell pondered the possibility of an amnesty. The Court might rule that those who had waited years on death row had already suffered cruel and unusual punishment. He found, however, no support in the law for such a move.

When the states began passing new death penalty laws right after the 1972 *Furman* decision, Stewart realized that he had miscalculated. "Professor [Anthony] Amsterdam promised us that if we decided his way this would be the last death case," Stewart told his clerks after *Furman.* Of course, Amsterdam had assumed that the Court would rule all death penalties "cruel and unusual" under the Eighth Amendment. Stewart and White had specifically declined to do that.

Unlike Stewart, White was not suprised by the overwhelming enthusiasm of state legislatures for the death penalty after the 1972 decision. He had predicted these new mandatory laws; and he was not about to have any role now in striking those laws. The standards of society were not evolving against the death penalty. Those new laws requiring juries to consider all mitigating circumstances also satisfied him. If that was what the states wanted, he found nothing unconstitutional about it. White expected that he might be the fifth vote to uphold all five laws if the Nixon appointees held firm.

Brennan was despondent. He anticipated that White would vote to uphold the new laws, and he had no hope for the four Nixon appointees. There was another problem too. Douglas was still trying to participate in the work of the Court. He had called Brennan to announce that he wanted to listen to the oral arguments in the five death penalty cases. Brennan had told him that would be impossible. There were only nine chairs at the bench. Douglas suggested a tenth chair could be brought in.

"No," Brennan said emphatically, "the statute governing the Court clearly calls for only nine Justices. John has taken your place."

"Not you too," Douglas said, and hung up.

The conference decided that the Justices would have to put an end to Douglas's attempts to interfere. They agreed to draft an unequivocal letter to him explaining that since he had resigned, he had no official duties on the Court. He could not sit for oral argument, vote, speak at conference, write or publish opinions. Burger wrote the letter and had it hand-carried to each Justice for his signature. It was painful for Brennan to sign, but he did.

Douglas stopped trying to rejoin the Court.

On March 30 and 31, at oral argument, Amsterdam called for a total ban on capital punishment. Without spending much time trying to distinguish among the five state laws, he argued that they should all be struck as "cruel and unusual."

Stewart wanted to be sure that Amsterdam was taking an absolute view that the death penalty for "any person in any state for any crime is cruel and unusual punishment, no matter what the technique, no matter how serious the offense, no matter how fair the procedure."

"That is precisely the contention," Amsterdam replied. The life-or-death decision was of such magnitude that asking juries to find differences was unjustifiable. "Our argument is that death is different. If you don't accept the argument that it is constitutionally different, we lose this case."

Brennan, Stewart and White were all upset at Amsterdam's self-righteousness. Amsterdam had lectured them, and, at one point, had even bordered on being rude to Blackmun.

The conference met on Friday, April 2. After the traditional handshakes, the Justices sat down. They first voted whether the death penalty was in all cases "cruel and unusual." The vote was 7 to 2, with only Brennan and Marshall taking such an absolute position.

Then they voted on each of the five state laws individually. Burger, White and Rehnquist voted to uphold all five; Brennan and Marshall voted to strike all of them. The other four Justices split on the various laws.

Stewart thought the main issue was how the death penalty was imposed. He felt that the Georgia and Florida laws provided the soundest sentencing procedures, since they allowed the best chance of consideration of individual circumstances. North Carolina and Louisiana, with mandatory laws, were the least likely to provide fair sentencing. On the fifth case, Texas, he was uncertain.

Blackmun, while still morally opposed to the death penalty, could find no legal ground to vote against it. But in North Carolina, with about one hundred people on death row, there was some evidence that a disproportionate number of blacks had been sentenced to death. Under its new mandatory law, about five times as many people had been sentenced to death than under the pre-1972 discretionary law. The possibility of racial discrimination troubled Blackmun, but he was not sure that he could accept a theory that would uphold some of the death penalty laws and strike others. For the moment, he passed on North Carolina.

Powell said he favored the death penalty for heinous crimes. But he disliked the compulsory death sentence. "What this country needs is for public executions to be reinstated," he said. If the public had to witness executions, it would be less likely to favor mandatory laws. Minimally the laws should provide a rational way for judges and juries to impose the extreme penalty. State laws providing guidelines, standards and separate sentencing hearings, went a long way toward ensuring that no injustice would be done.

And laws like those in Georgia and Florida—providing for automatic state Supreme Court review—would put a check on erratic jury verdicts. He tentatively voted to uphold all the laws, but said he also was unsure about North Carolina.

Stevens voted to strike the Texas, Louisiana and North Carolina laws. He called the mandatory North Carolina law a "monster" that, he said, amounted to a "lawless use of the legal system." He felt that the 1972 *Furman* decision was the governing precedent and that the essence of it was to provide procedural safeguards. But separate sentencing hearings and review by the state's highest courts could guarantee due process and uniformity, so he voted to uphold Georgia and Florida.

The final tally was:

Georgia: 7 to 2 to uphold. Only Brennan and Marshall dissented.

Florida: 7 to 2 to uphold. Again only Brennan and Marshall dissented.

Texas: 5 to 3 to uphold. Stevens joined Brennan and Marshall in dissenting while Stewart passed.

Louisiana: 5 to 4 to uphold. Stevens and Stewart joined Brennan and Marshall in dissent.

North Carolina: 4 to 3 to 2 to strike. Brennan, Marshall, Stewart and Stevens were in the majority while Blackmun and Powell passed.

Brennan emerged from the conference drained and saddened. The Court now had seven Justices who felt that the death penalty did not necessarily violate the Eighth Amendment. There were not five votes to strike any one law. The best vote on his side was 4 to 3 to strike North Carolina, but the two passes were Powell and Blackmun, who had voted to uphold all other laws. Brennan was so discouraged that he virtually turned the cases over to one of his clerks.

Burger saw a rare opportunity to assign all five cases. He was in the majority in four, and in the North Carolina case there was not yet a five-man majority either way. Accordingly, it was logical that he assign it. He was tempted to take the decisions himself, or give them to Rehnquist. But White was the key. He was for upholding all five state laws, but given his 1972 rationale against the death penalty, his vote had to be guarded. The assignment would probably hold him. White was also the most likely to draft a technically proficient and consistent opinion which could pick up Powell's and Blackmun's votes in North Carolina, to give the pro-death-penalty side a clean sweep.

On Monday, April 5, Burger circulated the assignment sheet giving all five cases to White. White was pleased, and even a little excited, by the challenge of pulling together a majority in the North Carolina case. He geared up for the research and writing, giving all three of his clerks part of the work. As the chamber threw itself into the assignment, White alternately blew hot and cold on the prospects of bringing it off. For the next four weeks, he worked almost exclusively on the five cases.

Powell was surprised at the assignment. When he checked his notes, he felt there had to be some mistake. He had marked himself as a vote to *strike* the North Carolina law, providing the fifth vote. In his own mind, he had not passed as the others had apparently concluded.

Stevens, still unsure of the protocol after fewer than four months on the Court, was also perplexed. Whatever Powell's or Blackmun's vote in the North Carolina case had been, there were more votes to strike it than to uphold it.

Stewart understood the logic of the assignment to White, but he raised the matter of North Carolina with Powell. It was clear from what Powell said that he was now, or always had been, a vote to strike the North Carolina law. That meant there was a five-man majority to rule it unconstitutional.

Stewart and Powell shared a favorable impression of Stevens; they decided to talk with him. As they talked, it was apparent that they were all firm in wanting to strike the North Carolina law. Brennan and Marshall could be counted on to join them at least in the result, though probably not in the reasoning of the opinion. That was five votes. Stewart could see the possibility of a working centrist coalition on the other four cases as well.

Stewart, Powell and Stevens all favored upholding the discretionary Georgia and Florida laws. While the three were not in agreement on Louisiana and Texas, they might be able to work out a full opinion spelling out their reasoning and then agree on all five.

Stewart in particular was fairly certain that they could work out a compromise and formulate an overall theory covering all five.

But they needed to begin writing. Normally they would wait for White's opinion, then one of them would write a dissent in the North Carolina case and pick up the votes, making the dissent a majority. But the term was about to enter its frenetic final two months. If they waited, they probably would not get out their own opinion in time. That could mean reargument the next year.

They went to see the Chief to explain their emerging consensus. Burger was not very responsive. White still had the assignments. He would probably be circulating soon, Burger said, and there was no reason to do anything but wait. Then they could do what they felt was necessary.

Stevens left the meeting astounded. Burger was thwarting the will of the clear majority in the North Carolina case. The Chief was forcing them to work underground. Stewart and Powell told Stevens that now perhaps he could see what they all had been dealing with for years.

The three Justices—the troika, as they were soon dubbed— concluded that they had to inform White that at least one of his five cases had slipped away. White and his clerks had been working for a month. Stevens did not like sandbagging White. He would not go. As the senior of the troika, Stewart finally went to see White on one of the first working days in May. He began by telling White that Powell, Stevens and he had talked informally, that they had realized that they all wanted to strike the North Carolina law. With Brennan's and Marshall's vote, that would give them a majority. Avoiding White's gaze, Stewart forged ahead, explaining that they were also trying to develop a rationale to fit the other cases.

How can some laws be upheld and others struck? asked White. On what theory?

Stewart said they would work that out. But they wanted to let him know what they intended. It was too late in the term to wait for his circulations. At the same time, they did not want to work behind his back.

But what was their approach? White pressed. Maybe he could satisfy them?

Stewart was vague. He said simply that they knew the direction in which they were headed. The laws most like North Carolina's would be struck. Georgia's and Florida's, with separate sentencing hearings and guidance for the jury, would be upheld.

"Of course," White said, "you're going to overrule *McGautha.*" (*McGautha* said sentencing and guidance for juries were not constitutionally required.)

"No," replied Stewart. They would find a way around *McGautha.*

"How can you with a straight face not overrule *McGautha?*" White asked.

Stewart replied that they were not going to say that sentencing standards were absolutely, constitutionally required. *McGautha* could stand.

White didn't buy it.

Stewart was unmovable. After nearly an hour, he left on a very chilly note.

White, feeling both powerless and disappointed, rebuked himself for failure to focus on the weak case in the assignment, the North Carolina case. But he could see the moment Stewart walked out of his chambers that the struggle was effectively over. White went to his clerks. "There is now a three-man plurality in the death cases," he explained. "I want one of those opinions ready to go to the printer by the close of business today," White said coolly. He was going to play by the rules and carry out his assignment. White said he did not want their research shared with other chambers, particularly those of Stewart, Powell and Stevens. They were not to see drafts that were not circulated. White tensed slightly. "Can you believe it?" he added. "They're not going to overrule *McGautha.*" Another legal abomination was in the making. "I thought the reason I was writing these in the first place was for them to read and react," White said.

White knew that Stewart had instigated the effort to steal the opinions. Typically, Stewart was hiding behind another committee.

But recognizing the importance of the five cases being handled as a group with a consistent rationale, White formally submitted all five cases back to the conference for reassignment.

On Wednesday, May 5, a special conference was called to consider the reassignment of the death cases. Burger wanted only the Justices to know about the meeting. The normal preparations for conference were unnecessary. The buzzer did not have to be sounded, and no refreshments would be served. The conference would be short.

After the Justices sat down, Burger said there were clearly now five votes to strike the North Carolina law.

White said he could not join the rationale that Stewart, Powell and Stevens were developing, and was formally resubmitting all five cases for reassignment so that a moderately coherent principle might emerge.

Dealing first with North Carolina, Burger acknowledged that he was in the minority and could not assign the decision. That left it to Brennan. But Brennan declined to assign the case; he did not share the troika's reasoning; he thought that any death penalty was unconstitutional.

Stewart proposed that the three Justices in the center could be joined on the laws they wanted to strike by Brennan and Marshall, and on the laws the three wanted to uphold by the four on the other side.

Powell and Stevens elaborated on the theory they were developing. They suggested that the 1971 *McGautha* ruling—that standards guiding sentences by juries and separate hearings were not required—was inconsistent with the 1972 *Furman* opinion. They might have to acknowledge that *McGautha* was bad law or even overrule it.

Burger adjourned the conference after about twenty minutes.

Stewart had long felt that the Justices in the center controlled major cases, but they had always suffered from a real handicap. Burger, on the right, or Douglas and then Brennan, on the left, controlled the assignments. Now, by breaking protocol the center had effectively taken over an assignment for the first time.

The troika, however, had no draft opinion and very little time. Powell was also concerned that they had no clear-cut legal theory for these cases, were not fully agreed among themselves, and had only a working plurality, not a majority. The three met several times to discuss and divide the work. Each sensed that the effort might fail.

They all agreed that Stevens should take the facts. They also agreed that they needed a section holding that the death penalty did not invariably violate the Eighth Amendment. Powell agreed to do this section, since he could draw from the briefs and his long *Furman* dissent. This would probably go with the opinion in the Georgia case, because they agreed that Georgia had the best law. Next, they had to have a fully developed opinion striking the mandatory North Carolina law. Stewart agreed to undertake this draft that represented the biggest problem. None of them could articulate a clear rationale why North Carolina's law violated the Constitution.

Once these tasks were completed, they could try to fit each of the other laws into its proper category. It seemed almost certain that the Georgia and Florida laws would be upheld. The Louisiana and Texas laws were left in limbo.

Stewart and one of his clerks went to work on the North Carolina draft. The Court's 1972 *Furman* decision had clearly prompted North Carolina to enact a mandatory death penalty law. The state's brief defending the law maintained that it was enacted to eliminate "all sentencing discretion" so that "there would be no successful *Furman*-based attack" on the new law. Stewart had been disappointed when the states began passing mandatory laws after *Furman*. The North Carolina law was certainly one that he had been partly responsible for creating.

Stewart wanted to rely heavily on his separate opinion in the *Furman* case, which argued for striking the death laws as arbitrary and capricious. But the automatic penalty was regular, predictable, uniform. He soon developed a line of reasoning that made his point. "It is capricious to treat two similar things differently," he said. And by enacting mandatory death penalty laws in response to the Court's 1972 ruling, states like North Carolina had put an end to situations where some murderers got the death penalty and some did not. This ended the capriciousness of having no reason for some men being put to death while others were not. But now Stewart added, "It is capricious to treat two different things the same way." Since each defendant is different, to give all convicted murderers the same penalty, the death penalty, was just as capricious as imposing it randomly. Some sentencing guidelines were therefore necessary.

Stewart sent the draft to Powell and Stevens. Powell was dazzled; Stevens was satisfied.

Powell and his clerks, meanwhile, were working on their section. He worried that his rationale for upholding some capital punishment laws might sound contrived, since the Court had struck down other death penalty laws just four years before. He still believed in his own dissent, but *Furman* was precedent. Stewart and Stevens, however, liked Powell's draft. That left the troika with the two cases on which they did not yet agree.

Stewart and Stevens had voted to strike the Louisiana law, which was virtually mandatory. It was almost as inflexible as North Carolina's. Stewart presented some arguments on this to Powell, and he agreed to switch his vote.

Only Texas remained. It was the hardest to fit into either category—mandatory or discretionary. Though it did not specify as many procedural safeguards for the accused—with provisions for guidance or separate sentencing hearings—as the other discretionary laws, Powell wanted to uphold the Texas law. He had gone along with Stewart and Stevens on Louisiana; it was their turn to go along with him. Stewart changed his pass to uphold, and Stevens, who had originally voted to strike, also switched. But Stevens was uneasy. They were acting like a superlegislature, laying out a model law. Despite qualifying phrases that they were not requiring standards and separate sentencing procedures, no one could miss the point. It would have been clearer to overturn *McGautha* and state that standards and separate hearings were now constitutionally required.

As the joint project progressed, Stevens was amazed at Burger's brooding acquiescence to their work. If he were Chief, Stevens concluded, he would not abdicate the most important cases of the term.

The troika finally began stitching the various sections into appropriate places in all five opinions. Powell realized that the opinions read like a committee project, but he thought they were the best they could do. Stewart liked the committee approach. Points of view were expanded; the work and responsibility had been shared. Considering that they had spent just two months, Stewart felt they had done a good job.

Brennan's clerks wanted him to turn them loose to point out the logical inconsistencies in the troika's opinions, but this time Brennan said no. Rehnquist would handle that by attacking from the other side. Brennan wanted to keep his colleagues focused on the moral issue of killing people; that was what had been won in 1972 and was now lost. "Justice of this kind is obviously no less shocking than the crime itself," he wrote, "and the new 'official' murder, far from offering redress for the offense committed against society, adds instead a second defilement to the first." But the dissent had no effect on the outcome of the case.

After leaving his vote in doubt for months, Blackmun finally said he would not join the troika; he would vote to uphold all five state laws along with Burger, White and Rehnquist.

It was agreed that the plurality of three should announce the judgments. Friday, July 2, was set as the day. The troika produced 112 printed pages of opinions upholding three laws and striking two. The other six Justices added ninety-three pages of dissents and concurrences. Since there was no one majority opinion, the Chief suggested he should read his opinion first. The others insisted the troika go first. The Chief yielded.

On the morning of the announcement, the Justices were solemn and quiet in the robing room. A heavy cloud cover outside darkened the courtroom. Stewart's hand shook, and his voice cracked, as he read the lead case, Georgia, upholding the death penalty. Marshall delivered an angry, emotional dissent. The Justices were absolutely silent as they left the bench. Drained and discouraged, Marshall went home early. That night he had a mild heart attack.

The next day, the newspaper stories called attention to the fact that the decisions set the stage for the execution of about half of the 600 people on death row—all those who had been sentenced under discretionary laws. *The New York Times* predicted that it would probably be several months before an execution took place. "But the judgment today means that the main legal battle is over."

Two weeks after the announcement, Amsterdam filed a petition for rehearing in the three cases that were upheld. Since the Court was in recess, the petition was forwarded to Powell, the circuit Justice for these states. Executions could begin at the end of the month, unless Powell granted a temporary stay until the Court could meet to consider the petition.

Powell did not want the first blood on his hands; he was inclined to grant the stay. When Burger learned of Powell's intention, he tried to persuade him to deny. This was the kind of stalling and use of technical loopholes that was fouling up the law, Burger argued. Another delay would be interpreted as a last-minute shift by Powell, perhaps by the whole Court. There would be more doubt.

Powell told Burger that he could not act for the full Court. If any person were executed before the Court reconvened, he would have been denied his fair chance for a rehearing, no matter how unlikely it was that it would be granted.

Burger replied that if Powell granted the stay, he would have no alternative but to reconvene the Court in a special session to overturn the stay, and deny the petition for rehearing.* They both knew that a majority would do just that.

Powell called Brennan in Nantucket, and told him about Burger's threat. Brennan reminded Powell that the Chief had no power over him when he was acting as circuit Justice. Brennan suggested that Powell show some "backbone."

If Powell granted the stay, Brennan said, and Burger tried to summon all of them back, Brennan would not come. If Burger persisted, Brennan said he would write a full dissent from any action the Court took spelling out what happened in detail.

---

* The last time the Court had been convened in the summer to expedite an execution had been in 1953, when the Court overturned Douglas's order blocking the executions of convicted spies Julius and Ethel Rosenberg.

On July 22, Powell granted the stay. Burger did not summon the Court back into session.*

The chaos of his first half-term gave Stevens reason to pause. At conferences the Chief read verbatim from clerks' memos and tried to avoid committing himself to a position until the last minute. Brennan's bitterness at the direction of the Court's decisions made him a voice crying in the wilderness. It was sad. Stevens liked Brennan personally, but Brennan gave knee-jerk liberal reactions. Stewart was hard-working but distracted. Marshall parroted Brennan. Blackmun was tormented and indecisive, searching for a way to duck issues or narrow the final opinion as much as possible. Rehnquist was clearly very intelligent and hard-working but too right wing. His willingness to bend previous decisions to purposes for which they were never intended was surprising, but Stevens also liked Rehnquist. Powell seemed the most thoughtful, the best prepared, and the least doctrinaire. White was the most willing to discuss an issue informally before it was resolved, but he could become unnervingly harsh.

The absence of intellectual content or meaningful discussion at conference was the most depressing fact of Court life. Stevens thought that the nation's highest Court picked its way carelessly through the cases it selected. There was too little time for careful reflection. The lack of interest, of imagination and of open-mindedness was disquieting.

---

* In one of the first actions of the new term the next October, the Court issued a short order denying the petition for rehearing. There was not a single dissent. The states were technically free to begin executions. But Amsterdam and the lawyers for the Inc. Fund continued to fight each individual death sentence, and to file every conceivable motion in the federal courts to block them. They were successful in every case except that of convicted murderer Gary Gilmore, who asked the state of Utah in January 1977 to carry out his death sentence. He was executed by a firing squad. Involuntary executions began on May 25, 1979, at 10:12 A.M. with the electrocution of John A. Spenkelink, whose sentence had been stayed since the Court's 1972 decision declaring the death penalty unconstitutional.

By the end of the term, Stevens was accustomed to watching his colleagues make pragmatic rather than principled decisions—shading the facts, twisting the law, warping logic to reconcile the unreconcilable. Though it was not at all what he had anticipated, it was the reality. What Stevens could not accept, however, was the absence of real deliberation. Under the extreme pressures created by Stevens's arrival in the middle of the term, internal animosities that had been growing surfaced more openly and more regularly.

On Sunday, June 20, *Washington Star* reporter Lyle Denniston wrote a front-page story that was headlined "Supreme Court Is a Different Place Without Douglas." The story related how Douglas's former colleagues, even those who had disagreed with him, missed his outspokenness. Though Denniston did not name them in the story, two Justices had talked to him about the impact of Douglas's departure on Brennan and Marshall. One Justice was quoted as saying that the two remaining members of the liberal wing were "beleaguered." The other was quoted as saying that Brennan and Marshall were aware of their declining importance, and were reacting to their isolation with more strident dissents. The result, one Justice said, was that the majority felt less obliged to respond to the Brennan-Marshall dissents. "You don't go around chasing rabbits," one Justice was quoted as saying. "You don't need to answer every flag they run up."

A few days later at the end-of-the-year status conference to determine which cases were ready to be announced, one of Powell's Fourth Amendment cases came up for discussion.

"I'm ready," Powell said, "but I don't know if Bill Brennan is ready. He may have more dissenting to do."

"Well," Brennan said, "if the story in *The Star* on Sunday is correct, I don't know why you even have to ask me. I take it you don't feel you have to read my dissents or respond to them anyway."

"You don't believe that, Bill," Powell said.

Several of the others tried to calm Brennan, but Brennan answered them sharply. "Two of the brethren are quoted."

"You don't believe what you read in the papers, do you?" White asked.

Stevens said that he too wondered about the direct quotations attributed to unnamed Justices. Nearly everyone jumped in, voicing views about the article, the press, dissents, Douglas's retirement and its meaning. The discussion continued for some time.

Only Stewart and Rehnquist remained silent.

Brennan later toned down his dissent in Powell's case. It was one of the few that he softened, and it was still strong. It accused the majority of deception, charging that they had overruled the 1969 Warren Court case without saying so. The majority's action, he said, was "drastic," was "novel," foreshadows "future eviscerations," and amounts to a "denigration of constitutional guarantees." He pointedly retained a citation to a 1971 *Yale Law Journal* article entitled, "Some Anxious Observations on the Candor and Logic of the Emerging Nixon Majority."

Five separate Fourth Amendment cases were announced on July 6, the last day of the term. All five ruled against citizens' rights and in favor of the government. One case *(U.S. v. Martinez-Fuerte)* authorized the border patrol to stop cars at fixed checkpoints miles away from borders and without probable cause. Brennan, dissenting for himself and Marshall, listed it as one of nine such cases in the "continuing evisceration of the Fourth Amendment" during the term.

Because of the five cases announced on the last day, the clerks in most chambers began calling it "Black Tuesday." But if it was "black" and ran contrary to their liberal views, this turning away from the Warren Court was orchestrated and controlled not by Warren Burger, but by Stewart and White, who had served on the Warren Court, Powell, the most moderate of the four Nixon appointees, and by Stevens, the new moderate.

The center was in control.

Index